Routledge Revivals

The Mabinogi

The purpose of this collection, which was first published in 1996, is to provide both an overview of the major critical approaches to the Four Branches of the *Mabinogi* and a selection of the best essays dealing with them. The essays examine the origins of the *Mabinogion*, comparative analyses, and structural and thematic interpretations. This book is ideal for students of literature and Medieval studies.

The Mabinogi
A Book of Essays

Edited by
C. W. Sullivan III

First published in 1996
by Garland Publishing Inc

This edition first published in 2015 by Routledge
2 Park Square, Milton Park, Abingdon, Oxon, OX14 4RN
and by Routledge
711 Third Avenue, New York, NY 10017

Routledge is an imprint of the Taylor & Francis Group, an informa business

© 1996 C. W. Sullivan III

The right of C. W. Sullivan III to be identified as editor of this work has been asserted by him in accordance with sections 77 and 78 of the Copyright, Designs and Patents Act 1988.

All rights reserved. No part of this book may be reprinted or reproduced or utilised in any form or by any electronic, mechanical, or other means, now known or hereafter invented, including photocopying and recording, or in any information storage or retrieval system, without permission in writing from the publishers.

Publisher's Note
The publisher has gone to great lengths to ensure the quality of this reprint but points out that some imperfections in the original copies may be apparent.

Disclaimer
The publisher has made every effort to trace copyright holders and welcomes correspondence from those they have been unable to contact.

A Library of Congress record exists under LC control number: 95052929

ISBN 13: 978-1-138-85483-3 (hbk)
ISBN 13: 978-1-315-72071-5 (ebk)

The Mabinogi
A Book of Essays

Edited by
C.W. Sullivan III

Garland Publishing, Inc.
New York and London
1996

Copyright © 1996 by C.W. Sullivan III
All rights reserved

Library of Congress Cataloging-in-Publication Data

The Mabinogi : a book of essays / [edited by] C.W. Sullivan III.
       p.   cm. — (Garland reference library of the humanities ;
vol. 1791. Garland medieval casebooks ; v. 16)
    Includes bibliographical references.
    ISBN 0-8153-1482-5 (alk. paper)
    1. Mabinogion.   2. Welsh prose literature—To 1550—History and criticism.   3. Tales, Medieval—History and criticism.   4. Tales—Wales—History and criticism.   5. Mythology, Celtic, in literature.   6. Folklore in literature.   7. Folklore—Wales.   I. Sullivan, Charles Wm. (Charles William), 1944–   . II. Series: Garland reference library of the humanities ; vol. 1791.   III. Series: Garland reference library of the humanities. Garland medieval casebooks ; vol. 16.
PB2273.M33M28   1996
891.6'631—dc20   95-52929
                                                                                     CIP

Cover photograph of Pentre Ifan courtesy of C.W. Sullivan III.

Printed on acid-free, 250-year-life paper
Manufactured in the United States of America

COPYRIGHT ACKNOWLEDGMENTS

J.K. Bollard, "The Role of Myth and Tradition in *The Four Branches of the Mabinogi*," *CMCS* 6 (1983): 67–86; Juliette Wood, "The Calumniated Wife in Medieval Welsh Literature," *CMCS* 10 (1985): 25–38. Reprinted by permission of the authors and the editor of *Cambridge Medieval Celtic Studies*.

J.K. Bollard, "The Structure of the Four Branches of the Mabinogi," *THSC* (1974–1975): 250–276; Rachel Bromwich, "*The Mabinogion* and Lady Charlotte Guest,"*THSC* (1986): 127–141; T.M. Charles-Edwards, "The Date of the Four Branches of the Mabinogi," *THSC* (1970): 263–298; C.W. Sullivan III, "Inheritance and Lordship in *Math*," *THSC* (1990): 45–63. Reprinted by permission of the authors and the editors of *Transactions of the Honourable Society of Cymmrodorion*.

Patrick K. Ford, "Branwen: A Study of the Celtic Affinities," *SC* 22–23 (1987–1988): 29–41 and "Prolegomena to a Reading of the *Mabinogi*: 'Pwyll' and 'Manawydan,'" *SC* 16–17 (1981–1982): 110–125; Elizabeth Hanson-Smith, "*Pwyll Prince of Dyfed*: the narrative structure," *SC* 16–17 (1981–1982): 126–134; Sarah Larratt Keefer, "The Lost Tale of Dylan in the Fourth Branch of *The Mabinogi*," *SC* 24–25 (1989–1990): 26–37; Seán Ó Coileáin, "A Thematic Study of the Tale *Pwyll Pendeuic Dyuet*," *SC* 12–13 (1977–1978): 78–82. Reprinted by permission of the authors and the editor of *Studia Celtica*.

Jeffrey Gantz, "Thematic Structure of the Four Branches of the Mabinogi," *Medium Aevum* 47 (1978): 247–254. Reprinted by permission of the author and the editor.

R.M. Jones, "Narrative Structure in Medieval Welsh Prose Tales," *Proceedings of the Seventh International Congress of Celtic Studies*. Ed. D. Ellis Evans. 171–198. Oxford, 1986. Reprinted by permission of the author and the editor.

Catherine A. McKenna, "The Theme of Sovereignty in *Pwyll*," *BBCS* 29 (1980): 35–52; Roberta L. Valente, "Gwydion and Aranrhod: Crossing the Borders of Gender in *Math*," *BBCS* 35 (1988): 1–9. Reprinted by permission of the authors and the editor of *Bulletin of the Board of Celtic Studies*.

Andrew Welsh, "*Manawydan fab Llŷr*: Wales, England, and the 'New Man.'" *Celtic Languages and Celtic Peoples*. Ed. Cyril J. Byrne, et al. 389–362. St. Mary's University, 1989. Reprinted by permission of the author and the editors.

To Professors Barre Toelken and Hugh N. Maclean,
each of whom, in his own way,
set me onto this path;
and to Ann, my wife, who has shared the journey

Contents

Preface   xi

Introduction   xv

I. ORIGINS

1 *The Mabinogion* and Lady Charlotte Guest
    Rachel Bromwich   3
2 The Date of the Four Branches of the Mabinogi
    T.M. Charles-Edwards   19

II. COMPARATIVE ANALYSES

3 The Calumniated Wife in Medieval Welsh Literature
    Juliette Wood   61
4 The Lost Tale of Dylan in the Fourth Branch of
    The Mabinogi
    Sarah Larratt Keefer   79
5 Branwen: A Study of the Celtic Affinities
    Patrick K. Ford   99
6 *Manawydan fab Llŷr:* Wales, England, and the
    "New Man"
    Andrew Welsh   121

III. STRUCTURAL INTERPRETATIONS

7 A Thematic Study of the Tale *Pwyll Pendeuic Dyuet*
   Seán Ó Coileáin   145
8 *Pwyll Prince of Dyfed:* the narrative structure
   Elizabeth Hanson-Smith   153
9 The Structure of the Four Branches of the
   Mabinogi
   J.K. Bollard   165
10 Prolegomena to a Reading of the *Mabinogi:*
   "Pwyll" and "Manawydan"
   Patrick K. Ford   197
11 Narrative Structure in Medieval Welsh Prose
   Tales
   R.M. Jones   217

IV. THEMATIC INTERPRETATIONS

12 Thematic Structure in the Four Branches of the
   Mabinogi
   Jeffrey Gantz   265
13 The Role of Myth and Tradition in *The Four
   Branches of the Mabinogi*
   J.K. Bollard   277
14 The Theme of Sovereignty in *Pwyll*
   Catherine A. McKenna   303
15 Gwydion and Aranrhod: Crossing the Borders
   of Gender in *Math*
   Roberta L. Valente   331
16 Inheritance and Lordship in *Math*
   C.W. Sullivan III   347

Works Cited   367

About the Contributors   383

Preface

Anyone who spends much time with the Four Branches of the *Mabinogi* (and with the other prose pieces usually published with them as *The Mabinogion*) soon comes to recognize the truth of Gwyn Jones's and Thomas Jones's comment that the

> eleven stories known as the Mabinogion are among the finest flowerings of Celtic genius and, taken together, a masterpiece of our medieval European literature. Their excellence has been long, if intermittently, celebrated, and their influence deeply felt and widely recognized. (ix)

And anyone who has studied the Four Branches also recognizes that there is excellent scholarship in the field and that some of it is a bit hard to find, existing, as it does, in long-out-of-print journals or in journals found only in the most extensive Celtic Studies libraries, personal or academic.

The purpose of this collection is to provide both an overview of the major critical approaches to the Four Branches and a selection of the best essays dealing with the Four Branches. The divisions are somewhat arbitrary—the essays dealing with structure, for example, can hardly help but mention theme, and those dealing with theme cannot easily ignore structure; but I have tried to place each according to the author's primary intent.

Although the total number of essays in this field is by no means large, especially when compared with the number of essays on more well known medieval works, such as *Sir Gawain and the Green Knight*, there are still too many to be reproduced here. Therefore, I have elected not to include many of the older essays whose scholarship has been superseded by or incorporated into more recent essays. Also, in a pragmatic attempt to reach as wide an audience as possible and make this volume useful to students who are studying medieval literatures but who do not read Welsh, I have not included the many valuable essays written in that language. For reasons of length and in order to include as many essays as possible, I have chosen to limit the bibliography to a works-cited list. Finally, and again for reasons of space, I have had to eliminate such cogent cognate essays as Proinsias Mac Cana's "Aspects of the Theme of King and Goddess in Irish Literature," an essay that certainly sheds light on portions of the Four Branches.

Editing the essays themselves was fairly simple. I first standardized, insofar as it was possible, the use of italics and quotation marks, except in the titles of books and articles, in regard to the Welsh Celtic materials: *The Mabinogion* signifies the publications which include the Four Branches and the other prose pieces first translated by Lady Guest; the *Mabinogi* refers to the Four Branches themselves, the individual titles of which will also be in italics, even in their abbreviated forms (e.g., *Math*). Four Branches will be used as a designation, but without italics or quotation marks. Welsh Celtic words and passages will be as presented in the original articles. Otherwise, titles will appear according to Chicago style. The other major work of editing was to move all of the notes to the ends of the articles and edit them to conform to a style approved by Garland Publishing. In addition, I consolidated the individual bibliographies at the end of each article into a common bibliography at the end of the volume to reduce repetition. I believe that this standardization will serve to prevent minor confusions and will make the whole volume more readable without changing its content.

ACKNOWLEDGMENTS

I would, first and foremost, like to thank those authors and journal editors who had faith in this project and were kind enough to allow their articles to be reprinted here, and second, East Carolina University and the Southern Regional Education Board for the grants that enabled me to make several research expeditions to Wales, and third, the East Carolina University College of Arts and Sciences for a summer stipend which allowed me to finish this project almost on time.

I would also like to thank the staffs of the National Library of Wales and the Hugh Owen Library of the University College of Wales in Aberystwyth for their assistance; and I am indebted to Professor R. Geraint Gruffydd, then Director of the Centre for Advanced Welsh and Celtic Studies, for his assistance and, especially, for his encouragement.

Ms. Pat Guyette, head of ECU's Inter-Library Loan Service deserves special mention for finding, from incomplete bibliographic references, copies of some highly specialized sources referred to by the individual authors herein. My 1994–1995 graduate assistant, Robert Owens, was invaluable in scanning the various articles onto computer disks; 1995–1996 graduate assistant John A. Myers, Jr., was also invaluable in running down bibliographic data and helping proofread the final copy; and Laurie Evans, my Associate Editor on the *Children's Folklore Review*, was ultimately responsible for the layout and design of the manuscript that became this book and should be considered Associate Editor here as well.

All of these people made the job of editing *The Mabinogi: A Book of Essays* much lighter and more pleasant than it otherwise would have been.

C.W. Sullivan III

Introduction

The individual manuscripts which contain what we now know as the Four Branches of the *Mabinogi* —the White Book of Rhydderch (Llyfr Gwyn Rhydderch) and the Red Book of Hergest (Llyfr Coch Hergest), and MSS. Peniarth 6, 7, 14, and 16—were probably written down sometime between AD 1300 and 1325 (for the White Book) and AD 1375–1425 (for the Red Book). However, T.M. Charles-Edwards's careful linguistic and cultural arguments in "The Date of the Four Branches of the Mabinogi," reprinted in the first section of this collection, Origins, place the composition of the Four Branches themselves between AD 1050 and 1120, although they contain some materials, if not complete stories, which are certainly centuries older. Whatever their ages, the versions we have available to us today have long been considered masterpieces of medieval literature. Given their quality, it is ironic that relatively few scholarly translations of them have been published and that few otherwise well-read scholars outside of the field of Celtic Studies know much at all about them.

The first complete translation of the Four Branches and the other materials included in the Red Book of Hergest, as well as the story of Taliesin, was published between 1838 and 1849 by Lady Charlotte Guest—a rather remarkable person, according to Rachel Bromwich's *"The Mabinogion* and Lady Charlotte Guest,"also reprinted in the first section—and her translation has been reissued a number of times since, with and without the notes which accompanied the first; recent editions have included one from The Folio Society in 1980 and another, edited by Owen Edwards, in 1992.

In 1929, largely as a result of the discovery and publication of *The White Book of Rhydderch,* T.P. Ellis and John Lloyd published a new translation with commentary comparing the two manuscript sources. Almost 20 years later, Gwyn Jones and Thomas Jones published the Golden Cockerel *Mabinogion* (1948), which then appeared in Everyman's Library (1949)—subsequent editions of their quite formal translation were issued in 1974 and 1989. More recently, Jeffrey Gantz published *The Mabinogion* (1976) and Patrick K. Ford *The Mabinogi* (1977), both translations presenting the Welsh texts in more modern English versions. Ford's translation excludes the three Arthurian romances, "The Dream of Rhonabwy," and "The Dream of Maxen Wledig," included in the others, but he adds "The Tale of Gwion Bach" and "The Tale of Taliesin" and includes *Cad Goddeu* in an appendix. In addition, there have been numerous retellings, such as Sidney Lanier's *The Boy's Mabinogion,* published in 1881, based on one or more of these scholarly translations.

When scholars today refer to *The Mabinogion,* they generally refer to the Red Book materials Lady Guest translated and use the title under which she published that translation. Technically, the term *mabinogi* applies only to the first four tales in Red Book and White Book manuscripts, those stories called the Four Branches. The form *mabinogion* appears only once in the text (probably as a scribal error), at the end of the First Branch, and various spellings of *mabinogion* appear at the ends of the other Three Branches. The meaning of *mabinogion/mabinogi* has been the subject of much debate. Because of its similarity to the Welsh word *mab,* meaning "son" or "boy," William Owen Pughe, Lady Guest, and some subsequent scholars have felt that these stories were intended for young people, stories learned early in a bard's career, or stories about the youth, *enfance,* of a medieval hero—in this case, Pryderi. Recently, Eric Hamp has looked past the medieval style and sense of the Four Branches and into the mythological and linguistic roots of the word for a cogent explanation. Hamp concludes that "*Mabinogi* is to be understood as originally 'the material, or doings pertaining to (the family of) the divine Maponos'" and that part of what structures the Four Branches as we have them is the story of the father of Maponos, Gwri=Pryderi ("Mabinogi" 248–249).

As many critics have noted, another key to the mythological ancestry of the Welsh figures in the *Mabinogi* lies in comparing them with their Irish counterparts. The *Mabinogi's* Children of Dôn, for example, are descended from the goddess Dôn, just as the more clearly mythological Tuatha Dé Danann are descended from the Irish goddess Danu. Recently, in *Celtic Heritage,* Alwyn Rees and Brinley Rees assert that the traditional tales appearing in the Irish cycles contain "material which appears to belong to a common Indo-European heritage and which presumably was a part of the tradition of the Celtic peoples before they ever came to these islands" (26). The same would hold, of course, for the oldest Welsh Celtic materials in the Four Branches. As other critics have noted, however, mythological materials are not the only ones to be found in the Four Branches.

Matthew Arnold may be the godfather of the search for sources, for it was he who articulated the idea that the stories which we have contain bits and pieces of mythology, legend, history, folktale, and more. One of the most often quoted passages from his "On the Study of Celtic Literature" asserts the following:

> The very first thing that strikes one, in reading the *Mabinogion,* is how evidently the medieval storyteller is pillaging an antiquity of which he does not fully possess the secret; he is like a peasant building his hut on the site of Halicarnassus or Ephesus; he builds, but what he builds is full of materials of which he knows not the history, or knows only a glimmering tradition merely;— stones 'not of this building,' but of an older architecture, greater, cunninger, more majestical. (51)

Arnold's attention to the building blocks rather than the edifice itself was to guide *Mabinogi* criticism for almost 100 years.

W.J. Gruffydd's monumental studies, *Math vab Mathonwy* and *Rhiannon*, attempted to identify the elements of myth, folklore, legend, and history in the First, Third, and Fourth Branches; and Proinsias Mac Cana's *Branwen* did the same for the Second Branch. In *The International Popular Tale and Early Welsh Tradition* and other publications, Kenneth Jackson identified the international motifs and tale types in the Welsh stories while deriding their integrity, calling them "confused and senseless," "corrupt," "badly broken up," "clumsy," "unconnected," and "practically unintelligible" (78–95, *passim*). Many other critics writing in the first two-thirds of the twentieth century have made valuable source studies while commenting unfavorably on the stories *as* stories. However, as the essays in the second section of this volume illustrate, it is not necessary to denigrate the integrity of the Four Branches in the search for comparative motifs and tale types.

All of the essays in the second section of this collection, Comparative Analyses, look outside of the tales themselves for materials which will make those tales clearer. Juliette Wood, in "The Calumniated Wife in Medieval Welsh Literature," compares the fates of Rhiannon and Branwen with the larger body of medieval literature featuring the Calumniated Wife theme. In "The Lost Tale of Dylan in the Fourth Branch of *The Mabinogi*," Sarah Larratt Keefer looks to Scottish selkie legends and to a traditional British ballad to explain Dylan's heritage and unusual aquatic abilities. Patrick Ford's "Branwen: A Study of the Celtic Affinities" views the Second Branch as an essentially traditional tale which quite nicely incorporates specifically Celtic concepts of war and warriors. In "*Manawydan fab Llŷr*: Wales, England, and the 'New Man,'" Andrew Welsh looks at changing cultural worldview to explain the contrast between the actions of Manawydan in the Third Branch and the heroic ethic articulated there and elsewhere in the *Mabinogi*.

As a body of critical inquiry into the structure of traditional narrative began to develop in the middle of the twentieth century, best typified, perhaps, by Vladimir Propp's *The Morphology of the Folktale* and other works which looked at the structures of traditional oral literatures, a similar line of inquiry began to examine medieval literature. In an introduction to the 1974 edition of *The Mabinogion*, Gwyn Jones suggested:

> Many of the so-called structural imperfections of the Four Branches . . . cannot have been regarded

Introduction

> as faults by the author or by his audience. The tellers of the native tales knew no foreshadowings of nineteenth-century critical logistics; their hearer had not heard of the "well-made" novel; and it is in the nature of the wondertale to transcend factual consistency. (xxxviii)

Similar statements contrasting modern and medieval literary aesthetics have since been made by a number of commentators on the Four Branches, comments which echo J.R.R. Tolkien's belief about the *Beowulf* poet—that it is "improbable that such a man would write more than three thousand lines (wrought to a high finish) on matter that is not worth serious attention; that remains thin and cheap when he has finished with it" (61).

The essays in the third section, Structural Interpretations, all published within the last twenty-five years, break with previous analyses and offer various interpretations of the structure of the Four Branches, each interpretation arguing that, although modern readers may not recognize it, structure is there in each of the Four Branches. Attempts to understand the structure of the Four Branches have followed both traditional and non-traditional lines of inquiry. In "A Thematic Study of the Tale *Pwyll Pendeuic Dyuet*," Seán Ó Coileáin presents structural correspondences between the major sections of the tale which direct the reader toward the theme. Elizabeth Hanson-Smith, in "*Pwyll Prince of Dyfed*: the narrative structure," builds upon Ó Coileáin's analyses but suggests that the three structural segments each focus on the restoration of the wasteland. J.K. Bollard's "The Structure of the Four Branches of the Mabinogi" posits a more complex narrative than do the previous two essays; instead of parallel or reflective segments, Bollard sees an interlaced narrative, like that of *Beowulf*, in which several narrative lines are woven together, much as in a tapestry. Patrick K. Ford's "Prolegomena to a Reading of the *Mabinogi*: 'Pwyll' and 'Manawydan'" takes yet another step, suggesting that the Four Branches must be read as one would read a musical score, both vertically and horizontally at the same time. And in "Narrative Structure in Medieval Welsh Prose Tales," R.M. Jones surveys the field, discusses the ways in which modern attitudes might lead to misreading of medieval prose narratives, and posits a synchronic as well as a diachronic approach to the materials.

The attempt to discover structure in the Four Branches inevitably led to the attempt to find theme; indeed, to some extent, the two efforts occurred simultaneously, for, as the essays in section three indicate, it is difficult to discuss structure without discussing theme. What an author says is almost always inextricably tied to the form in which he says it. The essays in section four, Thematic Interpretations, all relatively recent publications, take structure in the Four Branches almost for granted, often referring to the major structural essays in passing or in footnotes. These authors, too, see their task, in part, as a reaction against the source studies of Jackson and others and, in part, as an attempt to find the thematic unity that must accompany structural unity. Each of the five essays in this section discusses what the Four Branches might be saying to and saying about the people of the time.

Jeffrey Gantz's 1978 "Thematic Structure in the Four Branches of the Mabinogi" was one of the earliest attempts to articulate the idea that the Four Branches might be thematically unified, arguing that the balanced structural elements also carry balanced statements of theme. J.K. Bollard focuses on "The Role of Myth and Tradition in *The Four Branches of the Mabinogi*" to explain how the author wove his materials together to create a story with a theme culturally relevant for the people of that time. Catherine A. McKenna examines the First Branch in "The Theme of Sovereignty in *Pwyll*" and suggests that the First Branch is about the characteristics of a good prince. Roberta Valente looks at Welsh law to explain the conflict between Gwydion and Aranrhod in the Fourth Branch in "Gwydion and Aranrhod: Crossing the Borders of Gender in *Math*." In "Inheritance and Lordship in *Math*," C.W. Sullivan III discusses matrilineal and patrilineal inheritance traditions to suggest cultural change as a major theme in the Fourth Branch.

The confluence of cultural changes which led to the Romantic movement, with its strong interest in Arthurian and other medieval materials, prompted a number of nineteenth-century scholars to look at the Celtic materials in general and the Four Branches in particular. Ernest Renan, "The Poetry of the Celtic Races" (1854), focused on the imaginative power of the

Celts and found it to be significantly different from that of the Mediterranean or Eastern peoples; Matthew Arnold, *On the Study of Celtic Literature* (1865) stressed the Celtic elements in the English spirit and in English literature; and William Butler Yeats, "The Celtic Element in Literature" (1903), felt that the Celtic myths and legends would reinvigorate European imagination and literature. All three argued that the Celtic literature and language were worth studying and that Celtic literature had had a significant influence on subsequent literatures, especially British. The result, as Rachel Bromwich argues in "Matthew Arnold and Celtic Literature, A Retrospect: 1865–1965," was that Arnold "inaugurated in this country a dispassionate and scholarly attitude towards Celtic Studies, which made possible their acceptance here as a serious academic discipline" (1). And while this scholarship has only occasionally included examinations of the influence of the Celtic materials on other literatures, the study of the Celtic materials themselves has indeed become, in Bromwich's words, "a serious academic discipline."

C.W. Sullivan III

I

Origins

1

The Mabinogion and Lady Charlotte Guest

Rachel Bromwich

> For thee, of English birth but British heart,
> Our bardic harp neglected and unstrung
> Moved to the soul, and at thy touch there start
> Old harmonies to life: our ancient tongue
> Opens, its buried treasure to impart.
> Rowland Williams (Goronva Camlan) *circa* 1850.

Today we regard the *Mabinogion* as the foremost Welsh prose classic of the Middle Ages. But this is very far from having been the case in the past; indeed it would seem that up till the end of the eighteenth century these tales were little known, at any rate in the final literary form in which we now have them. Consider the relatively small number of medieval manuscripts of these tales—the White Book of Rhydderch and the Red Book of Hergest, fragments in Peniarth MSS. 6 and 7, 14 and 16, Jesus MS. 20, and some later copies of these—in comparison with the very large number of medieval texts and versions of *Brut y Brenhinedd*[1] and the numerous texts and fragments of *Trioedd Ynys Prydain*.[2] This relative unfamiliarity is borne out by the fact that if we examine the allusions made by the Gogynfeirdd[3] to the traditional legendary characters it becomes very clear that the prime source of their knowledge was the *Triads* and the *Brut*, and the same is true, by and large, of the earlier *cywyddwyr*. The heroines of the past whom the poets cite as standards of beauty are Eigr, Esyllt, Luned, Dyfyr, Tegau—all of them names which would have been familiar to them from the *Triads*. There are sparse allusions to Branwen and to Rhiannon in the fourteenth century, to the first by Dafydd ap Gwilym and by Justus Llwyd, and to the second by Goronwy Gyriog; while there is no poetic allusion to Aranrhod before Tudur Aled, or to Olwen before Lewys Môn. Many of the traditional heroes and heroines appear both in the *Triads* and in the *Mabinogi*, of course, and this limits the force of the distinction I am trying to make. For this purpose one needs to pay especial attention to those *Mabinogion* characters who are *not* named in the Triads, such as Dafydd ap Gwilym's single allusion to Llwyd fab Cel Coed (sic),[4] or the earliest recorded allusion to Rhonabwy in a poem by Madog Dwygraig, after 1370. These two, and the allusions to Branwen, Olwen, and Rhiannon, are late enough to have been derived by the poets from written texts[5] of the stories: my point is that these heroines could not compare for popularity among the poets with those heroines previously named, although we know little enough of Dyfyr, Tegau, or even Esyllt (Isolt) from Welsh sources that have been preserved. For the poets the canonical texts continued down the ages to be *Brut y Brenhinedd* and *Trioedd Ynys Prydain*, together with the *Hengerdd*. These embodied the national *senchus*[6] (to employ an Irish term), the canonically accepted record of the nation's past. And in this record the *Mabinogi* and the other native *chwedlau* apparently played little part, although there can be no question but that the origins of the Four Branches of the *Mabinogi* and of *Culhwch and Olwen* go back to the very earliest times, being foreshadowed by several allusions in the *hengerdd*. Although the *Mabinogion* tales appear to have been widely known in oral tradition, and sometimes in variant forms, for the poets who were the custodians of this tradition, they bore no comparison in esteem with those works which were regarded as the pillars of the historical record. This apparent neglect, down the ages, of the ancient mythological tales, is difficult to account for, but it is nevertheless a fact. A number of triads were of course introduced into the written text of the *Mabinogi*, as it were to give the tales status and authority.

A partial explanation is that among scholars of the seventeenth and eighteenth centuries everything was deprecated which was not believed to contribute in any way to the historical record. Edward Lhuyd is somewhat ambivalent: in cataloguing the contents of the Red Book of Hergest he describes the Four Branches of the *Mabinogi* as *fabulosas quasdam historiolas* "certain fabulous stories"—evidently a slightly depreciative epithet—and the tale of *Owain* as *narratio fabulosus* "a fabulous narrative"—implying by this that "fables" are of little interest or value.[7] In contrast is the prestige he allots to the *Triads,* by quoting Robert Vaughan's opinion that these go back as far as the seventh century:[8] Robert Vaughan was of course the great champion of the antiquity and historicity of *Trioedd Ynys Prydain*. In 1717 Moses Williams completed his preparation for the press of a large collection of Triads from a number of sources,[9] and he intended to include the texts of *Breuddwyd Maxen* and *Lludd and Llefelys* in his projected edition, which however was never published. No mention of the tales is made by Theophilus Evans, though he admits in general terms that something is perhaps to be learned from *traddodiad a hen chwedlau*.[10] The Morris brothers appear to have been equally neglectful. In his *Celtic Remains* Lewis Morris quotes Lhuyd as defining the term *Mabinogi* as "a British romance under this title," but without further comment, and such references as he makes to the tales in his *Celtic Remains* are based entirely upon the Triads.[11] He describes *Trioedd Ynys Prydain* as "a book of greater authority than anything else extant." In the Constitution of the Honourable Society of Cymmrodorion, drawn up in 1755, the *Triads* head the list of subjects to be "occasionally considered and treated of" by the Society: the *Triads* are followed in the list, but only after an interval, by "the British History and its historicity."[12] But no mention is made of the *Mabinogi*. Nor does Iolo Morganwg appear to have known or felt any interest in the *Mabinogi* and the other tales, preoccupied as he was—among other activities—in re-writing the older Triads in order to convey through them his individual and personal myth of history.[13]

But a great change came about with the Romantic Revival in the latter years of the eighteenth century, for which the rediscovery of medieval literature was a main inspiration, and one which brought with it an appreciation of the records of the past for other values than the purely historical. As concerns the Celtic literatures, the publication of James Macpherson's *Ossian* in the 1760s was an epoch-making event, which created a receptive audience outside Wales, Ireland, and Scotland for the traditions of these countries. It came as a challenge both to the Irish and to the Welsh, and impelled both Celtic nations to search out and to disclose to the world such genuine early literature as they possessed, which could be set beside Macpherson's forgeries. (For these he had claimed an impossibly early third-century date.) One result of this was the publication in Wales of the great compendium of verse and prose contained in the *Myvyrian Archaiology*, published in 1801–1807, of which William Owen Pughe was the chief editor. This famous lexicographer deservedly enjoyed the reputation of being the chief Welsh scholar of his day, and he was in addition the prime informant on Welsh literature to a number of English medievalists, namely Joseph Ritson, George Ellis, Sharon Turner and Sir Walter Scott,[14] all of whom possessed names to conjure with in the field of antiquarian studies. Besides giving the earliest edition of the poems of Dafydd ap Gwilym (1789), and *The Heroic Elegies of Llywarch Hen* (1792), Pughe published in his journal *The Cambrian Register* the text with translation of the first half of *Mabinogi Pwyll* in 1796, and followed this subsequently with his versions of *Math fab Mathonwy* and of the *Hanes Taliesin*.[15] In another of his works, *The Cambrian Biography* (1803), he listed Welsh heroes alphabetically and gave notes on such *Mabinogi* figures as Bendigeidfran, Pryderi, Rhiannon, and Culhwch. He made a distinction between the "historical" and the "legendary" Arthur, and said of the latter, "It has generally been inferred that the great achievements of this hero created those illusory actions and scenes depicted in the *Mabinogion* or 'Juvenilities'"—and he contrasted the *Mabinogion* with the *Triads* which he described as "documents of undoubted credit"—again demonstrating the supposedly great historical value of *TYP* which had persisted down the ages. Note, incidentally, that the title *Mabinogion* originated with W.O. Pughe, and not with Lady Charlotte Guest who adopted it from him, as also she derived from him the notion that these tales were intended for children—in his *Dictionary* (1773–1803) W.O. Pughe defines *Mabinogi* as "Juvenile Romances"—and he went on to contrast the tales with the *Triads,* describing the latter as "documents of undoubted credit" thus demonstrating yet again the supposedly high historical value of *TYP,* which had persisted down the ages.

With the interest and enthusiastic encouragement of the English medievalists I have mentioned, W.O. Pughe conceived the plan, in the early years of the nineteenth century of publishing a translation of the whole of the *Mabinogion,* which he asserted to be "the earliest romance-writing in Europe." The original plan had been to include the texts of the Welsh tales in the total corpus of early prose and verse to be contained in the completed *Myvyrian Archaiology*—a plan which fell far short of accomplishment. In 1800 Pughe showed to Sir Walter Scott his completed translation of *Peredur,* and a few years later he showed his completed translation of *Math fab Mathonwy* to George Ellis.[16] Ellis referred in his correspondence to Pughe's translations as "infinitely curious" and stated his belief that they would "excite more curiosity" than any work since Macpherson's *Ossian.* However it seems that both Ellis and other English scholars felt that W.O. Pughe's style of translation and his English grammar left something to be desired, although Ellis promised to contribute a preface whenever Pughe's completed translation of the *Mabinogion* should be ready for the Press. For a number of years W.O. Pughe was distracted by other interests and by his personal affairs, but in the 1820s he was again working on his translation, and in 1825 he issued a prospectus in which he asked for subscriptions for his *Mabinogion,* to be published in two volumes with the original texts accompanied by a translation and notes. Various Welsh societies, the Cymmrodorion, Gwyneddigion, and others, strongly supported this plan and looked forward eagerly to the publication. The work was actually completed in manuscript[17] and partially prepared for press, when William Owen Pughe died in 1835.

Note well the date—1835. Because it was only three years afterwards, in 1838, that Lady Charlotte Guest published the first of her seven parts which were to contain her *Mabinogion,* later to be published together in three superb and luxurious volumes in 1849. These volumes contain the texts with translations of all the eleven tales, accompanied with copious notes, together with variant versions in other languages of the three Arthurian romances—*Peredur, Geraint,* and *Owain*—and with the addition of the story of Taliesin. Apart from this last, the texts were taken from copies made for her by Tegid (John Jones, 1792–1852), an Oxford scholar who was strongly under the influence of William Owen Pughe.

Who was Lady Charlotte? A young Englishwoman of 26, who in 1833 had married John Guest (later Sir John), a man who was more than twice her age, an extremely successful, intelligent, and philanthropic iron-founder, manager of the Dowlais works outside Merthyr.[18] Lady Charlotte Bertie was a sprig of the nobility, but in some ways a very unhappy one. Her father, who died when she was six years old, had been the Earl of Lindsey. Owing to her mother's re-marriage to a violent and drunken step-father, the Rev. Mr. Pegus, Lady Charlotte passed a miserable childhood, along with her two younger brothers, both of whom were apparently of weak intellect. It fell to her, indeed, to attempt to guard their interests throughout her life. As a refuge from her early troubles, she turned to the study of languages and learned French and Italian by herself, and with the help of her brothers' tutor, she studied also Greek, Latin, Hebrew and Persian. Her favourite English author was Chaucer, and in her old age she could still repeat by heart the whole of the Prologue to the Canterbury Tales, taking just 35 minutes to do so. I have not found any evidence that she had ever gone to Wales or had known anything of the Welsh language before her marriage, which took place within 3 months of her meeting, aged 21, with John Guest. But after her arrival at Dowlais she set to work to study literary Welsh (there is no evidence that she ever spoke it fluently) and in this she seems to have received active help and encouragement from several Welsh scholars: first and foremost from Thomas Price, (Carnhuanawc), cleric, scholar, and *eisteddfodwr*, and pioneer in re-establishing Welsh-Breton connections; John Jones (Tegid) who copied the tales for her from the Red Book of Hergest, and Gwallter Mechain; all of these being members of that band of clerics devoted to Welsh scholarship to whom Bedwyr Lewis-Jones has paid tribute in describing them in his book *Yr Hen Bersoniaid Llengar.*[19] Through Carnhuanawc she met with likeminded friends among the neighbouring gentry; with Sir Benjamin and Lady Hall of Llanover[20] (with the latter of whom she evidently had a certain rivalry, however) and with Sir Richard (Judge) Bosanquet of Dingestow Court near Monmouth, to whom she refers more than once as having lent her manuscripts, and who in fact first lent her Tegid's copy of *Culhwch and Olwen* from the Red Book. She also had contact with Taliesin Williams (Iolo's son), and refers to manuscripts lent her by Colonel Vaughan and Lord Mostyn.

In spite of the disparity of age, her marriage with John Guest seems to have been an ideally happy one. She produced ten children during the years that it lasted (till 1852), of whom the first four had already been born by 1838 when the first fascicle of the *Mabinogion* was published. By 1849 when the work was completed and published in a collected edition, her family was also complete—five boys and five girls. During all these years Lady Charlotte was closely concerned with her husband's business and evidently took a responsible share in many aspects of it (his firm sent railway-lines all over Europe, and to Poland, Russia and America, and the pair frequently travelled to Germany and to many parts of Britain). At Dowlais and nearby, Sir John and Lady Charlotte founded and financed six schools[21] and it was she who supervised these, as well as teaching her own daughters. She played the harp and the piano (Beethoven was her favourite composer), she etched and was fond of riding her horse, who was called "Llamrei" ("Swift Leaper"), after Arthur's horse in *Culhwch*. As she wrote in her journal "whatever I undertake I must reach an eminence in. I cannot endure anything in a second grade." Childbirth evidently she took in her stride and it caused her the bare minimum of disturbance; she would be up and about and busily correcting proofs or drafting her notes to the tales within a few days. All her children were exceedingly healthy, and all but one survived her. She kept a journal throughout her long life, from the age of ten until 1891 when she was almost 90, and nearly blind. The journal was so voluminous that only a relatively small part of it has so far been published, in the form of extracts, by her grandson the Earl of Bessborough. I have given here only a bare outline of all Lady Charlotte's voluminous activities and cares during the years in which she was simultaneously producing her *Mabinogion* and her family of ten. When her husband died in 1852 she was left for a time in sole charge of the Dowlais works, and she played an influential part in co-operating with other iron-masters in negotiations over a major strike in the South Wales coalfields in 1853. Her later life formed an equally vigorous sequel, as is shown in her later journals, after her second marriage.[22] But my chief concern here is to consider her work as translator and editor.

The Mabinogion was published simultaneously by Rees of Llandovery and by Longmans, in three volumes dated respectively 1838, 1840, and 1849. Pages of the Welsh texts and of the versions in other languages are reproduced in facsimile, and there are delightful head and tail pieces illustrating the tales. The sequence in which she tackled her work of translation is interesting. Priority is given to the Arthurian tales: vol. 1 contains *Owain* and *Peredur*, vol. 2 has *Geraint* followed by *Culhwch* and *Rhonabwy*, vol. 3 has the Four Branches of the *Mabinogi* followed by *Maxen, Lludd and Llefelys*, and the tale of *Taliesin* (this last from two MSS. in the British Library, written by William Morris and by Iolo Morganwg). It is clear that the three Arthurian romances were Lady Charlotte's primary interest and the task to which she turned first and which she first completed. These are accompanied by the corresponding French poems of Chrétien de Troyes, given either in full or in summary; she includes a summary of the German poem corresponding to *Erec et Enide*, and prints in full the English *Sir Percevale de Galles* (apparently copied by herself from the Thornton MS. in Lincoln Cathedral).[23] Although it was these romances which first claimed her attention and interest, she makes it clear in her preface that she recognised a fundamental difference in manners between these and the Four Branches "both as regards the manners they depict and the style of the language in which they are composed." She acknowledges the help of various people—Tegid, Judge Bosanquet, and Villemarqué, but oddly enough she does not mention Carnhuanawc, who was unquestionably her prime helper and informant. She concludes disarmingly:

> It may be considered rash in one who has but recently become acquainted with the Principality

> and its literature, to engage in a work like the present, while there are so many others by whom it would be much more ably executed. At the hazard, however, of incurring such an imputation, I have ventured upon this undertaking, in order to gratify the desire so generally and repeatedly expressed for the publication of these interesting remains.

She dedicates the work to her two elder sons, Ifor and Merthyr, as follows:

> My dear Children, Infants as you are, I feel that I cannot dedicate more fitly than to you these venerable relics of ancient lore, and I do so in the hope of inciting you to cultivate the literature of "Gwyllt Walia," in whose beautiful language you are being initiated, and amongst whose free mountains you were born. May you become early imbued with the chivalric and exalted sense of honour and the fervent patriotism for which its sons have ever been celebrated. May you learn to emulate the noble qualities of Ifor Bach, after whom the elder of you was named. I am your affectionate mother C.E. Guest.
>
> Dowlais, August 29, 1838.

But how much of Lady Guest's edition is in fact her own work, and how much of it is due to that of others? The diary repeatedly refers to the material help which she received from Carnhuanawc, and to the encouragement which she received from him and from the gentry of south Wales, the highly aristocratic members of the Cymreigyddion Society of Abergavenny.[24] She certainly knew of as much of William Owen Pughe's work as was available in print, which is to say the greater part of the Four Branches and the tale of Taliesin, and it was from Pughe that she adopted the title *Mabinogion* and with it the notion that these were stories for children—Pughe's "Juvenile Tales." By her own statement we know that she undertook the work primarily to entertain her own children, and it is this—apart from a general Victorian sense of decorum—which may account for the fact that she cut out the passage concerning Pwyll's relations with Arawn's wife (as indeed W.O. Pughe had also done). She used Pughe's Dictionary, but her translation clearly owes nothing to his, and in the several pieces of *Pwyll* and *Math* that I have compared, it is in several instances more accurate than his. And she began her undertaking, not with the *Mabinogi* tales which Pughe had already published, but with the three Arthurian romances, of which Pughe's translations existed at this date only in manuscript. Evidently it was the relationship between these Arthurian tales and the cognate European versions which had first inspired her to undertake her task of translation—indeed, it seems to have been these which initially had made English and European scholars curious to know more about the Welsh tales. We know that Lady Charlotte had been greatly interested previously in medieval literature—Chaucer was her life-long favourite as a poet—and in so far as I have yet been able to establish, it seems most probable that Lady Charlotte was the first person to discover and point out that closely parallel versions existed in French[25] and other languages to the three romances. It is certain that she was indebted to the Breton-French nobleman Theodore Hersart de la Villemarqué for a transcript of the *Yvain* of Chrétien de Troyes, which he made for her at her request in the Bibliothèque Nationale; she published this, after due acknowledgement, as an appendix to her first translation, the tale of *Owain*. In the event, Villemarqué turned out to be a thorn in her flesh, and caused not a little annoyance by his preposterous claim that his name should appear along with hers on the title-page of her book. Later he tried to forestall her book by bringing out a French version of *Peredur* and though the diary shows that he was defeated in this, he published in 1842 his *Romans de la Table Ronde des Anciens Bretons*, which gave his French translations of the Welsh tales, based without acknowledgement on her English text already published.[26] Villemarqué's whole intention at all times was to belittle the difference between Breton and Welsh, and to claim that much of the oldest Welsh literature really originated in Brittany, and was composed in a language which was intelligible to a Breton speaker of his day.[27]

Lady Charlotte Guest's easy, fluent, slightly archaic style has been much praised by subsequent generations. Gwyn

Jones and Thomas Jones describe her *Mabinogion* as "a classic in its own right," and say that they cannot too emphatically pay tribute to so splendid an achievement."[28] Alfred Nutt had written in similar terms in 1904. The poet Tennyson had told her that her style was "the finest English he knew, ranking with Malory's *Morte D'Arthur*."[29] He based on her translation his poem "Geraint and Enid" in his *Idylls of the King* (1859): all the other tales in this work were based on the *Morte D'Arthur*. Prior to the publication in 1887 of the diplomatic text of the *Mabinogion* by John Rhŷs and J. Gwenogvryn Evans, her text of the tales was the only complete text in print. Rhŷs in his introduction says guardedly of her translation that "it may be said to belong to the prescientific era" but nevertheless he awards her due praise, stating that "her text in her edition approximates to the original more nearly than that of any other Welsh text of any length"—but that her book is hard to obtain, and that "greater accuracy is now imperative, hence our effort to meet the requirements of a more exacting age."[30]

One cannot but suspect that all those years of diary-writing must have contributed towards the ease and fluency of Lady Charlotte's style. But I want to emphasize also that the extremely full and wide-ranging notes which she wrote to accompany the tales, are quite as remarkable as the translations themselves. The range of illustrative material which is covered in them is stupendous. She had read and studied all the contents of the *Myvyrian Archaiology of Wales* (available since 1801), and had culled from it a number of quotations from the Cynfeirdd and the Gogynfeirdd, the Triads and *Brut y Brenhinedd*. Nothing appears to have escaped her: for instance she has found the reference to the Twrch Trwyth in the *Gorchan Cynfelyn*, as well as those to Brân and to the sons of Llŷr and Morddwyd Tyllon in a poem in the Book of Taliesin.[31]

She cites the references to Branwen and to Blodeuwedd from Pughe's 1789 edition of Dafydd ap Gwilym, and has used his *Heroic Elegies of Llywarch Hen* (1792), as well as the poems of Lewis Glyn Cothi, edited by Tegid and Gwallter Mechain and published at Llandovery in 1837. She quotes from the *Book of Llan Dâv* (Llandovery 1840), and from the genealogies given in Lewis Dwnn's *Heraldic Visitations* (1846). All her quotations from Welsh verse and prose are invariably translated, even the quotations from the Books of Aneirin and Taliesin. She has a predilection for Iolo Morganwg's Third Series of Triads in the *Myvyrian*, over the two more ancient earlier series. But this was unfortunately only too common in her day, since the Third Series was much the most diffuse and informative of the three series in the *Myvyrian*, and also because it purported to record the earliest events relating to the pre-history of the Cymry, and therefore was generally presumed to be the most primitive version.[32] She was conversant with the Welsh learned journals of the late eighteenth and early nineteenth centuries—the *Cambro-Briton* and the *Cambrian Quarterly Magazine* of William Owen Pughe (from which she derived her knowledge of *Cyfraith Hywel*) and *Y Greal*. She knew of Edward Jones's *Welsh Bards* (1784) and his *Bardic Museum* (1802): from the latter she derived (in her Notes to *Culhwch and Olwen)* her long and informative version of the story of Huail fab Caw, which goes back ultimately to Elis Gruffydd's Chronicle. Her background reading further included Warton's *History of English Poetry*, Froissart's Chronicles, Ritson's *English Medieval Romances*, Gibbon's *Decline and Fall of the Roman Empire* (for her note on Maxen Wledig); Robert of Gloucester's Chronicles, Malory's *Morte D'Arthur* (for her note on Cai), Polwhele's *History of Cornwall* (for the site of Celli Wig), William Rees's *Welsh Saints*, Sharon Turner's *History of the Anglo-Saxons* (1799), Edward Davies's *Celtic Researches* (1804)—with which work, however, she did not always agree. She also used some MS. material—for instance, a text of the *Thirteen Treasures of the Island of Britain* from a MS. in the possession of Judge Bosanquet at Dingestow Court. The more recently published works on which she drew for her illustrative material can only have become available at the time when she was preparing the collective edition of the tales which was published in 1849. For her work as a whole she must have derived considerable help from her Welsh informants; indeed she refers several times in her diary to Carnhuanawc's having gone through some of her notes and translations with her. But for her knowledge of general medieval sources she drew on her own extensive reading and long-established interest in medieval literature—in Middle English, in French and German, Latin and Icelandic. She refers to her visits to the British

Museum, where she would sit and read and where she set others to work in search of the continental parallels to the Welsh romances—particularly those bearing on the theme of the Grail. She was interested in Welsh folklore, and gives references to beliefs about Gwyn ap Nudd and his *Cŵn Annwn*, and to Sarn Helen, which she explains as *Sarn y Lleng* "the road of the Legions." She was indeed particularly interested in the place-names associated with the stories, such as *Bryn y Cyfergir* and *Llyn y Morynion*, and in her introduction she argues interestingly (if hardly convincingly) that the antiquity of the tales is proved by the fact that these must ante-date the place-names which commemorate them. So great was her enthusiasm in pursuing place-name investigations that after discovering the reference in Nennius's *Historia Brittonum* to *Carn Cabal* as denoting the Radnorshire mountain of Corn Cafallt, which is said to preserve on its topmost cairn the paw-mark of Arthur's hound, she tells that she prevailed upon "a gentleman of her acquaintance" to undertake for her a pilgrimage to the summit of the mountain. On his return he reported that he had discovered such a stone with an oval indentation upon it, but there were no marks of toes or nails to be seen. Her comment is "but when we make allowance for the effect of 1000 winters in this high and stormy region, it is not too much to suppose that at one time the resemblance (to a paw-mark) was still more striking," and she adds cryptically that "a geologist might say that the indentation on the stone was due to natural wearing, but such an opinion scarcely requires a remark."

Whatever may have been the extent of the help which Lady Charlotte received from others, whether in scholarship or in mountaineering, it cannot detract from the magnitude of her achievment and her deep interest and involvement in her work. Her name will always remain indissolubly linked with the *Mabinogion*, whose publication was an epoch-making event in Welsh studies, even if she was more indebted to the assistance of others than she was always quite ready to acknowledge. Her translation had a penetrating influence both at home and abroad, as can be seen from the manner in which allusions and themes from the *Mabinogi* gained increasing prominence in the work of Welsh poets, while Tennyson's poetic rendering of "Geraint and Enid" and his praise of her work, followed by the warm praise of Alfred Nutt in his re-edition of her *Mabinogion* in 1904, did much to make the tales well-known in England. One result of the impact of the *Mabinogion* upon the outside world was that in France it stimulated Ernest Renan's *Essai sur la Poésie des Races Celtiques* (1854)—a belated review-article of Lady Charlotte's book, which he reviewed together with Villemarqué's work and ab Ithel's *Ecclesiastical Antiquities of the Cymry* (1844). Renan's essay was absolutely the first attempt ever made at any kind of comparative study of the Celtic literatures between themselves,[33] and an attempt to define their mutual characteristics. In it he describes the *Mabinogion* as "the true description of the Celtic genius," and one by which, as he says, in the twelfth century "the Celts transformed the imagination of Europe." He finds it surprising that "so curious a literature, the source of nearly all the romantic creations of Europe, should have remained unknown until our days." One can do no other than endorse Renan's expression of surprise, though I have tried to indicate how it came about that it was necessary to wait for the Romantic Revival before there could be any true appreciation of the qualities and interest of the tales brought together in the *Mabinogion*.

NOTES

1. Brinley Roberts gives the number as 60, *Brut y Brenhinedd* xxiv: Edmund Reiss lists 76 copies, "The Welsh Versions of Geoffrey of Monmouth's *Historia*,"106.

2. I have examined some 30 MSS. containing *Trioedd Ynys Prydein*, hereafter *TYP*.

3. For particulars see Lloyd, *Rhai Agweddau ar Ddysg y Gogynfeirdd*. For a newly discovered possible reference to Teyrnon and Rhiannon see Gruffydd and Roberts, "Rhiannon Gyda Theyrnon Yng Ngwent," 289–291.

4. Parry, *Gwaith Dafydd ap Gwilym*, 84, 46.

5. In *Aspects of the Poetry of Dafydd ap Gwilym*, ch. 5, I have suggested that Dafydd ap Gwilym derived his knowledge of *Mabinogion* figures from the White Book of Rhydderch, or its source. See also "Cyfeiriadau Daffydd ap Gwilym at Chwedl a Rhamant," 58.

6. Compare *TYP*, lxxi–ii.

7. *Archaeologia Britannica*, 710, 262.
8. *Archeologica Britannica*, 264; *TYP* liv. Compare Bromwich, *Trioedd Ynys Prydian in Welsh Literature and Scholarship*, 11-12.
9. Davies, *Bywyd a Gwaith Moses Williams*, 15; *TYP*, lvi-lix.
10. Evans, *Drych y Prif Oesoedd: Y Rhan Gyntaf*, 17.
11. Morris, *Celtic Remains*, 286.
12. Jenkins and Ramage, *History of the Honourable Society of Cymmrodorion*, 241.
13. Bromwich,*Trioedd Ynys Prydain in Welsh Literature and Scholarship, passim*; "*TYP:* The *Myvyrian* 'Third Series,'" I, 299-338, "*TYP:* The *Myvyrian* 'Third Series,'" II, 127-156.
14. On these writers see Johnston, *Enchanted Ground: The Study of Medieval Romance in the Eighteenth Century*. For William Owen Pughe, see now Glenda Carr's biography.
15. In *The Cambrian Quarterly* I (1829). The text of *Math* was not reproduced from the Red Book of Hergest, but from an inexact copy: possibly that of Moses Williams in one of the Llanstephan MSS. 90, 91, 93, 126. The translation is by Idrison (John Jones, 1804-1887). Vol. V (1833) gives the tale of Taliesin "from a MS. of Hopcyn Thomas Phillip, c. 1370."
16. George Ellis was entirely English, and had no knowledge of Welsh matters; see Johnston, *Enchanted Ground*, ch. VI.
17. National Library of Wales MS. 13242. On Pughe's translations of the *Mabinogion* tales and his associations with English scholars in connection with the work, see Arthur Johnston's important article, "William Owen-Pughe and the Mabinogion." In the same issue, there is a letter written in 1831 by Aneurin Owen to Arthur Johnes, referring to his father's plans to print the *Mabinogion* by Gee and Co., Denbigh, and referring to a list of subscribers to the work, 244.
18. I have derived all biographical details from *The Diaries of Lady Charlotte Guest*, edited by her grandson the Earl of Bessborough. An earlier publication, *Lady Charlotte Guest and the Mabinogion* by D. Rhys Phillips gives extracts from the diary referring specifically to her work of translation.
19. B. Jones, *Yr Hen Bersoniaid Llengar*.
20. See Fraser, "Lady Llanover and Her Circle," 181-184. On the Llanover family see the latter's articles in *National Library of Wales Journal* XI, XII, XIII, and Thomas, *Afiaith yng Ngwent*.
21. "From the standpoint of established schools for the education of the working classes, the Guest family of Dowlais . . . was undoubtedly the most important and also the most progressive in the industrial history, not only of south Wales, but of the whole of Britain in the nineteenth century." Evans, *Education in Industrial Wales 1700-1900*.

22. *Lady Charlotte Schreiber*, by the Earl of Bessborough, gives extracts from her diaries relating to her life after the death of her first husband in 1852. See now Revel Guest and Angela John, *Lady Charlotte: A Biography of the Nineteenth Century*, London, 1989.

23. Professor R.S. Loomis performed the same task a century later, and notes that whereas Lady Charlotte appears to have copied the text within a week, it took him nearly a month to do so ("Pioneers of Arthurian Scholarship," 104).

24. Thomas, *Afiaith yng Ngwent*, and Roberts, "Y Dr. John Davies O Fallwyd," 97ff.

25. The late Professor C. E. Pickford informed me that none of the poems of Chrétien de Troyes were published before the late 1840s (firstly by the German Immanuel Becker, predecessor of Wendelin Forster). Editions followed in England, America, and Germany. But apart from Potvin's editions of the Grail romances (1866–1871) no French edition was published until the 1950s. Dr. Roger Middleton has suggested to me that Lady Charlotte may have learned of the various continental versions of the three Welsh romances of *Peredur*, *Owain*, and *Geraint* from the summaries to be found in the *Bibliotheque Universelle des Romans*, of which a copy would have been available to her in the British Museum.

26. See her diary, 84–87, and Phillips, *Lady Charlotte Guest and the Mabinogion*, 33; also Gourvil,*Theodore Hersart de la Villemarqué et le "Barzaz-Breiz,"* 70–72, 96–97. As Gourvil points out, Villemarqué had no more than a smattering of modern Welsh, which was quite insufficient to enable him to understand the language and orthography of the Red Book of Hergest.

27. Gourvil, *Theodore Hersart de la Villemarqué et le "Barzaz-Breiz,"* 73.

28. Jones and Jones, ed. and trans.,*The Mabinogion*, xxxi. Nutt speaks of "the charm and splendour of her translation," *The Mabinogion translated by Lady Charlotte Guest, with Notes by A. Nutt*, 324.

29. Bessborough, ed., *The Diaries of Lady Charlotte Guest*, 111. On page 68 she refers to Tennyson's acknowledgement of the source in her book of his poem *Geraint and Enid*.

30. Rhŷs and Evans, eds.,*The Text of the Mabinogion from the Red Book of Hergest*, vii–viii.

31. I. Williams, ed., *Canu Aneirin*, l. 1340; Evans, *The Book of Taliesin*, 33, 25.

32. See my *Trioedd Ynys Prydain in Welsh Literature and Scholarship*, 10–29.

33. In this he was followed shortly after by Matthew Arnold. On both writers see my *Matthew Arnold and Celtic Literature: A Retrospect*.

2

The Date of the Four Branches of the Mabinogi[1]

T.M. Charles-Edwards

The generally accepted view on the date when the Four Branches were given the form in which we have them is that of Sir Ifor Williams, who said in the introduction to his edition: "the theory which corresponds to the facts known to me, then, is that a man from Dyfed joined together old stories of Gwent, Dyfed and Gwynedd around 1060 when the three kingdoms had been united."[2] Professors Gwyn Jones and Thomas Jones, in the introduction to their translation of the *Mabinogion*, agree saying, "the likeliest date for the Four Branches would appear to be early in the second half of the eleventh century."[3]

Since Sir Ifor Williams published his edition there have been two important dissenting voices. Professor Morgan Watkins in *La Civilisation française dans les Mabinogion* has argued for a date in the first half or middle of the thirteenth century, and Mr. Saunders Lewis has recently published some articles in support of a date between 1170 and 1190.[4] The disagreement between them and Sir Ifor Williams is an important one, for what they are arguing about is whether the man who wrote the Four Branches was indebted to French and Anglo-Norman literature and ways of thought and life, or on the contrary, belonged to the period of Welsh literature which preceded the Norman conquest of much of Wales.

The main purpose of this paper is to discuss the arguments put forward by Mr. Saunders Lewis, but I shall first give a short account of Sir Ifor Williams's case.

His arguments—and here there is a clear contrast between him and Mr. Saunders Lewis—were mainly linguistic. He thought that the thirteenth century manuscripts still retained a few clues of spelling and phonology which pointed to an original manuscript written before 1100. He pointed to four examples in the White Book of *t* standing for *th*. This spelling is found in the early legal manuscript, Peniarth 28, written towards the end of the twelfth century but containing several OW. features. On the other hand, there are also three examples of *t* for [*th*] in another legal manuscript, containing a law book, part of which is attributed to a thirteenth-century lawyer.[5] This spelling habit, therefore, lasted well into the thirteenth century, and so does not show that the original manuscript of the Four Branches was any older than the earliest surviving manuscript containing part of the Four Branches, which is believed to have been written about 1225. In this early manuscript, however, there are two words, both belonging to the Second Branch, which are spelt without the initial *y* which they always have in MW., *stlys* and *stryw* instead of *ystlys* and *ystryw*.[6] Sir Ifor Williams shows that the poets regard such words as having an initial *y*, which counted as a full syllable, at the latest by 1106. Professor Jackson argues that this prosthetic *y*, while being produced as early as the ninth century did not count as a separate syllable until the accent shift took place in the eleventh century. *Stlys* and *stryw* reflect, therefore, OW. spellings. Another orthographical argument is that in the White Book copy of the Four Branches *makwyf* from Irish *macc cóem* is still spelt with a final *f* and its plural *makwyueit* still shows the intervocalic [*v*], even though Cynddelw rhymes *maccuy* with words without a final [*v*]. This argument is not entirely convincing since the White Book copy of *Gereint*, a story showing undeniable French or Norman features, also spells *makwyf* with a final *f* and its plural with *f* or *u* standing for [*v*]. In this case Welsh orthography seems to have kept the *f* or *u* long after [*v*] had ceased to be pronounced. Though the rhymes of Cynddelw show that it was no longer pronounced in the middle of the twelfth century, the old spelling survived for more than a hundred years after that. This being so, the spellings *makwyf* and *makwyueit* do not show that the Four Branches were compiled any earlier than the surviving manu-

The Date of the Four Branches

scripts, since they prove nothing about how the author would have pronounced *makwyf*. The evidence of orthography for an original manuscript written before the Norman influence became powerful is reduced to just two forms, *stlys* and *stryw*. Since the history of MW. orthography has not yet been properly worked out, this is not enough by itself to prove that the Four Branches had been written down by 1100.

Sir Ifor Williams also put forward one purely phonological argument from the metre of the second *englyn* which Gwydion sang to Lleu:

> Dar a dyf yn ard uaes
> Nis gwlych glaw, nis mwy tawd tes,
> Naw ugein angerd porthes,
> Yn y blaen, Lleu Llaw Gyffes.[7]

The first line should have seven syllables. This, together with the rhyme in *-es*, shows that *uaes* is disyllabic, *uaës* and not *uaes*. *Maes* is from **mag-est-*, so that the disyllabic pronunciation would be predictable for OW.; but already by the time of the earliest Gogynfeirdd *maes* was regularly treated as one syllable for metrical purposes. The englyn, therefore, belongs to the OW. period.

Sir Ifor treats this, without any further discussion, as good evidence for the date of the final redaction of the Four Branches. But is this correct? Sir Ifor Williams himself, when he came to discuss the Welsh version of the Tristan story, pointed out that the *englynion* were linguistically older than the prose.[8] There are plenty of examples in Irish of stories which contain poems older than the date of the final redaction of the stories themselves. So, although the argument from *maës* is formally correct, it does not take one nearly far enough. It shows that the englyn is old, but proves nothing about the Four Branches in the form in which we have them. The three *englynion* sung by Gwydion could, and very probably did, exist before the final redactor got to work.

The last of his linguistic arguments is from the scarcity of French loanwords in the text. Only three seem certain, *pali*, *cordwal* and *swmer*. These he maintains could be either later scribal substitutions, or borrowed from the Normans settled at Hereford in 1052, or borrowed through merchants. This number of loanwords, three in eighty pages of the Red Book Mabinogion, is contrasted with the dozen or so French loanwords in the sixteen pages of the Red Book copy of *Breuddwyd Rhonabwy*. Since Sir Ifor Williams is comparing the Four Branches with *Breuddwyd Rhonabwy*, it becomes important to establish the date of the latter. It seems to me that the opinion of Loth and others, that it was composed during the lifetime of Madog ab Maredudd, who died in 1160, or shortly after his death, is preferable to Professor Melville Richards's view that it was written about 1220, still more to Dr. Parry's date of about 1250.[9] Madog ab Maredudd is mentioned as Prince of Powys at the beginning of the story, and circumstantial details are given about his difficulties with his younger brother Iorwerth. One of the main themes of the whole story is the sad contrast between the miserable physique and appearance of Rhonabwy and his companions, Madog's soldiers, and the strength and splendour of Arthur and his men. Take, for example, the passage in which Rhonabwy and his companions are brought before Arthur:

> "May God bless you," said Arthur. "Where Iddawg did you find those little men?"
> "I found them, Lord over there on the road."
> Then the emperor smiled a grey half-smile.
> "Lord," said Iddawg, "What are you laughing at?"
> "Iddawg," said Arthur, "I am not laughing but I am so sad that men so weak as these should be guarding this island after men as fine as those who once guarded it."

Now this looks very much like satire aimed at contemporaries. There would be much less point to it if it were written two generations later, and so aimed at the generation of the author's grandparents. And, given that the story has this satirical purpose, I do not see any force in the argument put forward by Professor Richards and Dr. Parry that some time must have elapsed between the death of Madog and the use of his name in a story. If, then, *Breuddwyd Rhonabwy* is a guide to the extent of French influence on Welsh vocabulary about 1150–1160, the Four Branches must be put back at least to the beginning of the twelfth century. But this is not enough to show that the Four Branches cannot have been influenced by

The Date of the Four Branches

French culture. It may not be obvious in the vocabulary, but that does not prove that there was no French influence on the choice and treatment of subject matter.

So much for linguistics. The evidence it has provided is not sufficient to decide which view is correct, though it does show that the Four Branches cannot be later than the early Medieval Welsh period.

Sir Ifor Williams also put forward historical arguments. Indeed, it was an historical argument which gave the fairly precise date *c.* 1160. One of these I shall leave until later, since it turns on the question of whether the author of the Four Branches used language which betrays a knowledge of Anglo-Norman feudalism, and this question is at the heart of many of Mr. Saunders Lewis's arguments.

There are two other historical arguments which Sir Ifor Williams puts forward. One is from the fact that the king goes on circuit, *cylch,* around his kingdom. This circuit was a journey during which the king and his entourage were entertained by his subjects. Sir Ifor Williams argues correctly that in the Welsh laws kings do not go on *cylch,* even though other members of the court do. Therefore, he concludes, if the earliest Welsh lawbooks (*c.* 1175–*c.* 1250) know nothing of a king's *cylch,* then the Four Branches, which do, must be about a century earlier at least. In other words they must belong to the end of the eleventh century at the latest. A point which he did not mention, but which is important, is that the name for the tribute exacted by the king from his free subjects, *gwestfa,* shows that the entertainment which had once been owing to the king when on *cylch* had been changed to a tribute of food and, later still, money. *Gwest* is cognate with Irish *feiss,* "spending the night," which is just what the Irish king, or any Irish lord, did at the homes of his vassals during the *aimser chue,* the season of entertainment between New Year's Day and Shrovetide. By the thirteenth century *gwestfa* was a money rent, often called *twnc,* but the word *gwestfa* shows that the king's vassals had once had to entertain their lord since it means "spending-the-night-place." It must have referred originally to any house in which the king was entitled to entertainment when he was on *cylch*. The institution, then, went through three stages in its development: at first it was an obligation on the part of the vassal to entertain the king (and, doubtless, anyone who was his lord); next it was a food-rent; and, finally, it was money-rent. This third stage was reached in the thirteenth contury, but it is the first stage which is reflected in the Four Branches.

The Four Branches, then, contain old law obsolete by the time of the earliest Welsh lawbook. Does this mean that the Four Branches were themselves old by the time of the earliest Welsh lawbook? To this the answer must be, not necessarily. In all cases of this kind the difficulty is to prove that the writer or storyteller is not being deliberately archaic, but is referring to an institution or rule current in his own day. To cite only one example, the sagas of the Irish Ulster cycle assume a political situation in which the kingdom of Ulster embraces roughly what is now the province of Ulster, something which ceased to be true after the middle of the fifth century.[10] The sagas themselves, however, belong to the seventh, eighth and subsequent centuries. The lateness of a saga may emerge from details which are taken from contemporary life and where there are no such tell-tale details there is a presumption that the saga is old. It is, however, a presumption and not a proof.

The reason why Sir Ifor Williams chose c. 1060 as the date of the Four Branches lies in the political situation at the time. By 1055 Gruffudd ap Llywelyn had made himself king of all Wales and from then until his death in 1063 he ruled Gwynedd, Powys, Deheubarth, Morgannwg and Gwent Is Coed. He therefore united under his rule all the territories which provided the local traditions and tales used by the author of the Four Branches. During his reign poets and storytellers could move easily around Wales. In this way the author of the Four Branches could have gathered the materials for his stories. This argument is not particularly convincing. Even MW. prose is relatively, though by no means entirely, free from dialectal differences, and MW. poetry uses a uniform, fixed, literary language. The situation is similar to that for Old Irish and Classical Modern Irish. It implies that poets and storytellers could move freely around Wales, just as they are assumed to do in the text of the Four Branches. We know, in fact, that poets did often move from one patron to another; Cynddelw is an example. When the Lord Rhys held his court at Cardigan at Christmas 1176, and organized competitions

The Date of the Four Branches

between poets and between musicians, the poets of Gwynedd were not only able to attend but defeated the poets of the Lord Rhys's own kingdom.[11] The history of both Ireland and Wales shows how political disunity and cultural unity can march hand in hand. It is not necessary, therefore, to look for a period when Wales was unified under one king to explain the use of local traditions from different areas in the Four Branches. And furthermore, it is by no means clear how far the Four Branches do make use of local traditions. A tradition about people from a particular place is one thing; a local tradition is quite another.

Mr. Saunders Lewis has published a series of four articles each on one of the Four Branches. His is the most recent voice, and since, whether right or wrong, his case is always incisively, and sometimes ingeniously, argued, it deserves careful consideration. His arguments appear persuasive, and if we are not to be persuaded too easily, we must examine them at leisure.

I shall first concentrate on one specific point he made, for the simple reason that I found it very telling when I first read it; and then I shall examine the whole knotty problem of the supposed influence of French and Norman feudalism.

This specific point is one he makes about a passage in *Manawydan*.[12] Pryderi, Manawydan and Rhiannon are living in Dyfed and Manawydan and Rhiannon have just been married. Pryderi is lord of Dyfed having failed to give his kingdom to Manawydan. After the marrriage, he tells the others that he intends to go off to England to do homage to Caswallon, who is now king of the Island of the Mighty (Britain). Rhiannon dissuades him, saying that Caswallon is now in Kent, and Pryderi can stay for the rest of the marriage feast, and go to meet Caswallon when he is nearer. He agrees, and they go on *cylch* around Dyfed (normally a winter activity) and hunt and enjoy themselves. Apparently before the *cylch* is over, Pryderi goes off to Oxford, where Caswallon now is, and becomes Caswallon's vassal. He is received with delight and gratitude, after which he returns to Dyfed.

At this stage in the article Mr. Saunders Lewis has already made the suggestion that the story reflects the conditions of Henry II's reign, and he therefore proceeds to look at this passage to see whether Caswallon resembles Henry II, and whether the sequence of events resembles a sequence of events in his reign. His answer to both questions is, yes. Caswallon, like Henry II, gained his throne by force, had only a doubtful right to the throne, and so valued highly acts of homage by his vassals. On the 12th July 1174 Henry went to Canterbury to do penance for the murder of Thomas Becket, one of the famous events of his reign; and at the end of May 1177 he held a great council at Oxford which was attended by nearly all the Welsh princes of the time. The two events would have been well known to contemporary Welshmen. Mr. Saunders Lewis's theory is, then, that Rhiannon knew Caswallon was in Kent because all western Christendom knew Henry II was doing penance there; and they knew Caswallon would be in Oxford because of the Great Council to be held there at which so many Welsh princes would be present.

He also suggests that the author may have been a Cistercian monk of Strata Florida, since he holds that certain narrative features of the Four Branches owe much to the Welsh annals, and Strata Florida was the main centre for the writing of annals.

Attractive though it is, there are certain objections to the argument. The picture of Caswallon is undoubtedly true of Henry II, except that it was a treaty between himself and Stephen which finally gave him the throne. But it is just as true, or even more so, of every English king since 1066. William the Conqueror, William II, Henry I, Stephen, all seized the throne in spite of good or even superior rival claims, and had to fight for their kingdoms either before or soon after their accessions. Some of them spent most of their reigns defending their positions by war. It is not until the thirteenth century that son regularly succeeds to father. The rule of primogeniture was not established for royal succession until then. It displaced a quite different rule of succession by which the reigning king would normally choose an heir-apparent from a close circle of kinsmen.[13] This circle of kinsmen included, for example, a nephew or a brother, besides the son. According to this scheme, Henry II's succession was the most unimpeachably legal succession since that of William Rufus, who was designated as his successor by William the Conqueror in a letter to Lanfranc. Caswallon, as a first cousin of Bendigeidfran, was probably within the circle of those who had a claim to the throne according to Welsh law. All these kings, of course, were like Caswallon in attaching great importance to homage. This was true of all the kings and lords of early medieval Western Europe. Homage was felt to be the main unifying force of society.

Mr. Saunders Lewis's source for his picture of the Council of Oxford is Lloyd's *History of Wales*.[14] If, however, you read Lloyd himself, you will find that he never mentions any act of homage as having been performed at the Council of Oxford by a Welsh prince. Some weeks earlier, apparently, oaths of fealty were sworn by some Welshmen to the king, but this was not at Oxford, and fealty is a quite different thing from homage. On the other hand, if you go back behind Lloyd to his source, the chronicler Benedict Abbas,[15] you will find that two Welsh princes, Dafydd of Gwynedd and Rhys of Deheubarth, were given extra lordships by Henry II, Ellesmere going to Dafydd and Maelienydd to Rhys. For these they swore fealty and became the liege vassals of the king. But nobody performed any act of homage for Dyfed. That had already been done by Rhys years before.

To see what was involved in these transactions it is necessary to bear in mind some of the main features of vassalage.[16] The contract of vassalage was a ceremony with two essential stages. The first of these was homage, an act by which a man placed his hands in those of another and declared that he was becoming the other's man. The second was fealty, by which the man swore to be faithful to his lord placing his hand upon the Bible or on relics. Fealty was the specifically Christian part of the ceremony. There is an important difference between homage and fealty. The act of homage was normally effective for a lifetime. Once the lord's man, always the lord's man. In theory, homage, like baptism,[17] changed a man for life, and was, therefore, not renewable. The same attitude was not taken towards fealty. A vassal might swear an oath of fealty more than once to the same lord. Men who would not be expected to do homage, royal officials for example, were expected to swear fealty. The act of homage, then, was the core of the contract of vassalage. The other important point about vassalage, for our purposes, is that one man was often the vassal of more than one lord. This meant a risk of a conflict of loyalties. The popular method of avoiding this risk in the twelfth century was the institution known as liege homage. This involved a promise by the vassal that he gave allegiance without reservation to his liege lord, and therefore that in any conflict of loyalties the liege lord would come first. This system decayed quickly on the continent, so that a man could have more than one liege lord—something which made nonsense of the original purpose of the institution. In England, however, the crown made use of the system for its own benefit, and it retained its character until the end of the twelfth century.

It is clear from the chronicler's account that it was quite specifically liege homage which was at stake at the Council of Oxford. Dafydd and Rhys were already the king's men. What the grants of Ellesmere and Maelienydd secured was that they now became the liege men of the king. Their allegiance to him was now absolute in law. The events in *Manawydan*, therefore, fail to correspond to those of Henry II's reign in two ways: Pryderi was doing homage to Caswallon, and he was doing it specifically as lord of Dyfed; the Lord Rhys, on the other hand, was doing liege homage, and the only land involved was Maelienydd. The two situations were quite different, both politically and in law.

Mr. Saunders Lewis suggests that the two events, the penance of Henry II and the Council of Oxford, would have been well known to a Welshman such as the author of the Four Branches, and also that the author was a monk of Strata Florida. This theory can easily be tested. The abbey, founded in 1165, became the main centre in Wales for the writing of annals.[18] The C version of the *Annales Cambriae* and another set of Latin annals, called in the *Brut y Tywysogion* the Annals of Strata Florida, were both compiled there. The Annals of Strata Florida were, it seems, from 1175 until 1282 the main source of yet another set of Latin annals of which the Welsh *Bruts* are three independent translations. This means we have two independent witnesses, *Annales Cambriae*, version C, and the three Welsh annals translated from one Latin original, which will tell us whether the monks of Strata Florida were so well informed or so interested as these suggestions presume. As it turns out, neither of the two events is mentioned by any Welsh chronicle.

This is not because they never do mention events which take place in England. Only two years before the Council of Oxford, at the end of July 1175, the princes of South Wales had met Henry II at a council at Gloucester. This meeting is duly recorded in the Welsh annals. And it suggests a further objection. Pryderi, it will be remembered, did not wait long before he set off to Oxford. The impression given is that it was only a matter of a few months at the most. Yet almost three years went by between Henry II's penance at Canterbury and the Council of Oxford. The interval between the penance and the Gloucester council was only one year; but Mr. Saunders Lewis has to ignore that meeting in favour of the later one because he wants Henry II in Kent first and then in Oxford.

Here we may ask a further question: how often did the Anglo-Norman kings visit first Kent, and then, within a year or two, Oxford? Just outside Oxford was the royal hunting-lodge of Woodstock. In May 1122 Henry I was in Kent and in January and March 1123 he was at Woodstock. In May 1130 he was at Canterbury and in April 1132 he was at Woodstock and in March 1133 he was at Oxford. In December 1135 Stephen was at Canterbury having just arrived in England. In January 1136 and March or April 1136 he was at Oxford where a charter of liberties for the church was issued, having among its witnesses Bernard, Bishop of St. David's. In 1139, in January, Stephen was at Canterbury for the consecration of Theobald as archbishop, and in June he was at Oxford.[19] This is only a space of twenty years, but it shows that the sequence of events supposedly alluded to in *Manawydan* was quite a common one. There is no need to attribute them to Henry II's reign.

Since Sir Ifor Williams's theory puts the date of the Four Branches in the eleventh century, it is worth pointing out that the early eleventh century, and not the twelfth, has been called "Oxford's most glorious period."[20] Several royal councils were held there up to 1066, some of great importance. Domesday Oxford appears as a relatively large town which has known better days.

The theory that the allusion to Caswallon being in Kent in the conversation between Rhiannon and Pryderi, and Pryderi's journey to Oxford to do homage to Caswallon, reflect two events in Henry II's reign is attractive; but it seems to fail every available historical test.

The heart of the debate lies in the question of whether the Four Branches do or do not reflect the language and customs of English and French feudalism. This was the point which gave Sir Ifor Williams the most trouble when he was arguing for a date about 1060. He was faced with a number of words of an institutional character which seemed to be quite foreign to the society which existed in Wales before the twelfth and thirteenth centuries. These words were *gwr* meaning a vassal, "man" in the feudal sense, *gwrogaeth* meaning "homage," *estyn* meaning "to grant, to invest." His only argument in face of this evidence is that, since no Welsh lawbook is earlier than the second half of the twelfth century, we have no means of knowing what Welsh society or social vocabulary was like in the eleventh century. We, therefore, cannot be certain that these terms were not then in use.

Mr. Saunders Lewis has more to say on the same theme. In *Pwyll*, he maintains, the conversation between Pwyll and Arawn contains feudal technical terms; the customs of Arawn's court show a feudal concern for ceremony and grades of honour; the term *iarll* puts one at once into the world of the Arthurian tales; and the fight between Pwyll and Hafgan at the ford is a tournament. He further maintains that the description of the tournament is borrowed from *Gereint*, and, therefore, that the first part of *Pwyll*, the story of how Pwyll became known as Pwyll Pen Annwfn, is much later than the rest of *Pwyll*, and did not originally form part of the Four Branches. He claims that, in *Manawydan*, the description of the events leading up to the marriage of Rhiannon and Manawydan reflects the language of twelfth-century humanism; that some of the crafts practised by Pryderi and Manawydan when in England show a knowledge of the provisions of the Assize of Arms (1181); and that the fear of Manawydan, that Caswallon and his men would punish them if they slew their enemies among the townspeople, shows that the judicial system of Henry II, in particular the system of judicial circuits, was in existence. The point is that Manawydan fears the king's justice rather than the lord's justice. In *Math*, the military tactics, the references to knights arming themselves or being armed, the giving and releasing of hostages and the judicial duel between Pryderi and Gwydion, all reflect the conditions of feudal warfare, and, for the most part, twelfth-century feudal warfare. It is then, the mature feudalism of Angevin England, when the royal administration had considerable power and when intellectual life had been renewed, that he sees as the background to the Four Branches.

Before discussing this case, it is necessary to have some idea of what we mean when we say that certain words or customs are feudal. The feudalism in which we are interested is not feudalism in the narrow legal sense. The term "feudal" is used in this debate to characterise words, customs or institutions which were (1) part of the fabric of society in Anglo-Norman England or Capetian France, and (2) not part of the fabric of either Anglo-Saxon society or pre-Norman Welsh society. The point about Anglo-Saxon society is a vital one. If the word, custom or institution either certainly existed in Anglo-Saxon England, or may well, for all we know, have done so, then it is of no use whatever in an argument designed to prove that the Four Branches were written under the influence of Norman ideas or customs. The element in question may not be pure-bred Welsh, but that does not show that it was not borrowed long before 1066.

An example will help to drive this point home. Sir Ifor Williams was inclined to think, and others appear to assume, that the phrase "man of so-and-so" meaning "vassal of so-and-so" must be of Norman or French origin. Thus, when in *Pwyll* we have the sentence about Teirnon, "Ansawdd Pwyll hyspys oed gantaw ef, canys gwr uuassei idaw kynn no hynny," "the appearance of Pwyll was familiar to him, because he had previously been his man,"[21] we are apparently to take it as evidence for Norman influence. This inference, however, is quite wrong, since these phrases could have been borrowed centuries earlier from the Anglo-Saxons. Consider the evidence of the Anglo-Saxon laws. Alfred says in his code: "moreover we declare that a man may fight on behalf of his lord, if the lord is being attacked, without incurring a vendetta. Similarly the lord may fight on behalf of his man."[22] Athelstan, in the code issued at Grately says: "and we pronounce about these lordless men from whom no justice can be obtained, that one should order their kindred to fetch such a person to justice and to find him a lord in public meeting."[23] Cnut, in his ecclesiastical code declares: "and also every lord has great benefit from treating his men justly."[24] When Domesday Book talks about the time of King Edward it frequently describes A as the man of B. In Old English one can talk of a *man-dryhten*, a "lord of men," and about *man-bot*, the compensation paid to a lord for injury to his man. This last term is attested as early as Ine's laws.[25] Even the word *vassellus* itself is found in Anglo-Saxon sources, at first under the form *fasellus* which reflects Old English spelling habits.[26] There is then no need whatever to suppose that *gwr* meaning "vassal" and *gwrogaeth* meaning "homage" owe anything to Norman influence. Indeed, since vassalage existed in Ireland in the seventh century, and is clearly present in the Welsh laws, it is almost certainly a native institution.

There is even evidence from the passage about Teirnon which I have quoted that *gŵr* did not have exactly the meaning one would expect if it were simply an equivalent to Anglo-Norman Latin *homo* in the sense of "vassal." The passage went in translation: "the appearance of Pwyll was familiar to him, because he had previously been his man." When a contract of vassalage was made, it was made for life. It was legally possible for a vassal to renounce his homage, but this was an unfriendly act and normally a prelude to rebellion. In the text the noticeable thing is that Teirnon no longer is Pwyll's vassal, and yet "gwr goreu yn y byt oed," "he was the noblest man in the world." He was also on excellent terms with Pwyll. This situation would hardly be possible in Anglo-Norman England. It all becomes much less puzzling if we remember the Anglo-Saxon use of the term *vassallus*. This could be used as the equivalent of the Latin *minister*,[27] and *minister* is the normal translation of *thegn*, which originally just meant "servant," like Celtic **wassos* > Ir. *foss*, W. *gwas*.[28] By the end of the Anglo-Saxon period, though a thegn was not necessarily a royal servant, he still well might be. In the eleventh century a man who hoped to become a thegn was expected to do a period of service at the royal court. If, then, *gwr* might be used as a rough equivalent of thegn, the passage would make better sense. It would mean that he had been Pwyll's servant, *minister*, and had spent a period at the court of Dyfed. He had been a *makwyf*, perhaps, or a *gwas ieuanc*. When he ceased to be Pwyll's man, he was not renouncing his homage, but simply ending his period of service at Pwyll's court.

There are similar difficulties about the terms *gwr* and *gwrogaeth* in the passage describing Pwyll's conquest of Hafgan's kingdom after Hafgan's defeat.[29] He instructs his nobles to discover who should be his men, and they reply that everyone should, since Pwyll is now the only king of Annwfn. He then receives the *gwrogaeth* of the men of Hafgan's kingdom. If, in this passage, *gwr* and *gwrogaeth* meant "vassal" and "homage" in the Norman sense, the reasoning attributed to Pwyll's nobles would be obviously fallacious. In the Anglo-Norman state the king did not have the right to receive everyone's homage. Only in exceptional circumstances, as at Salisbury in 1086, did he even demand the vassalage of the principal tenants of his tenants-in-chief. It is clear enough that *gwrogaeth* means something like "submission" or "allegiance" here rather than homage. All the men of Hafgan's kingdom could be expected to submit to Pwyll; they could not be expected to become his vassals.

Gwrogaeth, in this sense, reminds one of the Irish term *uréirge*, literally "rising up before," which referred to a ceremonial act which a vassal performed to his lord as an acknowledgement of their relationship, but which was also performed by an inferior to a superior without there being any suggestion that the inferior was the vassal of the superior, an acknowledgement of authority rather than of personal dependence.[30] Welsh vassalage, then, appears to be a native institution containing elements reminiscent of both Irish and Anglo-Saxon vassalage.

One of the characteristics of the case put forward by Mr. Saunders Lewis is that it consists of a large number of short arguments. He uses the tactics of the medieval Turk: he attacks quickly and suddenly from all possible directions. I shall group his arguments, I hope not unfairly, under three main headings: the language and ceremonial of the court and the nobility, evidence about society and government in England, and warfare, including tournaments.

First, the language and ceremonial of the court. Pwyll, you will remember, was so rash as to drive away Arawn's pack from the stag it had just killed, and to give the stag to his own hounds. The conversation between the two kings which followed contains several interesting ideas.[31] It shows that there were definite rules as to who should first speak when two men met. The man of lower status had to greet his superior. It also shows that Pwyll's offence against Arawn's dignity was sufficient to merit either direct revenge or a satire. Arawn says to Pwyll, "a chyn nyt ymdialwyf a thi, y rof i a Duw . . . mi a wnaf o anglot itt guerth can carw." This sentence is full of old legal ideas and is, therefore, hard to translate accurately. The best rendering I can offer is, "and though I shall not revenge myself on you, I swear to God that I shall cause you to be satirized to the value of a hundred stags." The word for satire, *anglot*, is the negative of *clod* "praise, a praise-poem." Its meaning is made clear by a passage in *Culhwch and Olwen* in which Culhwch threatens to satirize Arthur, if he does not obtain his request. In the White Book the phrase used is "dwyn dy wyneb,"[32] but in the Red Book "dwyn dy agclot."[33] *Wyneb*, literally "face," was used in Welsh to mean "honour."*Wynebwerth* meant the honour-price of a man, according to which he was compensated for offences against his honour or person. It is a very old term since it appears also in Old Breton, and has an equivalent, *lóg n-enech*, in Old Irish. "Dwyn dy wyneb" meant "remove your honour" and came to be a phrase meaning simply "dishonour." In the White Book text Culhwch threatens to take away Arthur's honour, in other words to dishonour him, as far as the farthest corners of the earth. In the Red Book text, however, Culhwch threatens to carry Arthur's "dis-praise," in other words to satirize him, as far as the farthest corners of the earth.

Arawn, then, is threatening to have Pwyll satirized. The value of the satire was to be a hundred stags. This is probably an allusion to the hundred cows due to a king of a *cantref*, the lowest rank of king, as compensation when his honour was outraged (*sarhâd*).[34] Arawn is threatening to injure Pwyll's honour by the smallest amount by which Pwyll could be considered to have injured Arawn's honour. The idea that a satire could remove a man's honour-price so that he was no longer entitled to his proper compensation for injuries done to him, is found in the Old Irish laws.[35] In *Pwyll* we have the corresponding Welsh institution. Arawn is going to cause *aglot* to Pwyll, to the value of a hundred stags, *guerth can carw*, which means that the satire will deprive Pwyll of a hundred stags' worth of his honour-price, *wynebwerth*. The passages in *Pwyll* and *Culhwch and Olwen* show the connection between the words *wyneb, aglot, guerth*, the legal term *wynebwerth*, and the old law of satire.

Pwyll is duly impressed by Arawn's threat, and offers to buy Arawn's *cerennyd*, Modern Welsh *carennydd* "friendship." Professors Gwyn Jones and Thomas Jones translate *cerennyd* as "friendship," but this is not an adequate rendering of the word as it is used in *Pwyll*. In the next paragraph Arawn makes a strong pact of friendship, *cedymdeithas*, with Pwyll by promising to put him in his own, Arawn's, place in Annwfn and to give him his wife to sleep with. This does not, however, produce *cerennyd*, which is only secured later when Pwyll has killed Hafgan, Arawn's enemy, and so recompensed Arawn for the insult done to him. *Cerennyd*, then, is the formal, legal relationship, *cedymdeithas* the personal friendship. In *Math, cerennyd* is used together with *tangneued*, Modern Welsh *tangnefedd*, in such a way as to show that they mean the same thing. When Gwydion and Gilfaethwy have undergone their punishment for the rape of Goewin, Math says to them "tangneued a gawsawch, a cherennyd a geffwch," "you have obtained *tangnefedd*, and you shall have *carennydd*'."[36] *Tangnefedd* and *carennydd* mean the state of legal peace between two parties when outstanding claims between them have been satisfied. *Tanc* is used in just this way in Old Welsh in the *Surrexit* memorandum in the Lichfield Gospels.[37]

In *Pwyll* the *cerennyd* is between two kings. This is of considerable interest, for it means that *cerennyd* is there used in the same way as its Old Irish cognate *cairde* (both *cerennyd* and *cairde* are from Celtic **karantion*). In the Old Irish laws *cairde* is used as a term for a treaty between two tribal kingdoms which secures peace between them. It is also used for the peace thus secured, and even for the kingdoms at peace.[38] Neither Irish nor Welsh law would distinguish hostility between kings from hostility between kingdoms, so the two terms *cerennyd* (as used in *Pwyll*) and *cairde* are equivalent. The old legal meaning of *cerennyd* is found in early Welsh poetry,[39] and even in the Court Poets, those masters of archaic language, but only once or twice in MW. prose, and not at all in the laws. It is an archaic survival by the MW. period.

Mr. Saunders Lewis, although he recognizes the legal influence on this passage, also thinks that there is an element of feudal custom in it, particularly in such terms as *teilygdawt, anryded, anwybot* and *ansyberwyt*. They show a preoccupation with hierarchy and with rules of honourable behaviour, such as the one about which man should greet which first. If, however, one compares this with Old Irish society, one will find that there is nothing un-Celtic about hierarchy and related rules. One only has to think of the rule already cited, that a man must rise up before his superior, and that a man need only raise his knee when his equal approaches.[40] This shows the same attitude as the courtly feudal one. After all, the modern idea that a man must rise up when a woman enters the room can be explained from the courtly pretence that the lover was the vassal of his lady.

Mr. Saunders Lewis also sees signs of feudalism in the customs of Arawn's court, and positive proof of a late date in the occurrence of the word *iarll*. On the first point, I can only reply that I see no such signs, and on the second, he does not appear to have noticed Professor Jackson's argument that *iarll* was borrowed as [iarL], in other words before the tenth century.[41] If it had been borrowed after [L] > *ll*, we should, no doubt, have had MW. *iarl. Futhermore, Irish *iarla*, also from ON., is used in a poem by Fland Mainistrech (ob. 1056), who, if Sir Ifor Williams is right, would have been an older contemporary of the author of the Four Branches.[42] *Iarll* may have been more popular with post-Norman Welsh prose-writers than it was earlier, though we have no means of telling whether this was the case; but it still does not show that *Pwyll* is a twelfth- or thirteenth-century text merely because it uses the word once.

In *Manawydan*, it is the conversation leading up to the marriage of Manawydan and Rhiannon which is taken to bear the mark of twelfth century date.[43] It seems to Mr. Saunders Lewis remarkably mature, "so unaffected and yet so tender and accurate"; and he sees in it the influence of late twelfth-century humanism. Here, two difficulties spring to mind. We have hardly anything of the probably extensive

OW. literature with which we can compare this passage. Where we have such an extensive literature in a Celtic country before the twelfth century, namely in Ireland, we then have a story which has just the characteristics which Mr. Saunders Lewis so rightly sees in *Manawydan*, the story of *Líadain and Cuirithir*.[44] This tale is probably late ninth century. The other difficulty lies in the association of twelfth-century humanism with the literary and imaginative quality of *Manawydan*. "Humanism" is a word of many slippery meanings. It does not imply, and I do not believe that it has been shown, that the humanists of the twelfth century were men who, on the whole, had an unusual imaginative sympathy for the passions of men, or that they were unusually successful in conveying this sympathy in literary form. One only has to think of that distinguished humanist, Gerald of Wales, who, though a passionate man himself, and a shrewd one too, could hardly have written anything with the quality of *Manawydan*.

The evidence of English society and government all comes from *Manawydan*. Manawydan and Pryderi spent some time in England, in Hereford and other towns, as craftsmen. There is, therefore, a certain amount of information about the making of saddles, shields and shoes, and also a little about the social life of towns. An archaeologist may, perhaps, some day be able to give definite dates to some of the methods of work described, but this is not Mr. Saunders Lewis's approach. He shows, entirely successfully, that the description would fit the conditions of Henry II's day but he does not prove that they could not fit the conditions of, say, 1050. His argument is that the warfare during Gruffudd ap Llywelyn's reign would have prevented Welsh craftsmen from working in towns like Hereford, as Pryderi and Manawydan do. Gruffudd's first attack in the region of Herefordshire seems to have been in 1049, and it was followed by others. If, however, a man wrote the Four Branches about 1050–1060 he had no obligation to be so topical and up-to-date as this argument presupposes. He also points to the remark of Manawydan that, if they were to attack their enemies in one of the English towns where they worked, "Caswallon would hear of it, and so would his men, and we should be ruined."[45] He suggests that this reflects the judicial system of Henry II's reign, by which the royal justices went on circuit to hear local cases. There are two objections to this argument. First, Henry II was anticipated, at least by Henry I, in the use of itinerant justices. Secondly, in the Anglo-Saxon period most boroughs were royal boroughs, and, therefore, the king as lord had direct judicial interest in the normal borough. This was true, for example, of Hereford.[46]

The last heading under which I have put Mr. Saunders Lewis's arguments is that of warfare and the tournament. He shows, entirely successfully, that some features of the tactics and strategy of the armies of Math and Pryderi in the Fourth Branch are reminiscent of the wars of Gruffudd ap Cynan and later Welsh princes. Some of these features simply reflect the influence of topography on warfare, and since tactics which are dictated by the lay of the land are as ancient as the hills, they are of no use in a problem of dating. He also claims, however, that the war of Math and Pryderi is a feudal war. He points to the contrast between the *pedyt*, the foot-soldiers, Latin *pedites*, and the *marchogion*, the horsemen or knights, and at the same time to Lloyd's statement that, by the beginning of Stephen's reign, the Welsh had learnt the use of heavy cavalry.[47] *Math*, he concludes, must be later than this development in Welsh military skill. He points, too, to the arming of Lleu by Aranrhod as showing that Lleu wore armour of the feudal period.[48] There are a number of difficulties in this argument which are worth pointing out. First, it is not entirely certain that the English learnt the art of fighting on horseback from the Normans. The normal view has been that the housecarls of the eleventh century rode to battle and then dismounted before fighting started. This, they undoubtedly sometimes did; and their successors, the Norman knights, sometimes used the same tactic, for example, at the Battle of the Standard. The housecarls may on occasion, however, have fought on horseback.[49] Until the discussion on this point has finally settled the question, it would not be wise to assert that the Welsh must have learnt the art of cavalry fighting from the Normans. Furthermore, if we go back several centuries, we find the *marchogion* of the *Gododdin* quite heavily armed and fighting on horseback. The word *pedyt* occurs in the *Gwarchan Tudfwlch*. Let us, then, suppose, for the sake of argument, that the eleventh-century Welsh nobleman did not know, unlike his ancestor of the sixth and seventh centuries, how to fight on horseback. Would that prove that the author of *Math* lived in the twelfth century? The answer is, not at all. In the Book of Leinster version of the Irish saga *Táin Bó Cúalnge*, a work of the early twelfth century, warriors use chariots as in the pre-historic heroic age of Ireland. We do not have to assume that the teller of tales must be up-to-date in these matters. He often took great care to be as archaic as possible.

Finally, the tournament. Pwyll and Hafgan fought each other at a ford.[50] The fight was between the two of them. A *marchog* was in charge, and he warned all the kings' men not to take part. He stated the purpose of the encounter: the two kings had claimed each other's land, and the fight was to decide between them. The encounter is described as an *oet*, and as a *cyfranc*. The land at issue is described by the standard legal phrase *tir a daear*. They attack each other across the ford, and at the first onset Pwyll splits Hafgan's shield, breaks all his arms, throws Hafgan back across the hind quarters of his horse, the length of his spear and his arm, to the ground, and mortally wounds him.

Mr. Saunders Lewis makes two points about this passage. First, he quotes Dr. R.M. Jones for the opinion that the description is of a tournament; secondly, he quotes a passage from *Gereint*, which uses very similar phraseology about the actual encounter, as distinct from the background and purpose of the encounter, and refers to two other similar passages. He asssers that the author of *Pwyll* took the description from *Gereint* and adapted it to his own purposes. This would imply that the first part of *Pwyll* is later than *Gereint*, and much later than the rest of the Four Branches including the rest of *Pwyll*. I shall take the second point first. If two passages resemble each other so closely that the resemblance can hardly be fortuitous, there may be three different explanations. A may have borrowed from B, or B from A, or both A and B may have borrowed from some other passage, perhaps no longer extant. In order to prove that one passage depends on another, therefore, one has to show that the dependence is not the other way round, and that they cannot both be dependent on a third passage. Mr. Saunders Lewis does not attempt these two proofs.

A point which he makes in support of the idea that the story of *Pwyll Pen Annwfn* was not originally part of the First Branch is that the remainder of the story begins with the phrases "A threigylgueith yd oed yn Arberth, priflys idaw," "and on one occasion he was at Arberth, his principal court."[51] At the beginning of the First Branch the same phrases occur. He takes this, then, as a formula used when beginning a story, and this implies that the First Branch, as we have it, is made up of two separate tales. In arguments of this kind it is essential to distinguish between tale and sub-tale. None of the Four Branches consists of only one story. *Math*, for example, contains three: the story of the rape of Goewin and the death of Pryderi, the story of how the fate sworn upon Lleu by his mother Aranrhod was defeated by the wiles of Gwydion, and the story of Blodeuwedd's adultery with Gronw Pebr. These three stories are interconnected, the first two, however, only loosely; but they remain distinct stories. This does not prove that they were ever separate tales. They may have been, but not every sub-tale has once been an independent tale. Even if they were once independent tales, this does not mean that they had not become united as sub-tales of one independent tale when the author of the Four Branches got to work. It is essential, then, for Mr. Saunders Lewis to prove that the *treigylgueith* opening formula is only used for full tales and not for sub-tales. This he has not done; and, indeed, the opening sentence of the sub-tale of Blodeuwedd's adultery uses this very word *treigylgueith*.[52]

Mr. Saunders Lewis quotes Dr. R.M. Jones as saying that the encounter between Pwyll and Hafgan was a tournament.[53] Dr. Jones's argument is, however, rather different from what Mr. Saunders Lewis's use of this idea would lead one to believe. The general direction of his argument is against the theory that the three romances, *Peredur*, *Owein* and *Gereint*, are heavily indebted to French literature and culture. He makes the suggestion that the origin of the tournament may be Celtic, and, as a Celtic version of the tournament, he quotes our passage. He is arguing that, since *Pwyll* is not affected by French influence, and since it contains a tournament, there was a Celtic tournament, called an *oet*. This Celtic tournament could have been the source, *via* the fashionable enthusiasm for things Arthurian, of the French

The Date of the Four Branches

and English tournaments. Mr. Saunders Lewis has turned this argument on its head. The argument, however, is not convincing whichever way round it is pointed. The reason for this is simple. The Welsh *oet*, as it is found in *Pwyll*, is essentially a single combat, a fight between two men. The early form of the tournament, on the other hand, was not a fight between two men, but a general mêlée. It only acquired the form of a single combat in the thirteenth century.[54]

Dr. R.M. Jones is, however, quite correct in regarding the *oet* between Pwyll and Hafgan as a native and not a French institution. Indeed, it is one of the oldest elements in the story. To see this one must remember, first, that it is an ordeal by battle. It is a fight under strict rules for the purpose of deciding a legal question. This question is about two claims to land, and the standard legal phrase for land, *tir a daear*, is used. Mr. Saunders Lewis quite rightly calls the similar fight between Pryderi and Gwydion a *duel judiciaire*. You will, however, look in vain in the Welsh law books, and for that matter, in the Anglo-Saxon law codes, for the ordeal by battle. It was introduced into England by the Normans. One might think that here was a good argument in favour of the thesis that the Four Branches have been influenced by Norman and, therefore, French ways of thought and life; but the truth is otherwise.

If you have read *Culhwch and Olwen*, you may remember the phrase *gwir Duw*, literally "truth of God." It is used in an exclamation, and also in two questions.[55] The promise of *gwir Duw* appears as a solemn binding oath. By looking at the cognate Irish phrase, *fír nDé*, one can see why this is so. The *fír nDé* was a method of deciding a legal case when all else failed. Thurneysen translates it as "divine verdict" or "ordeal."[56] It involved an oath on relics or on the altar. This, no doubt, replaced other solemn forms of oath which were used in the pre-Christian period. The *fír nDé* is a procedure which belongs to the first of the five types of action in Irish law.[57] This first type is entitled *fír* "truth." Two other methods of proof were, probably, attached to this type of action, the *fír [n]daíne* "truth of men" (the Welsh equivalent would have been *gwir dynion*), and *fír fer* "truth of men" (Welsh *gwir gwŷr*).[58] The *fír [n]daíne* was proof by oath-helpers, the *fír fer* ordeal by battle. Though Welsh has the phrase *gwir Duw*, corresponding to *fír nDé*, it has no phrases *gwir dynion* or *gwir gwŷr*. Welsh has, however, the ordeal by battle as in *Pwyll*. Since the *gwir Duw* corresponds in meaning and etymology to the *fír nDé*, and the *rhaith*, "(proof by) a body of oath-helpers," is similar to the *fír [n]daíne*, it is likely that the Welsh and Irish ordeals by battle both descend from the one Celtic institution.

Two further considerations make this theory probable. The type of action called *fír* in Irish law was the one appropriate for a certain range of legal topics. Thus, if, for example, one was faced by perjury on the part of one's opponents, one proceeded by the *fír* type of action. To this same type also belonged cases about hereditary right to land and about the right of a lord to be acknowledged as lord by his vassal.[59] This means that the legal issues at stake in *Pwyll*, the right to *tir a daear* and to the *gwrogaeth* of the men of Annwfn, would, in Irish law, have come under the *fír* heading. This makes more probable the identification of the Welsh ordeal by battle with the Irish *fír fer*.

The evidence for the rules by which the *fír fer* proceeded comes from the saga literature. The *fír fer* in the sagas is a single combat fought according to definite rules. Only the two opponents may take part, and the fight is usually at a ford. Occasionally, it seems, more than two men took part, but even then the numbers on each side had to be equal. In the early version of *Táin Bó Cúailnge*, Óengus mac Óenláma would, "the experts say," have driven the men of Ireland as far as Emain Macha if only they had encountered him "ar galaib óenfir," "in fights of one man (on either side)."[60] But on the contrary, they broke the *fír fer* and slew him in *écomlond*. The term *écomlond* is the negative of *comlann, comlonn*, which means, etymologically, "equal number."[61] The men of Ireland had broken the rules of *fír fer* by attacking Óengus, not one man at a time, but in *écomlond*, "an encounter with unequal numbers." *Écomlond* is the opposite of *fír fer*. The men of Ireland were suffering so many casualties by night from Cú Chulainn's attacks that they sent a messenger to negotiate with him. He refused their terms until Fergus, his foster-father, told the men of Ireland what terms he would accept. The chief of his demands was "a ford upon which his fighting and his encounter with one man will be done."[62] The encounter with one man, *comrac fri hóenfer*, on the ford is the same thing as the *fír fer*.

The encounter between Pwyll and Hafgan has all the features of the *fír fer, comrac fri hóenfer* or *comlann*. It was fought between two men. The *marchog* in charge warns everyone else not to take part. It was fought at a ford. One of the words used to describe it, *cyfranc*, is cognate with the Irish *comrac* used for the *fír fer* encounter. This form of fighting is found elswhere in Welsh literature in *Canu Llywarch Hen* when Gwên arms himself and goes off to meet his enemy at the ford.[63] The suggestion there, however, is that the English broke the *fír fer* and attacked in a group. The *fír fer* was, probably, fundamentally a legal institution, but the name was used also of the single combat when no specifically legal issue was involved. In *Pwyll*, however, the *cyfranc* is still the legal ordeal by battle. This ordeal by battle must have been long obsolete by the twelfth century, and even in *Culhwch and Olwen* the *gwir Duw* is only a survival.

If this theory about the fight between Pwyll and Hafgan is correct, it shows that it is not possible to analyse adequately the ideas and themes of early Welsh literature without taking into account the possible Irish parallels. A knowledge of Irish literature is the only remedy for the fact that so little has survived of OW. literature: to gain some idea of what an early Celtic literature is like one must turn to Ireland.

Professor Morgan Watkins provides an example of what can happen when the Irish evidence is ignored. *Pwyll* begins with the description of a stag-hunt in which Pwyll's hounds are beaten to the mark by the hounds of Arawn king of Annwfn, the other-world. Pwyll is amazed by the colour of Arawn's hounds, white with red ears. Watkins quotes four medieval French descriptions of hounds in which they are said to be white and in one of which the hounds are said to have black ears. He concludes that the colours of Arawn's hounds are an example of the influence of French literature. This argument is not plausible even when one only takes into account the passage from the Welsh laws quoted in Sir Ifor Williams's note; but the Irish examples of animals with white bodies and red ears put the theory quite out of court.[64] Here is just one example from Old Irish story, *Táin Bó Fraich*:

"dobert a máthair dí báe déc dó assint síd, it é finda óiderga," "his mother gave him twelve cows from the *síd* (other-world mound), and they were white with red ears."[65]

Mr. Saunders Lewis provides another example with his theory that the opening formula found at the beginning of *Math* ("Math uab Mathonwy oed arglwyd ar Wyned, a Pryderi uab Pwyll oed arglwyd ar un cantref ar ugeint yn y Deheu.") reflects the phraseology of the Welsh annals. This is extremely unlikely in the light of the corresponding Irish opening formula: "Boí rí amrae for Érinn, x a ainm," "there was a famous king of Ireland called x" and its numerous variants.[66]

Sometimes, however, Mr. Saunders Lewis's arguments fail to convince because he has not studied the Welsh evidence closely enough. An example of this is in his article on *Math*. He is arguing that the war in *Math* shows signs of twelfth-century date, and he points to one particular correspondence. Pryderi gave twenty-four hostages for a truce. When Henry II came through Wales on his way to Ireland in 1171 he demanded from the Lord Rhys twenty-four hostages. This is the statement of the Red Book of Hergest version of the *Brut y Tywysogyon*. This kind of detailed correspondence lends considerable force to an argument, but in this case the whole thing depends on a scribal error. There are three versions of the *Brut*, all independent translations of one lost Latin chronicle. The other two versions have, not twenty-four hostages, but fourteen. A scribe must have put xxiiii instead of xiiii.[67]

I do not think that any precise date for the Four Branches can yet be given. The arguments of Mr. Saunders Lewis and, before him, Sir Ifor Williams, are not sufficiently convincing. On the other hand, Sir Ifor Williams's date, though too precise, may well, on the available evidence, be quite close to the truth. The verbal system of the Four Branches, unlike that of *Culhwch and Olwen*, is all MW. with the sole exception of the 3rd sing. imperfect form *seui*.[68] This means that the Four Branches cannot be earlier than the eleventh century. On the other hand, the evidence of the two forms *stlys* and *stryw*, the rarity of French loanwords (*pali*, *cordwal* and *swmer* were very probably borrowed through merchants well before 1100, or even 1066), and the archaic form of society depicted suggest that the date of composition cannot be much later than 1100.

The work of Mr. Arwyn Watkins and Professor P. Mac Cana on the syntax of the copula has confirmed that *Culhwch and Olwen* is older than the Four Branches;[69] but I doubt whether their criteria will help much to decide the relative date of MW. texts. Too many of the examples of the old syntax in MW. prose consist of set phrases like "ys gwir." Nonetheless, similar research may yet determine the true date of the Four Branches.

APPENDIX: BRANWEN

Mr. Saunders Lewis's article on *Branwen* has now appeared in *Ysgrifau Beirniadol V*.[1] Its main thesis is that *Branwen* was composed between 1172 and 1174, no later because it is alluded to in a poem by Prydydd y Moch early in 1174, and no earlier for the reasons I shall now discuss.

His arguments fall under two headings. First, he maintains that the author of *Branwen* used Geoffrey of Monmouth in a Welsh translation. Secondly, he argues that there are several allusions in *Branwen* to the Norman invasion of Ireland, in particular to events between 1 August 1166 when Diarmait mac Murchada fled from Wexford to Bristol and 17 April 1172 when Henry II returned from Ireland.

His reasons for maintaining that *Branwen* is dependent on Geoffrey are these:
1. The opening sentence of *Branwen* ("Bendigeiduran uab Llyr a oed urenhin coronawc ar yr ynys hon ac ardyrchawc o goron Lundein"; "Bendigeiduran uab Llyr was crowned king over this island and adorned with the crown of London") shows influence of Geoffrey in its vocabulary and syntax. The same vocabulary is used later in the story.
2. *Branwen* shows close similarities to *Cyfranc Lludd a Llevelys*, a story which has certainly been influenced by Geoffrey.
3. He accepts Gruffydd's theory that the name *Ynys y Kedyrn*, "Island of the Mighty," was originally a name for the island paradise to which the Irishman Bran mac Febail sailed, and only became a name for Britain when Bran himself was made into a British king.[2] He then quotes a passage from the Red Book *Brut y Brenhinedd* which tells how giants brought healing stones from Africa to Ireland.[3] When a bath was made within the square of the stones and some of the stones were brought and put in the bath, then anyone who entered the bath would be healed of his disease. This bath, he maintains, was a clear precursor of the Cauldron of Re-

birth (*Peir Dadeni*) in *Branwen*, by which dead warriors were brought to life again even though they remained dumb. He also holds, if I understand him rightly, that between the old version which calls one of the Isles of the Blest *Ynys y Kedyrn*, and the new version, as in *Branwen*, according to which Britain is the Island of the Mighty, there stood a third version, as in Geoffrey, which makes Ireland the Island of the Mighty, namely the *kewri*, the giants who brought the healing stones from Africa.

The fundamental objection to his arguments is that they take no account of the problem of the sources which Geoffrey of Monmouth used. It is essential to his case that *Branwen* should be indebted to Geoffrey and not to Geoffrey's sources, and yet there is no argument in his article to show this.

On the first point, it is quite true that both Geoffrey and *Branwen* use the idea of a unified kingdom of Britain with a capital at London; but we know for certain that the idea of a kingdom of Britain is as old as the Venerable Bede, and that Gregory the Great assumed that London and York were the two chief cities of Britain.[4] He was out-of-date, it is true, but that does not change the fact that if one can prove that the traditions which Geoffrey used show a great interest in the relationship between Rome and Britain, and therefore in Roman Britain, one can show how the idea of a kingdom of Britain with a capital at London might have taken root long before the twelfth century. In the Harleian genealogies and in Nennius there is just the evidence required. One of the most noticeable features of the genealogies is that three of the pedigrees are traced back to Roman emperors.[5] Nennius contains the earliest versions of the origin legend of the British, the story of Brutus, or Britto, the grandson of Aeneas the Trojan. According to one of the versions Brutus came to Britain and after him the island was called Britain.[6] This origin legend was probably fabricated for good political reasons: to establish the kinship of the Britons and the Romans, and, therefore, the political respectability of the native British ruling families. It is not unlike some of the Irish origin legends, in which Nennius shows an interest, but unlike them it presumes at least an outline knowledge of the Roman origin legend, the *Aeneid*. It is likely that its origins lie in the Romano-British period, for that is the time when the reasons for composing such a story would be most compelling. The same reasons lie behind the introduction of a large Christian element into the story, and also into the genealogies: it was now important to establish the place of the Britons in sacred history, and the means by which this was done, the creation of a genealogical link, were the same as those used to establish the connection with Rome. In the same way, when the early Irish genealogists wished to prove that two ruling families were connected they did so by pushing their pedigrees back to

The Date of the Four Branches

a point where they met. It is quite possible, then, that the leading position of London in Roman Britain was remembered in Wales, even though Nennius does not mention it. The scanty sources show that the Welsh were interested in their Roman past, and London was part of that past.[7]

On the second point, the similarity between *Branwen* and *Cyfranc Lludd a Llefelys*, Mr. Saunders Lewis advances two arguments. First, he points to the similarity between their opening passages. This is not a question of the phraseology of their opening sentences, but rather of the situation described: Llefelys, the brother of Lludd king of the Britons, wished to marry the daughter and heiress of the king of France who had just died. Lludd and Llefelys set out for France with a fleet to achieve this. Like *Branwen*, therefore, *Cyfranc Lludd a Llefelys* starts with the story of a dynastic marriage. Secondly, *Branwen* contains a reference to a triad about the three men who broke their hearts from bewilderment, and *Cyfranc Lludd a Llefelys* to the three *cynweissieid* who broke their hearts from bewilderment. The difficulty with the argument from the similarity of the opening passages is that their common theme, dynastic marriage, is an obvious one. If the passages corresponded in several points of detail then the argument would be more attractive, but they do not. They correspond only in that the suitors set out to press their case with a fleet. The argument from the triads is valueless, since the triad of the three *cynweissieid* is a very old one; and, furthermore, it is very likely, as Mrs. Bromwich has pointed out, that *Cyfranc Lludd a Llefelys* is here dependent on *Branwen*, which, of course, does not suggest that *Branwen*, like *Cyfranc Lludd a Llefelys*, is dependent on Geoffrey.[8]

On the third point, the name *Ynys y Kedyrn* and the *Peir Dadeni*, "Cauldron of Rebirth," the difficulty is not so much with Mr. Saunders Lewis's argument as with Gruffydd's theory on which it depends. For example, it is essential to Gruffydd's theory that one of the names for the island paradise in the original Irish form of the Bran story should have been something like *Ynys y Kewri*, perhaps *Inis na Curad;* but no such name occurs in the Old Irish story of the voyage of Bran mac Febail. I suggest, also, that Mr. Saunders Lewis has done less than justice to Professor Mac Cana's theory of the origin of the idea of the *Peir Dadeni*, which seems to me the best explanation which has yet been put forward. While, therefore, the passage in Geoffrey to which Mr. Lewis draws attention certainly deserves to be included in any discussion of the *peir dadeni* theme, I do not believe that he has shown it to be a precursor of the *peir dadeni* in *Branwen*.[9]

The other arguments which Mr. Saunders Lewis puts forward are designed to prove that *Branwen* was composed by a man familiar with the story of the Norman invasion of Ireland. He suggests that Matholwch, king of Ireland, sailing to Harlech from the south of Ireland in order to ask for the hand of Branwen is to be compared with Diarmait mac Murchada, who sailed from Wexford to Bristol, went to do homage to Henry II, and offered the hand of his daughter and the succession to his kingdom of Leinster to Richard Earl of Pembroke. He suggests that the purpose of Diarmait's offer of his daughter was the same as that of Matholwch in asking for Branwen, namely "ymrwymaw ynys y Kedyrn ac Iwerdon y gyt, ual y bydynt gadarnach," "to bind together the island of the Mighty and Ireland, so that they should be stronger."[10]

Against this theory the following objections may be offered. Mr. Saunders Lewis says that Matholwch is to be thought of as sailing, like Diarmait mac Murchada, from Wexford, and quotes in support of this the phrase from *Branwen* "teir llong ar dec yn dyuot o deheu Iwerdon," "thirteen ships coming from the south of Ireland."[11] This is an unjustifiable interpretation of the evidence. The author of *Branwen* knew about the traditional divisions of Ireland, for example the five provinces. Another of these divisions was one between the north of Ireland, *Leth Cuinn* (Conn's half); and the south of Ireland, *Leth Moga* (Mug's half). On the east coast the boundary seems to have been the mouth of the Liffey.[12] This means that Matholwch could have sailed from anywhere from Dublin southwards, and still have been sailing from the south of Ireland. Diarmait mac Murchada's main support was concentrated in the south of Leinster around Ferns, the area called after its old ruling family, to which he belonged, *Uí Chenselaig*.[13] This is why he sailed from Wexford and later returned there.

Mr. Saunders Lewis was right to call attention to the sentence in *Branwen* which describes Matholwch as sailing from the south of Ireland; but it constitutes important evidence against his thesis. The point is that the author of *Branwen* is supposing the king of Ireland to have sailed from the south of Ireland, from Leinster or Munster. This would have been a reasonable supposition in the eleventh century, but it would not have been a reasonable supposition in the twelfth century. In 1002 Brian Bórama of the Dál Cais (a people in what is now County Clare) achieved the position of high-king of Ireland when he "took the hostages of Connachta at Áth Luain, and the hostages of Mael Sechnaill (King of Mide)."[14] From then until 1116 when Diarmait Ua Briain unseated his brother Muirchertach Ua Briain, the descendants of Brian Bórama were generally the most powerful kings in Ireland except perhaps for a period in the middle of the eleventh century when Diarmait mac Mael na mBó, king of Leinster, is said to have been king of Ireland "with opposition."[15] After 1116 the kings of Connaught were dominant. This means that after 1116, or perhaps a few years later, it would no longer have been a natural thing for a Welshman so well

The Date of the Four Branches

informed about Irish affairs as the author of *Branwen* to assume that the king of Ireland would come from the south of Ireland, namely from Leinster or Munster.

It is also a misunderstanding of Irish political history to suggest that Diarmait mac Murchada's purpose in offering his daughter to the Earl of Pembroke, together with the succession to Leinster, was to bind together Britain and Ireland. His purpose, it is clear, was to recover control of Leinster, and he needed outside support to do it. Diarmait is not a plausible counterpart to Matholwch. Matholwch sailed to Britain as the king of Ireland, Diarmait only as the ex-king of Leinster. It is noticeable that elsewhere in the article Matholwch is compared to Ruaidri Ua Conchobair, king of Connaught and high king, and not to Diarmait.

In the summer of 1171 Henry II led an expedition to Ireland. Mr. Saunders Lewis maintains that the author of *Branwen* had this expedition in mind when he told the story of Bendigeidfran's expedition to Ireland. In support of this idea he puts forward several arguments. I shall confine myself to discussing the three which seem to me to have the most weight.

The first of these is that just as Matholwch, having retired behind the Shannon into Connaught, was obliged to do homage to Bendigeidfran and to grant the kingdom to Gwern, his son by Branwen, so was Ruaidri Ua Conchobair, king of Connaught, obliged to do homage to Henry II on the Shannon. Mr. Saunders Lewis points both to the similarity between the two situations, and also to the language used in *Branwen* by which Matholwch is described as granting (*ystynnu*) the kingdom to Gwern. Mr. Lewis's authority for saying that Ruaidri did homage to Henry II on the Shannon is Giraldus Cambrensis.[16] Unfortunately for his case, however, this statement of Giraldus is not supported by any other authority. Several Irish annals give lists of who submitted to Henry, but none mentions Ruaidri; and two English sources say explicitly that Ruaidri did not submit.[17] It is generally accepted that Giraldus's statement is false. The author of *Branwen* cannot have used Giraldus's *Expugnatio Hibernica* which appeared several years after 1175, so Mr. Saunders Lewis's theory requires us to assume that the author made, independently, the same mistake as Giraldus.

Mr. Saunders Lewis is on more familiar ground in holding that the phraseology of the following sentence is feudal: "Ac y mae Matholwch yn rodi brenhinaeth Iwerdon y Wern uab Matholwch, dy nei ditheu, uab dy chwaer, ac yn y ystynnu y'th wyd di."[18] The Everyman translation is: "And Matholwch is giving the kingship of Ireland to Gwern son of Matholwch, thy nephew, thy sister's son, and is investing him in thy presence."[19] In translating "yn y ystynnu" "by investing him" Professors Gwyn Jones and Thomas Jones are following Sir Ifor Williams who says in his note on the passage,

"Cynnig M(atholwch), felly, yw arwisgo Gwern yn frenin yng ngwydd ei ewythr." If the translation of "yn y ystynnu" faithfully reflects the meaning of the original then this passage is good evidence for assigning a twelfth-century date to the Four Branches. Sir Ifor Williams's suggestion that the Norman settlement at Hereford in the Confessor's reign was responsible for this early evidence of French influence reads like a counsel of despair.

The first objection to the translation is that it assumes that the infixed pronoun *y* in *yn y ystynnu* refers to Gwern. It is more likely to refer to *brenhinaeth*. In this construction the infixed pronoun is the direct object of the verb, and this raises the question whether *ystynnu* normally takes a personal direct object or whether the thing granted is regularly the direct object. The sentence in *Branwen* uses the two verbs *rhoddi* and *estynnu/ystynnu*, and is, therefore, an example of the legal phrase most common in its nominal form *rhodd ac estyn*. The usage of the laws is quite clear: *estynnu* takes a direct object of the thing granted and an indirect object of the person to whom it is granted. One example is: "gan pob un ed estenno er argluyd e svyd ydav," "from everyone to whom the king may grant his office."[20]

Usually *estynnu* simply means "to grant" "to give" in the laws, but when used together with *rhoddi* it can have a more limited meaning as in this example: "Ef (*the* pengwastrawt) bieu estynnu pop march a rotho y brenhin," "He (the chief groom) is entitled to hand over every horse which the king may give."[21] In this sentence *estynnu* stands for the physical act of giving, but *rhoddi* for the legal act of giving. The horse belongs to the king and only he can legally give it; but the law gives the chief groom of the court the right to hand the horse over. In *Branwen*, similarly, *estynnu* refers to the ceremony by which Matholwch will give the kingdom to Gwern, but *rhoddi* to the whole legal transaction. The correct literal translation of the sentence is: "And Matholwch is giving the kingship of Ireland to Gwern son of Matholwch, your nephew, your sister's son, and is handing it over in your presence."

Sir Ifor Williams gave a few examples of *estynnu* when it is used for the feudal ceremony of investiture. There are, however, good reasons why the evidence of the laws is to be preferred on the question of the meaning of *estynnu* in *Branwen*. First of all, it is essential to remember that kings and lords give offices and land whether they belong to feudal societies or not, and that such gifts are usually made by means of a legal ceremony in front of witnesses. The feudal-ness of investiture lies in the form of the ceremony, and even here there is nothing which is feudal in the strict sense about investiture, nothing which limits it to societies properly called feudal. Investiture followed the ceremonies of homage and fealty, and was performed by the lord handing over some

The Date of the Four Branches

physical object, a wand, ring, glove, etc., which stood for the object of the gift.[22] In the examples quoted by Sir Ifor Williams the symbolic objects are a rod, a glove and a bow. Now, there is no evidence that the ceremony in *Branwen* was of the feudal character. The examples which Sir Ifor quotes are all from the Welsh Charlemagne stories, later on any showing than *Branwen* and inevitably largely French in atmosphere. By contrast with the examples from them, the example in *Branwen*, like those in the laws, makes no mention of any such objects as a rod or glove. Furthermore, investiture was an element in a gift by a lord to a vassal or at least a *fidelis*, one who had sworn fealty; but the passage in *Branwen* in no way suggests that Matholwch will be Gwern's lord after the translation is over. Matholwch even offers to live in Britain. The ceremony in *Branwen*, then, is not investiture.

Estynnu remains, however, a puzzling term. It is a borrowing from Latin *extendo*, and outside the laws it preserves many of the characteristic meanings of the Latin verb, in particular its fundamental meaning "to stretch out." The legal meaning of *estynnu*, however, is not easily explicable. In classical Latin *extendo* appears not to be used, either by itself or in phrases, to mean "give."[23] In late Latin there are a few examples in Christian sources, of which the most important is 2 Maccabees 15.15 in the Vulgate: "Extendisse autem Jeremiam dextram, et dedisse Judae gladium aureum." This is clearly one possible source of the phrase *rhodd ac estyn*, but it is not a sufficient explanation. In the Vulgate example, the right hand is the direct object of *extendo*. The verb is still being used with its basic meaning. In the Welsh examples, however, *estynnu* is used with a direct object of the thing given; in other words *estynnu* now has a metaphorical sense. It is a natural and common development, but it may well have been encouraged by the way in which the Celtic verb which it replaced was used. This verb was **reg-e-ti*, OIr. *rigid* "stretches, extends." There was also an old causative form **rog-eye-ti*, OIr. *roigid*. Both verbs have important uses in the Old Irish laws. *Roigid* and its verbal noun *rogad* were used together with *lám* "hand" to mean "recover," "take back." *Rigid* is used in an explanation of *rí* "king": "Rí why is he so called? Because he stretches (*riges*) over his peoples with coercive power."[24] From *rigid* "stretches" came the meaning "protects" and then "rules." In the example a different aspect of royal power is emphasized, but this is due to a confusion between *rigid* "stretches," "rules," and *rigid* "binds." *Estynnu*, then, borrowed from Latin, replaced one of the Celtic verbs most important in its legal and social vocabulary, a verb etymologically related to the word for a king, **rīx*, Ir. *rí*, W. *rhi*, and used to express the characteristic activity of the king.[25] One such characteristic activity has always been the dispensing of gifts, and I therefore suggest that the Welsh verb *estynnu* shows, in its legal usage, the influence both of late Latin *extendo manum* and also Celtic **reg-e-ti*.

Mr. Saunders Lewis argues that the house which Matholwch built to contain Bendigeidfran is a reminiscence of the house built on the Thingmote at Dublin for Henry II. There are two difficulties with this theory. First, Ruaidri Ua Conchobair, Matholwch's counterpart, was not present in Dublin, and had no part in the proceedings. Secondly, both the incident in *Branwen* and that in Dublin in 1171 are examples of a common Irish political custom. Up to the eleventh century the normal way of saying that one king had made another submit was to say that he took the hostages of the country concerned, for example, "tuc gíallu Muman," "he took the hostages of the Munstermen." If one wanted to put it the other way round, one said "gíallais dó," "he gave hostages to him." In the middle of the eleventh century a new way of saying that a king submitted to another king became popular. A common form of it is "tánic ina thech," "he came into his house." The first example of this phrase in the *Annals of Inisfallen* is under the year 1059, and in the *Chronicon Scotorum* under 1057 = 1059.[26] After that date it is the phrase regularly used in the *Annals of Inisfallen*, and it is used alongside the old phrase in the *Chronicon Scotorum*. There must have been a change of political custom some time before 1059 by which a submitting king no longer simply handed over hostages but was obliged to go himself to the house of his over-king as a sign of his submission. It may be that this policy was inaugurated by Brian Bóroma whose under-kings came to his fortress at Cenn Corad.[27] The policy was continued by his son Donnchad, for the *Annals of Inisfallen* say that in 1026 the coarb of Patrick and the king of Osraige were in Donnchad's house at Cenn Corad for Easter. It seems that after fifty years of the new policy "he came to his house" became a set phrase for submission alongside the older set phrases.

This Irish phrase shows what was involved when Henry II received several Irish princes in his house in Dublin in 1171. It was all arranged because it was the standard method of submission to an over-king. It may even have been more than that. Brian Bóroma was the first really effective king of Ireland. No one before him could truthfully be described as *imperator Scottorum*.[28] If the two things are connected, then the new ceremony began life as a symbol of submission to the king of Ireland and not just any over-king. Most of the examples in the *Annals of Inisfallen* of the use of the phrase between 1059 and 1171, when it is used of the gathering at Dublin, belong to the years 1092 to 1095 when Muirchertach Ua Briain asserted his power over most of Ireland. This theory would also explain why, in *Branwen* Matholwch's second offer is such a definite improvement on his first one. In the first, he simply offered to hand over the kingdom to Gwern in Bendigeidfran's presence; in the second, he offered to have a house built which would be sufficiently large to contain a giant like Bendigeidfran, and into which he and the Irish would come, thus submitting to Bendigeidfran and putting the kingdom at his disposal. *Branwen* makes it clear that the house would be a particular honour to Bendigeidfran because he had never before had a house big enough for him, but the Irish custom of submission explains why it should be so important in the eyes of the Irish king and his advisers to have a house at all. If all this is correct it shows, first, that the incident in *Branwen* resembles the incident in Henry II's invasion of Ireland only because both assume the existence of a particular Irish political custom; and, second, that *Branwen* is probably not earlier than, at the earliest, about 1050. It seems unlikely that this custom would have been something to be taken for granted by a storyteller any earlier than it became something to be taken for granted by an annalist. Since the set phrase for submission begins to be used in 1059, *c.* 1050 seems a reasonable *terminus post quem* for *Branwen*.

I have already argued that *Branwen* was probably not composed after 1120, because of the assumption that the king of Ireland comes from the south of Ireland. It is likely that all four of the Four Branches were composed in their final form by one man. It is, therefore, likely that the Four Branches belong to sometime between about 1050 and about 1120.

NOTES

1. An earlier draft of this paper was read to the Oxford and Cambridge Celtic Society.
2. Ifor Williams, ed. *Pedeir Keinc y Mabinogi*. 2nd ed. Cardiff: University of Wales Press, 1951, xli. This, the standard edition of the Four Branches, will be referred to as *PKM*.
3. Jones and Jones, ed. and trans., *The Mabinogion*, ix.
4. "Pwyll Pen Annwfn," "Manawydan Fab Llyr," and "Math." An article on *Branwen* is to appear in *Ysgrifau Beirniadol, V*, ed. J. Caerwyn Williams (see the appendix on *Branwen*).
5. See the section on orthography in the introduction to *Llyfr Iorwerth*, ed. Wiliam, xiiff.
6. *PKM* 306.
7. *PKM* 90. The emendations given in the notes to the "Everyman" translation have been adopted. They do not affect the argument.
8. Williams, "Trystan ac Esyllt," 115–129.
9. Richard's date is given in the introduction to his edition, *Breudwyt Ronabwy*, xxxix; Parry's in his book *Hanes Llenyddiaeth Gymraeg hyd 1900*, 66.

10. Binchy, "St. Patrick and His Biographers," esp. 150 ff. For other archaisms in the Ulster cycle see Jackson, *The Oldest Irish Tradition: A Window on the Iron Age.*

11. T. Jones, ed., *Brut y Tywysogion* (Peniarth MS. 20 version), 127–128. The text is vol. 6 of the University of Wales Press, History and Law series, the translation and notes vol. 11. The Red Book of Hergest version is edited and translated, also by Professor Jones, in vol. 16. The following abbreviations will be used: *Brut y Tywysogion*, Pen. 20 (text), *Brut y Tywysogion*, Pen. 20 (transl.) and *Brut y Tywysogion, RBH.*

12. *PKM* 50–51.

13. Compare Poole, *Domesday Book to Magna Carta*, 1087–1216, 2.

14. Lloyd, *A History of Wales,* II, 552–553.

15. Stubbs, ed., *The Chronicle of the Reigns of Henry II and Richard I commonly known as Benedict of Peterborough,* I, 162.

16. This paragraph summarizes the relevant portions of the two classical works on feudalism: Ganshof, *Feudalism,* esp. 69–105; Bloch, *Feudal Society,* chapters XI, XV, XVII.

17. The joined hands of the Christian at prayer are a gesture borrowed from the ceremony of the contract of vassalage, Bloch, *Feudal Society,* 233.

18. On the different Welsh annals and their provenance see, especially, the introduction to *Brut y Tywysogion,* Pen. 20 (transl.).

19. For the itineraries of Henry I and Stephen see the introductions to *Regesta Regum Anglo-Normannorum,* II, ed. Johnson and Cronne, and III, ed. Cronne and Davis.

20. Salter, *Medieval Oxford,* 16.

21. *PKM* 24.

22. Alfred, 42.5. The translation is from Whitelock, ed., *English Historical Documents,* I, 380.

23. II Athelstan 2, *English Historical Documents,* I, 382.

24. I Cnut, 20.2, *English Historical Documents,* I, 419.

25. Ine 70, *Die Gresetze der Aryelsachsen,* ed., Lieberman, I., 118.

26. Stevenson, ed., *Asser's Life of King Alfred,* 254–255.

27. Stevenson, ed., *Asser's Life of King Alfred,* 255 n. 2.

28. Celtic **wassos* was borrowed into Gallo-Latin as *vassus,* which is the early word for a vassal. From *vassus* was formed an adjective *vassalis* and from *vassalis* the noun *vassallus* (thus correct Ganshof, *Feudalism,* 5).

29. *PKM* 6.

30. For *uréirge* see Thurneysen "Aus dem irischen Recht II," 240, § 2 (the note is not entirely accurate); Binchy, ed., *Críth Gablach,* lines 605–606, and the legal Glossary under *sóerrath.*

31. *PKM* 2.
32. Evans, ed., *The White Book Mabinogion*, col. 459, 1.22. Examples of *anglot*: col. 457.2–3.
33. Rhŷs and Evans, eds., *The Text of the Mabinogion from the Red Book of Hergest*, 105, line 23.
34. Emanuel, ed., *The Latin Text of the Welsh Laws*, 110. Williams and Powell, eds., *Llyfr Blegywryd*, 3.
35. See *Críth Gablach*, ed. Binchy, legal glossary under *áer*.
36. *PKM* 77.
37. Printed in the preface to Evans and Rhŷs, eds., *The Text of the Book of Llan Dav*, xliii.
38. *Críth Gablach*, ed. Binchy, legal glossary under *cairde*.
39. See Lloyd-Jones, *Geirfa Barddoniaeth Gynnar Gymraeg*, s.v.
40. *Críth Gablach*, ed. Binchy, lines 605–606.
41. Jackson, *Language and History in Early Britain*, 476.
42. Best and O'Brien, eds., *The Book of Leinster*, IV, 814.
43. *PKM* 50.
44. Meyer, ed., *Líadain and Cuirithir*.
45. *PKM* 54.
46. Stenton, *Anglo-Saxon England*, 523, 524.
47. Lloyd, *History of Wales*, II, 472.
48. *PKM* 82, 83.
49. Glover, "English warfare in 1066," 1–18. Hollister, *Anglo-Saxon Military Institutions*, chapter VII.
50. *PKM* 5–6.
51. *PKM* 8.
52. *PKM* 84.
53. R.M. Jones, "Y Rhamantau Cymraeg a'u Cysylltiad â'r Rhamantau Ffrangeg," 208–225, especially 212.
54. Denholm-Young, "The Tournament in the thirteenth century," esp. 240–242.
55. Evans, ed., *White Book Mabinogion*, cols. 459.8; 459.33–37; 460.15–16.
56. Thurneysen, *Cóic Conara Fugill*, 8.
57. *Cóic Conara Fugill* is a law tract, probably of the seventh century, but with later glosses, which describes the "Five Paths to a Verdict." The five paths are five types of action each with its own procedure.
58. For *fir [n]daine* see *Cóic Conara Fugill*, 8 (exx. confined to commentaries, *Ancient Laws* IV, 294). The following are some examples of *fír fer*: *Táin Bó Cúailnge*, ed. Strachan and O'Keeffe. This is the early version of the *Táin*. The language is of the eighth or the ninth century: 31, 1.809; 77, 1.2138. *Táin Bó Cúalnge*, ed. O'Rahilly. This is an early twelfth-century version, 1.4025. *fír catha* (= *fír fer*) 1. 4222. *Togail Bruidne Dá Derga*, ed. Knott 1.411 (*fír fer*). See also

Royal Irish Academy, *Dictionary of the Irish Language* under *fír* and esp. the note by Professor Binchy, "The Saga of Fergus Mac Léti," 42.

59. *Cóic Conara Fugill*, ed. Thurneysen, 16, § 3.

60. *Táin Bó Cúailnge*, ed. Strachan and O'Keeffe, 76–77, lines 2133–2139.

61. This word is discussed by O'Rahilly, "Notes, Mainly Etymological," 173–176, according to whom it is an old compound of *com* + *lán*. The later compound *comlán* does not show the effect of MacNeill's law. See also the note by David Greene, "Miscellanea," 46, where he suggests that the noun *comlann* is a compound of *lín*, and the adjective a compound of *lán*.

62. *Táin Bó Cúailnge*, ed. Strachan and O'Keeffe, 43, lines 1139–1140.

63. *Canu Llywarch Hen*, ed. I. Williams, 1–5.

64. Discussed by Bergin, "White Red-eared Cows," 170.

65. *Tain Bo Fraích*, ed. Meid, 1, lines 5–6.

66. Some examples of the formula are: *Lebor na hUidre*, ed. Best and Bergin, lines 1644, 4041, 10114. Examples of variants in this formula are: *Lebor na hUidre* lines 2926, 3136, 10707, 10940.

67. See *Brut y Tywysogion Pen. 20* (text), 117 (181 of the MS.), col. b., *Brut y Tywysogion Pen. 20* (transl.), 66 and note on 185. Professor Thomas Jones contradicted himself, doubtless by accident, when he wrote the corresponding note to the Red Book version, saying that the *Brut y Saeson* version agrees with the Red Book version. But in the note in Pen. 20 (transl.) he quotes the *Brut y Saeson* reading and it is "xiiii o wystlon."

68. *PKM* 92.

69. Watkins and Mac Cana, "Cystrawennau'r Cyplad mewn Hen Gymraeg," 1–25.

NOTES: APPENDIX

1. ed. J. E. Caerwyn Williams, 30–43

2. Gruffydd's views are summarized by Professor Jarman, "Mabinogi Branwen: Crynodeb o Ddadansoddiad W.J. Gruffydd," 129–134.

3. Rhŷs and Evans, eds., *The Red Book of Hergest*, II, 166–167; compare *Brut Dingestow*, ed. Lewis, 126–127.

4. Bede, *Historia Ecclesiastica*, iii, 6 (ed. Plummer, 137–138); compare Adamnán, *Life of Columba*, 9a (ed. Anderson and Anderson, 200). For Gregory the Great see Bede, *Historia Ecclesiastica*, i, 29 (ed. Plummer, 63).

5. Bartrum, ed., *Early Welsh Genealogical Tracts*, 10, no. 2, 4: 11, no. 16.

The Date of the Four Branches

6. Nennius, *Historia Brittonumn* (ed. Mommsen), 149–153, 159–161. Nennius took a great deal from Latin sources (for which see Mommsen's remarks, 114 f.) but the basis of the origin legend is likely to be Welsh, just as Nennius's account of the legendary pre-history of Ireland depends on an early version, now lost, of the *Lebor Gabála*.

7. Mr. Saunders Lewis has himself argued in favour of the theory that Latin literature, in particular Vergil, was known to Taliesin, either directly or through Gildas, "The Tradition of Taliesin," 293–298.

8. Bromwich, ed., *Trioedd Ynys Prydein*, 23–24.

9. Gruffydd's theory is criticized by Prof. Mac Cana, *Branwen Daughter of Llyr*, 191–194. For his own discussion of the *peir dadeni* see 50–64.

10. *PKM* 30.

11. *PKM* 29.

12. O'Rahilly, *Early Irish History and Mythology*, 191–192; *The Annals of Inisfallen*, ed. Mac Airt, 35, 257.

13. His genealogy is in *Corpus Genealogiarum Hiberniae*, ed. O'Brien, 10. The text gives the pedigree of his older brother Enna, but the Book of Leinster has substituted his name.

14. Mac Airt, ed., *Annals of Inisfallen*, s.a.

15. See the king-list in the *Book of Leinster*, I, ed. Best, Bergin and O'Brien, 98, line 25.

16. *Giraldi Cambrensis Opera*, ed. Dimock, 279.

17. Otway-Ruthven, *A History of Medieval Ireland*, 49.

18. *PKM* 41.

19. Jones and Jones, ed. and trans., *The Mabinogion*, 35.

20. *Llyfr Iorwerth*, ed. Wiliam, 11, § 15, 1.8. See also §§ 71.12; 94.4, 10 (the last two exx. are of *estynnu* in the passive with a subject of the thing given and the person to whom it is given referred to by *ydau* (mod.W.*iddo*).

21. Wade-Evans, ed., *Welsh Medieval Law*, 21, lines 8–9. On page 47, I. 12 there is an example of *estynu* with an infixed pronoun as object which refers to *rantir* (l. 11).

22. Ganshof, *Feudalism*, 111.

23. *Thesaurus Linguae Latinae*, s.v.

24. Examples of *roigid*: Meyer, "Mitteilungen aus irischen Handschriften," 20 (=Thurneysen, *Die Burgschaft im irischen Recht*, 8, § 11); Thurneysen, "Aus dem irischen Recht II," 248; *The Oldest Fragments of the Senchas Már*, ed. Best and Thurneyson, 5, MS. f.15b, 1.7). Example of *rigid*: *Críth Gablach*, ed. Binchy, lines 444–445.

25. Binchy, *Celtic and Anglo-Saxon Kingship*, 3–4.

26. *Chronicon Scotorum*, ed. Hennessy, 284.

27. Hughes in her introductory chapter in Otway-Ruthven, *A History of Medieval Ireland*, compares Brian's policy to that of

Athelstan. The principle targets of Athelstan's policy seem to have been familiar with the idea from then on. Cf. *Armes Prydein*, ed. Williams, xiv–v.

28. A contemporary note in the *Book of Armagh* gives this title to Brian. Compare Athelstan's use of the title *imperator*.

II

Comparative Analyses

3

The Calumniated Wife in Medieval Welsh Literature

Juliette Wood

The influence of folklore on medieval Welsh literature has long been a topic for study and speculation. A work which has attracted particular attention is the Four Branches of the *Mabinogi* which, with its rich and controlled use of language and its wealth of intricate, and often frustratingly complex, narrative detail, has caused numerous scholars to speculate on what lies behind the texts as they exist in their present form. In his recent essay, *The Mabinogi,* Proinsias Mac Cana has described and evaluated both the older historical approach to this text and the increasing emphasis on its unity and aesthetic quality which characterizes several more recent studies. Although modern scholarship has tended to move away from the exclusively historical approach with its often highly speculative search for origins, Mac Cana warns, quite rightly, that in dealing with pre-modern traditional literature such factors as "social milieu, artistic convention and the extent to which the author retains or discards the matter and form of traditional oral literature" must be taken into account.[1] This is particularly true of the Four Branches, where so much of the material is rooted in Celtic myths, in which themes concerning the birth and adventures of a semi-divine hero and sovereignty in both human and divine realms abound, and in international folktale motifs dealing with magic and the Otherworld and its inhabitants. In handling material such as this, a medieval writer's "creativity" lies less in creating novelty than in his ability to incorporate the disparate elements into a smoothly flowing work. However, the author's skill may be hampered by the state of the narrative as he inherits it, and this is certainly one of the imponderables in any historical consideration of the Four Branches.

Although there are a few references in Welsh poetry, the *Triads,* and other prose tales which hint at versions of events different from those described in the Four Branches, little is actually known about the development of the text, and the modern reader must turn to analogous material from other cultures, material whose history and development is itself often obscure. In dealing with the international motifs, however, one is at least dealing with a structure which remains remarkably constant and recognizable, and where these occur it is often easier to establish how precisely a motif has been integrated into the text.

The scope of this article is to consider the relationship between the international folktale motifs and their literary context—specifically the material which clusters around the Calumniated Wife motif (K 2110.1) in the first two Branches, *Pwyll* and *Branwen*—and to examine the relationship of this material to its cultural environment. This approach is particularly suited to the Calumniated Wife motif and to the *Mabinogi* tales because the Calumniated Wife story forms an important part of both tales and because variants of the Calumniated Wife are sufficiently numerous for cultural comparisons to be made.

The Welsh heroines in the First and Second Branches of the Four Branches, Rhiannon and Branwen, are very different in character, but they both share the experience of persecution after marriage. The link between the two is further strengthened by the fact that the stories share a number of folktale motifs. Branwen is a Welsh woman who marries an Irish king; Rhiannon, an inhabitant of the Otherworld who marries a mortal. Both are rejected after marriage like the women in other Calumniated Wife tales, and ultimately their persecution stems from the fact that these women are foreigners, intruders, as it were, into a world which will not readily accept them. On a literary level, the Calumniated Wife motif contributes to the complex characterization of two very different heroines; but it also reflects cultural factors which created a situation in which foreign wives would be open to persecution.

A prominent aspect of attitudes to foreigners is the tendency to identify what is rejected in the foreign with what is culturally outcast. Those individuals who cannot be clearly classified in a culture, for example aliens, are relegated to a special class which is "unclassifiable" in terms of all the usual social categories.[2] A characteristic often attributed to foreigners (and social pariahs) is the use of supernatural power.[3] William of Auvergne attempted to give a rational justification for this link between magic and foreignness. Magic, he says, is seldom practiced in Europe because the demons have been stopped by Christianity and because gems and other occult materials are not plentiful, while in the East, magic is common because the people are not Christian and bizarre plants and animals abound.[4] The reasoning may seem a little circular for modern tastes, but William was expressing a common feeling about the nature of magic and the character of the foreign. Giraldus Cambrensis says much the same thing in his comparison of West and East in which he calls the East a "fountain of poison" where men have more subtle minds.[5]

Interplay between the real world of cultural experience and the imaginative world of literature occurs on all levels, and it is not surprising to find cultural concerns and preoccupations reflected in literary works. The treatment of Medea in Euripides' play is a literary view of the foreigner as possessor of diabolic power, which has some bearing on the Calumniated Wife theme as it is found in Welsh tradition. The theme of Medea as a homeless foreigner pervades the play, and she is conscious that this puts her at a disadvantage in Greek society,[6] and describes herself to Jason as "your barbarian bride."[7] In *Medea*, the witch and foreigner concepts have merged completely. She is a witch, and she does murder her children, whereas the Calumniated Wife figure is an innocent victim of these accusations. Yet their situations have much in common. As a foreigner, Medea is not well integrated into the structure of Greek society, and is thus a natural focus for hostility. The Calumniated Wife is also a foreigner and often accused of witchcraft, and here too her relatively unstable position in society makes her vulnerable.

The Calumniated Wife has been part of European folk tradition since at least the twelfth century and forms an important episode in several folktales. The motif The Woman Charged with Eating her Children (K 2116.1.1) concerns a king who marries a mysterious girl. The king's mother hates the young queen, and when children are born, the mother-in-law steals them, often smears the queen's mouth with blood, and tells the king his wife has eaten the children. Eventually the mother-in-law is punished and the wife exonerated.

The Maiden Without Hands story (AT 706) is frequently introduced by the motif The King who Wants to Marry his Daughter (S 322.1.2). The girl cuts off her hands and sends them to her father. She is found wandering in a forest by a king who marries her despite her mutilation, but she incurs the enmity of someone at court (usually his mother). This jealous person substitutes letters saying she has given birth to a monster and another saying she should be banished. The wife wanders again, during which time her hands are restored, and is finally reunited with her husband. The motif also occurs in the Crescentia tale (AT 712), in which the banished wife becomes renowned for her saintliness and is eventually reunited with her husband and children.

A third tale in which the Calumniated Wife motif plays an important part is The Maiden Who Seeks Her Brothers (AT 451). The girl is attempting to free her brothers from a spell when a king finds and marries her. After their child is born, the mother-in-law steals the baby and accuses the queen, who cannot defend herself because of her vow of silence. The motif appears as an important sub-plot in three other tales: The Three Golden Sons (AT 707), Our Lady's Child (AT 710), and The Prince Whose Wishes Always Came True (AT 6532). In the first tale, the queen is imprisoned and it is her children who eventually rescue her. In Our Lady's Child, a supernatural being steals the baby because the mother, who was the fosterling of this being, had been disobedient. In the Prince, a supernatural child is born to the queen, someone steals it and accuses the mother, who is eventually rescued by her own child. In these last three tales, the Calumniated Wife is a subsidiary theme since they focus on the adventures of the children rather than the mother.

The Calumniated Wife

The Calumniated Wife motif in the Welsh tales has already been the subject of a great deal of comment.[8] W.J. Gruffydd deals with it extensively in his study, *Rhiannon*.[9] He feels that the influence of the Calumniated Wife märchen in medieval times "overshadowed all others," but gives no evidence for this opinion. According to Gruffydd, Rhiannon was accused of giving birth to a foal and her punishment was to act as a mare.[10] Similarly Branwen was accused of being a fairy and of giving birth to a supernatural child, and Efnisien's subsequent burning of the child is seen by Gruffydd as an attempt to refute this charge. As the accusation of infanticide does not occur in *Branwen* and is very unclear in *Pwyll*, although both women are punished, Gruffydd has to rely on very speculative reconstructions to support his thesis. Gruffydd's instincts are more correct than his arguments, however, when he points out that the motivation for the wife's persecution is the hostility she engenders because she is a foreigner or a supernatural being.[11]

Recently Proinsias Mac Cana has re-evaluated Gruffydd's reconstruction of *Branwen*.[12] Mac Cana accepts Gruffydd's suggestion that hatred of foreigners and the accusation of the wife by the people are regular features of the Calumniated Wife motif.[13] However, specific mention that the wife is a foreigner, together with the name of her native country, is more characteristic of the literary variants; in oral tales, the wife is found living in exile, thereby a foreigner by implication, but details about her background are seldom given. The accusation of the wife by her husband's people is unique to the Welsh tales. Even here the motivations are complex. Rhiannon is merely accused of barrenness, whereas Branwen is clearly the victim of a wider xenophobia:

> ... llyma ymodwrd yn Iwerdon am y guaradwyd a gawssei Matholwch yg Kymry, a'r somm a wnathoedit idaw am y ueirch. A hynny y urodyr maeth, a'r gwyr nessaf gantaw, yn lliwaw idaw hynny, a heb y gelu. A nachaf y dygyuor yn Iwerdon hyt nat oed lonyd idaw ony chaei dial y sarahet. Sef dial a wnaethant, gyrru Branwen o un ystauell ac ef ...

> ... lo, a murmuring in Ireland, on account of the insult which Matholwch had suffered in Wales, and the shameful trick played on him over his horses. Moreover, his foster-brothers and the men close to him taunted him therewith, and did not conceal it. And lo, an uprising in Ireland till there was no peace for him unless he avenge the disgrace. The vengence they took was to drive away Branwen from the same chamber with him ... [14]

Professor Jackson does not mention the appearance of the Calumniated Wife motif in *Branwen*, although he recognizes its importance in *Pwyll*. He considers that the Calumniated Wife motif in its form K 2116.1.1.1 (The Woman Charged with Eating her Children) was the last element to enter the story in an attempt to provide motivation and characterization in the original version,[15] but it is difficult to establish a temporal sequence for tale elements such as these. Jackson's analysis, while it classifies a number of motifs in the Four Branches, leaves the texts in a rather dissected state. This is perhaps an inevitable result of this type of historical-analytical approach; however, it is at variance with the impressions one gets in reading the Four Branches, and recent work on the prose and the internal structure of the tales would tend to support the thesis that the author has suceeded in imposing a degree of order on his material.[16] In addition, an analysis of other Calumniated Wife stories does not suggest that the Four Branches present a particularly fragmented version. The motif occurs in some half-dozen tale types and within these one finds variants which echo features in the Four Branches.[17] These similarities are purely coincidental, but they do illustrate the degree of fluidity that can exist without the tale losing the essential structure that allows us to classify it as a particular type.

A Florentine version of the Calumniated Wife tells how a king out hunting frees a lady from an enchanted castle.[18] The initial situation resembles that in *Pwyll*, in which the hero rescues his bride from danger in the Otherworld. There are also a number of tales in which the character of the heroine is elaborately drawn and she is depicted as taking an active part in her fate.[19] In one of the *Arabian Nights* tales, a girl marries a sultan and her sisters substitute a puppy for the child. The mother is confined at the door of a mosque and everyone who passes is compelled to spit at her. Her son refuses to do so and frees her.[20] The situation is not unlike that in *Pwyll* where Rhiannon is forced to sit by the horseblock and carry guests to the court. Pryderi refuses to allow this and soon frees his mother.

Italian tradition contains a number of Calumniated Wife tales. The two motifs prominent in nearly all Italian variants are mutilation and the exchange of letters. The best known example is probably the one included in Basile's collection *Il Pentamerone* (1634),[21] although the story appears much earlier. The sixteenth-century *Pecarone* contains a version in which the king of England marries the disguised sister of the king of France.[22] The king's mother objects that she is a low-born foreigner and here we have some indication of a motivation for the persecution. The version in the fifteenth-century *I Reali di Francia* also says that the mother objects on the grounds that the girl is a foreigner and she plots with two other women to discredit her.[23] Multiple persecutions are rare, but the motif occurs in both *Branwen* and *Pwyll*.

Italian tradition contains a whole cycle of stories about St. Uliva (the Crescentia tale), many of them in the form of popular drama and chapbooks.[24] In most of these the mother-in-law objects to the marriage, claiming that the girl is a foreigner, but a more striking feature is the piety and patience of the heroine, which are reminiscent of Branwen's character.

The English variants, almost without exception, include an exchanged letter motif. They are also very specific about the motivation for the persecution. Gower's Constance is accused of being a fairy, and the king is advised to kill the "devill."[25] In *Emaré*, the heroine says vaguely that she comes from a "ferre lande" and the king's mother calls her a "fende."[26] Chaucer's Constance is called an "elf" who works "by charms or by sorcerie."[27] In Matthew Paris's *Vitae Duorum Offarum*, one of the earliest variants, the girl is accused of witchcraft.[28]

In a fifteenth-century Catalan version, the heroine takes shelter with a couple who pity the beautiful girl "from a foreign land," while the accusation brought against her clearly reflects the prevailing xenophobia, since she is accused of giving birth to a child "black and having the shape of a Saracen."[29] Examples such as this could be multiplied indefinitely, but it is clear that one factor underlying all the tales is a polarity between that which is within the boundaries of society and that which is foreign or intrusive.

Welsh and Irish laws dealing with foreigners, with kinship, and with marriage reflect the tension between an integrated social unit and external, but tangential, elements. In Ireland laws applied only between members of a *túath*, the basic jurisdictional unit, and a man lost his legal and political status once he crossed the boundary in which his kin resided.[30] This kind of social ordering created problems when marriage occured outside the *túath*, since it failed to achieve one of the expected benefits of such an alliance, that is, the strengthening of kin groups. One of Matholwch's reasons for marrying Branwen is that the alliance will benefit both islands.[31] Since this is marriage outside the *túath*, conflict results. Branwen is removed from the protection of her kin and becomes a resented foreign element among her husband's people. Eventually the Welsh try to avenge their kinswoman. Much of the tale's irony lies in the fact that the two islands are destroyed, not strengthened, by the alliance. Branwen's comment about the war and her part in the destruction of Wales and Ireland emphasizes her pivotal role in the relationship between the two countries, as well as her personal tragedy as a rejected wife:

> "Oy a uab Duw," heb hi, "guae ui o'm ganedigeath.
> Da a dwy ynys a diffeithwyt o'm achaws i."
>
> "Alas, Son of God," she said, "woe is me that ever
> I was born: two good islands have been laid waste
> because of me!"[32]

The Laws refer contemptuously to men and women who marry foreigners.[33] A wife who moved to her husband's *túath* might naturally be brought into conflict with her husband's kin and in most of the Calumniated Wife tales the accusers are members of the husband's family.[34] In the stories of Branwen and Rhiannon, the accusers emphasize that they are foster-brothers *(brodyr maeth)* of the husband and in this role of kin-substitute would naturally resent a foreign wife in the group.

However, no direct prohibition existed against the marriage of a Welshman and a foreign woman,[35] and no doubt such marriages did occur. Foreigners, whatever the feelings towards them, had definite duties and rights under law. The Latin texts of the Welsh laws refer to men "De aliena patria . . . de uno pago . . . de uno commoto"[36] as having different degrees of responsibility under law. This classification is similar to that reflected in the Irish laws between an *ambue*, an exile from another *túath* in Ireland, and a *cú glas*, an exile from outside Ireland.[37] *Cú glas* means "grey dog" or "wolf," and this may reflect a certain contempt for this type of foreigner. There are several references to children of marriages between foreigners and Irish women. In one law tract the offspring of such unions are called *glasfine*, the grey kin.[38] Here too the term may contain a slighting reference to children possessing alien blood, and therefore not fully members of the social group. This attitude both to the alien spouse and to the half-alien offspring of these unions helps to clarify why such tension surrounds the birth of the Calumniated Wife's children. In many tales, a member or members of the husband's family are openly resentful of the marriage. The mothers-in-law in Chaucer's Man of Law's Tale and in Giovanni Fiorentino's tale of Dionigia in *Il Pecarone* retire from the court after their sons' unwanted marriages, but when grandchildren are born, they take a more active role (falsifying letters) in bringing about the expulsion of their daughters-in-law. *Branwen* may reflect this negative attitude to alien offspring, since it is not until after the birth of her son that the Irish cause her humiliation.

The Welsh versions of the Calumniated Wife as they appear in the first two Branches of the *Mabinogi* differ from other variants on a number of points, but the Welsh stories preserve both the structure and the cultural tensions of the Calumniated Wife motif. Rhiannon claims that she is being forced into an unwelcome marriage, an assertion which can be compared to the other Calumniated Wife stories where the girl is escaping an unwelcome, usually incestuous, alliance. Furthermore, the proposed marriage of Rhiannon to Gwawl is a logical substitute for the unwanted incestuous alliance.

The wedding generally occurs without comment in the märchen, but in *Pwyll* it is the setting for the Badger in the Bag episode and in *Branwen* for the mutilation of the horses, both of them incidents which influence the subsequent persecution of the women.

Another distinctive feature is Rhiannon's initiative in seeking out Pwyll once he has placed himself on Gorsedd Arberth. The Calumniated Wife is usually a passive figure, while it is the opposite quality in Rhiannon that gives the Welsh version much of its artistry. The Badger in the Bag episode is not part of the Calumniated Wife tradition, but it develops the dramatic possibilities inherent in Rhiannon's preference for Pwyll and helps to link the First and Third Branches through the vengeance motif which motivates Llwyd Cil Coed's activities in Dyfed.

The men of Dyfed bring the charge of barrenness against Rhiannon and this precipitates the major conflict of the Calumniated Wife section. They regard Pwyll as a foster-brother and in the context of this assumed kinship relationship their concern over the queen's barrenness is understandable. They advise Pwyll to take another wife, but he delays them for a year. This action is paralleled in some folktales[39] in which the wife is often reprieved twice through her husband's intercession before being condemned.

Rhiannon's child disappears despite the guardian nurses, who later implicate the queen. In most versions of the Calumniated Wife, the same person accuses the queen, steals the child, and implicates the mother. In the Welsh tale, the men of Dyfed accuse the queen of barrenness, not infanticide, while the nurses' actions stem from fear of reprisal, not hatred.[40] It is not stated who steals the child, but later the culprit seems to be a mysterious supernatural claw. The *Pwyll* version is clearly more complicated than the ordinary folktale, and it is likely that elements of another tale, The Hand and the Child, have entered the story.[41] Jackson assumes that the theft of Teyrnon's colt occurs some time after the theft of Pryderi, but it is just as likely that both actions occurred on the same night with the author bringing the Rhiannon situation to its logical conclusion then backtracking; the technique of narrating simultaneous action is always difficult, and this would be a natural, and not uncommon, way of solving the problem. One can see why Jackson should raise so many questions about action and motivation at this point. If, however, a variant of Our Lady's Child formed part of the background for the First Branch, then the motif of supernatural persecution would already be part of the tale and some at least of the seeming confusion in this episode would be dispelled.

Rhiannon refuses to defend herself against the women. Dramatically this helps to elucidate her character. In The Maiden Who Seeks Her Brothers, the heroine is often silent in the face of accusation in order to release her enchanted brothers. Although Rhiannon is punished, she retains her position at court. Interestingly, the language used to describe her, and particularly that used in direct address, is respectful. The correct terms for a woman of her status are used and this further underlines the impression that the relationship between the husband and wife remains intact.[42]

Rhiannon's penance is an interesting feature of the story. Although this is the only instance in which it is associated with the Calumniated Wife, it occurs as a motif elsewhere (Q 493: Punishment of Being Saddled and Ridden as a Horse), and frequently appears in medieval literature, sometimes in fabliaux.[43] The character of Rhiannon is strong and memorable and much of its quality is due to the fusion of traditional and literary elements. Rhiannon is an Otherworld being who takes the initiative in seeking out her lover. This puts her within the tradition of the fairy mistress, which is a strong one in Celtic tradition. Rhiannon appears riding a white horse which cannot be overtaken, and only stops when Pwyll himself addresses her. It is nowhere stated that Rhiannon is an Otherworld being, but from the manner of her appearance, she clearly comes from Annwn. The impossibility of anyone overtaking her, the fact that her father's court lies outside the bounds of Pwyll's kingdom, and her appearance after Pwyll places himself on a mound, Gorsedd Arberth, provide clear indications of her supernatural nature. At the wedding, Gwawl almost tricks Pwyll out of his bride, and it is Rhiannon who comes to the rescue. Yet once she and Pwyll return to his world, Rhiannon seems to become more vulnerable. She becomes a foreigner, in effect, and the initial roles are reversed, with Pwyll and later Pryderi having to protect her.

Rhiannon is first accused of barrenness, an accusation which fits in with the legal and social consequences of marriage in Welsh society. It is not, however, an accusation that figures much in the Calumniated Wife märchen. The second accusation, brought by the nurses, is more usual. They are multiple accusers, an uncommon but not unknown motif. The fact that the women persist despite Rhiannon's reassurance gives the author an opportunity to portray her as a dignified and noble woman. The text says that she prefers penance to wrangling with the women.[44] Both Pwyll and the kings in other fairy tales are reluctant to punish their wives, despite the seeming evidence against them. In the Four Branches, this aspect of the tale is developed into a convincingly real and sustained husband-wife relationship.

Gwawl's character also reveals much about the use of folklore in the work. Gwawl is a rejected suitor who shares some of the qualities of the incestuous father and the supernatural being in Our Lady's Child. He does not accuse the wife, but, by implication, is the reason for the vengeance taken against her and, later, her son. It is not clear in the First Branch to whom the mysterious claw belongs, but in the Third Branch it seems, in retrospect, to be part of a plot against Rhiannon and her family.[45] Motivation in folktales is usually very clear, whereas here a motif initiated in the Calumniated Wife section of the First Branch forms a link with material in the Third. Motivation in the Four Branches is more complicated than in märchen, but the structure underlying the story, the persecution of a queen who is an outsider in her husband's kingdom, is a constant feature no matter how complicated or how literary the tale.

The return of Pryderi follows the pattern in tales such as The Prince Whose Wishes Always Came True and Our Lady's Child, in which the son returns to vindicate the mother. The court recognizes that Pryderi is Pwyll's son, and Rhiannon's penance is at an end. There is, however, no punishment of the accuser as is customary in the märchen since, as yet, he has not been identified.

The Calumniated Wife episode in *Branwen* contains no attempted incest, but there is mutilation, of the horses rather than of the heroine. Branwen marries Matholwch with the consent of her family, except Efnisien who is a perennial

The Calumniated Wife

trouble-maker. Efnisien is angry because he has not been consulted about Branwen's marriage and he mutilates the horses in revenge.[46] In Ireland all goes well for a while and when her son is born, he is put out to fosterage according to custom. Once again, it is the king's "foster-brothers" who cause trouble. They do not accuse Branwen directly, but they remind Matholwch of the insult of the mutilated horses. Since Bendigeidfran made restitution for the horses and since the Irish king accepted the restitution, it is clear that this is not the real point. Rather, the insult committed against the Irish during their stay in Wales is being transferred to Branwen, the alien Welshwoman in Ireland.

The men of Ireland are more successful in turning Matholwch against his wife, and Branwen is driven from the court and made to work in the kitchen. Again the language reflects the change in circumstances.[47] She is a much more passive figure than Rhiannon, and in this her character is closer to that of the folktale queen, even though her story diverges more from the structure of other Calumniated Wife folktales than does Rhiannon's. The description of how she raises a starling in her kneading trough to inform her brother of her plight gives her both individuality and a tragic dimension. The relation of *Branwen* to the Calumniated Wife folktales is complex. There is no flight motif, no incest, and no mutilation. Branwen's child is born before she is persecuted. He is not stolen, nor is she accused of murdering him. She is exonerated and reunited with her child and her family, but not with Matholwch, who shows none of the belief in his wife's innocence characteristic of the märchen husband. Whatever the author's intention, the section presents an interesting contrast to the treatment of Rhiannon. Both women are punished as the outcome of popular unrest, but the personal relationship between Pwyll and Rhiannon survives, unlike that of Branwen and Matholwch.

The shadowy figure of Efnisien takes on some of the qualities of the persecutor in the Maiden Without Hands tale. He causes trouble before Branwen's marriage and later murders her son. This aspect of *Branwen* is not characteristic of the folktale, where conflicts are resolved happily, and the Calumniated Wife theme which appears in *Branwen* is clearly to be considered a literary adaptation of a folktale. In structure, the theme in *Branwen* is most like the Crescentia tale (AT 712) in the patient endurance shown by the heroine. In *Branwen*, the theme provides a poignant characterization of the heroine, although it appears to be slightly removed from the main narrative, while in *Pwyll*, with the exception of the Pwyll-Arawn material, the theme is a motivating factor throughout the story.

There is one other possible example of the Calumniated Wife in Welsh tradition. This occurs in an episode in *Culhwch and Olwen* in which Arthur and his men set out to rescue the prisoner Mabon, who was stolen from his mother when three nights old.[48] Jackson points out that the abduction of a child takes place in both myth and folktale.[49] Here Mabon, not his mother, is the prisoner and the tale is, in any case, too fragmentary for real analysis. However, if Celtic mythology contained a story about a stolen son of one of its goddesses, then this would have been a possible way in which the Calumniated Wife tale could have entered Welsh tradition.

Whatever the particular variations, the tale clearly reflects a number of attitudes towards that which is foreign and to the foreigner's role within the familiar bounds of society. The fact that there were laws referring to aliens and to the children of alien marriages indicates that society recognized their existence and needed to define their position within the social system.

The position of the *fiana* in Irish law and literature provides a model for the process by which aliens could be integrated into the dominant social structure. It also illustrates the similarities between attitudes to members of the social periphery and attitudes to foreigners, and in this sense is relevant to the foregoing discussion of the Calumniated Wife theme. The position of the Irish *fiana*, roving bands of independent fighting men, was similar to the legal status of the Welshman or Irishman who travelled outside his own country. A *féinnid* was *écland* (clanless), which meant that, like the Welsh *alltud*, he lost his legal status and the protection of his kin.[50] However, he was an outsider, not an outlaw, and his position entailed certain duties and privileges.[51] Much of what can be said of Celtic society's attitude to the *fiana* can be applied to its attitude to foreigners as well:

> Every society and specially a closed society organized in rigid classes like that of the Celts includes certain abnormal elements. . . . Celtic society provides its own antidote (the *fiana*) and copes with what is asocial by expelling it, while at the same time recognizing its right and assigning it a particular domain.[52]

The foreigner does not need to be expelled, as he is already outside the social structure, but he does need to have his place in society defined and what Sjoestedt says in the above quotation can be applied to the position of the foreign wife in the Calumniated Wife tales; she is an acknowledged but unnatural element in the social system. Her position is a weak one, and she is subject to rejection in times of stress.

This examination of the parallels between the Four Branches and folktales that contain the Calumniated Wife episode does not imply that these tales were direct sources for the author of the Four Branches. Reconstruction of sources is always difficult, and the author may have known one or several versions of the tale. What seems unlikely is that he created a pastiche out of half-remembered folklore motifs, which is the impression that one gets from Jackson's book, or that he was trying to make sense out of a contaminated mythology, as Gruffydd implies. Rather, his use of folklore sources was a creative and very controlled activity. The many parallels between the events of the Welsh tales and folklore tradition indicate that the latter was a major source for these tales, but it is also evident from the text that the author reworked the stories, developing the dramatic possibilities and adding characterization. This is particularly clear in Rhiannon's story, where the Calumniated Wife motif is pivotal to much of the action in the First Branch and ultimately affects events in the Third Branch as well. The Calumniated Wife theme is much less pronounced in *Branwen*. Here the motif is closely tied to a feud and an eventual war between two national groups and this clearly demonstrates the way in which elements of the theme relate to negative attitudes to foreigners. The motif functions on at least two important levels in the Four Branches. As a dramatic theme forming part of an integrated work, it adds further motivation, and therefore further meaning, to the persecution of the two queens, and contributes substantially to the characterization of both figures. As a folktale motif incorporated into a literary work, it reveals something about the nature of the connection between these medieval Welsh stories and their cultural context which can help to clarify the meaning and significance of these works for the modern reader.

NOTES

1. Mac Cana, *The Mabinogi*, 4. References to tales and motifs in this article are followed by letters and numbers which refer to the appropriate tale-type or motif as laid out respectively in Antti Aarne, *The Types of the Folktale*, and in Stith Thompson, *Motif Index of Folk Literature*. The abbreviation AT refers to tale-types in the Aarne-Thompson*Type* Index, while motifs are preceded by the relevant classifying letter in the *Motif Index*.
2. Douglas, *Purity and Danger: An Analysis of Concepts of Pollution and Taboo*, 53–57.
3. Newell, "The Jew as Witch," 100–102 and 104.
4. William of Auvergne, *De Universo*, II. iii. 23, quoted by Lynn Thorndike, *A History of Magic and Experimental Science*, II, 236.
5. Giraldus Cambrensis, *Topographia Hibernica*, Chapters xxxiv–xl.
6. Euripides, *Medea*, lines 222–223.
7. Euripides, *Medea*, line 591.
8. Jackson, *The International Popular Tale and Early Welsh Tradition*; Gruffydd, *Math vab Mathonwy* and *Rhiannon*; Ó Coileáin, "A Thematic Study of the Tale *Pwyll Pendeuic Dyuet*"; Bollard, "The Structure of the Four Branches of the Mabinogi," and "The Role of Myth and Tradition in *The Four Branches of the Mabinogi*."
9. Gruffydd, *Rhiannon*, 60–67.
10. Gruffydd, *Rhiannon*, 110–111.
11. Gruffydd, *Rhiannon*, 65; Gruffydd, *Folklore and Myth in the Mabinogion*, 17.
12. Mac Cana, *Branwen*, 154 and 162, and *The Mabinogi*, 28–30.
13. Mac Cana, *Branwen*, 49 and 161.
14. Thomson, ed., *Branwen Uerch Lyr*, lines 213–218; Jones and Jones, ed. and trans., *The Mabinogion*, 32.
15. Jackson, *International Popular Tale*, 92–95.
16. Mac Cana, *The Mabinogi*, 44–61; Bollard, "A Literary Assessment of the Four Branches of the Mabinogion" (unpublished M.A. dissertation, University of Wales, Aberystwyth, 1970); Sioned

Davies, "A Study of Narrative Methods in The Mabinogion" (unpublished D.Phil. dissertation, University of Oxford, 1982); and Catherine A. McKenna, "The Theme of Sovereignty in *Pwyll,*" 35–52.

17. Barbulesçu, "The Maiden Without Hands: AT 706 in Romania," 319–367. This study examines twenty-one examples of AT 706 collected from Romanian folk tradition. All can be classified as The Maiden Without Hands on the basis of the mutilation and exile motifs, but within even this rather restricted group of variants, the author identifies three sub-types. Furthermore, examination of the tale summaries reveals that very few of the variants do not differ in some way from the type-plot given in the Aarne-Thompson Index.

18. Imbriani, *La Novellaja Fiorentina, Fiabe e Novelline,* 232.

19. Schlauch, *Chaucer's Constance and Accused Queens,* 102–103.

20. Burton,"Two Sisters Who Envied Their Cadette," III, 491–510; analogues, 647–648.

21. Basile, Day 3, Tale ii, "La Bella dalle Mani Mozze."

22. Battaglia, Tale iv, 36–42.

23. Vandelli, ed., *I Reali di Francia di Andrea da Barberino,* II, Book 2, Chapters 42, 49, and 52–53.

24. d'Ancona, ed., "Rappresentazione di Santa Uliva," III, 235–316; Florentinus, "Historia de La Regina Oliva," 19.

25. Gower, "The Tale of Constance," lines 1919–1929.

26. Rickert, ed., *The Romance of Emaré,* lines 442 and 446.

27. Chaucer, "The Man of Law's Tale," lines 754–755.

28. Wats, ed., *Vitae Duorum Offarum,* 6–7.

29. Suchier, "La Fille Sans Mains," 525–526 and 531.

30. Charles-Edwards, "Some Celtic Kinship Terms," 115; and Binchy, *Celtic and Anglo-Saxon Kingship,* 5.

31. Thomson, ed., *Branwen Uerch Lyr,* lines 35–39.

32. Thomson, ed., *Branwen Uerch Lyr,* lines 406–407; Jones and Jones, ed. and trans., *The Mabinogion,* 38.

33. Charles-Edwards, "Some Celtic Kinship Terms," 116 and 119.

34. Schlauch, *Chaucer's Constance,* 32.

35. Ellis, *Welsh Tribal Law and Custom in the Middle Ages,* I, 425. The author cites several examples of royal marriages between Welsh princes and foreign women.

36. Emanuel, ed., *The Latin Texts of the Welsh Laws,* 211.

37. Charles-Edwards, "Some Celtic Kinship Terms," 116; Jackson, "*Varia* II: Gildas and the Names of the British Princes," 33.

38. Charles-Edwards, "Some Celtic Kinship Terms," 119.

39. Schlauch, *Chaucer's Constance,* 28–30; Wats, ed., *Vitae Duorum Offarum,* 6–7; and Campbell, *Popular Tales of the West Highlands,* I, 226.

40. Thomson, ed., *Pwyll Pendeuic Dyuet*, lines 449–508.

41. Jackson, *International Popular Tale*, 90–95; Ford, *The Mabinogi and Other Medieval Welsh Tales*, 4–5; and Bollard, "Role of Myth and Tradition," 78.

42. Charles-Edwards, "Honour and Status in Some Irish and Welsh Prose Tales," 127–129. Charles-Edwards points out, however, that one incident differs from this apparent consistency in the use of honour titles. When Teyrnon brings Pryderi to court he initially addresses Rhiannon as *gwreicda* and *eneit*, and only after her innocence is proved does he use *arglwydes*.

43. Roberts, "Penyd Rhiannon," 325–337.

44. Thomson, ed., *Pwyll Pendeuic Dyuet*, lines 449–501.

45. I. Williams, ed., *Pedeir Keinc y Mabinogi*, 2nd ed., 64–65.

46. Thomson, ed., *Pwyll Pendeuic Dyuet*, lines 58–77.

47. Owen, "Shame and Reparation: A Woman's Place in the Kin," 58–59; and Charles-Edwards, "Honour and Status," 129–130.

48. Jones and Jones, ed. and trans., *The Mabinogi*, 118 and 126.

49. Jackson, *International Popular Tale*, 128–129.

50. Sjoestedt, *Gods and Heroes of the Celts*, 102.

51. Sjoestedt, *Gods and Heroes of the Celts*, 100, 103, and 108.

52. Sjoestedt, *Gods and Heroes of the Celts*, 109.

4

The Lost Tale of Dylan in the Fourth Branch of *The Mabinogi*

Sarah Larratt Keefer

In his presentation of the compiler of the Four Branches as a "man of literature," Proinsias Mac Cana draws our attention to the "subsequent interpolation of miscellaneous matter from Irish and other sources."[1] Through the following discussion, I hope to open yet another new line of thought by which we may further understand the complex relationships existing between Gaelic and Britannic[2] sources of Celtic tales. Throughout the Four Branches of the *Mabinogi*, the mystical Otherworld encroaches upon the realm of mortal kind, and one of the more powerful appearances of it takes the form of animals that participate in metamorphoses with human figures. These can signify an Otherworld incursion into mortal nature in several different ways. They can signal a thinning of the barriers between the realms of the Otherworld and this world; they can represent characteristics associated with the mysteries of fertility and tribal magic; and they can appear to enhance or, at times, take the place of the principal figures in the tales. It is this third role of Otherworld animals that I wish to concentrate on, because among the many named, and hence *characterized* animal shapes into which figures are transformed, we come across an *unnamed* animal whose disclosure may shed light on the puzzle of the lost tale of Dylan in the Fourth Branch. Jeffrey Gantz describes the "appearance of Dylan" as "an unintegrated tradition."[3] W.J. Gruffydd assumes that Dylan "makes for the sea and becomes a fish . . . or probably a merman."[4] It is only a modern popular study by Caitlin Matthews that makes what I believe to be the appropriate animal identification of a seal in attempting to reconstruct "Dylan's lost story,"[5] but it does not place the Dylan fragment into the correct context of analogue tales. It has therefore remained an enigma, despite scholarly exploration into its sources.[6]

Metamorphoses of mortals into animals are far more numerous in the Fourth Branch than in the earlier three. In the First Branch, *Pwyll Pendeuic Dyuet*, Rhiannon and Pryderi are clearly to be identified with horses if we seek the mythical origins of the tale,[7] but they do not appear in the narrative *as* horses. Similarly, the identification of Gwawl with a badger[8] seems less an animal connection or a transposed shape-changing than a complex metaphor drawn from fertility rite and sympathetic magic. Within the complexity of insult and revenge linking the First and Third Branches together through the Badger-in-the-Bag game, the importance of "badger" as an animal seems lost in the greater theme of outrage. When the narrative thread from Gwawl to Llwyd is considered as a whole, we can see the overshadowing importance of the bag motif, perhaps as a fertility signifier, with the consequent subordination of the badger element to it.

Branwen, the Second Branch, deals less with animal metamorphoses than with animals linked associatively through a beast-symbol that formed part of the base-myth. Regardless of their origins in the oral versions of this Branch, Matholwch's horses only serve in the textualized narrative to provide Efnisien with a target for intentional insult-giving. In the same fashion, the starling that Branwen rears "on the edge of her kneading trough" (Jones 32) may once have been associated symbolically with Bendigeiduran (Brân) and hence Branwen, whose names may be etymologically linked with the Welsh word *brân*, for "crow";[9] however, as with Rhiannon and Pryderi in the First Branch, we once again find a division in place between the tale-figures and what may once have been their symbolic animal counterparts.

In *Manawydan*, the Third Branch, the "shining white" boar (Jones 46) that lures Pryderi to the Otherworld fortress is more a harbinger of Llwyd's ominous approach than an animal to be identified with any principal figure in the tale. There is, however, one animal metamorphosis to be found in the Third Branch—the appearance of Llwyd's pregnant wife in mouse form—which is, both in the narrative and the emblem that the narrative creates, perhaps as closely linked to fertility as Gwawl's role of Badger-in-the-Bag in the First Branch. What is different here is that now the association between narrative emblem and fertility is explicitly effected, not implicitly suggested: Gwawl was *like* a badger, but the wife of Llwyd *is*, in fact, the mouse whom Manawydan captures in his glove. She represents the sole true animal metamorphosis in all of the first three Branches, and her function is the important one of completing the narrative thread begun with the Badger-in-the-Bag game. The visualization of this metamorphosis, which occurs when we see the mouse-queen returned to "the fairest young woman that any one had seen" (Jones 54), underlines the importance of an actualized shape-change from character to animal or vice versa. It is one thing to be *told* that the mouse is Llwyd's wife, already transformed into animal shape before we first see her, but when the narrative describes the process of actual transformation, we are effectively being provided with a graphic equation. By demonstrating a shape-change in front of us, the narrative asks us to ponder the nature of the elements which changed from one to the other, and their significance to the thematic narrative thread within which they function.

As distinct from the first three Branches, the Fourth, *Math uab Mathonwy*, is full of animal metamorphoses. The most memorable is perhaps the dramatic punishment[10] levelled by Math on Gilfaethwy and Gwydion for the rape of Goewin such that, with genders exchanged annually, they become a hind and stag, a boar and sow, and a she- and he-wolf. We also remember the transformation at the end of the tale, of the faithless Blodeuedd into an owl by Gwydion who, with Math, had created her of flowers in order to overcome Aranrhod's curse of wifelessness for Lleu. In this last Branch, animal metamorphoses may be the result of either a change inflicted upon one figure by the agency of another, or a change adopted and effected by one figure himself. Both of the foregoing punitive transformations are wrought upon unwilling subjects by wrathful magicians. Math takes revenge on behalf of his violated footholder, while Gwydion punishes Blodeuedd for his betrayed foster-son. However, even here we notice a distinction drawn between the means by which these two metamorphoses occur. Math, like Llwyd before him, uses physical contact with his wand to reinforce the pronouncement of shape-change, while Gwydion relies upon the potency of the spoken word alone. The authority of verbalization over enactment, the word over the ritual, is here depicted as an alternative means of power. However, these episodes both remain metamorphoses caused by one character but affecting another. The change from human to animal form is split into an agent who creates the transformation but is not himself transformed, and at least one recipient whose shape is consequently changed against his or her will.

In contrast to these, there are two other animal metamorphoses in the Fourth Branch which make use of self-agency in transforming from mortal to bestial shape. One is the changing of Lleu, presumably by his own volition, into an eagle after Gronw has cast the doomed spear through him; his subsequent return to human form, however, must be effected by Gwydion through spell-singing and a ritual blow from a magic staff. The other is contained in the brief but extraordinary fragment which Gruffydd describes as having an "abundantly established . . . connection with a sea-transformation of some kind" (Gruffydd 221). It appears to be the shape-changing of a human being, by no evident agent other than himself, into an unnamed creature, which occurs in the following passage after Aranrhod's virginity test:

> Yna y camawd hitheu dros yr hutlath, ac ar y cam hwnnw, adaw mab brasuelyn mawr a oruc. Sef a wnaeth y mab, dodi diaspat uchel. . . ."Ie," heb Math uab Mathonwy, "mi a baraf uedydyaw hwn," wrth y mab brasuelyn. "Sef enw a baraf, Dylan." Bedydyaw a wnaethpwyt y mab, ac y gyt ac y bedydywyt, y mor a gyrchwys. Ac yn y lle, y gyt ac y doeth y'r mor, annyan y mor a gauas, a chystal y nouyei a'r pysc goreu yn y mor, ac o achaws hynny y gelwit Dylan Eil Ton. Ny thorres tonn adanaw eiryoet. A'r ergyt y doeth y angheu ohonaw, a

The Lost Tale of Dylan

> uyrywys Gouannon y ewythyr. A hwnnw a uu trydyd anuat ergyt.[11]
>
> Then she stepped over the magic wand, and with that step she dropped a fine boy-child with rich yellow hair. The boy uttered a loud cry.... "Why," said Math son of Mathonwy, "I will have this one baptized"—of the rich yellow-haired boy. "The name I will give him is Dylan."
>
> The boy was baptized and the moment he was baptized he made for the sea. And there and then, as soon as he came to the sea he received the sea's nature, and swam as well as the best fish in the sea. And for that reason he was called Dylan Eil Ton. No wave ever broke beneath him. And the blow whereby his death came, his uncle Gofannon aimed. And that was one of the Three Unhappy Blows. (Jones 63–64)

"Whether we look upon it as an instance of the Twin legend, or as an example of the savage ritual of the placenta, or as a story of the Child committed to the Sea, it bristles with interesting points" (Gruffydd 211).[12] Gruffydd assumes a relationship, to be discussed in detail later on, between this tale and two versions of the Irish *Balor on Tory Island*, in which children, in one case born like Aranrhod's in multiple birth to one mother, fall into the sea and either drown or become seals, yet he insists that Dylan becomes a fish (Gruffydd 212). Only Matthews's modern and somewhat fanciful reconstruction of the lost tale has Dylan enter the sea, "whereupon Gwydion gifted him with the ability to turn into a seal, so that the boy had two natures."[13] Yet this is only partially sound: in the Fourth Branch with which we are here concerned, we see Gwydion showing no interest whatsoever in the golden-haired Dylan, only in the "small something" which turns into Lleu. In fact, one may easily infer from the passage that Dylan and Lleu have different fathers, and that Gwydion is responsible for Lleu alone (Gruffydd 137, 198). Nor is it Gwydion who baptizes the child—the pagan naming ceremony was doubtless Christianized into baptism at the scribal stage of narrative transmission as the author was probably a cleric[14]—but Math who takes responsibility for naming, and hence characterizing the child with an identifier that is of great importance. The significance attached to the naming of children in the Four Branches, as in the cases of Pryderi and Lleu, should cause us to pay closer attention here. I suspect that the fact that Math *knows* to call him "Dylan" contains the key to the lost tale underlying this narrative gesture. While the etymology for the early Welsh *dylan* should not be over-simplified, attempts to link it to the thorn-pin, *dealg*, which loosens to release the children into the sea in the Irish *Balor* tale (Gruffydd 214), are not as convincing as the definitions *môr, cefnfor, eigion* or *ton*, glossed "sea, ocean, the deep" and "wave,"[15] and rendered in the Jones translation as "Sea" (Jones 64, n1). The subsequent events reiterate the appropriateness of this name for the child, for "the moment he was baptized" (Jones 63), Dylan "straightway" (Gruffydd 19) heads for the ocean as if in response to the identifier which he has been given. Once there, he "received the sea's nature" (Gruffydd 19; Jones 63) "and swam as well as the best fish in the sea" (Jones 63–64). The narrative rationalizes this occurrence by repeating and augmenting the name. Despite the lack of identified paternity for the boy, the *eil* of "Dylan Eil Ton" ("Dylan Like-a-Wave" or "Dylan Mate of the Wave") "may be also rendered, metaphorically, 'son'" (Gruffydd 214, 221), and the Jones translation reinforces such an association by translating "Dylan Eil Ton" as "Sea Son of Wave" (Jones 64, n1). With this, we are told that "no wave ever broke beneath him" (Jones 64). Gruffydd asks, in connection with the Irish *Balor* tale, "which is more likely to be the older form of the legend, the simple drowning, as in Irish, or the transformation into a sea-being as in Welsh?" (Gruffydd 216). Yet he either asserts that Dylan became a fish, or contradicts himself by proposing that Dylan turns into a sea-being or merman, and never suggests the evident alternative, implicit in the *Balor* tale, of a seal. It seems a logical assumption to make that a seal is the creature into which Dylan is transformed, and by which I hope to propose a very close analogue tale for the lost story behind the Dylan fragment. That the child never had a wave break *beneath* him suggests that he swam by diving under the breaking waves, as a seal does. He is clearly not a fish, for he is likened to one solely in his ability to swim, not in his appearance. We therefore need analogues from the seal-lore and seal-tales of the Scottish islands and Irish coasts to shine light on the Dylan fragment.

The grey seal *(Halichoerus grypus)* or "selchie" has very large breeding grounds in the Orkney, Shetland and Hebrides Islands, on the Isles of Man, North Rona and Ramsey, and, critical to our study, along the mainland Welsh coast down through North Devon to Cornwall and all around the Irish coastline.[16] The Welsh seal colonies have their pups in August, and we are told that, even in babyhood, "in the water, the Grey Seal displays a true mastery of its aquatic environment; it is equally at home streaking through the water face down or on its back, or hovering vertically in one spot."[17] In both Scottish and Irish coastal folklore, seals have been identified as supernatural creatures with the power to transform themselves into humans when on land. In some places they were regarded as a race of fallen angels, while in others they were believed to be supernatural children under a spell. For northern Orkney dwellers, seals were identified with the "Blue Men of the Minch" and were thought of as dangerous. "Pagan supernatural seal-folk were confused with human beings, and ultimately the superstitions were tinged with Christianity."[18] In the Scottish island of Harris (part of Lewis), seal-meat was once widely eaten, and one specially caught seal, called the "Virgin Mary's seal," was offered annually as a food-gift to the minister."[19]

What is important for our purpose is that, in most of these folklores, seals were regarded as ancestral.[20] Certain families in both Scotland and Ireland claim descent from a seal progenitor, once a human whose sins had brought punishment in the form of soul-transmigration into a seal-body: it was believed that members of these families would never drown if they fell into water, nor would they kill seals or eat seal-meat. When sealing ceased entirely on the coast of County Down, the explanation was that an ancient seal had spoken in a human voice to the seal-killers as they slaughtered seals in a cave on Downpatrick Head; they were warned that by killing seals they were destroying the bodies serving as homes for their ancestors' spirits, who would then be forced to inhabit less felicitous creatures such as sharks.[21] Finally, "a photograph has been exhibited before the Folk-Lore Society of an old Scotch woman who proudly claims to be the granddaughter of a seal, and tells the story of her grandfather's capturing and marrying the seal maid."[22] This wide-spread identification with seals is clearly the expression of early tribal beast-association, confirmed by the visual similarity between the head of a human when swimming out from shore and that of a seal, or the audible one between the cry of a seal in pain and that of a human being.[23] These ancient associations have given rise to many seal-tales which serve both to explain and, in turn, rationalize the belief in seal-ancestry held by the peoples of this region. "Most of the stories are based on the motif 'Marriage to seal in human form' (seal-maidens are among the commonest of fairy brides) and deal with the tragedy inherent in such a union"[24]: a seal-woman is tricked out of her "seal covering,"[25] and must remain on land with her captor until the day when she discovers the hiding place of the "covering" or "hood," and can escape to the sea once more.[26] In each case, there is a return to seal-nature and to the ocean at the tale's end. A similar story to these, and the only such tale in Welsh is Glasynys's *Y Fôr Forwyn*, "The Mermaid," which actually makes mention of Dylan in an aside part-way through the narrative. It is quoted by Sir John Rhŷs, and tells of a mermaid, said to be niece of Gwydion, son of Dôn, who is won by a mortal fisherman.[27] She has a "cap of wonderful workmanship"[28] which she must have hidden from her in order for her to stay on land with her husband. Rhŷs links this motif to an Irish tale in which "a beautiful girl with a cap of salmon skin"[29] is captured, like the seal-maidens of the afore-mentioned stories, by theft of the cap, and is free to go back to the water only when she finds her stolen cap. This in turn leads Rhŷs to Welsh lake-fairy tales in which a water-dweller must return to her natural element when her husband breaks the command "never to strike her with steel or clay."[30] While there are no true seal-tales in Welsh, we come across these very motifs of broken-command-broken-marriage and hidden caps or hoods of sea-nature in the Irish seal-tales, and should recall Gruffydd's use of "cognate tales in Ireland [to] throw considerable light" upon problems in the Fourth Branch (Gruffydd 52).

The Irish seal-tales are therefore important for the purpose of understanding the Dylan fragment because they contain certain elements that appear to be similar to those in the lost story. In many of the seal-tales, the bearing of children and subsequent abandonment of them by the mother when she returns to her seal-nature is a prevalent motif. While this stands back to front with the Dylan story, in which Aranrhod abandons Dylan who then becomes a seal, it serves as an introduction to a similar, but correctly ordered analogous tale to which I shall turn in a moment. In addition to the abandoning of child by mother, we find another similarity: Dylan is described as *brasuelyn mawr a oruc* (PKM 77), being "big stout yellow-haired" (Gruffydd 19) or, more colloquially, "fine . . . with rich yellow hair" (Jones 63). In "The Conneelys and the Seals" (O'Sullivan #21), we are told of the three seal-maidens who were daughters of the King of the Sea, that "as soon as they took off their hoods, they became the three finest women that the sun ever shone upon, and they would go out swimming, each with a golden head of hair."[31] However, despite these echoes, the seal-maiden stories by themselves do not provide enough evidence to be considered cognate with the Dylan episode.

In order to locate a more accurate analogue to the implied configuration in the Dylan fragment, we must find tales about mortals turning into seal-men instead of seal-maidens. These are rarer but nevertheless exist as well. Irish folklore tells the story of an old man who identifies a wound in his head as having been given by the sealer to whom he speaks, when he was in seal form.[32] In "The Seal Hunter and the Water Man," a sealer is convinced to abandon his pursuit of seals by being transformed into a "great brown seal" by a mysterious horseman in black silk who is himself a seal-lord when in the water.[33] Finally, "The Daughter of the King Ron," which is primarily a seal-maiden tale, includes details about the maiden Fionna's father the Ron Mor or Seal King, whose name was Ailean Mor, or "Great Rock."[34] He is a "great man" on the land but, like his offspring, a seal when in the water. It is he who gives permission for Fionna to marry the Lord of the Isles, but also he who is the prophet of her doom to return to seal life if her mortal husband ever speaks to her in anger. In these last two tales, we notice the recurring motif of the seal-lord who allows relationships with humans but assumes a didactic or prophetic role in these associations.

If Dylan's mother is the mortal Aranrhod[35] and Dylan himself turns into a seal upon entering the ocean, then we should assume that his father is a seal-lord, and must look for analogue tales with a mortal woman/seal-man configuration instead of the mortal man/seal-maiden motif which is more frequent. I have located three such stories which have in them some but not all the elements of the Dylan episode. The first is "Annie Norn and the Fin Folk,"[36] in which a mortal maiden from the Orkney Islands is carried off by the Fin or seal-folk, to Hildaland, their secret home. She rescues her human relatives from shipwreck and entertains them with her seal-husband in Hildaland, but does not return because she is happy and has three children whom she loves. This resembles the Dylan fragment in that a mortal woman bears children to what must be a seal-lord but, unlike Aranrhod, Annie Norn dwells with the seal-folk, and is happily married to an identifiable father of children whom she will not abandon.

The second tale is found in David Thomson's important exploration of eastern Scottish seal-lore.[37] He reports a conversation said to have been held about a woman named Brita, who, like Aranrhod, scorned men but took a seal-lover at the time of the Lammas stream or summer high tide, and bore children whose fingers and toes were webbed.[38] The third tale, "King Cormac and King Conn," is also found in Thomson's study.[39] However, this story is from the first not quite an analogue, as it concerns an otter-lord instead of a seal, who lies by the daughter of King Cormac as she is swimming, and fathers the child Conn on her. Conn is raised as Cormac's heir, and his adventures pit him against the posthumous child of Cormac's second wife whose father is Gaibhne Gow the blacksmith. Yet, while the early part of the tale has Conn follow folklore hero motifs when he tricks Finn Mac Cuil into helping him wrest the kingdom from Cormac, the later part shows Conn as a tyrannous villain, while the hero-role is taken over by Cormac's true son who defeats Conn and causes his death by the very otter-lord who sired him. This lengthy story holds some interest for us, in that the king's daughter is found to be mysteriously with child like Aranrhod. We might be tempted to connect Gaibhne Gow with Gofannon, the uncle of Dylan, since both are smiths,[40]

The Lost Tale of Dylan

but since Gaibhne Gow makes no attempt on Conn's life, the potential link between him and Gofannon, whose blow killed Dylan, is tenuous. The "smith" role alone without cognate actions cannot convincingly point to an analogue here for our Fourth Branch episode.

In none of these unions do we find the offspring of the mortal women and seal-men turning *into* seals and swimming out to sea, away from their mothers. Annie Norn lives with the Fin Folk in Hildaland, but her children are never specified as being seals only when in the water. Both Conn and the children of Brita live on land as humans with their mothers, and show no inclination to return to seal life in the ocean. It is here that we must consider the peripherally linked Irish tale-group *Balor on Tory Island,* to which I have referred earlier. It is peripheral to our study in that it does not concern itself directly with seal-transformations, but is important in that such a transformation does in fact occur in passing within one version of it. Briefly, the tale-group treats the theme of "The King and his prophesied Death," which Gruffydd sees as the dominating motif of the Fourth Branch (Gruffydd 46–47): in two versions, the child (Lui Lavada or Lugh) who is to slay his grandfather (Balor) is sired by the trickster (Fin or MacKinealy) on the king's daughter (in one tale called Ethnea). But this Otherworld trickster sires other children at the same time, who are thus at least half-siblings to Lui Lavada/Lugh; in one version, they are born to the twelve women guarding the princess from men, while in the other they are the two brothers of Lugh, born to Ethnea at the same time as he. In each instance, an escape by water is needed, with the children wrapped in a blanket pinned with a thorn. In the first version, when the thorn-pin breaks, the twelve children fall from the blanket into the sea and become seals, unlike Lui Lavada, who is held on Fin's breast instead, while in the second, only Lugh falls but is saved by MacKinealy, while the other two are drowned by a servant (Gruffydd 65–73). All that needs to concern us here about the rest of each version, and the other analogues to them, is that there was once an original tale about the doings of Lugh (or Lui Lavada or Lleu) which was common to both the *Balor* stories and the Fourth Branch (Gruffydd 79–91). This means that Lugh, whose birth-brothers were drowned, and Lui

Lavada, whose half-brothers were turned into seals, are the same character as Lleu in the Fourth Branch, whose half-brother Dylan, born at the same time as he, "received the sea's nature, and swam as well as the best fish in the sea" (Jones 63–64). An equation is almost irresistible.

However, in all of these tales, there is still much left unaccounted for in relation to the Dylan fragment. We would have to leave the search for a seal-tale analogue to it as possible but inconclusive, if it were not for the existence of a single ballad which first appeared in print in the "Proceedings of the Society of Antiquaries of Scotland" in 1852, and was said to have been taken down by one Captain F.W.L. Thomas "from the dictation of a venerable lady of Snarra Voe, Shetland."[41] This ballad was collected from the 1864 issue of Cockburn's *New Monthly Magazine* by F.J. Child as #113, and was subsequently published as "The Great Selchie of Sule Skerrie" in volume II of his *The English and Scottish Popular Ballads*.[42] Despite its relatively late appearance, it is clearly of great antiquity, and the evident lack of any written source prior to 1852 does not detract from the existence of what must be a long oral tradition preserved in the northern islands where it was found. I believe that it is important to our discussion of the Dylan fragment, and I reproduce the 1852 text here in full,[43] as it would seem to represent the closest extant analogue of the tale-family to which the "unintegrated tradition"[44] of the Dylan-story belong.[45]

The Great Selchie of Sule Skerrie

An earthy nourrice sits and sings,
And aye she sings, "Ba, lily wean!
Little ken I my bairn's father,
Far less the land that he staps in."

Then ane arose at her bed-fit,
An' a grumly guest I'm sure was he:
"Here am I, thy bairn's father,
Although that I be not comelie.

"I am a man, upo' the lan',
An' I am a silkie in the sea;
And when I'm far and far frae lan',
My dwelling is in Sule Skerrie."

"It was na weel," quo' the maiden fair,
"It was na weel' indeed," quo' she,
"That the Great Silkie of Sule Skerrie
Suld hae come and aught a bairn to me."

Now he has ta'en a purse of goud,
And he has pat it upo' her knee,
Sayin', "Gie to me my little young son,
An' tak thee up thy nourrice-fee.

"An' it sall pass on a simmer's day,
When the sin shines het on evera stane,
That I will tak my little young son,
An' teach him for to swim his lane.

"An' thu sall marry a proud gunner,
An' a proud gunner I'm sure he'll be,
An' the very first schot that ere he schoots,
He'll schoot baith my young son and me."

Child identifies seals as "finns" or "denizens of a region below the depths of the ocean," and explains that "the Great Selchie, or Big Seal, of Shul Kerry, had had commerce with a woman during an excursion to the upper world."[46] The Shiant Islands are also the reputed home of a gigantic seal, "the father of all the seals."[47] This echoes the tradition concerning a great seal-king which exists throughout the Hebridean and Irish Sea regions, and appears in "The Daughter of the King Ron" and "The Seal Hunter and the Water Man." Thomson also mentions the King Seal,[48] and describes Sule Skerry as a great rock where seals could always be found: this again recalls the meaning of the King Ron's name, "Ailean Mor." The Great Selchie may have fallen out of the Dylan story as the boy's parent, but the selchie son remains in the form of the mysterious child who swims "as well as the best fish" (Jones 64).

If we look at the Great Selchie ballad in relation to the Dylan fragment of the Fourth Branch, we find the following equations. We note that the "earthly nourrice" like Aranrhod is human, while the unknown father of each child is eventually revealed as being of the sea, either explicitly (the Selchie's self-identification) or implicitly (Dylan's naming and his consequent assumption of the ocean's nature). This runs counter to the seal-maiden/mortal man configuration, and echoes "Annie Norn and the Fin Folk," "King Cormac and King Conn," and the Brita story. Yet in only the Dylan fragment and the Selchie ballad are the maidens unable to identify their Otherworld lovers at all. "Little ken I my bairn's father, / Far less the land that he staps in," sings the "earthly nourrice" in the first stanza, such that the Selchie himself must appear in order to explain and prophesy the future, a fact in keeping with the tales we have looked at and with Hebridean lore. When Math asks Aranrhod, "'art thou a maiden?', she answers, 'I do not know but that I am'" (Jones 63). In spite of this reply, she then bears through magic a child she has claimed to know nothing about. While different in setting and tone, the two tales each display a woman lacking a critical piece of knowledge concerning a child which she will bear to a father whose name she does not know. This is distinctly different from their closest analogous character, King Cormac's daughter, who is able to identify the otter-lord as the probable father of her child, with no prompting from the Otherworld sea-creature himself. Even in the *Balor* tales, the king's daughter appears to have had some consenting relationship with the father of her child (Gruffydd 66, 71, 73, 75).

We remember, too, that in the seal-maiden tales, the mothers are loving, and weep for their children,[49] bring them presents,[50] or drive fish to their hooks and even come onto land once to protect a son from blows.[51] The mortal Annie Norn is loving to her three children and refuses to leave them,[52] and neither Brita nor Cormac's daughter abandons her offspring, but appears to value her motherhood. In the ballad, however, the Selchie's maiden shows only alarm at her condition ("It was na weel . . . / That the Great Selchie . . . / Suld hae come and aught a bairn to me"), while in the Fourth Branch, Aranrhod is both alarmed, and spitefully angry (Jones 64, 66, 68) because of her loss of reputation. In the ballad, there is a clear exchange of money for child, with no emotional attachment between Selchie and maiden;[53] perhaps such an arrangement once existed in the Dylan fragment, which accounts for Aranrhod's ready abandonment of a baby who is of full term, and recognizably her own offspring.

The Selchie's arrangement to come and fetch his seal-child "An teach him for to swim his lane" is an element shared solely by the Fourth Branch, and the designated time of year, "When the sin shines het of evera stane" may recall the August whelping of the Welsh seal-colonies. Dylan is "baptized" by Math (perhaps standing here in the role of the Selchie-father) with a name which may mean "ocean," forming the identification with his rightful element implied by the Selchie's advent in the ballad; he then apparently either teaches himself "to swim his lane," or the naming itself in some way imparts a knowledge of his seal-nature to him. In each case, the child becomes a seal on entering the sea for the first time, and swims in all probability as naturally underwater as above: swimming "his lane" in the ballad, and "as well as the best fish in the sea . . . no wave ever broke beneath him" (Jones 63-64) in the Fourth Branch. While this description of Dylan clearly tallies with that of the "selchie" in the water,[54] it is surely also significant that no seal story other than the Great Selchie ballad shows the child of human and seal parentage deliberately exchanging the land for the ocean.

A final analogue element, also lacking in all other seal-tales, is the Selchie's prophecy of the deaths of his son and himself by "the very first schot" from the "gunner" husband of the "earthly nourice." This "gunner" is obviously a seal-hunter, whose traditional weapons for sealing were the club, the spear and the gun.[55] The prophecy of the mortal blow, to be given by what is effectively the selchie-child's stepfather, should remind us of another prophecy, concerning a mortal blow from perhaps another seal-hunting weapon, which closes the Dylan fragment. The Fourth Branch narrative states that Dylan's death is caused by a blow, from what was probably a spear, given by his uncle Gofannon, again a close tribal kin member to the doomed child. Gruffydd tells us that this addition "is in the nature of a gloss, and was probably incorporated in the story by one of its redactors as many of the triads were" (Gruffydd 145). Yet when we turn to the *Trioedd Ynys Prydein,*[56] we find that no extant text of the Welsh Triads preserves Dylan's slaying, noted as "hwnnw a uu trydyd anuat ergyt" (*PKM* 18), "that was one of the Three Unhappy Blows" (Jones 64). While the extant manuscripts of the Triads date from the thirteenth to the eighteenth centuries, and the book texts from the sixteenth century on (Bromwich xviii–xlvi), the original triad material clearly antedates any written source (Bromwich lxv). While dating of the original composition of the Four Branches has been a matter of scholarly speculation,[57] the manuscripts preserving the text seem roughly contemporary (*c.* 1300–1400) with the earliest of the *Trioedd Ynys Prydein*. Therefore, it is less likely that the Dylan slaying was left out of the Triads through a time lapse between manuscript compilations, than that "an episode in the *Mabinogi* has been adapted to make it fit in with a pre-existing triad. . . . The reference to the death of Dylan is one which would find a natural place in the group of triads which celebrate events which were *anfad* or 'unfortunate'" (Bromwich lxxxvii–lxxxviii). However, such an element, suggested perhaps by an ancient analogue tale about seal-hunting, might have been adopted into the Fourth Branch to secure that part of the narrative into the "bardic inheritance" (Bromwich lxxxvii) of the Triads. Returning to our motif comparison, then, in each case a seal-child, who affirms his selchie nature by returning to the ocean, has his death foretold at the hands of a close male member of tribal kin status, who will use a seal-hunting weapon to strike him down.

As we have already seen, the accidental nature of these mortal wounds is explicit in each tale. In the ballad, the "gunner" or seal-hunter evidently slaughters a seal whose identity he could not possibly have guessed at. Other similar stories, which usually end with someone's horrified but tardy recognition, abound in both Scottish and Irish lore. In the later version of our ballad itself, collected by Fergusson in 1883, the Great Selchie puts a golden chain as an identifying token for his mother about the selchie son's neck, and it is evidently this marvel, brought home by the unsuspecting "gunner," which lets the maiden know that the prophecy has been fulfilled.[58] It is also possible that because it was the "gunner"'s "very first schot," it was perhaps a trial or poorly aimed attempt, although the necessary identification of "gunner" with "seal-hunter" makes this suggestion less likely than the first. In the Fourth Branch, we have seen the spear-thrust from Gofannon termed "one of the Three Unhappy Blows" (Jones 64), and therefore, it was evidently not intended for Dylan at all. A modern tale-reconstruction would have "Dylan return[ing] to his foster-father's forge [where he] was accidentally slain in place of Lleu, for whom Math intended the spear,"[59] but this would straightway require that Dylan come back from the sea to the land, and no reason is offered for such a return. It is more in keeping with the narrative of the Fourth Branch to leave Dylan as a selchie in the waves and to identify Gofannon and his spear with some ancient seal-hunting legend which was perhaps once as much a part of the northern Welsh coast-dwellers' existence as it continued to be in the Scottish Hebrides and Shetlands. It may therefore be that the misidentification of "dual-natured selchie" for "seal as food" by a mythical seal-hunter was the original and underlying impulse behind the inclusion of this triad-like reference to the unfortunate nature of Gofannon's blow.

From the foregoing, we can see that even the sketchiest of incidents in the *Mabinogi* can prove to be rewarding if more closely examined. The many true animal metamorphoses which set the Fourth Branch apart from the first three, serve to confirm the need to search for similar transformations in cognate folklore stories, in order to uncover the puzzling origin of the Dylan fragment. The selchie legends, found in so many folktales from the Celtic coasts and islands, provide both a viable explanation for the Dylan episode, and plausible evidence indicating the tradition from which it may have come.

NOTES

1. Mac Cana, *The Mabinogi*, 45, 31.
2. I refer to the linguistic aspects of these terms as they are used by Baugh and Cable in *A History of the English Language*, 33.
3. Gantz, trans., *The Mabinogion*, 97.
4. Gruffydd, *Math Vab Mathonwy*, 135–136, 215. Hereafter in the text as Gruffydd.
5. Matthews, *Mabon and the Mysteries of Britain*, 131.
6. The most comprehensive study of the Dylan fragment to date remains that of Gruffydd in *Math Vab Mathonwy*, 210–234.
7. Gantz, trans., *The Mabinogion*, 18; for a more general background to this aspect of Celtic study, see Gimbutas' *Goddesses and Gods of Old Europe*.

8. "'What is here?' 'A badger,' they replied," from Jones and Jones, ed. and trans., *The Mabinogion* (rpt 1973), 15. Hereafter in the text as Jones.

9. Brân is glossed as "crow," "rook" or "raven" in Rhan V (1952), *Geiriadur Prifysgol Cymru*.

10. Gruffydd raises important questions about the lack of "punishment fitting the crime" in these transformations, 51.

11. I. Williams, ed., *Pedeir Keinc Y Mabinogi* (rpt 1951), 77–78. Hereafter in the text as *PKM*.

12. See Gruffyd, *Math Vab Mathonwy*, 227–228, for a discussion of twins, and 231–233, for an examination of the possible role played in the Fourth Branch by the placenta or the caul.

13. Matthews, *Mabon and the Mysteries of Britain*, 87.

14. Mac Cana, *The Mabinogi*, 51.

15. These entries are taken from Rhan XVIII (1964), *Geiriadur Prifysgol Cymru*.

16. Maxwell, *Seals of the World*, 112.

17. Maxwell, *Seals of the World*, 114.

18. Mackenzie, *Scottish Folklore and Folk-Life*, 87 and 90; and Gomme, *Folklore as an Historical Science* (rpt 1968), 280.

19. Gomme, *Folklore as an Historical Science*, 281.

20. Mackenzie, *Scottish Folklore and Folk-Life*, 87; and Gomme, *Folklore as an Historical Science*, 280.

21. Gomme, *Folklore as an Historical Science*, 280, n. 2.

22. Cox, *An Introduction to Folklore*, 101.

23. Clarkson and Cross, eds., *World Folktales*, 137.

24. Clarkson and Cross, eds., *World Folktales*, 138.

25. Mackenzie, *Scottish Folklore and Folk-Life*, 87.

26. A sample group of these consists of "The Conneelys and the Seals" in O'Sullivan's *The Folklore of Ireland*, #21; "The Silkie Wife" in Kennedy's *Legendary Fictions of the Irish Celts*, (rpt 1968) 122–124; "The Seal's Skin" in Simpson's *Icelandic Folktales and Legends*, 100–102, quoted in Clarkson and Cross, eds., *World Folktales*, 136–137; "The Woman of the Sea" from Shetland in Crossley-Holland's *Folktales from Great Britain*, 39–42; "The Daughter of the King Ron" in Leodhas's *Heather and Broom*, 81–93; "MacCodrum and the Seals" in Wilson's *Scottish Folk-Tales and Legends*, 1–7; and "The Fisherman and the Seal Maid" in Sheppard-Jones's *Scottish Legendary Tales*, 145–149.

27. Rhŷs, *Celtic Folklore* (rpt 1972), 117–125.

28. Rhŷs, *Celtic Folklore* (rpt 1972), 118.

29. Rhŷs, *Celtic Folklore* (rpt 1972), 124.

30. Rhŷs, *Celtic Folklore* (rpt 1972), 128.

31. O'Sullivan, *The Folkore of Ireland*, 117.

32. Andrews, *Ulster Folklore*, 82.

33. From Protter and Protter, eds., *Celtic Folk and Fairy Tales*, 127–131.
34. Leodhas, *Heather and Broom*, 81–93.
35. I view Aranrhod's role in the Fourth Branch as that of a mortal, despite Gruffyd's proposal and discussion of her "other role as a Sea Fairy," 224–226.
36. Cutt and Cutt, *The Hogboon of Hell*, 147–151.
37. Thomson, *The People of the Sea*, 144.
38. Thomson, *The People of the Sea*, 145.
39. Thomson, *The People of the Sea*, 49–63.
40. See Gruffyd on "smiths," 145–146.
41. Sargent and Kittredge, eds., *English and Scottish Popular Ballads*, 240.
42. Child, ed., *The English and Scottish Popular Ballads* (rpt 1965), vol II, 494.
43. There is a second, more expanded text, starting "In Norway lands there lived a maid," first collected in 1883 by Fergusson on page 140 in his *Rambling Sketches in the Far North*, and reproduced in Freidman, ed., *The Viking Book of Folk-Ballads of the English Speaking World*, 29–30.
44. Gantz, trans., *The Mabinogion*, 97.
45. Briggs, *A Dictionary of British Folk-Tales in the English Language*, the Great Selchie ballad is listed as an analogue to the "seal maiden" tale-type, but it does not appear as a type itself, or as having other tales standing as analogues to it.
46. Child, ed., *The English and Scottish Popular Ballads* (rpt 1965), 494.
47. Mackenzie, *Scottish Folklore and Folk-Life*, 87.
48. Thomson, *The People of the Sea*, 31.
49. Simpson, in Clarkson and Cross, eds., *World Folktales*, 137.
50. O'Sullivan, *The Folklore of Ireland*, 118.
51. Sheppard-Jones, *Scottish Legendary Tales*, 148–149.
52. Cutt and Cutt, *The Hogboon of Hell*, 150.
53. The 1883 version contains more sentimental elements; its modern editor describes both the references to marriage and the traditional prophetic ending as "a contrived literary device" on page 27, but to which of the two he refers is not wholly clear.
54. Maxwell, *Seals of the World*, 114.
55. Thomson, *The People of the Sea*, 106.
56. Rachel Bromwich, ed., *Trioedd Ynys Prydein*, lxxxvii. Hereafter in the text as Bromwich.
57. Mac Cana, *The Mabinogi*, 22–24.
58. Thomson, *The People of the Sea*, 205.
59. Matthews, *Mabon and the Mysteries of Britain*, 88.

5

Branwen: A Study of the Celtic Affinities

Patrick K. Ford

The critical analysis and understanding of such medieval narratives as the tale of *Branwen,* the Second Branch of the *Mabinogi,* is by no means at a very advanced state. In the present century, there were the pioneering interpretative efforts of W.J. Gruffydd on the Four Branches,[1] work that was carried forward and enhanced in certain respects by Proinsias Mac Cana in *Branwen: A Study of the Irish Affinities.*[2] The learned tradition of Branwen is discussed by Rachel Bromwich in *Trioedd Ynys Prydein,*[3] along with some of the archaeological connections to her name. The social background of the tale has been admirably discussed recently by Morfydd Owen,[4] and various other literary and linguistic matters relating to *Branwen* have seen print recently.[5] Among the Four Branches, *Branwen* has perhaps the most appeal for modern readers, dealing, as it does, with family relationships, domestic alienation, vengeance for the honour of one's family, heartbreak, and so on. Also, it is perhaps the simplest of the Four Branches with respect to its plot. But as the scholarly literature continually compels us to do, we must always remind ourselves that *Branwen,* like all of our literature, must be read at the several levels it occupies in our culture. As Morfydd Owen has shown, it has a precise synchronic social meaning, most profitably read against the background of the legal tradition of shame and reparation. In that respect, the traditional narrative *reflects* social values, mirrors contemporary concerns about "woman's place in the kin." But traditional narratives are encoded with more than just exemplary or non-exemplary social behaviour, they carry codes that relate to purely cultural (non-social) concerns and values. In other words, "women in society" is a subject different from "women in culture,"[6] which is why (at one level of the story) Branwen is such a different heroine than Rhiannon. Rhiannon reflects the idealized women of Celtic culture, the type of woman elevated and immortalized in the accounts of Dio Cassius,[7] Posidonius,[8] Ammianus Marcellinus,[9] Tacitus,[10] Pomponius Mela,[11] and who emerges from the traditional literature of Ireland in figures such as Medb, Macha, and her ilk.

And yet even the tale of one so profoundly embedded in Celtic cultural notions of women can be turned to social purposes, as Brinley Rees's recent important contribution shows.[12] Rees shows that Welsh analogues to the three kinds of kings depicted in the Irish *Audacht Morainn:* to wit, *fírfhlaith, tarbfhlaith,* and *cíallfhlaith* may be discovered in the Four Branches of the *Mabinogi.*[13] He goes on to show that Pwyll (cognate of Ir. *cíall*) represents, as it were, a lordship characterized by the learning of restraint of various kinds (the limits to which one can justly exercise one's authority) and the wisdom of just counsel, and thereby the perfection of rule.[14] This theme is emphasized in the name of his son and successor, Pryderi "care, concern," and is manifested in another way in the restraint and patience demonstrated by Manawydan, who takes Pwyll's place as spouse of Rhiannon and father of Pryderi. Rees adduces further evidence to show that *cíallfhlaith* (= W. *pwyllwledig*) is characterized by special attention to the cultivation of peace, counsel, well-being, prosperity, etc.[15] A similar approach was taken by Roberta Valente of Cornell University, in an unpublished paper, "Woman's Words: The Function of Rhiannon in the *Mabinogi,*" except that Valente concentrated on Rhiannon as the giver of wisdom.[16]

But the fact that a traditional narrative may demonstrably mean one thing does not mean that it cannot signify other cultural and social things as well. *Pwyll* is surely a Welsh version of a *speculum principis,* as Rees suggests, and just as surely contains elements of an inherited myth about the

Branwen: A Study of the Celtic Affinities

Celtic horse goddess.[17] And just as *Branwen* is set firmly in medieval Welsh legal tradition, so is it firmly anchored in cultural values not concerned with social realities.[18]

My own approach to these tales is essentially cultural and the method is basically structural, though admittedly idiosyncratically so. I believe, however, that the traditional narrative yields a great deal when its sequentially presented events are perceived paradigmatically or "vertically." At least this method is preferable to the once fashionable reconstruction of the *ur*-tale, a reconstruction made possible by the Historic-Geographic method of folktale research. It is also preferable to the allied motif-oriented approach, wherein a traditional tale may be seen as little more than the sum total of its motifs, and whereby any tale may be compared with any other that possesses the same assortment of motifs. The latter approach allowed scholars to posit wholesale borrowings and make one culture heavily dependent on another (where these motifs were first—or more abundantly—discovered) for its body of traditional narrative.[19]

The basic premise of the discussion that follows here, then, is that the text makes sense as we have it; our problem with it is that we don't yet know *how* the text means. When we have explored that problem, we might eventually be in a position to discover *what* the text means. We are all familiar with the counsels of despair offered by earlier (and some modern) commentators on the *Mabinogi*, who declared that the tales represent a mythology in decline and that their original shapes are probably lost to us forever. W.J. Gruffydd in particular sought to discover what those original shapes had been, and in the process he attempted reconstructions that were feasible in their own right, but that had dubious value for our understanding of the texts as we find them. And, we might add, as medieval Welsh audiences found them. For example, Proinsias Mac Cana paraphrases W.J. Gruffydd thus: "The outstanding characteristic of the existing Second Branch, i.e. *Branwen*, is the 'excessively large number of "loose ends" in the narrative and a vast amount of incoherence and confusion.'"[20] Professor Mac Cana's approach was to dissect the narrative episode by episode, motif by motif, and identify the medieval Irish narratives from which those episodes and motifs were borrowed. In the process, he supports the notion that the tale has loose ends, is at times incoherent and confused (though he stresses the literary skill of the "author" of the Branch in deploying these Irish borrowings in his tale). Referring, for example, to the iron house episode in *Branwen,* Mac Cana notes that it "has little more than a superficial connection with its context" (10). He believes that this particular episode was borrowed by the redactor from *Mesca Ulad* and inserted into the text. Toward the end of his study, he declares, "the Second Branch is largely a composite of diverse elements chosen arbitrarily from Welsh and Irish literature" (172). Though the Welsh author's favourite source seems to have been *Togail Bruidne Da Derga,* he was also closely familiar with and borrowed extensively from *Fled Bricrenn, Lebor Gabála Érenn,* and numerous other ancient Irish tales.[21]

Professor Mac Cana's insistence that *Branwen* was the conscious literary creation of a "scholar with the leisure and the inclination to divert his gifts of learning to the creation of such literature of entertainment" (182), and that the tale is an "almost entirely untraditional piece of work" (189) scarcely seems defensible any longer. Literary relations between Ireland and Wales in the early period have been studied often, but I can think of no more reasoned conclusions than those offered by Patrick Sims-Williams in his "The Evidence for Vernacular Irish Literary Influence on Early Mediaeval Welsh Literature."[22] Sims-Williams quotes Mac Cana himself (in the latter's review of Jackson's *International Popular Tale*) as saying that "one can scarcely doubt that most of the similarities between Welsh and Irish literary usage and content are to be ascribed to common origins" (236–237). It is true that there were channels and opportunities for Irish narrative material to pass over to Wales, and Mac Cana is but one of many scholars to propose that that is precisely what did happen. But as Sims-Williams says, "In itself the thesis is plausible enough, but it is quite unproven and perhaps unprovable." And later, "Future literary historians not wishing to put too much faith in Slover's 'countless opportunities' will do better to regard mediaeval Irish literature as a rich and indispensable quarry for analogues rather than for sources."[23] Given the cumulative evidence of twentieth-century scholarship on the questions, I think that most would agree that it is

Branwen: A Study of the Celtic Affinities

entirely possible that Welsh poets and storytellers were acquainted with a considerable amount of Irish story and lore. The converse is equally true. The tendency to isolate individual episodes which can be found in both Welsh and Irish and then assume borrowing from Ireland to Wales perhaps stems from the undeniable fact that vastly more Irish material has survived. Mac Cana is aware of this fact and addresses it on the first page of his study. Given the parallel development of the two traditions, I don't see how we can argue against the notion that there was an extensive narrative corpus in Welsh that simply has not survived. And if it were proportionately smaller, that would still not allow us to decide on the basis of such negative evidence just which "motifs" were borrowed. In the rare instance where borrowing could be absolutely proved, we should have to invoke the notion of "community acceptance" (see footnote 33 below), and argue that the borrowing was possible only because there was a "cultural fit"; in other words, the motif or theme was as much at home in the receiving culture as in the donor culture.

In my view, however, the approach represented by Mac Cana's study is misguided from the outset.[24] One does not have to look far from Wales (or even outside Wales) to find cauldrons, monstrous men and women, deaths of chieftains in burning houses (iron or otherwise), sinister trickster figures, or any of the other motifs, themes and incidents isolated by Mac Cana. The real question is, what do these incidents have to do with one another within the tale of *Branwen*?[25] Let us try a different mode of analysis then, one which begins by assuming that *Branwen*, like the other Branches of the *Mabinogi* is a traditional tale with (mostly) traditional characters. As a traditional tale, it is culturally anchored, and we shall find little in it that does not belong to inherited Celtic tradition as preserved and maintained in early Wales. Conversely, the elements in it will cohere in a special way, no matter how difficult it may be for us to see or understand that coherence. The present exercise, then, stresses the integrity of the text as we have it.

The concept of "narrative attention" is one that I think has been overlooked in our analyses of medieval Welsh texts. Narrative attention means simply observing those parts of the narrative that receive considerable attention from the author/redactor and those that receive little. It also means that apparently irrelevant matter introduced into the text, however brief, is probably there for a reason and deserves our attention. It remains to be seen what value such approaches may have, but the least we can do is to explore them, for as yet no single method or critical approach has revealed to us the complexity of meanings represented by medieval Irish and Welsh tales. I wonder, for example, how many have noticed how the individual Branches of the *Mabinogi* begin.[26] Is it significant? If the narratives are traditional, we might well expect that they would begin in a traditional way, and that their beginnings would tell us something about the tale. Let us consider the beginnings of the Four Branches.

The First Branch, *Pwyll*, begins: "Pwyll, Prince of Dyfed, was lord over the seven cantrefs of Dyfed."[27] The Fourth Branch, *Math son of Mathonwy*, begins: "Math son of Mathonwy was lord of Gwynedd, and Pryderi son of Pwyll was lord over twenty-one cantrefs in the South." The Third Branch, which follows sequentially on the Second Branch, and which is titled *Manawydan son of Llyr*, begins: "(after the seven men we have spoken of above buried Bendigeidfran's head in Gwynfryn in London with his face toward France,) Manawydan looked at the town of London and at his companions." The Second Branch, *Branwen daughter of Llyr*, begins: "Bendigeidfran son of Llyr was crowned king of this island, and was invested with the crown of London." Branwen doesn't turn up until many lines later.

Now evidence of this sort might well be supportive of Gruffydd's old contention that the Second Branch was originally about Bendigeidfran, and that Branwen was secondarily drawn into it. He argued chiefly from the fact that Branwen doesn't have a very great role in the tale, that it really is about Bendigeidfran. But as we have seen, it seems likely and plausible that these particular narratives we call the "branches" of the *Mabinogi* utilized a common stylistic device of opening the tale with reference to the chief character in it, so that on that ground the Second Branch is certainly Bendigeidfran's Branch. But if it is, why do we know it by the name of Branwen? The colophon of the tale says:

> And that is how this branch of the *Mabinogi* ends: the incident of Branwen's Slap—which was one of the three unfortunate slaps in this island, the occasion of The Assembly of Bran—when the hosts of one hundred and fifty-four districts went to Ireland to revenge Branwen's slap, The Feasting in Harlech—which lasted seven years, The Singing of the Birds of Rhiannon, and The Assembly of the Head—which lasted eighty years.

It would have it, thus, that the tale recounts events particular to both Branwen and Bendigeidfran.

Now the curious thing about these names, as I have pointed out,[28] is that one is apparently old, the other post-Christian. The first is a compound of *bran*, a feminine noun, with the adjective (fem.) *gwen*, "white, holy." The other, of course, is our noun compounded with *bendigeid* "blessed, holy," from Latin *benedic-*. It might be argued, then, that *Branwen* and *Bendigeidfran* (*Bran fendigeid*) are one and the same name, the latter reflecting the later and borrowed word for "holy," etc., the former representing a purely native development.[29] The fact that the order of the elements in the compound are inverted in the latter case need not disturb us, for **Bran Fendigeid* is possible if not attested;[30] cf., for example, *Cadwaladr Fendigaid, Gwrthefyr Fendigaid*.[31] On the other hand, *gwen-* may occur as the first element in such compounds, just as does the calque *bendigeid-*; e.g. *Gwendor(y)f* "blessed host."[32] One notes, too, that Branwen seems to be a female name because of the feminine form of the adjective, *gwen*. But of course the feminine form is required here, since the noun *bran* is feminine, although Bran is clearly conceived as a male deity in Welsh (cf. the Irish Bran). The point I wish to make here is simply that the opening formula of the tale may tell us something significant about its meaning.

The concept of "narrative attention" compels us to pay special attention to the so-called interpolation toward the beginning of *Branwen*, an interpolation that in fact occupies roughly one-sixth of the narrative and takes up much more space than, say, the marriage of Branwen, Efnisien's mutilation of the horses, the death of Gwern, or the Otherworldly feasting. It is, in short, one of the most fully developed episodes in the tale.

Matholwch, offended by the action of Efnisien, departs from the court of Bendigeidfran, who in turn lures him back by promising him sound horses for those that had been maimed and gold and silver as prescribed by law. In addition, but only after Matholwch has returned to the court, Bendigeidfran promises him a magical cauldron, a cauldron that revivifies slain warriors, except that they return to life without the gift of speech. On the next day, horses are paid out to Matholwch as promised, and this event is used to explain the name *Talebolion,* said to be the name of the district in which the horses were paid out to Matholwch and explained in the usual onomastic fashion as a compound of *tâl* "payment" and *ebol-ion* "horse-s" (though *ebol* is more properly "colt").

Following immediately upon this etymology, Matholwch asks how Bendigeidfran happened to come by the cauldron. The story that follows is a remarkable one, and Bendigeidfran is amazed as we are that Matholwch does not seem to know anything about it, especially since the whole business started in Matholwch's kingdom. The ragged narrative seam[33] shows us that we can expect some sort of structural shift here, and I believe that to understand this episode we have to conceptualize it vertically, to use Lévi-Strauss's orientation. To put it another way, viewed as part of the horizontal (linear) development of the narrative, the episode seems to be an interpolation or digression; in fact, it stands not in syntagmatic relation to the rest of the text but in paradigmatic relation.

Matholwch relates that he was one day hunting atop the mound[34] above the Lake of the Cauldron when he saw a great yellowish-red-haired man coming from the lake with a cauldron on his back. He was of enormous stature, but if he was big, his wife was more than twice his size. (We will remember that this story is being told to Bendigeidfran, himself a giant of such stature that he has never enjoyed the comfort of a house and is able to cross the Irish Sea by wading.) The man's name is Llassar Llaes Gyfnewid and his wife is Cymidei Cymeinfoll. In response to Matholwch's query, the man says that "at the end of a fortnight and a month this woman will conceive, and the boy born of that pregnancy at the end of a fortnight and a month will be a fully armed warrior."

Branwen: A Study of the Celtic Affinities

Matholwch took them in and within a short time she had borne more children, that is, fully armed warriors, and they were making themselves unwanted—insulting (that is, verbally annoying) people, and molesting noble men and women. The realm was not able to get rid of them on its own, and the warlike race did not choose to go willingly. So an iron house was constructed, and the man, his wife, and their children were induced to go into it. They were provided with food and drink, which they proceeded to consume, while outside a great fire had been built and men stationed at bellows all around the house to fan the flames. At the crucial moment, when the wall was white hot, Llassar, with his wife behind him, broke out through the wall and escaped the flames and the iron house. Only the man and his wife escaped from there; the children apparently perished. The warlike pair then went over to Britain.

> "How did you receive them, Lord?" asks Matholwch.
> "I divided them throughout the land, and they are numerous and thriving everywhere, and strengthening the places in which they happen to be with the best men and arms anyone has ever seen."[35]

Following this account of the cauldron, Matholwch and Branwen return to Ireland, she has a child, Gwern, and he is placed in fosterage. Then, Matholwch's nobles remind him of the insult he had received over the horses, and in a belated retaliation, Branwen is humiliated, being forced to cook for the court, and submit to a blow by the butcher each day (presumably accounting thereby for the phrase *Palfawd Branwen*, the title embedded in the colophon to the tale, although we notice that what she indeed receives each day is not a *palfawd* but a *bonclust*). With the aid of a helper bird, Branwen informs her brother Bendigeidfran of her plight, and he assembles an invasion force and heads for Ireland.

After some negotiations, it turns out that the only way Bendigeidfran can be appeased and come to terms with Matholwch is for the latter and his men to construct a special house for him—the one thing he has never had. It is so done, but the Irish are deceitful and they "fixed a peg on every side of each of the one hundred columns that were in the house, and hung a hidebag on each peg, with an armed warrior inside each." Efnisien comes into the house before the rest and succeeds in foiling the Irish plan.

Here again, narrative attention compels us to pause over the singular events that ensue. As I read the text, Efnisien is alone when he enters the house except for the hidden Irishmen. Admittedly, this is not the usual reading, for scholars (and my students) often assume it is some Irishman accompanying Efnisien who is doing the talking and who is addressed by the wily Welshman. But it seems to me that there are at least two things to support my view. The first is rational: if Efnisien were speaking in the presence of or directly to one of the Irish, why would such a person allow Efnisien to proceed from bag to bag dispatching the hapless warriors? Compare Mac Cana's comment: "the Irishman who was by him either did not notice what was going on or else, for some strange unknown reason, held his peace."[36] The second thing is the evidence of the text: after the event and after the *englyn* recited by Efnisien, the text says, "After that the hosts entered the house: the man of the Isle of Ireland on one side and the men of the Isle of the Mighty on the other." Reading the text in the way I have suggested then, let us review what happens. Efnisien goes up to one of the bags:

> "What's in this bag?" he asked one of the Irishmen.
> "Flour, friend," said he [from the bag].
> What the other did then was to feel around him until he found his head, and squeezed his head until he could feel his fingers meet in the brain, through the bone. Then he left him and put his hand on another, saying, "What do we have here?"

That one suffers the same fate, and then the text says that Efnisien did that to each in turn until only one of the two hundred remained. He went up to that one and repeated his question, got the same answer, and killed him. Then he recited an *englyn* as follows:

There is in this bag a form of flour,
Champions, battlers, fighters in the fray,
From warriors, battle-ready.

The story resumes and the two hosts come into the specially constructed house, and in the course of events, Branwen's child is destroyed in the fire. A great battle arises between the two hosts then, and because they have the cauldron, the Irish enjoy the upper hand for a while. Finally, however, Efnisien regrets his actions, crawls in among the slain Irish, is put into the cauldron and, stretching himself, succeeds in shattering the cauldron. Only seven of the British escape, and when they return home, they find that their country has been conquered.

Let us briefly recapitulate the events in the preceding summary. It is not my intention here to reduce the narrative to serve the purposes of my argument, only to call attention in a different way to episodes already heavily marked in the text itself.

   a. The explanation of the name *Talebolion*.
   b. The prodigious woman who gives birth to fully armed warriors.
   c. The cauldron of rebirth.
   d. The iron house and the destruction of Cymidei's children.
   e. The special house constructed for Bran.
   f. The armed warriors lurking in bags.
   g. The destruction of Branwen's child.
   h. The destruction of the cauldron of rebirth.
   i. The fall of Britain.

Most of these points are concerned with the generation of warriors and with the containment of warriors in various ways.

First, let us look at the woman Cymidei Cymeinfoll. Sir Ifor Williams (following Loth) noted, and I would agree, that her first name appears to be an extension of the ordinary noun *cymid* "battle."[37] Her second name is compound of *cymaint* and *boll* and would therefore mean something like "equally" or "so much" "distended."[38] The phrase that constitutes her full name, then, suggests something like "pregnant" or "bloated" with "war" or "warriors." In other words, her name is simply a description of her capacity and her function. She conceives and gives birth with alarming rapidity, and her offspring are fully armed (and I suppose we should assume fully grown, too) warriors—perhaps not so great a feat considering the fact that she is enormous in stature. In respect of her unique abilities, she is virtually identical with the *peir dadeni* "the cauldron of regeneration or rebirth," which revivifies fully armed warriors. We notice further that the *peir dadeni* requires a fire beneath it, and so it is fitting that the mate of Cymidei—the one who bears the cauldron upon his back—is appropriately named "fire."[39] Indeed, the very name *cymidei cymeinfoll* would be a perfectly appropriate name for the cauldron itself: "distended, bloated with warriors."

In the episode in which the Irish have hidden two hundred warriors in bags along the pillars of the great house, the phrase for bag is *boly croen*. W. *bol, boly*, cognate with Ir. *bolg* means "bag, pouch," but is also used commonly in the sense of "belly, womb." The fully armed warriors hiding out in the bags hanging on the pegs are, as it were, by metonymy, in wombs. After Efnisien has destroyed each of them, while still in their womb-like bags, he recites the *englyn* that begins *Yssit yn y boly hwn* . . . , referring to the warrior in the *boly*. It is a striking fact that this *englyn*, the only one in the Second Branch, could equally well have been recited by Llassar Llaes Gyfnewid, husband (consort) of Cymidei Cymeinfoll, when Matholwch first encountered them. He asked after their business, and Llassar replied that the woman would conceive and would bring forth a fully armed warrior. He might well have said, *Yssit yn y boly hwnn* . . . , placing his hands on her belly, as Efnisien placed his on the bags containing the armed Irish.[40]

We need not pause long over the cauldron of rebirth itself, for its role in the (re-)generation of warriors is clear; what is interesting is that the warriors so regenerated are without the faculty of speech. Cymidei and her brood made themselves unwelcome by overstepping their bounds in society. They became obnoxious and, among other things, they verbally abused people. It was this that cost them their lives and drove Cymidei and her mate from the land. In Efnisien's encounter with the warriors in the bags, it was their speech that betrayed them: they didn't know when to keep their mouths shut. The text is quite explicit about that, detailing the dialogue that passed between Efnisien and his adversaries: "what's in here?" he would say. And when they would respond, he would reach out and snuff their lives.[41] The cauldron of rebirth of warriors seems to do the job right from the beginning: it brings warriors back to life but without the gift of speech. We might be tempted to venture some modern parallels here and recall that outspoken members of the professional military class, that is, those who have verbally encroached on the civilian domain, have brought down the wrath of their civilian commanders-in-chief (e.g. Generals Patton, MacArthur in twentieth-century US military history).[42] But there is plenty of evidence from within early Indo-European society itself to show that the warrior function is always perceived as a threat to the society it protects; as in the case of Cú Chulainn in the Irish heroic age, the rest of the society had to constantly be on guard against the potential of force being turned inward upon society itself.[43] Bendigeidfran seems to have avoided this potential difficulty with the warrior class by dividing it (i.e. Cymidei's brood) throughout the land (*eu rannu ym pob lle yn y kyuoeth*): "and they are numerous and thriving everywhere and strengthening the places in which they happen to be with the best men and arms anyone has ever seen." This, of course, is the same strategy adopted by Medb in the *Táin* with respect to the dreaded Gailioin.[44] But there may be other reasons why Bendigeidfran himself should have no trouble controlling warriors.

While *talebolion* "payment of colts" may have a reasonable—if somewhat folksy—explanation in the text, one cannot help but perceive at least a pun on an alternative meaning: *tal y bolion* "payment of the bags," i.e. bags in the senses in which it is used elsewhere in the text.[45] The morphology is common, echoing such commonplaces as *Talybont* "edge, end, of the bridge," English *Bridgend*. Thus, although *-ebolion* is an acceptable explanation in terms of the episode in which the name is adduced, *-bolion* suits the "bag, womb" theme of the tale and would be very much at home in the cluster of episodes we have been considering.

Taken individually and viewed only in terms of the linear development of the tale, these episodes might well seem at best to have a loose and arbitrary connection with one another. But when we look at the events in paradigmatic relation to one another they fit neatly. The prolific and prodigious woman who gives birth to fully armed warriors has, in this contrapuntal scheme, a corresponding element in the numerous bags that conceal fully armed warriors. Both are undone by speech. The cauldron of rebirth belongs to the same scheme, as perhaps does the collocation *tal-y-bolion*, and the whole makes some sort of statement about the role of military might in society.

The iron house seems to have something to do with the cauldron, since both are made of iron and both are shattered by the action of a man inside. But its closer affinities (or perhaps "its other affinities") in the text seem rather to be with the house of Bran. Both are special constructions, made ostensibly to appease their occupants. In both, the offspring of the inhabitants are killed in flames; the inhabitants of both escape to Britain after an ensuing battle. The big difference between the two is that Cymidei and her mate escape with the cauldron, and as a result bring prosperity to Britain and fortify the land. In the case of Branwen and Bendigeidfran, the cauldron is shattered, Bendigeidfran is destroyed, Branwen dies, and Britain's defenses collapse and the land is conquered. Perhaps part of the message is that cauldrons and other gifts from the Otherworld must be maintained in safe keeping, and that he who gives them away dooms himself and his race—as does Pryderi in the Fourth Branch when he barters away the swine entrusted to him from Annwfn.

In the article I have already referred to, Mr. Brinley Rees has shown that the types of sovereign or lordship characterized in Irish as *fírfhlaith, tarbfhlaith,* and *cíallfhlaith* are to be found in the Four Branches. *Tarbfhlaith* is defined as follows: "The bull ruler strikes [and] is struck, wards off [and] is warded off, roots out [and] is rooted out, attacks [and] is attacked, pursues [and] is pursued. Against him there is always bellowing with horns."[46] Just as those three *flatha* form a triad, argues Rees, so do the three families whose story is told in the *Mabinogi*: the family of the magician-lord of Gwynedd, and their story revolving around knowing the truth, hiding it and revealing it, words that determine or delimit truth, and deceit; the family of the huge and awesome king of the Isle of the *Mighty*, with their attempt to secure stronger territories leading to anger, revenge, and horrible war; and the family of Pwyll. Thus, from an entirely separate analytical view, *Branwen* may be seen as concerned with the warrior class and the fortunes of war and warriors.

As I have argued here, too, *Branwen* is about war. It is first of all the story of Bran, the divinity whose zoomorphic (ornithomorphic) manifestation is the raven or carrion crow. The divinity's epithet, whether native (*gwen*) or Christianized (*benedigeid*) clarifies its divine nature. In Irish tradition—in this instance representing the Celtic state of affairs—the divinity in charge of war, warriors, and the battlefield is consistently female. She goes by a variety of names, but is either represented as single or triple. Thus, she is the Mórrígan or the three Mórrígan, or the Mórrígan and her three sisters Badb, Nemain, and Macha, or the three sisters themselves. The Second Branch has altered the sex of the war divinity, but has not fully divested itself of the female Bran figure. In Celtic terms and minus the Christian epithet, the war goddess Branwen would have been one of the triple "great queens" (in Irish, *mór-rígan*).[47] In fact, the Welsh text does call her *trydedd prif rieni yn yr ynys hon*.[48] This triad has caused all sorts of problems and discussion. Sir Ifor, following Morris-Jones (WG), understood it to mean "parent(s)," that is, a word susceptible of either singular or collective meaning—like *etifedd* "heir, heirs."[49] In so doing, he opposed both Loth ("maidens") and Gruffydd, who with his usually sharp perception (if sometimes flawed by his method), sought to link it to a word cognate with Ir. *rígain* "queen," hence, he said, "rhieni, pl. of *rigan*—means in Welsh both *parents* and *ladies;* trydydd prif *rieni* 'one of the three greatest "ladies" or "queens".'"[50] Sir Ifor settled on the meaning of "ancestress," and suggested that the triad referred to Rhiannon as mother of Pryderi, Branwen as mother of Gwern, and Aranrhod as mother of Lleu Llaw Gyffes. He was aware of the fact that at the time the triad is mentioned in the text she was not yet a mother (nor was she married!). He does not mention the further difficulty that since her son Gwern died young and Branwen herself shortly thereafter, she is no ancestress at all.

The present argument virtually compels us to accept Gruffydd's analysis, for the cultural context of the tale places Branwen alongside the Mórrígan and the other Celtic manifestations of the goddess of war.

And so, seen as a traditional tale with traditional (for the most part) characters, *Branwen* fits very comfortably indeed in Celtic cultural notions about war and warriors. The Celtic war divinity has become male, though her former sex is upheld in the character of Branwen. The names of two characters fundamental to the opposition inherent in the theme of this tale have been reduced to labels: Mr. Peace (Nisien) and Mr. Un-Peace (Efnisien). And, naturally, Branwen's land is known by the military designation "Isle of the Mighty." It has not been my purpose to rationalize or explain every single detail in this intricate narrative. But I hope that enough has been said to show that *Branwen* is essentially traditional and that its principal episodes form a coherent nucleus of inherited cultural notions, notions for which one may find analogues elsewhere in the Celtic realms.

This brief exercise is designed primarily to show that the texts we have inherited from the Middle Welsh period are susceptible of serious scrutiny of more than one kind. The method may have its weaknesses and its application may not be uniformly appropriate, but it is motivated by the conviction that, until we can prove otherwise, the text is still the authority and that our excursions into its deeper meanings must come to grips with that authority.

NOTES

1. Gruffydd, *Math vab Mathonwy, Rhiannon*, and a host of articles.
2. Mac Cana, *Branwen: A Study in Irish Affinities.*
3. Bromwich, *Trioedd Ynys Prydein.*
4. Owen, "Shame and Reparation: Woman's Place in the Kin."
5. Jones, "Bedd-Branwen—The Literary Evidence," 32–37; Ford, "On the Significance of Some Arthurian Names in Early Welsh."
6. See, for example, Walters, "The European Context of the Welsh Law of Matrimonial Property," 115.

7. Dio Cassius, *Roman History*, 77.16.5.
8. See Tierney, "The Celtic Ethnography of Posidonius," 252.
9. Quoted in Anne Ross, *Everyday Life of the Pagan Celts*, 44.
10. As quoted in Chadwick and Dillion, *The Celtic Realms*, 26.
11. Pomponius Mela, *De Chorographia*, III. 6.48.
12. Rees, "Apair fris, ni fil inge cethri flathemna and . . . ," 686–689.
13. There are actually four kinds of kings, three of which have the same formation (those cited here); the fourth is *fhlaith congbále co slógaib díanechtair*. Kelly, ed. and trans., *Audacht Morainn*, 19.
14. Kelly, ed. and trans., *Audacht Morainn*, defines *cíallfhlaith* as follows: "§60 The wily ruler defends borders and tribes, they yield their valuables and dues to him" (19).
15. This, of course, represents a sovereignty that fits the third-function slot of Dumézil's tripartite structure of Indo-European society; *fírfhlaith* is first function, *tarbfhlaith* second function. Rees objects to Kelly's rendering of "Wily ruler," and though he does not advert to Dumézil, he does rearrange the list of sovereigns as it is given in the *Audacht* to conform to the canonical first, second, and third functions.
16. 8th Annual University of California Celtic Studies Conference, 2–4 May 1986, Los Angeles.
17. As I attempted to show in "Prolegomena to a Reading of the *Mabinogi*: 'Pwyll' and 'Manawydan.'"
18. Still, there are limits to our searches for meaning. As Eric Hamp observed from the floor at the UC Celtic conference already referred to, (my paraphrase): "Our task is not only to discover all the meanings in our texts, but also to discover and to define what our texts do *not* mean." In other words, meaning must be circumscribed by social and cultural parameters, and whenever we argue a particular meaning, it must be carefully justified within the social and cultural context.
19. This approach characterizes the work of Proinsias Mac Cana, *Branwen: A Study of the Irish Affinities*, and Kenneth Jackson, *The International Popular Tale and Early Welsh Tradition*. Whereas Mac Cana was concerned primarily with identifying the Irish analogues (which he takes for the most part to be sources) to the motifs and themes of *Branwen*, Jackson casts his net much wider, as the title of his work indicates.
20. Mac Cana, *Branwen*, 4.
21. Scholars continue to be fascinated with the idea of "borrowing"—even when the matter under consideration is demonstrably traditional. John Morris-Jones reacted strongly against the notion seventy years ago, when commenting on Alfred Nutt's theories about the origins of the *Mabinogi*: "But why all this as-

sumption of borrowing? It rests on the perfectly gratuitous supposition that the British had no traditional lore of their own" ("*Taliesin*," 239); and see Mac Cana's comments on this, *Branwen*, 2. And further on, ". . . it is sufficient to insist on the obvious truth that the two races *inherited* the fundamental conceptions of their respective mythologies from their common ancestor" (240). He later diluted somewhat this sound pronouncement by conceding that "It is also true, no doubt, that they contain elements which have been borrowed from Irish and other sources" (240). Among other things, he had in mind the suffix that turned *Manawyd* into *Manawyd-an*. And he may have had in mind the Irish personal names in *KO*: see now Patrick Sims-Williams, "The Significance of the Irish Personal Names in *Culhwch ac Olwen*." But Morris-Jones' final words on the subject would seem to be these: "it is inconceivable that British names of British gods could have survived except in traditions concerning them" (240). Therefore, where we have British names, let us look to British traditions, which we may assume to be *cognate* with extant comparable Goidelic traditions, not *borrowed* from them.

22. Sims-Williams, "The Evidence for Vernacular Irish Literary Influence on Early Mediaeval Welsh Literature;" see also Sims-Williams, "The Significance of the Irish Personal Names in *Culhwch ac Olwen*" and "The Riddling Treatment of the 'Watchman Device' in *Branwen* and *Togail Bruidne Da Derga*."

23. Sims-Williams, "The Evidence for Vernacular Irish Literary Influence on Early Welsh Medieval Literature," 257; the reference is to Clark Slover, "Early Literary Channels between Britain and Ireland," *Studies in English*, 6 (1926), 5–52, esp. 42.

24. Even Jackson, who also pays almost exclusive attention to motifs and tale types in his study, rejects the notion of borrowing from Irish into Welsh. His purpose, however, is to show that the motifs of early Welsh literature (and early Irish literature, for that matter) are often to be traced to extra-Celtic sources and are usually international. When they are found exclusively in Celtic sources, however, he insists that if borrowing were involved, it could have gone either way (*The International Popular Tale*, 122 f.).

25. Neither Mac Cana nor Jackson seem terribly interested in the question of meaning, apart from the question of *how* the tales came to have their present (corrupt) shapes. For Jackson, the word "meaning" would seem to be anathema. He uses it in quotation marks when referring to the "corrupted myth" theory of folktales (*The International Popular Tale*, 39). Myth appears to be inextricably entwined with "solar" and with other outdated theories in Jackson's view. "By and large, however," he says, "I think it is wise to regard mythological explanations of even the non-international episodes

Branwen: A Study of the Celtic Affinities

in the *Mabinogion* with cautious scepticism. Such interpretations can be tailored to fit anything, and hence they are a favourite device in the hands of the unscholarly. This is not to say that they cannot be handled in a scholarly manner, but as a common rule when a mythological explanation is fore-shadowed one suspects that a speculation is likely to be on its way, and probably a series of others erected on the basis of that one. In any case, no theory involving the supposition of a myth should even be advanced until one has made sure that the motif one is studying is not an international one" (129). The message is clear: myths may have meaning, but it is dangerous to look for it; folklore and folktales are the aggregate of motifs and tale-types, and these have no meaning outside their relationship to other tales with the same motifs or outside their participation in the international community of motifs. Therefore, meaning is out of the question, and since that is true, motifs—international or otherwise—cannot function "locally" in tales as signifiers; they are only there to be identified and numbered. As to theories to explain the existence of such narratives, "whether by supposing it to represent the detritus of old myths, or the expression of rituals, or the dreams of hashish-eaters and others (as has been suggested). Such hypotheses are dangerous attempts to be too clever—dangerous because they invariably lead to their author's attempting to force the facts to fit the theory. No explantion is needed, it seems to me, other than the fact that man has always loved stories and story-telling for their own sake as entertainment and always will love them for that reason. This is a universal human activity, and does not require to be accounted for" (43).

26. I know that Brynley Roberts has: "Stories normally open with a phrase naming the hero and giving his status, kingdom, etc." And "... the formulaic tale opening had as its primary purpose the presenting of the hero's name and status"; "From Traditional Tale to Literary Story: Middle Welsh Prose Narratives," 216, 222.

27. Quotations are from Ford, *The Mabinogi and Other Medieval Welsh Tales*.

28. Ford, "On the Significance of Some Arthurian Names in Welsh."

29. This is apparently what Gruffydd argued, according to Jarman, "Mabinogi Branwen: Crynodeb o Ddadanspddiad W.J. Gruffydd," 133. Bromwich could not accept this; *Trioedd Ynys Prydein*, 2nd ed., 287n. For other conjectures on Bran's epithet, see *TYP*, 2nd ed., 285, 545.

30. Bromwich has *Bran fendigeid* in *TYP*, 284, though she cites no source for this form.

31. Bromwich, *TYP*, 386 and note to Triad 37.

32. *Geirfa*, s.v., *gwen*. Also, compare index of epithets, s.v. *gwyn* in Bartrum, *Early Welsh Genealogical Tracts*.

33. The "fabric of fiction" metaphor employed here suggests that the cauldron digression is a kind of patch clumsily applied to the story; as Mac Cana puts it, "The Iron House episode has little more than a superficial connection with its context,"*Branwen*, 10. And here is Jackson on *Pwyll:* "It was the clumsy patching at this stage of the tale, consequent on the violent introduction of the Calumniated Wife, which has left it practically unintelligible in its present form"*(International Popular Tale*, 93). But until we can prove otherwise, we must begin our criticism with the principle of the integrity of the text; the text as preserved is the text we critique, and before we reject any part of it as invalid (borrowed, misunderstood, miscopied, concocted), we must satisfy ourselves that we have exhausted the resources of the culture that produced it. It has been argued that cultures do not retain what is no longer useful or relevant: "Community acceptance . . . is the major factor in deciding whether a piece of oral folk literature or popular literature will survive to the point where it may be recorded and brought into the realm of written literature" (Wittig, *Stylistic and Narrative Structures in the Middle English Romances*, 181, referring to the work of Roman Jakobsen and P. Bogatyrev). Therefore, even borrowings will not take hold if there isn't a cultural fit readily available (see further footnote 21). Thus, the patchwork appearance of the text doesn't necessarily mean something borrowed has been struck in; more likely it signifies a structural shift—an episode is being introduced that does not fit neatly into the linear or syntagmatic development of the narrative and so it must be perceived in its paradigmatic relationship to the narrative. To use Wittig's words, surface textual transformations of one sort and another (e.g. "flashbacks" and other "out of order" or "extraneous" episodes) serve as vehicles for important cultural information vital to the narrative process; they may present "information (which may be obscured, especially for observers from another culture, by the complexities of the narrative process) [which] is encoded within the deeper structure of the stories and is exemplified in the repetition of certain narrative components; it quite clearly has to do with the reinforcement and perpetuation of certain social and political beliefs held by the community" (180–181).

34. It should be noted that the mound and the hunt place the episode squarely in the environment of the Otherworldly encounter.

35. Again, "the best anyone has ever seen" no doubt points to the Otherworldly origin of the arms. Compare Pwyll's visit to Annwfn: "the most splendid and best equipped troop that anyone

had ever seen . . . the fairest woman anyone had ever seen . . . the noblest and gentlest in her nature and her discourse of any he had ever seen. . . . Of all the courts he had seen on earth, this was the court best supplied with food and drink, gold vessels, and royal treasures" (Ford, *The Mabinogi*, 39).

36. Ford, *The Mabinogi*, 69.

37. I. Williams, ed., *Pedeir Keinc y Mabinogi*, 180. Hereafter as *PKM*.

38. I. Williams: "cestog?"—*PKM*, 180.

39. See I. William's discussion of the name, *PKM*, 179–180.

40. Had that been the case, then the problem of singular *boly* with plural nouns in the second line would cease to exist; compare Mac Cana, *Branwen:* "As it stands it refers to only one bag, and we know from the preceding passage that there is only one warrior in each; yet the three nouns in the second line are in the plural. If the *boly* of the englyn referred to the wonderfully productive womb of Cymidei, then the reference to plural warriors would be quite appropriate" (70).

41. On the function of redundancy in narrative, see Wittig, *Stylistic and Narrative Structures in Middle English Romances*, 181; for redundancy in myth in particular, 125–126 (quoting Edmund Leach).

42. The "otherness" of the military is noticed even at the popular level in contemporary Western society: "A soldier ain't suppose to talk, just fight!" spoken by a minor character in the 1935 American movie *Red Salute*, starring Robert Young and Barbara Stanwyck.

43. See, for example, *LL Táin*, ll. 1177–1185.

44. O'Rahilly, ed. and trans., *Táin Bó Cúalnge*, ll. 345–350.

45. Gruffydd saw *tal y bolion* as the original form; *Math vab Mathonwy*, 305.

46. Kelly, ed. and trans., *Audacht Morainn*, 19.

47. According to Fergus Kelly, the first element in the Irish name is probably **mor*—"specter, phantom, mare" (cognate with OE *Mære* "female spirit or monster"; *Audacht Morainn*, 22.

48. I. Williams, *PKM*, 31.1.

49. Thomas Jones took this argument a step further, showing that in the sixteenth-century Mostyn MS 158 (Elis Gruffydd) at least, *rhieni* could mean all that Latin *progenies* meant: "ancestry," "race" or "family," and "descendants." See his "Rhieni," 131–133.

50. I. Williams, *PKM*, 166. Gruffydd's discussion is in "Mabon ab Modron," 455.

6

Manawydan fab Llŷr: Wales, England, and the "New Man"

Andrew Welsh

I.

Manawydan fab Llŷr, the Third Branch of the Four Branches of the *Mabinogi*, is the shortest and simplest story in that cycle of Middle Welsh prose narratives. Yet its meaning is far from settled. Much of the best work done on it has in fact not worried about its meaning at all, but has investigated possible sources and earlier forms of the tale in Celtic tradition. Around the beginning of the century, for example, Celticists such as John Rhŷs, Edward Anwyl, and John MacCulloch were relatively sure that the main character of the story, Manawydan, corresponded to the Irish figure Manannán mac Lir, who—they were relatively sure—was a sea god of some kind; this suggested sources for the Third Branch and explanations of its story in Irish (or at least Gwydelic) mythology.[1] Such "diachronic" views (as they are often called) of the Third Branch, and of the Four Branches as a whole, look below the medieval surface of the text and find there level beneath level of tradition, history, mythology, and ideology—a cultural dark backward and abysm of time. Their focus is different from that of this paper, which is primarily concerned with literary interpretation of the medieval narrative. But I need to turn first to a few of those studies, for though their interests lie elsewhere, they nonetheless identify central questions and provide key suggestions for this one.

An important and influential example of such a study came at mid-century in W.J. Gruffydd's book *Rhiannon*.[2] For Gruffydd, the name of Manawydan may derive, as the earlier scholars believed, from the Irish figure Manannán mac Lir, but the humble and forbearing temperament of the Welsh figure seems to be a complete transformation of that of the mythic trickster, sorcerer, and seducer of Irish tradition. In Gruffydd's hypothetical reconstruction, the original story of the Third Branch was not at all about the Irish "magician and shape-shifter *par excellence,* the Other-world trickster who harries the heroes and heroines, the ruthless King of Faery who entices men and women to their destruction."[3] Instead, it told of a "Great Mother" goddess (*Modron* < Gallo-Brittonic *Mātronā*), whose euhemerized form appears in the tale as Rhiannon; of the abduction of her young son by the Otherworld powers of Annwn; of a terrible desolation, during which "all life and all growth" disappeared, that simultaneously fell upon the land; and of the subsequent long search for the missing son by the goddess and her consort. That "myth of Rhiannon" concluded with a two-fold restoration, the son restored to the goddess and fertility restored to the land: "When they at last deliver him from captivity, prosperity is restored to the land and all life and growth re-appear."[4] As Gruffydd recognized, this wonderful story is better known from Frazer's *Golden Bough* than from medieval Welsh tradition, literary or mythological. It is in fact a "waste land" myth, in which the Welsh "Great Mother" is seen as a fertility goddess analogous to Greek Demeter and Asiatic Cybele.[5]

In the long processes of transmission, however (Gruffydd's argument runs), that story underwent major transformations both in structure and meaning, from sacred myth to heroic saga to medieval wondertale. Finally, in the last stages of transformation, two quite separate tales were added to the main structure. About the time "when the final recensions of the Four Branches were made," the popular saint's legend of St. Eustace was adapted from English versions and incorporated into the Third Branch. That homiletic story, which stresses the forbearance and humility of its central character, first contributed to the Third Branch the episodes of the two journeys into England by the survivors of the enchantment on Dyfed; eventually, it transformed the story of Manawydan as a whole into one depicting "the ideal Christian gentleman—patient, tolerant, pacific, and above all, chaste."[6] A second late addition, again according to Gruffydd, is the final episode of "The Mice in the Corn," as he called it, which was adapted from an independent folktale and tacked onto the end of the Third Branch.[7] Both the journeys into England and the ravaged wheat fields, in short, were seen by Gruffydd as extraneous to the central tale, as late interpolations which have no bearing on that story and are interesting primarily as signs of the disintegration of the original tale.

A somewhat different diachronic approach to the Third Branch appears in a recent article by John T. Koch, who argues that the sources of the Third Branch lie not in a conjectural fertility-goddess mythology but in something far more definite: in a specific historical figure.[8] The figure is Mandubracios, a British chieftain who at the time of Caesar's invasion of Britain in 54 BC endeavored to further the interests of his own tribe by providing the Romans with food and military intelligence.[9] His story is briefly told in Caesar's *De Bello Gallico* (5.20–22), but was also remembered, Koch suggests, in native British oral tradition, which quickly assimilated this early quisling into the traditional "Common Celtic theme of the Unrightful King"—the story of a king who shirks battle with his enemies, who instead flees into exile, who thus cannot defend the crops of his people, and whose own failings (weakness, disfigurement, or injustice) are finally responsible for the infertility of his land and his people.[10] This mystic connection between the physical or moral condition of a king and the fertility of his land is familiar in Irish tradition, and it also brings us back once again to the waste land myth.[11]

Manawydan is Mandubracios, Koch suggests, as he is remembered by native British tradition for a millennium or more, and the traditional form of the story of Manawydan is best understood "as a prolonged exemplary tale of Unrightful Kingship."[12] If that is not the story we have, it is because at a very late stage—perhaps at the hands of the "final redactor"—the story of the Unrightful King was radically reinterpreted so as to present Manawydan in a positive light, as a man of virtuous forbearance and prudent counsel. Nevertheless, the tale itself retains all those incidents which in earlier versions presented Manawydan very negatively: episodes such as his refusing to contest the usurpation of the kingship of Britain by Caswallawn, his retreat in the face of the hostile English craftsmen, his refraining from entering the enchanted fort in which first his companion Pryderi and then his wife Rhiannon are trapped, his failure to protect his crops, and his own social degradation to the level of a common craftsman, then a crofter, and finally a rodent exterminator. "The redactor has in fact handled his traditional material with great conservatism," Koch writes. "Though clearly siding with Manawydan, he has preserved every episode so that the protagonist has remained in every wise the exact antithesis of the rightful king of the older value system."[13]

The studies of the Third Branch by Gruffydd and Koch, one old and one new, both see some form of "waste land" theme in its tale of the enchantment on Dyfed. Both also see in the Third Branch as a whole a narrative structure originally made to tell a very different story—in one case the "myth of Rhiannon," and in the other the story of "The Unrightful King." Both are thus strongly concerned with the sources of the story material of the Third Branch, though they present differing views of the nature of that material:

(1) The material comes ultimately from an ancient Celtic mythology, the major outlines of which are cognate with the fertility goddesses and waste land myths of other ancient Indo-European cultures, such as Greek and Phrygian.

(2) The story of Manawydan begins with certain events in early British history, accounts of which were preserved but also substantially modified over the centuries by the conventions and patterns of Celtic oral tradition.

A third view of that story material, however, demonstrates that at least some elements of it have a provenance much broader than either mythological or historical Celtic tradition.

Some time ago Kenneth Jackson pointed out that a significant number of the incidents in the narratives of the Four

Branches were also widely known in other, non-Celtic, narrative traditions—that they were in fact the "motifs," or basic story elements, of the traditional folktale, or (as Jackson more accurately called it) "the international popular tale."[14] In the First Branch, for example, to which Jackson gave most of his attention, he identified about a dozen international motifs—widely known narrative elements such as two people magically exchanging shapes (motif D45); the wife of one of them mistaking the other for her husband (K1311.1); the man and woman sleeping together chastely (T350), sometimes (though not in the First Branch) with a naked "sword of chastity" between them (T351); a prohibition against striking more than one blow against a magic or demonic opponent, or else he will revive and not be harmed by further blows (C742); an enemy tricked into a magic bag and beaten (D1193 and K711); a "demon hand" which reaches down a chimney or through a window to snatch a baby (G369.5); an innocent woman accused of killing her newborn children (K2116.1.1).[15] The presence of so many international motifs in the Four Branches places much of the story material, if not the finished product, in the context of a worldwide storytelling tradition which includes not only oral folktales known from Ireland to India and from Russia to Africa, but also the great literary collections of traditional tales made in ancient India and the classical world, in medieval and Renaissance Europe, and in the *Arabian Nights* and Grimms' *Household Tales*.

Jackson's approach to the story material of the Four Branches is again fundamentally diachronic, just as much so as those which look for the sources of that material in Celtic mythology or early British history. He is concerned with the sources of the Four Branches in traditional storytelling, and with understanding the process of how—through time—the narratives of the Four Branches were "built up" into coherent stories from traditional motifs and combinations of motifs, and then at a later date proceeded to break down, gradually disintegrating until the point at which they were caught in manuscripts and finally fixed in what he feels is their "extraordinarily confused and incoherent" present state.[16] The failure of a motif or of an episode in the Four Branches to correspond to the traditional form thus tends to be for Jackson a measure of the extent of the disintegration in the Welsh work.

The attention of "synchronic" scholarship and criticism is focused differently. Its distinguishing assumption is that the text we have—which after all, it argues, *someone* was responsible for, whether we call him "author," "redactor," or "scribe"—is not an accidental product but an intentional one, that it is a work of medieval literature. ("Diachronic" approaches do not necessarily deny that assumption, but neither does their archaeological work of recovery and reconstruction require it.) The work of the synchronic approach, then, is that of unfolding at least some of the principles of structure and patterns of meaning, which it assumes *are* there, in the text as it stands.

From among a number of good examples of this approach, most of them relatively recent, I will mention just one: Proinsias Mac Cana's discussion of the central character of the Third Branch. Manawydan, he writes, is "the pragmatist and the peace-maker," a figure of "patience and tolerance," and "the protagonist of reason and enlightenment." He is a figure whose conduct presents "a thoroughgoing criticism of the heroic ideal." Thus social and political values of the author's own time are reflected and also criticized in the story of Manawydan: "Vengeance and feud were part of the pattern of medieval life, but Manawydan shows how they may be rejected and circumvented by the exercise of fortitude and prudence." Through Manawydan, the author "subtly conveys a scale of values which, by implication, he commends to the practice of contemporary society."[17] These synchronic comments on the Third Branch (which actually occur in the context of an extended argument against exclusively synchronic criticism) point out a coherent meaning in the story, see that meaning as something intentionally "created" (rather than "inherited") by the late eleventh-century author, and draw out the relevance of that meaning to conditions and conflicts within the author's society.

From these various studies of the Third Branch, all very different from one another, three topics emerge that are of particular interest here. One is the idea that the "waste land" theme, the motif of a land made magically sterile, is in some way central to the story of Manawydan. Another is the sense that both the story and the character of Manawydan present a fundamental criticism of the actions and values of heroic

Manawydan fab Llŷr

society. Third is the view that the structure of the tale, with its apparently extraneous digressions or late interpolations, is a relatively loose and random product of the processes of transmission and cannot be thought of as carrying any significance for those meanings in the narrative. To that topic we now turn.

II.

When Kenneth Jackson came to the international motifs of the Third Branch, he discussed only two in the whole story. The first is the magic fountain which traps Pryderi and Rhiannon, a version, Jackson pointed out, of the central motif in a comic tale known all over Europe and also in the Near East, in which a series of people is made to stick to a magic basin (D1413.7)—or, in some instances, a magic chamber pot (D1413.8). The other international motif is the episode at the end of the story in which a great horde of mice steal Manawydan's wheat crop three nights in a row. Jackson found folktales from England and Ireland in which the same thing is done by elves or beetles.[18] It is actually one form of a large number of widespread "devastating animal" and "devastating monster" motifs (B16 and G346). On the whole, however, Jackson felt that the Third Branch "is very poor in international themes, and those it does contain are trifling." Thus "it is perhaps significant," he added, that it is "the least interesting and successful" Branch of the Four Branches.[19]

There are in fact many more than two international motifs in the narrative of the Third Branch. At least twenty can be identified, including such familiar ones as the "magic mist" (D902.1), the "deserted city" (F766), the "guiding beast" (N774), the "phantom house which disappears at dawn" (F771.6), the transformation of people into mice (D117.1), and the "watch for the devastating monster" (H1471). But it is also possible to take a synchronic approach when placing the Four Branches in the context of the traditional tale. One thing such an approach might do would be to look to traditional tales less for particular motifs used by the author than for general principles which he could have learned from traditional story and have put to use in his own work. Along this line, there are four points in particular which it helps to keep in mind if we are to understand his work from that perspective. They are not inflexible "laws" but general descriptions of how tales can change as they are "tradited," handed around and handed down, and also descriptions of how a tale can change in the competent hands of a particular storyteller.

(1) Perhaps the first thing to keep in mind is that a "traditional" tale is not necessarily an "oral" tale. Although "orality and literacy" is one of those familiar opposing pairs of current critical discourse, the fact remains that the basis of written tales by authors such as Boccaccio and Chaucer is almost entirely traditional, whether that tradition has been oral or literary.[20] Obviously, in the case of medieval literature we have no purely oral tales: all come to us through some kind of literary medium. On the other hand, even when we do have an unambiguous modern example of an oral tale—one scrupulously recorded in the field by a folklorist from an informant (preferably illiterate, and in possession of no radio, TV, CD player, or "Walkman")—even then we cannot assume that it was *always* an oral tale.[21] As Irish folklorists discovered, a tale taken down in the field in the twentieth century may well derive from a literary version written in the sixteenth.[22] In short, there need be no contradiction in saying that the Third Branch of the *Mabinogi* is both a "traditional" tale and the written work of an individual author.

(2) Jackson's motif-analysis of the Four Branches has been criticized for its "atomistic" perspective, for involving (in the words of one such critic) "an analytical method whose end result is fragmentation of each tale into its component parts."[23] And there is some justification for the criticism. Any procedure that considered only isolated motifs in a traditional tale would be misleading. For individual motifs occur not on their own but as part of an interlocking structure—the plot—of a complete tale. The stability of such traditional plot structures is another general principle of traditional storytelling. As a tale passes from age to age and from country to country, the basic plot remains stable and recognizable.[24] Even when an individual storyteller, some Boccaccio or some Chaucer, decides for reasons of his own to change that structure, he inevitably does so in accordance with those

principles of coherent and consistent plot construction that he has learned from the traditional tales themselves. Being aware of traditional material in the narratives of the Four Branches, then, means being aware of traditional structures as well as of traditional motifs.

(3) And yet, different versions of the same tale are . . . different. Even while the basic structure remains the same, a traditional tale does change as it passes from one storyteller to another, or even as it is told on different occasions by the same storyteller.[25] There are many ways in which these changes take place—local or contemporary details are added, for example, or characters' roles are switched—but what I want to focus on here is how tales are combined. In both oral tradition and literary tradition tales are put together in various ways. For example, two tales can be strung together, one tale becoming an introduction or a sequel for the other. Or one tale can be set inside the other, giving us a tale within a tale, or a "frame-tale" and "in-tale" structure. One classic combination which uses both techniques is the old traditional tale of "The Two Brothers" (AT 303), which regularly includes within itself the quite distinct tale of "The Dragon-Slayer" (AT 300).[26] Many versions, moreover, add yet another tale, "The Magic Bird-Heart" (AT 567), to the beginning of "The Two Brothers" as an introductory episode. And roughly twenty percent of all versions of "The Two Brothers" add the episode known as "The Jealous Brother" (motifs N342.3 and B512) to the end of the tale as a sequel.[27] In the Four Branches of the *Mabinogi*, we see the same structural principles in the Second Branch, which has both a tale within a tale (the story of the origin of the magic cauldron of resurrection) and a sequel to the main tale (the story of the Otherworld sojourn of the British survivors of the battle in Ireland).

(4) Within those structural conditions—conditions involving both stability and flexibility—any individual tale, it seems, is available for different emphases or different interpretations of its meaning by particular storytellers or authors. John T. Koch's suggestion that the Third Branch is a radical reinterpretation of an earlier story, one which completely changes the meaning while keeping intact the original structure, becomes particularly interesting in this light.[28]

More generally, Brynley F. Roberts has said, in the process of summarizing a range of recent critical work on oral tradition and Welsh literature, that the change from a traditional "storyteller" *(cyfarwydd)* to an "author" involves a significant change of cultural attitude, in particular a much greater freedom with respect to the handling of traditional material: "The 'author' is not as bound to his tradition as the *cyfarwydd*. He is free to derive his inspiration from a broader spectrum of influences, and his material ceases to be that of his community to be transmitted but his own to be interpreted or utilized."[29] The distinction is valuable, though the application may be too rigid; it seems likely that at least some *cyfarwyddiaid* assumed as much freedom as they needed in making good stories.

There are of course limits on this. First of all, not every storyteller or author has the interest, the insight, or the artistry to "develop" a story of coherent and significant meaning from a basic tale. And even when he does, there are constraints in the nature of the tale itself, in the shape of its plot structure. The tale of the Calumniated Wife, for example, an early version of which appears in the First Branch of the *Mabinogi*, was very popular in both medieval literary tradition and oral tradition. It is a tale which always enlists the sympathies of both storyteller and audience on behalf of the falsely accused and long-suffering wife: it seems that things just have to be that way with this tale. None of the hundreds of versions seems ever to have made the accuser of the wife—usually a mother-in-law or a rejected courtier—into the hero of the tale, clever and resourceful though she or he may be. Within those limits, however, versions of even this tale do differ markedly from one another—from the First Branch to Chaucer's Man of Law's Tale to modern Irish oral variants.[30] The same "tale" can be put in the service of different "stories" as individual storytellers or authors give to it different interpretations or discover in it different meanings. Rather than one meaning exclusively and eternally associated with a traditional tale, then, there are a number of inherent meanings, various possibilities of story latent in one tale structure. A storyteller or author will respect the integrity of that structure (otherwise he would be telling a different tale), but may also bend it quite a bit in this direction or that as he follows one or another of those possibilities.

III.

What does the Third Branch of the *Mabinogi* look like from this point of view? First of all, it appears structurally as a story which combines two very traditional tales. There is a primary tale of enchantment and disenchantment, one of the fundamental stories of traditional narrative. Set within that tale, "framed" by it, is the tale of the jealous craftsmen of England. The storyteller—author, final redactor, inventive scribe, or whoever produced the text we have—appears to have used that combination of two traditional tales to tell a unique story. He developed meanings which are inherent in the tales, which appear also to reflect his own temperament and society, and which, finally, connect in significant ways with the themes of the other three Branches of the *Mabinogi*.

The Third Branch is essentially about the enchantment and disenchantment of the land of Dyfed. The climactic act of disenchantment comes in the final "Mice in the Corn" episode, in which Manawydan successfully bargains with Llwyd son of Cil Coed (Llwyt fab Kil Coet), the sorcerer who laid the enchantment on Dyfed in the first place, to remove the spell forever. But in between those two defining episodes of enchantment and disenchantment are two journeys into England ("Lloygyr," i.e., Lloegr) by the main characters of the story. On the first journey there are four of them: Manawydan, Rhiannon, Pryderi, and Cigfa live in England by the crafts of saddle-making, shield-making, and shoemaking, abandoning each in turn as their success causes the English craftsmen to plot against their lives. Eventually they return to Wales, but there Pryderi and his mother Rhiannon are trapped in a fort (*caer*) which then magically disappears, taking them with it. Manawydan and Pryderi's wife, Cigfa, return to England, once more to practice the craft of shoemaking, and once again to meet with the same hostile response from the English shoemakers. And so they go back to Dyfed, where Manawydan finally accomplishes the disenchantment of the land.

The three crafts in succession, like the other patterns of "folktale threes," or triple repetition, which occur in the story, are a clear sign that we are in the world of the traditional European tale.[31] But why do those episodes happen at all, and why does the story dwell on the crafts which the exiles practice while they are in England? As we saw earlier, W.J. Gruffydd believed that both the journeys into England *and* the "Mice in the Corn" episode at the end of the tale were extraneous to the story and have no bearing on it. But the "Mice in the Corn" episode is where the disenchantment happens, and clearly it is essential to the tale's overall structure of enchantment and disenchantment. Take away the journeys into England, however, and that structure is still intact. Unlike the "Mice in the Corn," there seems not to be any necessity for the episode of the jealous craftsmen, much less for telling it twice.

True, the story does provide some motivation for those two journeys. After the enchantment empties Dyfed, the four people left live very pleasantly on their own for two years by hunting, fishing, and gathering wild honey. "And at last," the story says, "they grew weary" ("Ac yn y diwed, dygyaw a wnaethant"):

> "Dioer," heb y Manawydan, "ny bydwn ual hynn. Kyrchwn Loygyr, a cheisswn greft y caffom yn ymborth."
>
> "Faith," said Manawydan, "we cannot live thus. Let us make for Lloegyr and seek some craft whereby we may make our livelihood."[32]

On the second occasion, after Pryderi and Rhiannon have disappeared in the enchanted fort, and the hunting dogs with them, it is again Manawydan who says (to Cigfa, the only person left to say anything to):

> "Ie, eneit," heb y Manawydan, "nyt kyfle yni trigyaw yma. Yn cwn a gollyssam, ac ymborth ny allwn. Kyrchwn Loegyr. Hawssaf yw in ymborth yno."(*PKM* 57.28–58.3)
>
> "Indeed, friend," said Manawydan, "this is no place for us to stay. We have lost our dogs and can win no livelihood. Let us go into Lloegyr; it will be easiest for us to make a living there." (*The Mabinogion* 48)

But these explanations have a half-hearted feel to them, as if the author were rationalizing for us something which the story needs to do anyway, some internal logic that requires those journeys.

In the story of Manawydan, we noticed earlier, there is for at least some readers an explicit criticism of the heroic way of life. Proinsias Mac Cana, for example, along with the comments mentioned earlier, has said of the author: "For the exaggerated and impulsive ideals of heroic tradition—and, one suspects, of much of contemporary life—he projects the more Christian and more practical virtues of patience and compromise."[33] Nowhere is this seen more clearly than in the English episodes. Each time the Welsh exiles are threatened by the English craftsmen, one of the group responds to the crisis by giving voice to the "heroic" values that are natural to them all. Their first time in England it is Pryderi, who seems less to feel physically threatened than to be deeply offended that craftsmen could plot against noblemen, and he wants to attack and kill them all. The second time in England it is Cigfa, whose words echo the words and values of Pryderi. But in each instance Manawydan finds reasons for moving elsewhere rather than staying and fighting.

A similar pattern appears between the two journeys, in the episode of the mysterious fort. When Pryderi enters that fort and does not return, Manawydan waits for his companion but does not rush in after him. The fort has appeared from nowhere, an all-white boar has just led their hunting dogs into it, now Pryderi has disappeared into it, and Manawydan, it seems, is becoming suspicious. And so he chooses the better part of valor. For that, the high-spirited Rhiannon severely upbraids him, then rushes in herself—and is immediately captured. The episode of the fort makes clear that the real conflict in the English episodes is not between the Welsh aristocrats and the English craftsmen but between the Welsh themselves: between the aristocratic and heroic warrior code which they all have inherited and a different way of life which only Manawydan seems gradually to perceive and tentatively to reach toward. Because of the nature of the genre, we see only what he does and not what he knows. But his actions seem to show that he knows the time for heroic deeds—those brave conflicts of bold spirits driven by the ideals of honor and the satisfactions of vengeance—is past.

That point about Manawydan, however, could have been made with one journey into England, and one set of encounters with the English craftsmen. But we have two journeys, the same thing happening both times. Why repeat it? This has seemed to many to be a flaw in the story. For W.J. Gruffydd it was evidence of the incomplete assimilation of the "interpolated tale," which gave the Third Branch "a duplication which the author for all his artistry failed to conceal."[34] But the duplication need not be a sign of failed artistry. The author could have repeated the journey episode simply for the sake of emphasis, to make sure that we see his important contrast between two ways of responding to crisis—and he would have been working entirely within traditional techniques of storytelling had he done so.[35]

But in fact the second trip into England does not simply repeat the first: there are significant differences between them. The most obvious difference is that by the time of the second journey two powerful representatives of the heroic code have been lost by acting in accordance with that code. But a more important difference is that Manawydan returns from the second exile with seeds for a wheat crop, and it is that crop which becomes the instrument for disenchanting Dyfed. The first journey perhaps emphasizes what *not* to do: one should not always expect to fight one's way out of a problem, especially when one is a stranger in a strange land. Back in Dyfed, moreover, heroic battle appears again to be futile as a means for freeing the land from the spell. The second journey, we might say, adds important information on what one *should* do. In this case, that is to plant.

The "charm and enchantment on the seven cantrefs of Dyfed" ("yr hut a'r lledrith y ar seith cantref Dyuet," *PKM* 63.28–64.1) has long been seen by Arthurian scholars as a prototype of the fisher king and waste land motifs of the Grail romances. Celticists as well usually see some version of the waste land in that enchantment—the Irish version in which infertility of the land is brought about by the physical blemish or moral failure of the king, the Grail version in which the wounding of a king causes the barrenness of his land, or the *Golden Bough* version in which a universal infertility of the land and the people is brought about by the grief or the absence of a fertility goddess.[36] But Dyfed is not a waste land: it is deserted but not infertile. Even under the enchantment it abounds in game, fish, and wild honey. Only the refinements of civilized life are gone: domestic herds, dwellings with their hearth fires, the society of people. It is not nature but culture that has failed. When Manawydan plants his grain—apparently introducing agriculture into Wales—it grows, in fact it flourishes, "the wheat springing up the best in the world" ("y guenith yn kyuot yn oreu yn y byt," *PKM* 59.4). And it is that growth, again, that leads to the disenchantment of the country.

Manawydan is the hero of the story, but not a mythic hero restoring fertility to nature, and certainly not an epic hero recklessly risking death for the sake of honor. He is almost a "culture hero," quite literally in the sense that he introduces agriculture to Dyfed, but more significantly in that it is the culture of Wales—its society, institutions, and values—that has need of him. He is also a form of hero familiar from traditional tales (as well as from the *Odyssey*), using his wits more than his sword to redeem the prisoners and the country. The journeys into England—both initiated by him—now begin to appear central rather than irrelevant to the story. They occupy the structural position of the hero's quest or tasks in a traditional tale, those tests of prowess, virtue, or cunning which are necessary before a folktale hero can accomplish his final goal, a goal which is often a disenchantment of one kind or another. But beyond that, things are to be learned on journeys: without the journeys into England there would be no seed, and no new growth for Dyfed. Again there is a parallel to this in the humble folktale, for Manawydan succeeds in a way many heroes of traditional tales succeed, by introducing into a country something previously unknown but badly needed (motif N411). It may be introducing saddles and stirrups to a land where people ride bareback (N411.3), or taking a cat to a country plagued by mice (N411.1)—the first example familiar from Sindbad's "Fourth Voyage" in the *Arabian Nights,* the second from the tale of "Whittington's Cat" (AT 1651) and also the Grimms' tales (no. 70).[37]

There is a sense in the Third Branch, or so it seems to me, that after the terrible destruction that takes place in the Second Branch a new society, or a whole new civilization, needs to be established. But it will not be like the old one, with giant warriors such as Bendigeidfran or violently unpredictable ones such as Efnisien. It is not the warrior Pryderi who frees the land from its spell, but Manawydan, who does it in the process of establishing a new way of life with new values. Pryderi the warrior belongs to the old way, and is trapped in its values, literally paralyzed. (His days are numbered, and he is killed off early in the Fourth Branch.) The enchantment itself comes from the old values: it is the long-smoldering vengeance for the trick played upon Gwawl fab Clud by Pryderi's father in the First Branch. And both Cigfa and Llwyd the magician appeal to those values when each tries to dissuade Manawydan from hanging the one mouse he has caught of the many who plundered his fields: they say that it is degrading for a nobleman to handle vermin. But a farmer has different enemies than a warrior does. Manawydan continues his preparations for the execution of the mouse (who is, of course, the transformed wife of the magician, and pregnant at that) until Rhiannon and Pryderi are freed, herds and houses and human society are restored to the land, and, probably most significantly, he has extracted from the magician a promise that never again will there be an enchantment on Dyfed.

In different ways, the Second Branch and the Third both show the outcome of those relentless processes of honor and revenge which characterize the heroic code: apocalyptic destruction in the Second Branch, an empty land in the Third. Thus it seems right that Manawydan is no warrior-hero but a man of crafts and a man of agriculture. He is also a man of law, as we see in the careful details of his charging the mouse with theft and settling its ransom.[38] It is possible for legal settlement, or even hard bargaining, to replace revenge. But the crafts and the farming and the law seem also to suggest something larger than themselves, and finally to be metaphors for a new way of life that can replace the old way, which has proven too destructive.

It is interesting to notice in conclusion that Manawydan is a generation older than Pryderi, a point which appears to remove the last vestiges of Frazerian fertility-myth from the Third Branch. This is not a new "generation" but a new vision. It is also interesting that Manawydan is remembered in Welsh tradition by two absolutely unheroic Triads (as the Third Branch itself mentions, somewhat anachronistically). He is "trydyd lledyf unben," usually translated as "one of the three ungrasping chieftains," though it is not clear what *lledyf* really means here, or whether it is a good thing or a bad thing to be[39]—which seems to correspond with the attitude of most of the characters in the tale towards Manawydan. In the other Triad he is remembered as "tryded eurgryd" ("one of the three gold shoemakers")—"pan vu hut ar Dyuet" ("when the enchantment was on Dyfed").[40] The Triad identifies Manawydan by juxtaposing the plight of Dyfed with the lowly craft, the lowest of all, he practiced in England. In linking the two it may also remember the heart of the story, or at least remind us of it: a story of something gone badly wrong, of a journey for a remedy, of finding instead a new way of seeing things—which, it turns out, is the remedy. It is an old, traditional story.

NOTES

1. Rhŷs, *Lectures on the Origin and Growth of Religion as Illustrated by Celtic Heathendom*, 663–668; Rhŷs, *Celtic Folklore: Welsh and Manx*, II: 547, 619–620, 637; Anwyl, "The Four Branches of the Mabinogi," 285; MacCulloch, *The Religion of the Ancient Celts*, 100–101; MacCulloch, "Celtic Mythology," 102–103.

2. Gruffydd, *Rhiannon: An Inquiry into the Origins of the First and Third Branches of the Mabinogi*.

3. Gruffydd, *Rhiannon*, 80; the Irish Manannán, Gruffydd wrote, is like Manawydan a master craftsman (85), but nevertheless the transformation from "Manannán the evil wizard" to "Manawydan the passive cordwainer" (86) is so complete that the Welsh figure finally takes only the name of the Irish figure (80).

4. Gruffydd, *Rhiannon*, 77.

5. Gruffydd, *Rhiannon*, 100–103; Gruffydd wrote that the story of the Desolation of Dyfed in the Third Branch "is clothed in all or nearly all of the mythical as well as folk-lore traditions of the *Waste Land*" (76).

6. Gruffydd, *Rhiannon*, 72–75, 78. A study of the Eustace legend by Thomas J. Heffernan casts doubt on Gruffydd's idea that the "final form" of *Manawydan* is a version of that tale. Heffernan demonstrates that the Eustace legend clearly was not a secular tale based on the "Man Tried by Fate" folktale, as Gruffydd assumed,

but was primarily a "homiletic aid" or sermon *exemplum* which drew most of all on the biblical Job story. The central features of the legend are the main character's conversion, trials, and final martyrdom; it speaks of miracles and of dying for one's faith, and not as a folktale would of wonders and triumph ("An Analysis of the Narrative Motifs in the Legend of St. Eustace").

7. Gruffydd, *Rhiannon*, 71–72.

8. Koch, "A Welsh Window on the Iron Age: Manawydan, Mandubracios"; Koch explicitly points out that his is a "diachronic" study concerned "with the sources of the *stories'* traditional subject matter rather than the artistry and outlook of the medieval redactor(s) of the extant *texts*" (18).

9. The Third Branch "recollects in some detail the struggle between the chieftains known to Caesar's *De Bello Gallico* . . . as Cassivellaunus and Mandubracius son of 'Imanuentius.' It is the latter of whom Manawydan himself is a reflection" (Koch, "A Welsh Window," 18). For Koch, the association of Manawydan's name with that of "the Irish sea god Manannán mac Lir" came later as a piece of "popular etymology" (20).

10. Mandubracios was a chieftain of the Trinovantes, who as a result of his efforts were given Caesar's protection against their enemies, the Catuvellaunians. Eventually, however, the Catuvellaunians did conquer the Trinovantes (ca. AD 7), Koch shows, and the history of Mandubracios, now presented as a story of an Unrightful King, became (Koch surmises) part of an heroic saga celebrating the leaders of the Catuvellaunians and legitimizing their conquest of the Trinovantes ("A Welsh Window," 18).

11. Koch, "A Welsh Window," 38–40.

12. Koch, "A Welsh Window," 42.

13. Koch, "A Welsh Window," 36.

14. Jackson, *The International Popular Tale and Early Welsh Tradition*, 81–133; see also Jackson, "Some Popular Motifs in Early Welsh Tradition."

15. Traditional motifs are catalogued in Thompson, *Motif-Index of Folk-Literature*. I list the motifs of all Four Branches in "The Traditional Narrative Motifs of *The Four Branches of the Mabinogi*."

16. Jackson, *International Popular Tale*, 91, 124.

17. Mac Cana, *The Mabinogi*, 48–50, 59–61; see also Bollard, "The Structure of the Four Branches of the Mabinogi," especially 257–263.

18. Jackson, *International Popular Tale*, 104–105.

19. Jackson, *International Popular Tale*, 103–104.

20. The folklorist Stith Thompson defined the "traditional prose tale" as "the story which has been handed down from generation to generation either in writing or by word of mouth." He noted

further, "The great written collections of stories characteristic of India, the Near East, the classical world, and Medieval Europe are almost entirely traditional." While the individual genius of well-known writers who used those tales is clear, "a study of the sources of Chaucer or Boccaccio takes one directly into the stream of traditional narrative" (*The Folktale*, 4).

21. Thompson pointed out that tales from Aesop, Homer, Perrault, and the Grimms have all "entered the oral stream," and that "the oral story need not always have been oral" (*The Folktale*, 5). He also wrote, "That many of our European and Asiatic folktales go back to a literary source is as clear as any fact of scholarship can be made" (176).

22. See especially Bruford, *Gaelic Folk-Tales and Mediaeval Romances: A Study of the Early Modern Irish "Romantic Tales" and Their Oral Derivatives*.

23. McKenna, "The Theme of Sovereignty in *Pwyll*," 36. McKenna also writes that an approach to the stories of the Four Branches which explains, "by reference to oral traditional processes, their development out of a jumble of originally separate themes and motifs" is one which sees the work "as a patchwork whole, and is more interested in examining the seams which traverse it than in describing the design thereby created" (35).

24. Thus numerous individual versions of a complex tale can be grouped under one "tale-type," as tales from the European-Asiatic tradition are classified in Aarne and Thompson, *The Types of the Folktale: A Classification and Bibliography*. (Jackson was quite aware of this structural coherence and stability in traditional tales [see *International Popular Tale* 56–59], but did not find it in the Four Branches.)

25. A given tale, according to Thompson, may even move into a completely different "oral narrative form," or genre—*Märchen* becoming myths, animal tales, or local legends, for example—while remaining the same basic tale. "As stories transcend differences of age or of place and move from the ancient world to ours, or from ours to a primitive society, they often undergo protean transformations in style and narrative purpose. For the plot structure of the tale is much more stable and more persistent than its form" (*The Folktale*, 10).

26. Tale-type numbers refer to the classification in the Aarne-Thompson *Types of the Folktale*, abbreviated "AT."

27. See Thompson, *The Folktale*, 24–32.

28. Koch, "A Welsh Window," 36.

29. Roberts, "Oral Tradition and Welsh Literature: A Description and Survey," 73. Roberts adds, with respect to the Four Branches and the other "Mabinogion" narratives, "The freedom of interpre-

tation this change allows us, however, must be exercised within the bounds of our ignorance, since very little is known of these 'authors,' of the context and of the audience of the written stories, features which must be aspects of their intentionality" (73).

30. For the medieval tradition of the Calumniated Wife tale see Schlauch, *Chaucer's Constance and Accused Queens*. A modern Irish version, collected in Donegal in 1946, is in the tale "The Speckled Bull," in *Folktales of Ireland*, ed. and trans. O'Sullivan, 117–30.

31. In the final section of the story, Manawydan plants three fields of wheat, which are plundered three nights in succession. When he is about to hang the single mouse he caught on the third night, three figures appear in succession to attempt to ransom the mouse, with the third figure making three offers in succession.

32. I. Williams, ed., *Pedeir Keinc y Mabinogi*, 2nd ed., 52.16–19; all references are to page and line numbers of this edition, subsequently abbreviated *PKM*. Translations are from *The Mabinogion*, trans. Jones and Jones (1949); this passage appears on 43.

33. Mac Cana, *The Mabinogi*, 60.

34. Gruffydd, *Rhiannon*, 75; according to Gruffydd's reconstruction, the "interpolated tale" is the legend of St. Eustace, which unlike the story of Manawydan requires two exile-journeys.

35. Jones, "Narrative Structure in Medieval Welsh Prose Tales," justifies the repetition in purely formal terms, noting that it is a technique of traditional narrative and adding that "whatever may have been what the author had in mind regarding this incremental emphasis on the suffering, from a structural point of view the duplication, or balancing of or incident with another, causes no obscurity whatsoever" (179).

36. As noted above, Gruffydd saw behind the story of the enchantment of Dyfed a myth in which "all life and all growth disappear" from the land when the fertility goddess's son is abducted; when he is recovered "prosperity is restored to the land and all life and growth re-appear" (*Rhiannon* 77). Ford also sees the disenchantment as "restoring the productivity and fertility of the land" ("Prolegomena to a Reading of the *Mabinogi:* 'Pwyll' and 'Manawydan,'" 123). For Koch, the enchantment on Dyfed is an example of "the Celtic Waste Land theme," deriving from "the notion that both human well-being and the entire fecundity of nature depend on the rightfulness of the king" ("A Welsh Window," 38). The "waste land" idea is known well in Celtic and international tradition: examples of some relevant Celtic motifs are B11.12.2 "Dragon's shriek makes land barren," H1574.2 "Fruitfulness of nature as proof of kingly right," and M411.6.1 "Druid's curse makes land sterile"; examples of international motifs are

Manawydan fab Llŷr

D2081 "Land made magically sterile," Q153 "Nature benign and fruitful during reign of good king," and Q552.3 "Failure of crops during reign of wicked king." The "dragon's shriek" motif appears in the Welsh *Cyfranc Lludd a Lleuelys:* a piercing scream heard every May-eve causes barrenness (apparently temporary) in men and women, animals and trees, and the earth and water, an effect much closer to a true waste land than is the enchantment on Dyfed.

37. At about the time of the composition of the Four Branches, the Normans, as part of their occupation of South Wales, were introducing systematic, intensive agriculture into the fertile valleys and plains; the early Welsh preferred herding to farming and were primarily a pastoral society (Nelson, *The Normans in South Wales 1070–1171*, 6–9). Note also the Triad (no. 26) of the "Three Powerful Swineherds of the Island of Britain," who were Pryderi, Tristan, and Coll fab Collfrewy; as Coll pursued the magical sow Henwen through South Wales, she bestowed wheat, barley, and bees upon the land (Bromwich, *Trioedd Ynys Prydein: The Welsh Triads;* subsequently abbreviated *TYP*).

38. For Manawydan's knowledge and careful use of the Welsh Laws in this episode see Ellis, "Legal References, Terms and Conceptions in the 'Mabinogion,'" 111–113.

39. *PKM* 49.12; see *TYP*, lxxxviii–lxxxix and Triad no. 8.

40. *PKM* 54.18; see *TYP*, lxxxix–xc and Triad no. 67.

III

Structural Interpretations

7

A Thematic Study of the Tale *Pwyll Pendeuic Dyuet*

Seán Ó Coileáin

The purpose of this article is to show how a thematic analysis of a given tale may be important for an understanding of its structure and meaning. The tale in question has already been the subject of a good deal of investigation. The most comprehensive attempt to analyse it has been that of W.J. Gruffydd in his *Rhiannon*.[1] Kenneth Jackson has corrected and supplemented this study on several important points almost to the extent of negating Gruffydd's conclusions altogether.[2] I am particularly indebted to Jackson's observations as they concern the most critical points of the narrative and provide valuable evidence as to the nature of the tradition to which it belongs. Jackson, however, does not provide a comprehensive explanation of the tale as Gruffydd had, however unsatisfactory his theorizing may now seem in the light of Jackson's criticism. The explanation here provided is an attempt to supply this deficiency.

My principal thesis is that the tale may be understood as a unit and that there is no justification for Gruffydd's statement that "there is no connection between Part I of *Pwyll* and Part II in their present form. Part I describes one independent incident in the life of the Lord of Dyfed, which has no connection, whether stated or implied, with the latter portion beyond the fact that the same protagonist appears in both."[3] This division will be seen to be only an apparent one; what Gruffydd calls Part II is in fact a doublet of his Part I, and the reason for the duplication may be explained in terms of theme. Before entering into this explanation we may note the points of correspondence which appear with remarkable regularity between what I prefer to call Sections A and B, rather than Parts I and II:

Section A

Introductory verbal formula:
A threigylgweith yd oed yn Arberth, prif lys idaw

1. Features which suggest magic: colour of dogs.

2. Pwyll, separated from his companions, encounters stranger, Arawn, king of Annwn, and questions him as to his identity.

3. Arawn tells Pwyll of his fear of an enemy, Hafgan of Annwn.

4. Meeting arranged for Pwyll with Arawn's enemy, "a year from tonight."

5. Instructions as to how enemy may be overcome.

6. Journey to the court of Arawn and reception. Pwyll described feasting, "the queen on one side of him, and the earl, as he thought, on the other."

7. Encounter with enemy, Hafgan.

8. Enemy's request refused by Pwyll as instructed in 5.

Section B

Introductory verbal formula:
A threigylgweith yd oed yn Arberth, prif lys idaw . . .

1^1. Features which suggest magic: mound of wonders, inability to overtake lady.

2^1. Pwyll, separated from his companions, encounters stranger, Rhiannon, daughter of Hefeydd Hen, and questions her as to her identity.

3^1. Rhiannon tells Pwyll of her fear of a loathed suitor, Gwawl (who is not, however, named at this point).

4^1. Meeting arranged for Pwyll, ostensibly with Rhiannon but also with suitor/enemy as it turns out, "a year from tonight."

[5^1. Absent at this point leading to initial defeat of hero Pwyll and further duplication.]

6^1. Journey to the court of Rhiannon and reception. Pwyll described feasting, "Hefeydd Hen one side of Pwyll, and Rhiannon on the other."

7^1. Encounter with enemy, Gwawl.

8^1. Enemy's request granted by Pwyll leading to his temporary defeat.

4^2. Meeting again arranged for Pwyll, "a year from tonight."

5^1. Instructions as to how enemy may be overcome.

6^2. Journey to the court of Rhiannon. Arrival in time for feast, ostensibly prepared for Gwawl.

	7^2. Encounter with enemy, Gwawl.
	8^2. Two variations on theme of request: (a) Request granted by Gwawl to Pwyll as anticipated in 5^1 leading to latter's triumph. (b) Request granted by Pwyll to Gwawl: of no structural significance, merely emphasizing (a).
9. Enemy, Hafgan, finally vanquished.	9^1. Enemy, Gwawl, finally vanquished.
[10. Significantly absent: pattern has broken down by contamination with Chaste Friend/Brother theme leading to total duplication and continuation of Section A in Section B.]	10. Pwyll and Rhiannon spend the night together "in pleasure and contentment."

A number of points may be made at this stage. Jackson has already clearly shown that the theme of the Chaste Friend/Brother in what I call Section A is secondary. The real analogues to this section (and indeed to Section B also) are such Irish tales as *Echtra Láegaire* and *Serglige Con Culainn*, especially the former. In these a mortal is rewarded for his aid to an other world being with the love of a fairy woman. Of *Pwyll*, Jackson says: "The mortal hero's reward, the love of a beautiful woman, is evidently an integral part of the plot, but in the episode in *Pwyll* this has been very much modified by the introduction of the international themes of the transformation into the likeness of the husband and of the Chaste Brother."[4] These two themes are obviously mutually exclusive as in one sexual relationship is specifically granted and in the other specifically denied. What has not been realized, I think, is the extent to which the substitution of one for the other in the case of *Pwyll* has determined the shape of the tale. In *Pwyll* we have the added complication that the pattern must conclude with the birth of Gwri/Pryderi, and it is this which makes the substitution of the Chaste Friend/Brother theme completely unacceptable and leads to a new beginning in Section B. The author himself seems to have been uneasy about the substitution and it is possible that at one point in Section A a vestige of the earlier pattern remains. If we compare stages 6 and 6^1 above, we see that in 6^1 (Section B) Pwyll is seated at the feast with Hefeydd Hen on one side and Rhiannon on the other, whereas in 6 (Section A), the queen is on one side and "the earl, as he thought" on the other. Who is this mysterious earl? The structure would indicate that he is none other than Arawn himself. The introduction of the Chaste Friend/Brother theme demands the absence of Arawn, while the earlier pattern requires his presence as the man whom Pwyll has come to aid. Faced with this dilemma the author has compromised with the shadowy figure of the earl of whom he (rather than Pwyll) does not feel quite sure. This is a good example of the genesis of a traditional tale. Each theme brings with it the sum of its uses and associations in the tradition, and some of these may be at odds with the immediate context in a given tale. If the primary theme is then ousted by an associated secondary theme, as in this instance, the tale may be given an entirely new direction which has to be corrected in accordance with the felt purpose and pattern of the narrative. In this way a tension is created between theme and structure, and it is this tension and balance which generates the tale. Again, the underlying structural logic is not always fully consistent with the narrative as we can see from a comparison of 4/7 and $4^1/7^1$ above. While in 4^1 Rhiannon does not mention a contest with Gwawl in arranging the meeting with Pwyll, it is structurally inevitable that this contest take place at 7^1, as it does at the equivalent stage of Section A.

As Section A is wholly duplicated in Section B, so Section B is partially duplicated within itself from stages 4^2 to 8^2 inclusive. This duplication is of a more conventional and obvious kind similar to that which Propp describes as sometimes occurring in the folktale on the completion of Function XXII of his morphological scheme.[5] In *Pwyll* this repetition is brought about by the initial omission of stage 5^1 the presence of which is necessary for the completion of the pattern. A similar device, the theft of the child on birth, introduces what I would call Section C of the tale the relationship of which to the continuation of Section B may be represented as follows:

Section B (cont.)	Section C
11. Birth of child, associated with birth of puppies.	11^1. Birth of foals.
12. Theft of child.	12^1. Theft of foals.
[Section concludes with secondary Calumniated Wife theme.]	13. Finding of Child: equivalence to rebirth emphasized by feigned pregnancy of Teyrnon's wife.

Professor Jackson has provided us with an exhaustive analysis of these events in terms of their traditional associations. A factor in the duplication must have been the author's familiarity with two traditional options as regards the Congenital Helpful Animals (puppies, foals) leading him to include both in a confused manner, as explained by Jackson: "There is some reason to believe that Rhiannon was in some way associated with horses, if not originally actually a horse goddess. This fact, together with the motif of the congenital dogs already in our tale, gave some storyteller the idea of introducing the well-known motif of the congenital horse which is generally associated with the congenital dog in the international tale AT. 303, which he must have known."[6] The above set of comparisons expresses this in a different way. Here the pattern of structural relationships is arrived at by reading horizontally, as opposed to the sequence of events which is to be read vertically column by column.

Rather than see Teyrnon as a helper figure, as Jackson does, I would regard him and his wife as variants of Hefeydd and Rhiannon just as the latter in turn are multiforms of Arawn and his wife. (The fact that Hefeydd is Rhiannon's father rather than her husband is not of any real significance.) Part of the process of duplication is the creation of different male and female figures to whom the tale successively transfers itself as Sections A and B are in turn diverted from their purpose, the first being brought up short by the Chaste Friend/Brother theme and the second losing itself in the equally unproductive theme of the Calumniated Wife. The Calumniated Wife theme is not as fatal to the purpose of the tale as that of the Chaste Friend/Brother, so that the division between Sections A and B appears much more clearly than that between Sections B and C. There is even an unsatisfactory reconciliation scene between the protagonists of the latter sections, and in this scene we may have further evidence of the structural division in the differing names of the child. As Pryderi he is probably to be grouped with Hefeydd and Rhiannon and as Gwri with Teyrnon and his wife. Although he is not given a name within Section B proper, it is thought necessary to rename him on his being retransferred from the Section C to the Section B characters. So the verbal identification of Gwri with Pryderi in the reconciliation scene might be interpreted as an attempt to rationalize a difference in nomenclature which had its real origins in the development of the tale as described above.

The growth process envisaged here would suggest that the basic structure developed on the level of oral transmission, although one could not rule out the possibility that it might also arise in a literary tale belonging to what might be broadly described as a traditional milieu. The whole may be regarded as a *compert* or conception tale, although of a somewhat different kind to that proposed by Gruffydd.[7] The fact that the tale's Irish analogues, *Echtra Láegaire* and *Serglige Con Culainn* are not *comperta* does not seriously affect this view: the pattern of these tales has simply been continued to its logical conclusion in this instance.

Finally, although further correspondences may be discovered or the validity of some of the above disputed, the scheme of the tale may be set out as follows. XY represents the functional stages and YZ the duplicate stages of the narrative:

Section A Pwyll+Arawn and Wife X	Section B Pwyll+Hefeydd and Rhiannon	Section C Pwyll+Teyrnon and Wife
1	1	
2	2	
3	3	
4	4 4	
5	5	
6	6 6	
7	7 7	
8	8 8	
9	9	
	10	
	11	11
	12	12
Y		13 Z

NOTES

1. Gruffydd, *Rhiannon*.
2. Jackson, *The International Popular Tale and Early Welsh Tradition*, esp. 81–95, 122; "Some Popular Motifs in Early Welsh Tradition," esp. 83–99.
3. Gruffydd, *Rhiannon*, 22.
4. Jackson, "Some Popular Motifs in Early Welsh Literature," 86.
5. Propp, *Morphology of the Folktale*, 57.
6. Jackson, *The International Popular Tale*, 92.
7. Gruffydd, *Rhiannon*, 24 ff. Gruffydd's mistake was not so much in proposing a parallel with *Compert Mongáin*, to which the *Pwyll-Echtra Láegaire* pattern is related, but being unaware of the traditionally acceptable reversal of roles between mortal and god/fairy, leading to a quite unnecessary attempt to explain away what appeared to him as an anomaly.

8

Pwyll Prince of Dyfed: the narrative structure

Elizabeth Hanson-Smith

Readers generally agree that the Four Branches of the *Mabinogi* prose tales, preserved in medieval Welsh manuscripts from the thirteenth to fifteenth centuries, are masterpieces of swift and graceful style, enchanting equally in their vivid detail and succinct understatement. Yet the structure of the narratives as a whole remains a puzzle. The varied plot elements combined in each—remnants of archaic myths, bits of heroic legends, folk tales, onomastic interpretations, and even historical events—all these pieces, developed over several centuries in an oral repertoire before finding a place in written narrative, combine in an elusive, yet somehow meaningful, whole. Some scholars, such as W.J. Gruffydd and Bernard Harder, see the tales as organically unified by the hero Pryderi along the patterns of the archetypal myth of the hero native to all early literatures.[1] Others, such as K.H. Jackson and Proinsias Mac Cana, argue that the Four Branches had no continuous development in a pre-literary tradition and are in fact ill-woven remnants of a number of earlier stories pieced together by a clever writer who possibly did not fully understand his material.[2] None of the critics seems willing to deal with another problem in the Branches: although supposedly composed or compiled by a churchman of South Wales, possibly a bishop,[3] only *Manawydan Son of Llŷr* contains the slightest trace of Christianity, and there it is introduced as "local colour," the enchanter of Dyfed appearing in the disguises of clerk, priest, and bishop. None of the Branches can be made to have a religious significance, and critics treat them as pure entertainment.

Since each of the Branches presents a relatively complex narrative structure and an interplay of several related themes, I will not attempt to deal with all of them at this time. Rather, taking *Pwyll Prince of Dyfed*[4] as an integral whole, I will argue that it is in fact structured in a manner reflecting conscious artifice rather than simply organic association, and that the repetition of certain motifs and themes represents artistic intention rather than a naïve mishandling of sources. A similar analysis of structure has been undertaken by Seán Ó Coileáin in "A Thematic Study of the Tale *Pwyll Penduic Dyuet*." His presentation includes a most useful schema of the tale, dividing it into two parts—rather than three, as I will later suggest—with a kind of coda attached to the second. Although Ó Coileáin does approach the structure as a set of repetitive patterns, he does not suggest any overriding concept that would necessarily cause the artist to put together these particular incidents or to insert certain changes in the traditional shape of these *topoi*. I will suggest that a mythic reading of *Pwyll* provides us with the source of that artistic unity, but that the tale's underlying structure builds on the motif of the restoration of the wasteland, rather than on the life of the hero Pryderi. This submerged mythic structure, however, is put to use as the controlling metaphor for an instructive, if highly fictionalized and therefore entertaining, book of governance. If instruction as well as amusement lies at the core of *Pwyll*, its composition by a monk or religious is more readily understandable. I leave to some later exploration the possibility that the other Branches also reflect this motif, theme, and purpose, but I shall in passing suggest that the structure and meaning of *Pwyll* offer a line of inquiry into the interconnections of the Four Branches of the *Mabinogi*.

Critics seeing a mythic unity in the Four Branches generally base their readings on the cycle of the hero Pryderi's conception and birth *(Pwyll)*, his early exploits *(Branwen Daughter of Llŷr)*, his enchantment or imprisonment *(Manawydan)*, and his eventual death *(Math Son of Mathonwy)*. But such a reading must ignore much of the stories as they

Pwyll Prince of Dyfed

now exist. The conception and birth of Pryderi takes up only one of the three major parts of *Pwyll;* he is barely mentioned in *Branwen* as one of the seven survivors of the great battle of Ireland; and his role in both *Manawydan* and *Math* is secondary to those of the title characters. No doubt the archetype of the hero forms a part of the background of each Branch, but it cannot explain the actual form each narrative takes. As any creative artist must be, the writer (or writers) of each story was engrossed in the matter at hand; the critic should accept that artistic preoccupation and, having acknowledged the mythic possibilities, examine what the artist actually made of that material. In *Pwyll,* the "matter" is Pwyll; and while the story involves the conception and birth of Pryderi, it relies on the restoration of the wasteland as its primary plot motif and replicates that motif, as I shall demonstrate, in each of its three segments.

The restoration of the wasteland, familiar to most readers from Frazer, involves the enchantment of a once fertile land so that its fields lie fallow and its king becomes disabled, a disability usually taken as sexual and often symbolized by wounded foot, thigh, or eyes. Regenerative powers are restored by the arrival of a young hero in this "other world." He solves a puzzle, demonstrating wisdom (the Oedipus version), or defeats an enemy, often a dragon or other magical beast (as with Perseus). The kingdom then rejoices in a new prosperity and often the young hero marries the daughter of the old king and replaces him as ruler. Frazer's work and later archaeological findings, such as those by P.V. Glob,[5] indicate that the story had its origin in a rite of the calendar in which the old king, either in person or by surrogate, was sacrificed to the Earth Mother to ensure the return of Spring and fertility.

By the eleventh century (and probably much earlier), the folk-myth elements of the ritual were forgotten, but the plot-line and a number of the mythic *topoi* persisted in innumerable tales embellished by contemporary social forms and manners. For instance, the Chaste Friend/Brother motif, noted by Ó Coileáin, is a variation on the exchange of places between old king and new king; the stag-hunt and quest of the supernatural bride, elements of the Sovereignty theme, noted by I.C. Lovecy,[6] are revised in *Pwyll* to accord with certain medieval customs; and so on. The most important group of tales employing the wasteland motif, as pointed out by Jessie Weston, belongs to the Grail legend, in which the Chalice of the Last Supper merges with the fabulous cornucopia or Cauldron of Plenty in Gaelic and Celtic myth and receives a place in the Arthurian cycle cherished by Anglo-Norman knights. While in the Arthurian version the restoration of the wasteland becomes a metaphor for Christian duty and salvation, in *Pwyll Prince of Dyfed* the motif forms a plot within which the author may demonstrate the various secular virtues of the good ruler: wisdom, prudence, courtesy, concern for the people, respect for the law, and so on. Each of the three segments of the story replicates the wasteland motif, thereby revealing an architectonic rather than organic structure. The medieval trappings—hunting-scenes, courtly feasts, romantic dialogue—disguise the ancient myth, but provide it with contemporaneity.

In the first segment, Pwyll, riding out to hunt, baits his dogs on a stag run by another huntsman, Arawn prince of Annwn, the Celtic "other world." The hunting of magic animals, as Rachel Bromwich notes, is a recurrent episode in the Celtic dynastic tradition,[7] but here the motif is given a distinctly medieval and verisimilar flavour: Pwyll has committed a breach of medieval etiquette in running another man's quarry and now owes the lord a favour, a natural excuse for the two to change places. Yet Pwyll obviously has some special charm or power in him, for Arawn predicts, rightly, that Pwyll will easily defeat a long-time enemy in the other world, Hafgan of Annwn. Pwyll successfully proves his growth in courtesy by remaining chaste with Arawn's queen, by meeting Hafgan at the appointed tryst, and by refusing to slay his opponent as he lies wounded and helpless. The writer thus interweaves contemporary medieval preoccupations with manners and morals into the fabric of the older mythic "exchange" between a mortal and a supernatural being, an element of the calendar sacrifice in which the mortal becomes divine by dying and thereby ensures the return of the new year. As is often the case in medieval romance, the mythic elements, such as Pwyll's transformation, appear as "magic," and are thus "explained" or rationalized—both for the audience and for the author, who is dealing with symbolic elements whose original meaning is by now obscure. Thus Harder is incorrect in claiming that the chief conflict in the *Mabinogi* is "between the magical forces of chaos and the human need for social order and peace,"[8] for magic is in fact the chief means of achieving social order, both within this segment and in the courting of Rhiannon.

During the year of Pwyll's exchange, both kingdoms thrive: Hafgan's land is joined to Arawn's, and Pwyll's people exclaim they have never been so well ruled. While the medieval author is careful not to indicate that the previous rule has been bad, Dyfed has clearly been elevated to a higher state through the exchange. Pwyll's sojourn in the other world is both a demonstration of his worthiness and a means to increased wisdom in his rule: he promises to continue the reasonableness, love, and generosity which Arawn has demonstrated. Annwn, a land of death, becomes a gateway to rebirth both physical and spiritual, and to increased wisdom. Like other heroes who visit the other world, Pwyll's special powers enable him first, to be chosen for the journey, and second, to complete successfully the tasks posed in the other world.[9] His re-emergence to the mortal world and his new title, Lord of Annwn, connect him to the archetypal sacred corn king who, symbolically planted in the earth, rises again as the new king, both representing and effecting the renewal of the earth in Spring.

Harder and Gruffydd, in keeping with their interpretations of the *Mabinogi* as the story of the hero, insist that a continuing hostility must exist between Pwyll and Arawn, since Pryderi is later carried off to the other world, once in the third segment of *Pwyll* and a second time in the *Manawydan*. Harder suggests that Pwyll (presumably in some earlier version) slays Arawn, thereby replacing him, and that Pryderi is a son of the other world later mystically reborn to the mortal world. Gruffydd suggests that Pwyll is in fact the king of Annwn who, having always loved Rhiannon, tricks her mortal husband into changing places. The mortal husband later imprisons Pryderi in Annwn in revenge. But these versions, however valid as mythic archetypes, belie the actual narrative, which states that Pwyll and Arawn grow in friendship, each grateful for the other's good offices. This part of the Branch would be rendered nonsensical by continued hostility between the princes, but if, as I propose, the Branch displaces the myth in order to model courtesy and wisdom, the great strengths of the good ruler, the reconciliation of Pwyll and Arawn provides a satisfactory close to this segment. The focus here is not on Pryderi, who is yet to be conceived, but on the wise rule that promotes a prosperous kingdom.

The second episode, the courtship of Rhiannon, demonstrates again the need for courtesy and wisdom in a ruler. Underlying the plot structure is again the motif of the wasteland restored, for the marriage symbolizes, as is customary, the fertility of the prosperous kingdom. Rhiannon in Celtic mythology is a goddess from the other world, the Earth Mother herself. In this medieval version, her connections to the myth are called forth by the mound where Pwyll waits—traditionally a gateway to the other world—by the magic steed that outpaces all pursuers, by her possession of the unfillable bag (a womb symbol), and by her knowledge of the future and her wisdom in dealing with Gwawl. But the medieval Welsh author completely displaces the elements of Rhiannon's mythic divinity in the aura of magic, exactly as do his near-contemporaries, Marie de France and Chrétien de Troyes, in treating mythic themes. Her marriage to Pwyll at the end of this segment is a displacement of the ritual marriage of the sacred king to the earth goddess. But in this medieval version, the marriage takes second place to the courtship. And the couple's challenge by Gwawl becomes a test and demonstration of wisdom, although he is finally overcome through the magic powers of the goddess. The two parts of this segment, the courtship and the test by Gwawl, each provide a symmetrical parallel to the other episodes.

As in the first segment, Pwyll in courting Rhiannon learns courtesy. After two futile attempts to catch her, he finally addresses her politely: "For his sake whom thou lovest best, stay for me." Rhiannon responds with archaic understatement: "It had been better for the horse hadst thou asked this long since." But she soon reveals a long-standing passion for him. Surrounded by the aura of magic, the encounter none the less displays the author's regard for manners. The two open their hearts to each other, again through courteous speech, and the wedding feast is set for the magical year from that day.

In the second part of this episode, although Rhiannon has been won, Pwyll now faces other obstacles to their marriage: he demonstrates a lack of wisdom in his rash promise to Gwawl. But as is often the case in medieval romance, the woman who is the object of the quest or struggle reveals to the chosen hero the means to her rescue. So Olwen assists Culhwch, and Isolde aids Tristan. We might read into the narrative an earlier, mythic attempt by a usurper, Gwawl, to replace the sacred king before the end of his reign, or conversely, Pwyll may be the usurper who successfully removes the old priest or extends the duration of his own reign, since Gwawl claims Rhiannon was previously promised to him. However, the purposes of the medieval writer override whatever was in the earlier raw material of the story: Rhiannon urges granting the boon to Gwawl, lest dishonour fall on Pwyll, thus instructing the ruler in his duty. A year later, Gwawl at his wedding feast in turn rashly promises a boon to Pwyll, thereby providing a perfectly symmetrical parallel to the earlier scene. When Gwawl, tricked into entering the unfillable bag, the reverse cornucopia, is at last beaten, Pwyll, having learned his lesson, now demands sureties that Gwawl will not seek vengeance; he is ruled fully in this caution by the advice of Rhiannon and her father Hefeydd. Thus the folk motif of The Rash Promise becomes a lesson in prudent governance. The story demonstrates fully the need for caution in dealing with enemies, for seeking and following sage counsel, and for generosity in sharing prosperity in good fortune: no one leaves empty-handed either that feast or the subsequent celebration at Dyfed. The marriage represents peace and plenty and parallels the restored order found at the close of the first segment.

In the final sequence, the fertility of the married couple is tested, as is Pwyll's wisdom for a third time. Fertility, the birth of a son and heir, confirms the "restored" state of the kingdom, but it also remains a duty and practical necessity for the ruler in medieval politics. Pwyll's people "feel heaviness of heart" at seeing the royal marriage barren, a wasteland motif perhaps "caused" mythically by Rhiannon's use of her unfillable bag. Pwyll now wisely postpones the request that he put aside Rhiannon, and in a year she bears a child. Likewise, he refuses again to put her aside when she is unjustly accused of murder, yet he maintains order by allowing her to perform a penance: the claims on him as a private person must bow to the claims of public law. Their son Pryderi's theft by the Síd finds numerous parallels in Irish folk stories. But the author does not connect this theft to the Annwn of the first segment: Annwn is a place of light, music, poetry, and dance; the fearsome claw that Teyrnon fights belongs to the dark and horrifying aspects of the Night-Mare, the Hag. The threat to Pryderi's life is overcome by the good vassal, who, immediately upon realizing the boy's identity, returns him to his parents. Pwyll's wisdom, generosity, and love are thus repaid in kind by his people, as is appropriate in the well-ordered state. The author of *Pwyll* again deploys the magical elements primarily as a strategy for capturing the reader's interest and turning it to the lesson to be conveyed.

Rhiannon's bearing of strangers in penance probably goes back to an ancient rite of ritual prostitution, practised at one time throughout the Mediterranean as a means of ensuring fertility in the kingdom. Her son's refusal to be "borne" would then mean an avoidance of incest, a second, forbidden "bearing." But, for the medieval writer and audience, Pryderi's refusal marks his wisdom and justice at an early age; it confirms his identity as the true heir. The episode concludes satisfactorily with Rhiannon justified, the faithful retainer richly rewarded, the youth named and placed with Pendaran of Dyfed, and the nobles of the land pledged to an alliance with the acknowledged heir. Again, this third segment symmetrically parallels the other two: order and prosperity have been restored through heroic action, the demonstration of prudence and patience by the royal couple, and of strength, loyalty, and truth by their vassal. The narrator now swiftly ties up the ends of the story, taking us rapidly through the rearing of the youth, the uneventful years closing Pwyll and Rhiannon's reign, the peaceful death of the old king, and the rule of Pryderi up to his own marriage, ensuring potentially the continuity of Pwyll's line.

Each segment contains relatively little action of the sort typically found in medieval romances: quests and battles are virtually absent; the love element is but briefly entertained and then quickly submerged in the war of wits between

Pwyll Prince of Dyfed

Gwawl and Rhiannon. But each part demonstrates the growth in wisdom, courtesy, and generosity of the good king, first as youthful prince, then as married ruler, and finally as older father. While the incidents form a chronology, they also create a pattern of repetition: test of courtesy and wisdom, growth in knowledge, and restoration of order manifested in prosperity and gift-giving and the happiness of the subjects. *Pwyll*'s narrative structure depends upon this repeated pattern, rather than simply organic and chronological links, for coherence and unity. It is the type of architectonic pattern, repetition with variation, relished by medieval audiences,[10] and it might be schematized as follows, the uppermost points representing dramatic turns in each section:

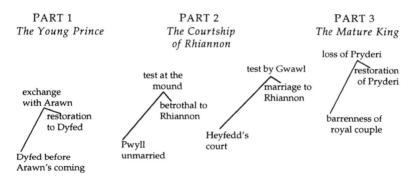

Underlying this pattern is the folk version of the wasteland myth, which usually involves a passage to the other world, the increase of wisdom and virtue, a marriage, and the restored fertility and prosperity of king and people.

The other Branches of the *Mabinogion* also demonstrate elements of the wasteland myth: in *Branwen* we find the cauldron with power to restore life and the years of forgetfulness in an "other world" as the surviving heroes feast merrily. The birds of Rhiannon, souls in the land of the dead, sing sweetly to the warriors. Bendigeidfran himself, wounded in the foot by a spear, as befits a sacred king, is the mythic prototype of the Fisher King in the Grail romances. In *Manawydan*, Dyfed is reduced to a wasteland by Llwyd's avenging of Gwawl, but it is restored by the penance and wit of Manawydan. In *Math,* Pryderi is tricked out of the magic swine of Annwn, symbols of both wisdom and fertility in Celtic myth, and the result is turmoil in the land and the rape of Math's maiden. The brothers Gwydion and Gilfaethwy, who destroy the peace, must perform penance as calendar animals, magically producing a child each of three years. The pursuit of a structuring order among these Branches is the task of another, much longer, work; however, the idea that Pryderi is the link among them must be taken into question. In *Branwen* we find a serious anachronism in that Pendaran Dyfed, the nobleman to whom Pryderi was entrusted for his education, is twice mentioned as a young lad on the expedition to Ireland while Pryderi is a grown warrior. In *Math* Pryderi's magic swine form an important element of the plot, but his death early in the story eliminates him completely from the audience's attention, and only by gross exaggeration could one claim the narrative is about him. In fact, although the Four Branches appear together in both the Red Book and the White Book, only the *Pwyll* and *Manawydan* are closely related in locale, chronology, and theme.

Pwyll Prince of Dyfed, whatever its connection to the other Branches, remains in itself an integral, skilfully woven narrative. If the work is viewed as a book of governance, designed, as I suggest, to both instruct and delight, we have a reasonable explanation of why an eleventh-century cleric of St. David's in South Wales might have created a work based on native pagan myth with almost no trace of Christianity. The myth of the wasteland restored provides a suitable vehicle for a pleasingly symmetrical plot and conveys admirably the lessons of wisdom and courtesy which the medieval author wished to set before a contemporary noble audience. The work need not contain Christian references, for it does not concern the individual soul, but rather the workings of the State. If Charles-Edwards is correct in dating the *Mabinogi* in the late eleventh century, its non-clerical nature may in fact have enhanced its credence for a not fully Christianized court, experiencing prosperity and prestige in a local cultural renaissance.

NOTES

1. Gruffydd, *Math vab Mathonwy;* and Harder, "Cradle of the Gods: Birth of the Hero in Medieval Narrative."
2. Jackson, *The International Popular Tale and Early Welsh Tradition,* and Mac Cana, *Branwen Daughter of Llŷr.* Glyn E. Jones, "Early Prose: *The Mabinogi,*" argues convincingly that the two feasts in *Branwen* represent the same feast from two separate versions, but he suggests that simple expedience determined the inclusion of both feasts: the author thereby "neatly sidestepped the difficulty arising from having two different localities for the feast in his sources" (195). I would suggest instead that the author favoured the symmetricality of repetition.
3. The identity of the author as a monk, Rhygyfarch, and the date of composition as around 1099 were first suggested by Sir Ifor Williams, and these opinions are generally accepted. See R.M. Jones, *Highlights in Welsh Literature: Talks with a Prince* (34). Glyn E. Jones, "Early Prose: *The Mabinogi,*" suggests Sulien, a bishop, or his son, as the author, 193; Charles-Edwards, "The Date of the Four Branches of the *Mabinogi,*" argues most persuasively for a date somewhere between 1050 and 1120.
4. The translation I use throughout is the readily available Everyman edition, *The Mabinogion,* ed. and trans. Gwyn Jones and Thomas Jones (1949; reprinted New York, 1974).
5. Glob, *The Bog People.* Glob's findings indicate the ritual was practised as late as the first century AD by tribes on the Jutland peninsula.
6. See "The Celtic Sovereignty Theme and the Structure of *Peredur,*" where Lovecy discusses Glenys Goetinck's *Peredur: A Study of Welsh Tradition in the Grail Legends.*
7. Bromwich, "Celtic Dynastic Themes and the Breton Lays."
8. Harder, "Cradle of the Gods: Birth of the Hero in Medieval Narrative," 49.
9. Chadwick, "The Borderland of the Spirit World in Early European Literature," notes that the voyage to the underworld is typically a brush with death and mentions that the king or hero usually "returns home enriched by the knowledge he has acquired through his super-natural experiences" (19). She finds it "curious" that the underworld sojourn is commonly one year (20), yet Frazer, Robert Graves, and Joseph Campbell all point to the associations of this journey with the calendar, the cycle of the seasons. As Harder points out in "Cradle of the Gods," both Jung and Campbell connect the theme of rebirth to the motif of the descent to the underworld, 47. All these themes are later displacements of the sacred king's escape from death and immortalization, either by offering a

surrogate to the goddess or outwitting her. Later still, as Neumann suggests, the motif comes to represent the search for wisdom.

10. Carson, in "The Structure and Meaning of *The Dream of Rhonabwy*," argues convincingly for a similar structure of repeated parallel patterns in this difficult narrative: a series of messengers pass between the camps of various fighters who are either intending war or playing at war in the chess game. The *Dream*, she claims, represents instruction in right and wrong wars and seeks to heal the factionalism in Welsh attitudes toward the English: the bards at the close of the narrative praise the truce offered by the Saxon king Osla, and lament the "bitter futility of brother being at odds with brother" (303). Although I would take exception to her dating of the *Dream*, her views on the purpose of the story, the instruction of Welsh nobility, coincide with my own opinions about *Pwyll* and lend some credence to the idea that the *Mabinogi* were considered instructive as well as entertaining literature.

9

The Structure of the Four Branches of the Mabinogi

J.K. Bollard

It has long been recognized that the Four Branches of the *Mabinogi* are among the finest literary creations of the Middle Welsh period, and represent a noteworthy contribution to European literature. Yet, in the search for ultimate origins, many studies of the Four Branches have tended to highlight a number of inconsistencies and to magnify certain weaknesses. The aim of this paper is to present an approach to these tales which will help to reveal the intricately formed pattern of the *Mabinogi*, leaving little room for doubt that it is the coherent and unified work of a single artist.

In a paper on "Form and Meaning in Medieval Romance," Professor Eugène Vinaver suggests that modern readers have difficulty in reading and understanding many medieval romances because we tend to approach them with a set of literary principles which "pre-suppose some permanent criteria of value."[1] The literary study of medieval texts is hampered by the fact that aesthetic criticism is rarely "practised in a disinterested way; it is there to strengthen the argument for or against a particular theory of the origins of early poetry; it is a means of discovering not what the poem is, but how it came to be composed."[2] Vinaver then goes on to suggest that the remedy "lies not in the search for other, more valid, general principles, but in the realization that all such principles are products of taste and sensibility, and that our taste and sensibility have a history—a long, varied and eventful history."[3]

The next step is obviously to determine what are some of the principles which underlie the creation of medieval tales and romance, and using the "Vulgate Cycle" of Arthurian romance as his chief example Vinaver shows that one great difference between medieval and modern literature is that much medieval literature is not composed according to the Aristotelian concept of beginning, middle and end, but rather "the author, or authors, had recourse to a narrative device known to earlier writers, including Ovid, but never before used on so great a scale, namely the device of interweaving two or more separate themes. . . . And since it is always possible, and often necessary, for several themes to be pursued simultaneously, they have to alternate like threads in a woven fabric, one theme interrupting another, and again another, and yet all remaining constantly present in the author's and the reader's mind."[4] Drawing an analogy with developments in twelfth- and thirteenth-century interlaced art forms, Professor Vinaver shows that in the thirteenth century the interlacing method becomes the chief manner of expression in the romance material.

The interlace method is not limited to the thirteenth-century romances, but is more highly developed in that period by writers recording and expanding the great body of romance material, much of which had been given meaning and shape in the Aristotelian sense by Chrétien de Troyes.[5] The Welsh prose romances, *Peredur, Iarlles y Ffynnawn* and *Gereint* are especially fine examples of the interlace structure used in the thirteenth-century, and in *Gereint* the author thrice makes explicit his use of this device with the formulae "Y chwedyl ef hyd yna," "Kyfranc gereint hyd yma," and "Eu chwedyl vynt hyd yna."[6] Yet the interlace method of tale-telling far antedates the twelfth and thirteenth centuries; for example, it reaches back into the Old English period and, as Professor John Leyerle has shown, it is one of the most significant structural elements of *Beowulf*.[7] The method of interlacing described by Vinaver is essentially a linear one; that is, episodes in the romances are alternated to allow the author to describe separate but simultaneous events.[8] Leyerle expands this concept and makes a distinction between two kinds of interlace in *Beowulf*. The first, which he calls "stylistic interlace,"[9] is a poetic device analogous to the *sangiadau* of the "Gogynfeirdd" and the "Cywyddwyr," and therefore is not relevant at present. The second type Leyerle defines is "structural interlace," and he sees a "counterpart in tapestries where positional patterning of threads establishes the shape and design of the fabric, whether the medium is thread in textile or words in a text."[10] This allows for the interlace of simultaneous episodes, and also for the juxtaposition or recollection of parallel or similar events and themes. My purpose in this paper is to examine the interlaced thematic elements of the Four Branches of the *Mabinogi* in the hopes of revealing something about the nature and form of the Four Branches which a study of origins cannot discover, for the study of origins has the disadvantage of fragmenting the text into more or less well-defined parts rather than seeking to find its unifying elements and its inherent meaning.

There are several major themes and a good number of minor and subsidiary themes which are interwoven to form the Four Branches. The material has developed and has been gathered from traditional and perhaps written tales from a number of sources,[11] and while at this point we may assume that many of the details of W.J. Gruffydd's analyses of the origins of the Four Branches are substantially correct, there is lacking in his work the realization that the component tales have been brought together in their present form quite consciously and for sound literary reasons. Often what Gruffydd and others consider to be contamination or unnecessary repetition is actually integral to the techniques not only of this particular work, but of a wide range of medieval literature in general.

The constant concern of the author of the Four Branches is the modes of personal conduct which are necessary for society to survive and progress. Yet he is not dogmatic, nor does he offer any explicit comment of his own upon the actions and statements of the characters. As R.L. Thomson notes in the introduction to his edition of *Pwyll Pendeuic Dyuet*, "The narrative is almost entirely a record of outward happenings open to the observation of all."[12] But this does not mean that there is no inherent meaning or "sentence" to be found in the tales by an audience which is familiar with the ways in which the tales work. As Leyerle has shown in "The Interlace Structure of Beowulf," the interlacing of themes "allows for the intersection of narrative events without regard for their distance in chronological time and shows the interrelated significance of episodes without the need for any explicit comment by the poet. The significance of the connections is left for the audience to work out for itself."[13] Thus it is the juxtaposition of the various episodes which makes the meaning implicit.

The fact that the *Mabinogi* is grouped into four "Branches" is significant in this context, for such a grouping takes the emphasis away from the tendency to regard the tales as a linear *continuum*. The four "Branches" have the effect of presenting the tales to us much the same way that decorative interlace designs form knots which help to create form within the interlace. The four tales are juxtaposed in order that the reader might compare the events of one with those of another, while each forms a complete tale in itself. The author expects his readers to keep in mind various themes, and when an episode arises, a slight reference to similar previous occurrences interlaces them together and we get a broader view of the entire pattern of the tales. There is no incident or detail which remains isolated or superfluous in the Four Branches.

The three major themes which the author develops in the Four Branches are three of the functions of society which bind together, or separate, various groups and elements of that society. These themes I have rather loosely termed Friendships, Marriages and Feuds. Each of these themes is presented in several episodes, and each occurrence of any one of them has some variation or different point of view from which it may be compared with other examples. If the reader can trace these themes throughout the Four Branches and keep in mind the pattern of the whole, he should then come to a greater understanding of the *Mabinogi*.

Friendships are noticeably an important theme in the *Mabinogi,* as we can tell quite early in our reading of the First Branch. When Pwyll is required to make amends for his ignorance and his incivility, Arawn begins by arranging a bond of friendship between them which is stated explicitly: "Mi a wnaf a thi gedymdeithas gadarn" (*PKM* 3).[14] From this point on the relationship between the two is not one of servility or indebtedness on Pwyll's part, but is a bond of mutual trust between them. And Pwyll not only satisfies the obligation he was under to meet with Hafgan at the end of the year, he far surpasses whatever was required of him by turning his back every night to Arawn's wife, when he could have made love to her, presumably without blame, had he so wished. It is this fact which is so greatly stressed after Arawn's return to his kingdom, and it is when he learns of Pwyll's faithfulness that their friendship is really strengthened:

> Ac o hynny allan, dechreu cadarnhau kedymdeithas y ryngthunt, ac anuon o pop un y gilid meirch a milgwn a hebogeu a fob gyfryw dlws, o'r a debygei bob un digrifhau medwl y gilid ohonaw. (*PKM* 8)

Even if this episode stood entirely free of other connections with the tales, the ties of friendship created between Pwyll and Arawn are impressive to the reader, because they are couched in such unrestricted terms.[15] However, there are connections with other parts of the Four Branches which make the episode even more significant. The friendship between Dyfed and Annwn is explicitly brought to mind in the Fourth Branch (*PKM* 68).[16] Not only does the reference there explain the origin of the swine from Annwn, it also brings to mind the reasons for the gifts being sent—the bond of friendship. The importance of this fact is that the episode in *Math* hinges on the friendship between Math and Pryderi. The connection between these two is brought out by the very clever interlacing of themes throughout the Fourth Branch. The opening sentences set the stage for the first half of the tale:

> Math uab Mathonwy oed arglwyd ar Wyned, a Pryderi uab Pwyll oed arglwyd ar un cantref ar ugeint yn y Deheu. (*PKM* 67)

From this formulaic beginning, which is a variant of the more usual identification of one character only, we know that the tale is going to deal with both Math and Pryderi. The author then goes on to develop another aspect of his tale—the *cyneddfau* of Math and the desire of Gilfaethwy for Goewin which of course leads to the stealing of the swine through the trickery and the magic of Gwydion. In this episode the generosity and good nature of Pryderi are portrayed alongside the deviousness and cunning of Gwydion, much the same as the contrasting characters of Pwyll and Gwawl were developed in the First Branch. The culmination of the episode is the fight between the two where Pryderi is defeated: "ac o nerth grym ac angerd, a hut a lledrith, Guydyon a oruu, a Phryderi a las" (*PKM* 73). The sense of loss felt by the men of the South is told with strong echoes of older heroic poetry:[17]

> Gwyr y Deheu a gerdassant ac argan truan ganthunt parth ac eu gwlat, ac nit oed ryued; eu harglwyd a gollyssynt, a llawer oc eu goreuguyr, ac eu meirch, ac eu haruen can mwyaf. (*PKM* 73)

But the full sense of the tragedy is not expressed until after the return of Math to Caer Dathyl and the discovery of the rape of Goewin. When Math says to Gwydion and Gilfaethwy upon their return, "Bei uy ewyllwys ny chollwn o wyr ac arueu a golleis. Vyg kywilyd ny ellwch chwi y dalu y mi, heb angheu Pryderi" (*PKM* 74), only then does the import of the episode strike home—that Math, through the designs of his sister's sons, has caused the death of a friend, and the tragedy here is as heavy as that of the similar events of the Icelandic saga of Njal.[18]

This episode in *Math* is thus closely related to the first part of *Pwyll,* for the bond of friendship with Annwn which Pryderi inherited from his father finally contributes significantly to the events surrounding his death. Thematically, the juxtaposition of the two episodes, which is brought about by the references to the swine from Annwn, expands the theme of friendship and feud by placing the two examples simultaneously in the reader's mind and thus inviting comparison between them. By carrying out this comparison we see that there is an implicit statement being made on the nature of friendship—that, unwittingly and with a sort of inevitability, the good intentions and bonds of friendship can lead to tragedy. In this instance the tragedy is two-fold. First, we see

Structure of the Four Branches of the Mabinogi

that the gifts from Annwn contribute to the death of Pryderi. The second tragic element of Pryderi's death which is important thematically to the structure of the Four Branches and which has close parallels elsewhere in the *Mabinogi,* is the breaking of the friendship between Math and Pryderi, and the resulting war. There seems to be but one explanation for the mustering of the men of Gwynedd. The situation is this: we have no reason to believe there was any antagonism between Math and Pryderi before the stealing of the swine by Gwydion. Math's sense of loss at the death of Pryderi, on the other hand, suggests a strong bond of friendship. Why then is he so quickly driven to war? The answer is found near the beginning of the Fourth Branch:

> Ac ny allei gylchu y wlat, namyn Giluathwy uab Don, [a Gwydyon] uab Don, y nyeint ueibon y chwaer, a'r teulu gyt ac wy [a aei] y gylchu y wlat drostaw. (*PKM* 67)

Whether we accept Sir Ifor Williams's emendation of the White Book reading as above, or rely on the reference several lines down to Gwydion as Gilfaethwy's brother, we still find and should keep in mind that Gwydion is Math's nephew, his sister's son, the closest tie between male relations in much of medieval literature. And this blood tie is stronger than the tie of friendship, so that when Gwydion is pursued by Pryderi, Math is required to muster the men of Gwynedd to his aid.

The opening episodes of *Branwen* are very similar in this respect. Efnisien, the quarrelsome half-brother, son to the same mother as Bendigeidfran, feels insulted and revenges himself by insulting Matholwch in turn. It is the blood relationship between Bendigeidfran and Efnisien which leads to the final tragedy of *Branwen,* because Bendigeidfran cannot take personal revenge on Efnisien, but can only offer the *sarhad* price and the restoration of his horses to Matholwch:

> "a menegwch ydaw pa ryw wr a wnaeth hynny, a phan yw o'm anuod inheu y gwnaethpwyt hynny; ac y may brawt un uam a mi a wnaeth hynny, ac nat hawd genhyf i na'e lad na'e diuetha; a doet y ymwelet a mi," heb ef, "a mi a wnaf y dangneued ar y llun y mynho e hun." (*PKM* 33)

Bendigeidfran attempts to prevent the inevitable feud from breaking out and tries to maintain his newly strengthened friendship with Matholwch by offering more payment for the *sarhad* to Matholwch than is legally required for the *sarhad* of a king. But he cannot easily punish Efnisien, and thus the men of Ireland (not insignificantly, Matholwch's foster-brothers) find excuse to renew the feud.

Interwoven into the second part of the First Branch is the account of the rearing of Pryderi by Teyrnon Twryf Liant, and his return to his rightful father, Pwyll. There is no need to dissect this section of the tale to try to prove that Teyrnon was originally someone else and that his inclusion is "again an instance of the cyvarwydd's invention in ironing out a contradiction."[19] The matter of Rhiannon's penance is dropped while the author develops and weaves the new thread into the story. The tale develops quite rapidly until the boy's fourth year, when Teyrnon hears tidings of the penance of Rhiannon and consequently recognises the boy as the son of Pwyll. In the events which follow, the author lays great stress on the friendship of Teyrnon and Pwyll, and also on the possibility of a future friendship with Pryderi,[20] and this alone is sufficient motivation for the episode. Thematically this episode can be viewed as an exemplum to which some of the other feuds and friendships may be compared. We have here an instance of the proper relation between friends which is raised a step above the level of obligation. By his unselfish actions Teyrnon strengthens his ties with Pwyll and prevents the possibility of any feud or friction which may have arisen had he kept the boy and been discovered.

The tale of *Manawydan* is the most developed and extended example of the theme of friendship in the Four Branches. The friendship between Manawydan and Pryderi is the central element of the entire tale, and all the action of the tale is concerned with the creation and examination of this close connection between them. To say that Pryderi is only of minor importance as a character in the Third Branch[21] is to ignore the author's constant comparison of Manawydan and Pryderi in their struggle to survive the enchantment of Dyfed and the threats of the craftsmen of England. Even when Pryderi and Rhiannon are spirited away in the magic *caer*, Manawydan's actions are directed towards keeping faith with Pryderi and towards the ultimate goal of restoring Pryderi and Rhiannon and all the population of Dyfed.

The Third Branch opens with the formation of the strong bonds of friendship between Manawydan and Pryderi. This is set in a larger sociological, almost feudal, setting with the references to Caswallawn and the triad of the *Tri Lleddf Unben*. Thematically the beginning of the Third Branch is important within the context of the Four Branches, for we see that Pryderi, by offering the seven cantrefs of Dyfed to Manawydan, is trying to prevent the outbreak of the potential feud between Manawydan and Caswallawn which would only lead to more destruction and grief. Pryderi's first suggestion is that Manawydan forget his complaint and live as the king's cousin, presumably a very good position:

> "Arglwyd," heb y Pryderi, "na uit kyn drymhet genhyt a hynny. Dy geuynderw yssyd urenhin yn Ynys y Kedyrn; a chyn gwnel gameu it," heb ef, "ny buost hawlwr tir a dayar eiryoet. Trydyd lledyf unben wyt." (*PKM* 49)

By not mentioning Caswallawn's name in this speech, the author insures that the reader must think back to the events given near the end of the Second Branch to identify *y cefnderw* and thus remember the full story of the trickery and treachery of Caswallawn and the tragic death of Cradawc. The reference there to the *Tri dyn a dorres ei galon o aniuyget* in turn recalls the full tragedy of Branwen which was the result of another feud which should not have been reopened. In *Manawydan*, rather than allow a similar development to take place, Pryderi offers the best part of his domain to Manawydan, as well as his own very exceptional and not displeasing mother as a wife. Here the friendship is formed between Manawydan and Pryderi and it is expressed in no less explicit terms than those we have seen at the formation of the friendship between Pwyll and Arawn in the First Branch:

> "A chyn bo enwedigaeth y kyuoeth y mi, bit y mwynant y ti a Riannon. A phei mynhut gyuoeth eiryoet, aduyd y caffut ti [waeth] hwnnw." "Na uynhaf, unben," heb ef, "Duw a dalo it dy

> gydymdeithas." "E gedymdeithas oreu a allwyf i,
> yti y byd, os mynny." "Mynnaf, eneit," heb ef.
> "Duw a dalo it. A mi a af gyt a thi y edrych
> Riannon, ac y edrych y kyuoeth." "Iawn a wney,"
> heb ynteu. (*PKM* 49)

And a little later:

> "Arglwydes," heb ef Pryderi, "mi a'th roessum yn
> wreic y Uanawydan uab Llyr." "A minheu a uydaf
> wrth hynny yn llawen," heb y Riannon. "Llawen
> yw genhyf inheu," heb y Manawydan, "a Duw a
> dalo y'r gwr yssyd yn rodi i minheu y
> gedymdeithas mor difleis a hynny." (*PKM* 50)

Note that here, as in the First Branch, stress is being laid on steadfastness as a particularly notable element of friendship.[22]

Once the friendship has been formed Pryderi's chief concern is to go to tender his homage to Caswallawn, even before the marriage feast of Rhiannon and Manawydan has ended, in order to do all he can to keep the peace. He has taken Manawydan under his own care, and by making a formal acknowledgement of homage to Caswallawn he guarantees that all those in his domain will remain peaceful, and this naturally includes Manawydan. After these "political" matters are resolved the scene shifts back to Dyfed and to the same rather unpredictable world which was the scene of most of the First Branch. Indeed, the feast in the Third Branch begins at Arberth and is couched in the same formulae as in *Pwyll*:

> A dechreu gwled a orugant yn Arberth, canys prif
> lys oed, ac o honei y dechreuit pob anryded. A
> guedy y bwyta kyntaf y nos honno... kyuodi allan
> o orugant, a chyrchu Gorssed Arberth a wnaethant
> yll pedwar, ac yniuer gyt ac wynt. (*PKM* 51)

This statement is obviously meant to remind the audience of the two previous occurrences of remarkably similar phraseology, before the hunt at Glyn Cuch and at the coming of Rhiannon.[23] These formulae prepare the audience for entering a particular kind of world, a world where most likely "y mae yno ryw ystyr hut" (*PKM* 10). Nor are they disappointed, for the following episodes are filled with enchantments even greater than before, and we find near the end of the tale that the very word *hut* takes on great significance in the dialogue between Manawydan and Llwyd fab Cil Coed.

The literary function of this kind of "world," which is subject to laws other than the natural ones we experience, is to provide a setting in which the characters of a tale may be seen in situations where their actions may be judged by the reader according to idealized concepts of Good and Evil. For though it is a world of enchantment, the principal characters are only required to act according to very human rules. If the characters succeed in living up to the ideals, the effects of the magic can be overcome, reversed, escaped, or turned to the good. This is seen time and time again throughout the whole body of romance literature: in *Sir Gawain and the Green Knight,* Gawain is tested under very strange circumstances (reminiscent of *Pwyll*), yet it is his actions within the framework of the human ideals of chastity, honesty, and bravery by which he is judged. The same is true in *Beowulf,* in *Le Roman de Tristan,* throughout the "Matter of Britain" and the Arthurian Cycle, and no less in the Four Branches of the *Mabinogi.* In *Manawydan* the situation is established by supernatural means whereby we can see how both Manawydan and Pryderi progress in their friendship. After two years of living in the Wasteland, Pryderi, Manawydan, Cigfa, and Rhiannon go to Lloegr to make a living, and we have roughly the same situation repeated three times; the craftsmen in each of the three towns grow angry because of their loss of profits and plot to kill the craftsmen—"y tayogeu lladron"[24] (*PKM* 54). This time, however, it is the prudence of Manawydan which prevents disaster and it is he who is concerned with the possible wider implications of killing the craftsmen:

> "Nac ef," heb ynteu, "Casswallawn a glywei hynny, a'e wyr, a rewin uydem. Kyrchu tref arall a wnawn." (*PKM* 54)

From the very beginning of the enchantment Manawydan takes control of the situation, and he supplies the knowledge, counsel, and craftsmanship by which they are able to survive.

The episode recounting the imprisonment of Pryderi and Rhiannon is a very crucial one in terms of the relationship between Pryderi and Manawydan. Pryderi may drop out of the action, but he should never be dropped from the reader's mind. The author's literary skill and dramatic sense are more evident in this last half of *Manawydan* than perhaps anywhere else in the Four Branches. To say with Professor Jackson that "Manawydan is the least interesting and successful of them all" is to miss a great deal of the drama and suspense of the tale.[25] At the magic *caer* Pryderi does not follow Manawydan's counsel as he had done in England, but enters the *caer* and is mysteriously trapped. Manawydan, on the other hand, does not seem to do a thing:

> A'e aros ynteu a wnaeth Manawydan hyt parth a diwed y dyd. A phrynhawn byrr, guedy bot yn diheu gantaw ef na chaei chwedleu y wrth Pryderi nac y wrth y cwn, dyuot a oruc parth a'r llys. (*PKM* 56)

When he returns to the court Rhiannon criticizes him for his lack of action and makes a very definite statement about the friendship he has shown to Pryderi:

> "Dioer," heb y Riannon, "ys drwc a gedymdeith uuosti, ac ys da a gedymdeith a golleisti." (*PKM* 56)

This is a very strong and unequivocal criticism, and it makes the reader reflect back upon Manawydan's actions to see if there could be an alternative by which he could save Pryderi and thus remain a good friend, rather than just waiting through the afternoon. In effect Rhiannon is saying that he should have gone in after Pryderi to try to save him, or, ideally, to die trying. Rhiannon attempts this herself and is trapped with Pryderi. At this point in the tale the reader still tends to sympathize with her criticism of Manawydan, for as far as we can tell he has done very little to rescue his friend.

The whole matter of the imprisonment of Pryderi is dropped at this point and the tale continues with the relationship between Manawydan and Cigfa. Manawydan makes a very strong affirmation of his friendship to Pryderi in order to reassure Cigfa:

> Y rof a Duw, bei et uwni yn dechreu uy ieuengtit, mi a gadwn gywirdeb wrth Pryderi, ac yrot titheu mi a'y cadwn. (*PKM* 57)[26]

The friendship between Pryderi and Manawydan, then, is still the prime theme of the tale, and the imprisonment of Pryderi gives us an opportunity to see how Manawydan reacts.

The episode of the Mice in the Corn provides the setting in which Manawydan very skilfully resolves the entire situation and proves his good faith and friendship. W.J. Gruffydd argues that the episode of the Mice in the Corn "could be lifted bodily out of Manawydan and presented as an independent short story."[27] This is a debatable point, but in any case it does not help us to understand why the episode *was* included in the tale and how it relates to the *Mabinogi* as a whole. The episode is not "merely utilised as the machinery for detecting the cause and cure of the traditional *Hud ar Ddyved*."[28] Within the context of the tale we must accept the sequence of events as they are narrated, and in this particular case the episode tells us much about the nature of Manawydan and it also links the tale thematically to the First Branch.

There is a strong link also between the section where Manawydan is hanging the mouse and the criticism which Rhiannon had for Manawydan after the disappearance of Pryderi. It seems that in both cases Manawydan is not acting according to the code by which a nobleman should act. Cigfa criticizes Manawydan for much the same reason when he decides to become a shoemaker (*PKM* 58) and when he is preparing to hang the mouse:

> "Arglwyd," heb hi, "diryued oed hynny. Ac eisswys anwymp yw guelet gwr kyuurd, kymoned, a thidi, yn crogi y ryw bryf hwnnw. A phei gwnelut iawn, nyt ymyrrut yn y pryf, namyn y ellwng e ymdeith." (*PKM* 61)

The reader too seriously begins to question Manawydan's course of action, if not his sanity, during this episode, especially as the repetition of similar scenes with the clerk, the priest, and the bishop makes the act seem even more petty and ridiculous. This, of course, is the author's intent and the dramatic tension increases throughout the episode.

At the climax of the episode, however, when everything is made clear the reader then has to re-evaluate Manawydan's actions. To do so it is necessary to go all the way back to the disappearance of Pryderi, and Rhiannon's criticism of Manawydan. In retrospect, now that we have seen Manawydan's subtlety and skill, we realize that he was being not merely prudent in resisting the temptation to run into the *caer* to rescue Pryderi, but that being acquainted with the nature of magic himself, he could see that any "heroic" or instinctive action, like that of Rhiannon, would not provide a solution. This would agree with the traditional character of Manawydan as echoed in the *Black Book of Carmarthen*, "Manawidan ab llyr. oet duis y cusil. Neustuc manauid eis tull o trywruid."[29] At the outcome we can see that Manawydan was much more aware of possible turns of events than were the other characters. When the occasion presents itself he seizes the opportunity quite masterfully, and proves himself to be neither a poor friend nor a pedantic vengeful man, but shows that he is largely concerned with the maintenance of peace and order.

The appearance of Llwyd fab Cil Coed in this final episode shows that the thematic unity of *Manawydan*, which is centred around the friendship of Pryderi and Manawydan, is quite closely interlaced with the other three Branches not only through the friendship theme and the marriage theme, but also through the predominant theme of feuds. All of these, of course, are very closely related and dependent upon each other, marriages and friendships being means of preventing feuds or, as in the case of Llwyd fab Cil Coed, means of continuing them. In *Manawydan* especially we can see how the author balances these themes and very carefully controls the dramatic elements of the tale, finally resolving all the loose ends at the last possible moment, making clear the significance of what had seemed irrelevant.

Structure of the Four Branches of the Mabinogi

The role of the women in the Four Branches of the *Mabinogi* has so far not been adequately defined or examined, though no one would deny that women play a significant part in the tales. This paper is not intended to answer completely the need for an examination of this aspect of the *Mabinogi*, but it is hoped that it will indicate the importance of the women in the tales, and that it will relate this theme to the other major themes which we are reviewing. The interdependence of themes and episodes makes it difficult to discuss any one theme in isolation from the others, as can be seen in two fairly obvious examples. In *Manawydan*, the marriage between Rhiannon and Manawydan greatly strengthens the bond of friendship between Manawydan and Pryderi and thus helps in the resolution of a feud from the First Branch, and in the tale of *Branwen* the marriage between Matholwch and Branwen is the fulcrum of the disastrous feud which follows.

It is quite striking that a marriage is related at some length in each of the Four Branches. This fact alone invites comparison between them, and such a comparison proves fruitful without stretching the facts beyond the framework of the extant redaction of the texts. Much of the First Branch is an account of the relationship between Pwyll and Rhiannon. The events leading up to their marriage, particularly the two feasts at the court of Hefeydd Hen, are thematically related to the *Mabinogi* as a whole in that ultimately they provide the motivation for much of the Third Branch: the complaint of Gwawl fab Clud against Pwyll. The theme of the Calumniated Wife links parts of the First and Second Branches. Many of the details and references in the latter portions of *Pwyll* are obscure, and this has led to several attempts to reconstruct the "original" form of the tale in such a way that it should be more comprehensible. However, most important in the tale are the events and motivations which the author stresses in his use of the material. That certain details may have been obscure to him and remain so to this day is secondary. Whether he understands certain of the inherited elements in his material or not, the author of the Four Branches is quite sure of his own particuiar handling of the material. For instance, his chief concern when the newborn boy is stolen is the relationship between Rhiannon and the women who had been set to watch and who conspire against her. It is, of course, only natural in any of the variations of the Calumniated Wife theme that the wife should be an important figure and that the sympathies of both the author and his audience should lie with her. Chaucer, in his version of the classic example of this theme—the tale of Constance—repeatedly invokes his (or at least, the Man of Law's) sorrow and sympathy for Dame Custance:

> O queenes, lyvynge in prosperitee,
> Duchesses, and ye ladyes everichone,
> Haveth som routhe on hire adversitee![30]

But for all his pleadings, Chaucer's main character is never as real or as touching as is Rhiannon in the short space which the author devotes to this episode. In his masterly handling of the dialogue the author brings Rhiannon to life with remarkable clarity when the women confront her with the loss of her son:

> "Neur diffetheeist du hun dy uab, ac na hawl ef ynni." "A druein," heb y Riannon, "yr yr Arglwyd Duw a wyr pob peth, na yrrwch geu arnaf. Duw, a wyr pob peth, a wyr bot yn eu hynny arnaf i. Ac os ouyn yssyd arnawchi, ym kyffes y Duw, mi a'ch differaf." "Dioer," heb wy, "ny adwn ni drwc arnam ny hunein yr dyn yn y byt." "A druein," heb hitheu, "ny chewch un drwc yr dywedut y wirioned." Yr a dywettei hi yn dec ac yn druan, ny chaffei namyn yr un atteb gan y gwraged. (*PKM* 20–21)

The author has carefully structured this passage to impress his audience with the characterization and moral implications in the tale and the sympathy which he arouses even in the modern reader is climaxed a few lines further:

> Hitheu Riannon a dyuynnwys attei athrawon a doethon. A gwedy bot yn degach genthi kymryt y phenyt nog ymdaeru a'r gwraged, y phenyt a gymerth. (*PKM* 21)

The confusion which many critics have seen in episodes such as this is primarily the result of obscurity of some details. In this case the presence of the bitch has not been accounted for by the author. It is interesting and in many ways a rewarding exercise to search out the origins and if possible the meanings, of such details, but we must not allow that search to eclipse what the author presents as the more relevant substance of the work.

The relationship between Pwyll and Rhiannon is subtly portrayed in the final portion of the tale. The first indication of this we might note is Pwyll's reluctance to take another wife when counselled to do so by the men of Dyfed both before the birth of the boy and again after the accusation against Rhiannon. Pwyll's reply to the latter incident is interesting in the light of earlier portions of the tale, for here too we can see the emphasis on the strict interpretation of words. Pwyll's reply is carefully guarded and he insists upon a literal interpretation of the first request the men made to him:

> Sef attep a rodes Pwyll, "Nyt oed achaws ganthunt wy y erchi y mi yscar a'm gwreic namyn na bydei plant idi. Plant a wnn i y uot idi hi. Ac nyt yscaraf a hi. O gwnaeth hitheu gam, kymeret y phenyt amdanaw." (*PKM* 21)

In other words, in this episode Pwyll is not to be led into a rash promise such as he had made earlier to Gwawl and which required a great deal of effort to reverse. Nor does Pwyll seem to be totally convinced that Rhiannon is guilty of the crime for which she has been accused, for his statement that she must do penance is expressed in much the same way as a conditional legal formula: "O gwnaeth hitheu gam . . ." We learn later, when Teyrnon comes to Arberth, that not only has Pwyll chosen to keep Rhiannon with him, but that, except for the penance which she still undergoes, she has kept her position of honour in the court at Pwyll's side, for at his arrival Teyrnon is given a place of honour between them: "Sef ual yd eistedyssont, Teirnon y rwg Pwyll a Rhiannon" (*PKM* 25).[31]

A comparison between this episode and the calumniation of Branwen reveals both significant differences and significant similarities. As in the First Branch, it is the men of the court who attempt to separate the king from his wife, though in this case they succeed. They do not approach him respectfully to make a request as did the men of Dyfed, however. Rather they taunt Matholwch until he is forced to take action:

> A hynny yn yr eil ulwydyn, llyma ymodwrd yn Iwerdon am y guaradwyd a gawssei Matholwch yg Kymry, a'r somm a wnathoedit idaw am y ueirch. A hynny y urodyr maeth, a'r gwyr nessaf gantaw, yn lliwaw idaw hynny, a heb gelu. A nachaf y dygyuor yn Iwerdon hyt nat oed lonyd idaw ony chaei dial y sarahet. (*PKM* 37)

There is in this passage none of the careful interpretation of words which we have seen in *Pwyll* and which recurs throughout the *Mabinogi*. The language used here gives us a picture of vindictiveness, coercion and almost motiveless spite which appears two years after the event, rather than of the formal deliberation found in the First Branch. It is perhaps significant that immediately preceding this episode we have been told of another case where Matholwch was similarly forced to take action through the instigation of the men of Iwerddon, after Llassar Llaes Gyfnewid and his wife have begun causing trouble in the land:

> O hynny allan y dygyuores uyg kyuoeth am ym pen, y erchi im ymuadeu ac wynt, a rodi dewis im, ae uyg kyuoeth, ae wynt. (*PKM* 36)

The punishment of Branwen is more extreme than that of Rhiannon, for she suffers the physical punishment of a blow daily as well as the humiliation of being driven from the king's chamber. The words *bonclust* (*PKM* 37) and *paluawt* (*PKM* 48) used to describe the blow to Branwen seem to indicate that this was meant as a humiliation to her rather than as a formal act of revenge for the *sarhad* originally done to Matholwch. In such a case we might expect a more formal word such as *dyrnawt*, which is used in *Llyfr Iorwerth* in the definition of *sarhad* to a queen: "eyl ev o tarav dyrnavt arney."[32] The men of Iwerddon apparently realize that the methods they have chosen to punish Branwen are extreme, for they find it necessary to set a ban on all travel to Wales lest Bendigeidfran hear of it. Thus the calumniation of Branwen differs considerably from that of Rhiannon in that not only is she unjustly punished, her tormentors as well are aware of her innocence. Pwyll, on the other hand, does not learn the truth of the matter for several years and thus must accept, however unwillingly, the testimony of the six women against that of Rhiannon alone. The point might be made, then, that Pwyll is acting honourably insofar as he is able, in contrast to Matholwch and his men who are aware of the wrongs they are committing, yet continue to dwell on an insult for which the price has been paid.

The author also considers aspects of the relationship between men and women beyond the functions of marriage within a social context. For instance, Pryderi offered Rhiannon as a wife for Manawydan in order to help prevent the outbreak of a feud between Manawydan and Caswallawn. The marriage is first viewed as a social expedient, and once it has been accomplished Manawydan has been given an honourable place in the society and thus he does not pursue his complaints against his cousin. As soon as this is established the author is free to develop the personal aspects of the friendly and marital relationships between the four characters within the wider framework of the tale. These relationships are put to the test and discussed explicitly in the interchanges between Manawydan and Rhiannon and between Manawydan and Cigfa.

In strong contrast to the faithfulness shown by Pwyll in the First Branch, first towards Arawn and his wife and later towards Rhiannon, his own wife, and the faithfulness shown by Manawydan towards Pryderi and Cigfa, there are three incidents in *Math* in which the author shows the negative aspects of such cases where the ties of friendship, faithfulness and social obligation are broken. Nor are these incidents ancillary to the tale, but rather they provide the motivations of the characters. Significantly, they all involve the women of the Fourth Branch: the desire of Gilfaethwy for Goewin brings about the war between Math and Pryderi; the shame of Aranrhod motivates the tale of Lleu's youth; and the unfaithfulness of his wife leads to the suffering of Lleu and finally to the transformation of Blodeuwedd and the death of Gronw Bebyr. Viewing the Fourth Branch with these three events as focal points largely eliminates the "four serious breaks in the story" upon which W.J. Gruffydd bases his reconstruction of the tale.[33]

It cannot reasonably be maintained that "Math is not even a secondary character like Gwydion, or a tertiary character like Pryderi or Gronw Pevr."[34] At the very least the action of the tale centres around Math and his court. It is his need for a virgin footholder which leads to the war with Pryderi and to the birth and adventures of Dylan Eil Ton and Lleu Llaw Gyffes, i.e., the greater part of the Fourth Branch. It is Math who punishes Gilfaethwy and Gwydion, who makes compensation to Goewin, who, with Gwydion, creates Blodeuwedd, and finally to whom Lleu comes to ask permission to seek redress from Gronw Bebyr. Far from being a secondary character, Math presides over the entire Fourth Branch.

Gruffydd's second objection is that while the king's footholder is raped, it is the king's niece, Aranrhod, who gives birth to a son. However, the switch in emphasis from Goewin to Aranrhod is sufficiently motivated in the text, and we have no evidence that Gilfaethwy (or anyone else, for that matter) was the father of Dylan and Lleu, nor have we any evidence that Aranrhod should be Math's footholder. Indeed, had she been the footholder and been raped there would be no need for the extreme shame which she feels. It is this shame which supplies an answer to Gruffydd's contention that no explanation is given for denying the boy a name, arms, or a wife. When Gwydion explains that the boy is her son Aranrhod replies,

> Oy a wr, ba doi arnat ti, uyg kywilydaw i, a dilyt uyg kywilyd, a'y gadw yn gyhyt a hynn? (*PKM* 78)[35]

The swearing of the destinies on him is an attempt by Aranrhod to deny existence to the boy. If he never gets a name he cannot exist as an individual in society and therefore he could not be a constant reminder of her shame.

Failing this she tries to prevent him from getting arms and thereby becoming a man, recognized by the court and by society in general. When this also fails she tries to keep him from marrying, to prevent him from possibly perpetuating the memory of her shame even in future generations. Gwydion recognizes that Aranrhod's chief concern is her shame, and he makes this explicit when he first confronts her:

> "Dygaf y Duw uyg kyffes," heb ef, "direit wreic wyt, a'r mab a geiff enw, kyt boet drwc genhyt ti. A thitheu," heb ef, "yr hwnn yd wyt ti, ac auar arnat am na'th elwir y uorwyn, ni'th elwir bellach byth yn uorwyn." (*PKM* 79)

With regard to Gruffydd's objection that the slaying of the paramour of Blodeuwedd is not in the fundamental framework of the tale, we can only put forward an opposite opinion. After Lleu is restored to his own form and nursed back to health he asks permission from Math to seek redress from Gronw Bebyr (*PKM* 90). Within the thematic context of the tale it is very relevant that Lleu should finish the feud which was begun with the betrayal of his wife and the lover's attempt to kill him. It is only fitting that Gronw should suffer the fate he had intended for Lleu, and the author thus completes the tale with the positions of the protagonists reversed; Lleu kills Gronw Bebyr in the same manner in which Gronw had tried to kill him.

This brings us to a discussion of the feud theme in the Four Branches, in many ways the most central theme of the *Mabinogi*, to which the other themes are related. In an article on "The Survival of the Bloodfeud in Medieval Wales," R.R. Davies has shown that the problem of feuds in Wales remained for a good many years even after the Edwardian conquest,[36] and thus we may safely assume that it was an important issue throughout the period in which the Four Branches reached their final form and were copied into the manuscripts which survive today. We must remember, however, that the Four Branches represent a literary treatment of the theme, and therefore the author is not bound to the strict legal definitions of the terms which he uses, though he shows himself to be somewhat conversant with legal usage and practice. The author's main concern (second, of course, to that of telling a good tale) is with the relationships between people in general, and the feuds and dissensions within the tales form only one facet of the total picture.

The opening episode of *Pwyll* contains the record of how Pwyll came to be known as Pwyll Pen Annwfn. This tale is set within the context of the insult or wrong (*cam, PKM* 2) which Pwyll did to Arawn and which provides the opening motivation for the tale. Pwyll's subsequent exemplary behaviour gives us an example of how one ought to act in such a situation, preventing the incident from leading into war or feud. The means of repaying his debt to Arawn is also the settling of a feud, that between Arawn and Hafgan, and stress is laid on the fact that Pwyll succeeded in uniting the two kingdoms:

> Ac o achaws i drigiant ef y ulwydyn honno yn Annwuyn, a gwledychu o honaw yno mor lwydannus, a dwyn y dwy dyrnas yn un drwy y dewred ef a'y uilwraeth, y diffygwys y enw ef ar Pwyll, Pendeuic Dyuet, ac y gelwit Pwyll Penn Annwuyn o hynny allan. (*PKM* 8)

With regard to the actual battle between Pwyll and Hafgan, there are close connections with a similar event in *Math*, the contest between Pryderi and Gwydion. In an article on the Fourth Branch Saunders Lewis states,

> Trown at hanes lladd Pryderi. Ef ei hun sy'n cynnig ornest rhyngddo a Gwydion er dwyn y rhyfel i ben ac arbed colledion trymach i'r ddau lu. Ni wn am ddigwydd tebyg yn hanes y ddeuddegfed ganrif.[37]

To find parallels to this episode Lewis turns to William of Malmesbury and to the *Historia* of Geoffrey Monmouth, but he neglects a very similar incident within the *Mabinogi* itself. In the First Branch a meeting is arranged for the two kings to settle the matter in single combat, and a horseman at the ford makes this perfectly clear before the battle begins:

> "A wyrda," heb ef, "ymwerendewch yn da. Y rwng y deu wrenhin y mae yr oet hwnn, a hynny y rwng

y deu gorff wylldeu ... A ssegur y digaun pawb o honawch uot, eithyr gadu y ryngthunt wylldeu." (*PKM* 5)[38]

The same general terms are expressed by two opponents in *Math* when Pryderi suggests that the matter be settled by Gwydion and himself:

"Dioer," heb y kennadeu, "teg, med Pryderi, oed y'r gwr a wnaeth hynn idaw ef o gam, dodi y gorf yn erbyn y eidaw ynteu, a gadu y deu lu yn segur." "Dygaf y Duw uyg kyffes," [heb y Guydyon], "nat archaf i y wyr Gwyned ymlad drossof i, a minheu uy hyn yn cael ymlad a Phryderi. Mi a dodaf uyg korf yn erbyn y eidaw yn llawen." (*PKM* 73)

In each case two elements are stressed, that the contest is "rwng y deu gorff wylldeu" and that the respective armies remain "yn segur." The similarity between these two episodes connects them in the reader's mind and having made this connection he may go on to contrast them, so that the implications of the two episodes becomes more explicit. Pwyll, on the one hand, was placed in the position of fighting Hafgan in order to repay the wrong done to Arawn, and to that extent he was obliged to perform the task to the best of his ability. Gwydion, on the other hand, is greatly at fault, as Math points out to him (*PKM* 74), for causing the trouble in the first place which resulted in the loss of many men. But he is even more to blame for the death of Pryderi, for he won the fight not only "o nerth grym ac angerd," but through "hut a lledrith" as well (*PKM* 73).[39] Throughout the entire first portion of this tale Gwydion's actions and motivations are dishonourable and contrary to the code of conduct which is developed within the Four Branches. We have already seen that the First and Fourth Branches are linked through the development of the theme of friendship and it is therefore all the more striking that the feuds which begin and end these episodes should be so closely related.

The First and Third Branches are linked by a feud carried over from one generation to the next, and there are significant comparative and contrastive elements to the feud theme in these tales. The enigmatic and rather humorous episode in which Manawydan prepares to hang the mouse for stealing suddenly becomes clear with the identification of Llwyd:

> Miui yw Llwyt uab Kil Coet, a mi a dodeis yr hut ar seith cantref Dyuet, ac y dial Guawl uab Clut, o gedymdeithas ac ef y dodeis i yr hut; ac ar Pryderi y dieleis i guare broch yghot a Guawl uab Clut, pan y gwnaeth Pwyll Penn Annwn; a hynny yn Llys Eueyd Hen y gwnaeth o aghynghor. (*PKM* 64)

This is the most extended textual link in the *Mabinogi* and it leaves no room for doubt about the connexion between the two tales. Just as Manawydan is seeking to restore his friend Pryderi, so Llwyd is taking revenge on behalf of his friend Gwawl. Once this has been revealed we see that the greater part of *Manawydan* is motivated by the continuation of a feud begun in the First Branch. A pledge had been made by Gwawl "na bo ammouyn na dial uyth amdanaw" (*PKM* 17). This seems to imply absolutely that there should be no revenge taken by anyone. Llwyd, though motivated by friendship, is acting dishonourably by breaking the pledge that his friend had made many years before. The revenge Llwyd takes is also reprehensible in that it extends the feud into the next generation, and it is only Manawydan's cleverness which ensures that there will be no further repercussions.

The most extended example of a feud in the Four Branches is the tale of *Branwen*, and the implications of the tale are clarified for the modern reader, at least, by several close correspondences with extant law texts. The payment which Bendigeidfran offers to Matholwch for the insult he has received is derived from an actual, though possibly never invoked, legal requirement. In addition to making reparation for the horses Bendigeidfran adds

> y gyt a hynny, ef a geif yn wynepwerth idaw, llathen aryant a uo kyuref [a'e uys bychan] a chyhyt ac ef e hun, a chlawr eur kyflet a'y wyneb. (*PKM* 33)

Though this does not give the exact conditions stated in the laws the correspondence between them is obvious.[40] This is not, however, the only passage in the episode to which the law texts have some relevance. If we turn to the actual *sarhad* done to Matholwch we can see another reference to legal practice. Efnisien, as he himself states, feels himself to be insulted: "Ny ellynt wy tremic uwy arnaf i" (*PKM* 31). Whether or not he has been insulted according to the law depends on whether he is related to Bendigeidfran closely enough to be a member of the particular kindred group or *cenedl* which has a hand in bestowing Branwen in marriage.[41] In the tale the relationship is subtly obscured by the fact that Efnisien is related to Bendigeidfran and Branwen only on his mother's side. In any case Efnisien himself considers his exclusion from the bestowal of Branwen as an insult, and his reaction, though extreme and rash, is not entirely without precedent. The disfiguring of horses is specifically mentioned in the law texts in terms similar to those used in describing Efnisien's actions. The relevant passage in *Llyfr Blegywryd* is the most compact:

> Rawn amws y maes o'r goloren, pedeir ar hugeint. Or trychir dim o'r goloren, gwerth yr amws oll a telir. Llygat amws a'e glust, pedeir ar hugeint a tal pob un. Or dellir oll, y werth oll a telir. Gwerth rawn rwnssi, deudec keinhawc, ac velly y lygeit a'e glusteu.[42]

This passage is highly significant in assessing the character of Efnisien, for it shows that he did not act purely out of malice; the vengeance he took can be seen, in the light of the law texts, to be a formal reply to the insult he feels was done to him.

Efnisien is the central character of the tale at two points, when he begins the feud with Matholwch and when he reopens it after peace has been made in Ireland (*PKM* 31, 43), and at these two points we should carefully examine the characterization of him. In both instances he is reacting to the fact that he has been ignored. From this we can see without much difficulty that he should be understood as an oversensitive character who reacts too quickly and too rashly when he feels he has not been accorded the rights which are due to him. This is not the only side of his character which the author develops, however, for on two occasions he saves the men of the Island of the Mighty from total defeat, when he cleverly destroys the men in the bags and when he sacrifices himself in the cauldron, though admittedly he was the cause of the battle as well. Efnisien can thus be seen as a complex, and in many ways, a very tragic figure. When Mac Cana states that "Efnisien is absolutely essential to the structure and motivation of the events in *Branwen*,"[43] he should perhaps add that this is because the author is very concerned with the character himself, making Efnisien more than simply a thread which gives unity to the tale. Mac Cana spends several pages pointing out the similarities between Efnisien and Bricriu Nemthenga.[44] This type of character, however, appears in several places in a wide range of medieval literature. A notable example is Unferþ in *Beowulf*, whose name (which may be rendered "mar-peace")[45] is remarkably similar to that of Efnisien (from *efnys*, "hostile, enemy," *PKM* 163), especially in the light of the role each plays in his respective tale. A much later example, in which this element is more fully developed, is found in both *Le Morte Arthur* and in the works of Sir Thomas Malory.[46] In this tale both Aggravayne and Gawain act similarly to Efnisien in that they repeatedly insist that attention be brought to a matter which ultimately leads to the destruction of the best men in the kingdom. There is no need, however, to go outside of Wales to find a parallel, for we can see traces of such a character in *Breuddwyd Rhonabwy* in the person of Iddawg Cordd Prydain, the Embroiler of Britain. Though his motives are different from Efnisien's the outcome of his actions is similar:

> A gwr ieuanc drythyll oedwn i yna, a rac vy chwannocket y vrwydyr y tervysgeis y rygtunt . . . Ac o hynny yd ystovet y Gatgamlan.[47]

Without going into greater detail it seems safe to suggest that the motif of a character wont to cause unnecessary trouble was widespread in both time and place, and in *Branwen* the characterisation of Efnisien is a very fine example of this motif.

Other examples of the feud theme have been mentioned above where they were relevant to the discussions of friendships and marriages, but we might touch on a few where these episodes throw light on each other. Efnisien, as we have seen, acts rashly and violently with little provocation, even when he can be fairly certain that the results will be disastrous. The author makes this clear when he gives us a glimpse into Efnisien's mind:

> "Y Duw y dygaf uyg kyffes," heb ynteu yn y uedwl, "ys anhebic a gyflauan gan y tylwyth y wneuthur, a wnaf i yr awr honn." (PKM 43)

Even so he thrusts the boy into the fire and thus begins the final massacre. To this we might contrast Manawydan's restraint at the beginning of the Third Branch when Pryderi dissuades him from taking action against Caswallawn, though his complaint has much more of a foundation than does Efnisien's. In this same vein we might call to mind Lleu's prudence in the Fourth Branch when he is careful to obtain Math's permission before seeking vengeance from Gronw Bebyr, establishing a legal right to seek reparation. Thus this feud is confined and does not disrupt society.

Throughout the *Mabinogi* the author has based his tales on a strict code of conduct which becomes most explicit in those episodes dealing with the feuds. The various examples which he develops survey the problem of feuds from a number of differing viewpoints and we are shown the disastrous results of rash actions and words as well as the more positive results of prudent action and respect for the bonds of kinship and friendship. The code of conduct which underlies the Four Branches is relevant not only to the society which the author depicts but also to the society within which the tales developed—that of both the author and his audience.[48]

In addition to the three major themes which we have discussed, there are a number of minor themes which appear intermittently throughout the Four Branches and which form an important element in the author's style. Since the events and thematic elements in the Four Branches are often interrelated in a non-sequential way, these minor themes work to increase the basic unity of the *Mabinogi,* and they often assist the reader or listener in making connections and comparisons with parts of the tales which are separated in the text itself. A brief mention of just a few of these should suffice.

The references to a number of triads are important in this respect. As Rachel Bromwich has pointed out, these references are integral to the *Mabinogi* and serve "(in a manner similar to the 'digressions' in *Beowulf*) to heighten the dramatic effect of his narrative by relating it to a wider field of tradition."[49]

Another such minor theme is the fairly frequent reference the author makes to the order of seating at a feast. In at least two instances he specifically uses such a reference to recall another example. In *Pwyll* it is one of the ways in which he establishes a sense of continuity of events. The two feasts at the court of Hefeydd Hen are linked by recounting the order of the seating at the first and then at the second remarking that the seating was the same (*PKM* 13,18). In the Second Branch also a feast is interrupted, in this case by Efnisien, and after reparation has been paid to Matholwch the feast is similarly resumed:

> Ac ual y dechreuyssant eisted ar dechreu y wled,
> yd eistedyssant yna. (*PKM* 34)

Such formulaic expressions and settings restore the development of the tale after a digression and provide the audience with a guide towards following the thematic and the narrative unity of the tales.[50] Parallelism of events works in a similar way to illuminate the thematic implications of the *Mabinogi*. For instance, after the weddings of both Rhiannon and Branwen, the brides travel to their new homes and distribute gifts among the people. In both cases they are received in great joy, and in both cases the people of each country soon forget the favours they received and both wives are wrongly accused and punished.

It is hoped that this thematic approach to the Four Branches has revealed some of the ways in which the author has utilized his material to create a work that is both meaningful and artistically unified. The intricate structure which can be seen throughout the *Mabinogi* is very closely woven, yet the author has sufficient control over his materials and over his own artistry to prevent the tales from becoming too complex in their interrelationships. The present study of these interweavings should serve at the very least to strengthen the belief that the *Mabinogi* in its final stage is the product of a single mind. That such an artist and such a work of art are products of generations of disintegration, corruption and forgetfulness is hard to believe. If a study of origins is undertaken, it should attempt to trace the development of literary aims and techniques from a more positive point of view, not searching for a "pure" form of story in the early stages, but for the ideals, both social and literary, which change and truly develop the various forms of literature.

Though there are some faults and gaps in the Four Branches, our present examination of the structure should show that these are the exception rather than the rule, and that the author possessed a deep understanding of the materials which he used in his tales in a sense which is far more important to him than the explication of various details. Consequently, though such explication is an important part of our criticism and study of his work, it is by no means the only method through which we should approach the tales. Combining his materials skilfully and permeating them with his own understanding of human nature the author has created a world in which all actions are relevant to the structure of society within that world, and by implication, the ideals and the very straightforward code of conduct which underlie these actions become relevant in the somewhat less controllable world of the author and his audience. The interlace method by which the tales are structured allows the author to develop the significance of the tales without intruding upon them himself, for the meaning is implicit within the amplification and variation of events. The reader, or listener, is left to draw his conclusions from the juxtaposition and interrelation of episodes and characters. The author succeeds in his aim to tell a tale both meaningful and captivating by following the advice given in a gnomic englyn found in the Red Book of Hergest:

> Eiry mynyd, eilion fraeth;
> gowlychyt tonneu glann traeth;
> keluyd kelet y aruaeth.[51]

NOTES

1. Vinaver, *Form and Meaning in Medieval Romance*, 3. Revised and enlarged in *The Rise of Romance*, chap. V.

2. Vinaver, *Form and Meaning*, 3.
3. Vinaver, *Form and Meaning*, 5.
4. Vinaver, *Form and Meaning*, 10 and 12.
5. See Vinaver, *Form and Meaning*, 6–7. Ferdinand Lot was among the first to recognize the principle of interlace in *Étude sur le Lancelot en Prose*.
6. Evans, ed., *The White Book Mabinogion*, cols. 399, 402, 406. Hereafter cited as *WBM*.
7. Leyerle, "The Interlace Structure of Beowulf," 1–17.
8. For an example of this in Welsh see *Peredur* (*WBM*, col. 125), where the scene shifts from Peredur's contention with the knight back to the court where Owein upbraids Kei.
9. Leyerle, "The Interlace Structure of Beowulf," 4.
10. Leyerle, "The Interlace Structure of Beowulf," 5.
11. See Mac Cana, *Branwen Daughter of Llŷr*, "Branwen bears all the characteristics of a work composed and written in the study, and, if my examination of the Irish borrowings has shown anything, it has shown that the Welsh writer himself possessed a very considerable knowledge of Irish literature, probably in written form, or else had constantly by him those who did" (182).
12. Thomson, ed. *Pwyll Pendeuic Dyuet*, xxi.
13. Leyerle, "The Interlace Structure of Beowulf," 8.
14. Sir Ifor Williams, ed., *Pedeir Keinc y Mabinogi*, second edition, 1951, 3. All references to the text will be to this edition, hereafter cited in the text as *PKM*. Compare also *PKM*, "ac ymgolli a'y gydymdeithon"(1).
15. See Jackson, *The International Popular Tale and Early Welsh Tradition*, 82–83; and Bar, "Le Mabinogi de Pwyll, Prince of Dyvet et la Légende d'Amis et Amile," 168 ff. While the chronology would seem to imply that the author of Pwyll could not have known the Welsh version of *Amis et Amile*, I am indebted to Dr. Brynley F. Roberts for the suggestion that the reverse may have been true, indicating a possibility that *Pwyll* may have been regarded as a tale of friendship.
16. The importance of friendship is also stressed in other tales in the *White Book*, e.g., *Peredur* (*WBM*, col. 144), "ath getymdeithas yssyd adolwyn genhyf. Keffy myn vyg cret. A dyro titheu imi y teu. ti ae keffy yn llawen heb y peredur." Interesting also is the following incident in Richards's *Breuddwyd Rhonabwy:* "Ac yna nachaf y marchawc yn eu gordiwes, ac yn gofyn y Idawc a gaffei ran o'r dynyon bychein hynny gantaw. 'Y ran a weda ymi y rodi mi a'e rodaf; bot yn gedymdeith undunt ual y bum ynneu.' A hynny a oruc y marchawc a mynet ymeith" (5–6).
17. Though this is a very subjective statement, the passage does have a very elegiac tone, comparable to that of much early Welsh poetry; e.g., see Ifor Williams's discussion of the "Juvencus

englynion" and the "Gododdin" in *Lectures on Early Welsh Poetry*, 28–29 and 65ff. Also compare the laments of Heledd for Cynddylan in Sir Ifor Williams's *Canu Llywarch Hen*, 33–38. The trappings of war, i.e., men, horses and arms, are a regular feature of the poetry of both the *Cynfeirdd* and the *Gogynfeirdd*; see for instance "Marwnad Owein" in Sir Ifor Williams's *The Poems of Taliesin*, 12. In an article on "Math fab Mathonwy" Lewis compares this passage to entries in the *Brut*, 192.

18. See Magnusson and Palsson, trans., *Njal's Saga*, esp. sections 33–45. Njal and Gunnar Hamunarson are continually trying to settle the feud between their families which their wives aggravate. Gunnar is eventually killed as a result of the enmities stirred up by his wife (section 77).

19. Gruffydd, *Rhiannon*, 99.

20. "Os gwr mwyn uyd y mab, mab maeth ynni uyd, a goreu a allo uyth a wna inni" (*PKM* 25).

21. See for example, R.L. Thomson, ed., *Pwyll*, xviii, and D.S. Thomson, ed., *Branwen Uerch Lyr*, xxviii.

22. The same word, *diffleeis*, is used in *Pwyll* (*PKM* 7).

23. *PKM* 1 and 8–9.

24. Pryderi's misuse of the term *taeog* (bondman, churl) reveals his feelings and concern for his own position. The author is very careful in his use of words, especially "legal" terms, and thus portrays Pryderi's resentment and impulsiveness both clearly and succinctly.

25. Jackson, *The International Popular Tale*, 104.

26. I am indebted to Dr. Brynley F. Roberts for pointing out that this statement suggests a parallel between the relationship which is made explicit here and that which is implied in the First Branch between Pwyll, Arawn and Arawn's wife.

27. Gruffydd, *Rhiannon*, 71. Jackson, *The International Popular Tale*, 104, cites the episode as a "trifling" example of an international theme and gives an analogue recorded in 1825.

28. Gruffydd, *Rhiannon*, 72.

29. Evans, ed., *The Black Book of Carmarthen*, 94. See also, Bromwich, *Trioedd Ynys Prydein*, 442n.

30. Robinson, ed., *The Works of Geoffrey Chaucer*, 69, lines 652–654.

31. Compare *PKM*, where the queen's customary place is beside Arawn (here "Pwyll"): "ac eisted a wnaethant ual hynn—y urenhines o'r neill parth idaw ef, a'r iarll, debygei ef, o'r parth arall" (4).

32. Wiliam, ed., *Llyfr Iorwerth*, 2. Bromwich, *Trioedd Ynys Prydein*, notes the distinction between "*Palfawt*, lit. 'a hand-slap' . . . as opposeed to *dyrnawt*, 'a blow with the fist'" (144). *Sarhaet* is

used, however, in conjunction with *bonclust* in *Peredur* (WBM, col. 122), though possibly it does not have the legal stress as when it is used in the *Mabinogi*. One might argue that the *sarhad* lay in snatching the goblet from Gwenhwyfar's hand.

33. Gruffydd, *Math vab Mathonwy*, 91–92.
34. Gruffydd, *Math vab Mathonwy*, 50.
35. Compare two proverbs from the White Book: "Hen bechot a wna kewilid newyd" (Phillimore, "A Fragment from Hengwrt MS. No 202," 142), "Gwell goleith meuyl noe diala" (ibid. 141).
36. Davies, "The Survival of Bloodfeud in Medieval Wales."
37. Lewis, "Math fab Mathonwy," 191.
38. A much earlier but very close literary parallel in Old English suggests that the motif of a single combat at a ford may have a more complicated history than has hitherto been recognized: see "Exaltatio Sancte Crucis" in Skeat, ed., *Ælfric's Lives of Saints*, II, 146, lines 52–58.
39. Compare, "trwy y hut ae letrith" in the Llanst. MS 1 (Shirburn MS 113) version of *Cyfranc Lludd a Llevelys*.
40. Though *Llyfr Iorwerth* has "guyalen eur" where *Llyfr Blegywryd* (eds. Williams and Powell), has "gwialen aryant" (3), the description in *Branwen* is closer to the text of the former: "a guyalen eur gyhyt ac ef ehun a chyn urasset a'y vys bychan, a chlawr eur cywlet a'y wyneb . . ." (2). See also Thomson's note on this passage and the emendation in *Branwen Uerch Lyr*, 25–26.
41. For this practice see Lloyd, *A History of Wales*, 289.
42. Williams and Powell, eds., *Llyfr Blegywryd*, 91. See also Wiliam, ed., *Llyfr Iorwerth*, 83.
43. Mac Cana, *Branwen*, 79.
44. Mac Cana, *Branwen*, 78–84.
45. For this name, see Klaeber, ed., *Beowulf*, 148.
46. Bruce, *Le Morte Arthur*, and Malory, *Works*, ed. Vinaver, 818 ff.
47. Richards, ed., *Breudwyt Ronabwy*, 4–5.
48. An interesting passage reflecting the role of literature in society, as well as noting the use of written tales, is found in the early fifteenth-century Llanstephan MS 3: "Hengerd, ac ystoryaeu yscriuenedic, ac gouyneu o anryued ac odidawc attebyon herwyd keluydyd a gwirioned, da yw y prydyd eu gwybod wrth ymddiddan a doethyon, a diddanhau rianed, a digrifhau gwyrda a gwraged da" (35), Williams and Jones, eds., *Gramadegau'r Penceirddiaid*.
49. Bromwich, *Trioedd Ynys Prydein*, lxxxvi.
50. For similar references to the order of seating, see *Peredur*, WBM, col. 154–155, 159, *Gereint*, WBM, 400–401: Wiliam, ed., *Llyfr Iorwerth*, 3.
51. Jackson, *Early Welsh Gnomic Poems*, 24.

10

Prolegomena to a Reading of the *Mabinogi*: 'Pwyll' and 'Manawydan'

Patrick K. Ford

In the Introduction to *The Mabinogi and Other Medieval Welsh Tales*, I attempted to give some account of the mythic structure underlying part of the tale of *Pwyll*.[1] Whatever the merits of that discussion may be, there are a great many other things that remain to be said about the tale of *Pwyll* and about the remaining Branches of the *Mabinogi*, as well as about other medieval Welsh tales. The same may be said of medieval Irish tales, for, in fact, there have been very few attempts to give an extended account and analysis of the levels of meaning in medieval Celtic literatures that venture beyond the historical approach—a notable exception being Tomás Ó Cathasaigh's *The Heroic Biography of Cormac Mac Airt*. What I wish to do here, then, is to supply some commentary on the *Mabinogi* that will go beyond the standard available treatments and, at the same time, fall short of a definitive attempt. Hence, I suggest the title of prolegomena.

One of the serious difficulties in attempting an analysis of *Pwyll* and the other Branches is that there are no alternative versions, no meaningful manuscript tradition. (Critics will note that I am refusing Lévi-Strauss's dictum that all its versions constitute the myth.[2] Therefore, I will not take into account antiquarians' collections, palaeographers' printings, or, for example, Sir Thomas Parry-Williams's rendition of the Four Branches into modern Welsh, Evangeline Walton's translations, or the colouring books published by Y Lolfa.) That means that, for better or for worse, we are constrained by virtually one manuscript version. But other literary traditions have not been more fortunate, by and large; the *Beowulf* poem exists in a single manuscript, and it was only very recently that a paper manuscript was discovered that provided an alternative version to Caxton's Malory. Such matters are not to be taken lightly, to be sure, for what we may seize upon as an extremely significant motif, lexical item, indeed, grammatical form, may be but a ghost. Still, the only alternative seems to be to wait for future generations in whose lives additional manuscripts may be discovered, and allow them the luxury of making midnight raids into our murky texts. Better for them to have the advantage of our myopic and limited vision.

What I propose to do here is to examine the tales as closely as I can, eschewing any one methodology for an eclectic approach, stating as clearly as I can that which is evident in the text, what its meaning may be first of all in the tradition of Welsh literature and Celtic mythology, then in the wider traditions of Indo-European—where that seems relevant. Wherever possible, I shall argue for inherited Welsh reflexes of Celtic, sprung from Indo-European, traditions, on the theory that one is usually richer in a less encumbered way from an inheritance than from a loan. Furthermore, if the metaphor is valid in this instance, an inheritance can be passed on: a loan cannot, at least not without resistance.

Matthew Arnold's assessment of the Four Branches of the *Mabinogi* has, no doubt, been a source of consolation for generations of students and scholars who have gone head to head with the tales, seeking to pry a modicum of meaning from their sternly resistant lines. Speaking of the redactor, Arnold supposed that he was pillaging an antiquity of which he scarcely possessed the secret.[3] It will be evident that Arnold meant that some medieval Welsh writer, scribe, author, redactor, or whatever we choose to call him, sat perplexed upon his stool, writing down things (from an informant? from an exemplar or exemplars?) that he did not understand, perhaps for his own puzzlement or for the puzzle-

Prolegomena to a Reading of the Mabinogi

ment of his patron. Such an activity would have consumed a considerable (albeit immeasurable) amount of time and was executed on costly velum. It seems to me that Arnold's assessment is, *a priori*, untenable. Everything known to me that came from the quills of medieval Welsh scribes served a purpose, be it aesthetic, moral, political, or social in some other context. The same is true for medieval Ireland, and, no doubt, the rest of medieval Europe.[4]

The notion of antiquity pillaged has been more or less pervasive in Welsh scholarship. The most prolific writer on the problems of the *Mabinogi* was W.J. Gruffydd. He concluded that the Four Branches originally told of the birth, exploits, marriage, and death of Pryderi, the only character to appear in each of the Branches. These are stages in the heroic biography pattern that seems to occur virtually throughout the world.[5] Such a pattern occurs in early Irish literature, and one might well expect to find it in Welsh also. But if one considers the Cú Chulainn cycle, which includes extensive narratives concerning the hero's conception, birth, youthful exploits, training in arms, wooing a bride, marriage, mature deeds, and death, it is clear that the *Mabinogi* contains no comparable cycle. The only element of the heroic biography that finds full expression here is the birth tale.

Professor Gruffydd supposed that the myth had become confused. By analogy with certain Irish tales, he suggested that the opening episode originally told how a mortal and an other-worldly figure changed places, in order that the divine hero might be begotten on the mortal's wife.[6] Subsequently, that theme was eroded so that when Pwyll went off to Annwfn, his activities there were controlled largely by the theme of chastity. Subsequent scholars have shared Gruffydd's view that the tales represent an artistic levelling of earlier traditional material that had become almost hopelessly confused, with the result that readers are frequently offered counsels of despair in their search to understand the tales. In recapitulating Gruffydd's reading, Thomas Jones and Gwyn Jones write, "In the first section of *Pwyll* we recognize the story of how the king of the Otherworld changes place with an earthly king, in order that he might beget a wonder-child on an earthly mother. But the story as we have it tells rather of the king of Dyfed's sojourn in Annwn, and of his loyalty and chastity there. Consequently no child is begotten, either in Dyfed or Annwn, and a fresh start must be made."[7] Such a process of literary creations, wherein a redactor or storyteller keeps trying various narratives until the right cluster of motifs is achieved, is completely unknown to me.

In discussing the literary merits of the *Mabinogi*, Gwyn Jones is compelled to admit, "In them we have a broken design and mutilated fragments, great confusions and unanswerable problems."[8] Glyn E. Jones, after surveying the views of Professors Kenneth Jackson and Proinsias Mac Cana, concludes that W.J. Gruffydd's theories still offer the best explanations of the origins and development of the Four Branches.[9] And Jeffrey Gantz asserts that "such myths as are preserved in these tales are so obscure and fragmentary that restoration [sic] is difficult if not impossible."[10] The key words, then, are confusion, fragmentation, obscurity, mutilation, and the like. Such formulations of despair are likely to discourage students and scholars alike from seeking new approaches to meaning in the tales.[11]

The basic assumption about the tales must be, it seems to me, *a fortiori*, that they did have a meaning for the scribe as well as for his audience, whoever and whatever that was. It is the only assumption, in fact, that in any way justifies our own excursions into their inner and outer meanings, and one that will guide the reflections and observations of this writer. That does not mean, of course, that our attempts to discover meaning will always if ever meet with success; but that is another matter. Out of justice, we might even say that Matthew Arnold's own judgement on the tales was simply another way of saying that *he* could not make head nor tail of the Four Branches. And we can sympathize with that.

The First Branch, *Pwyll, Prince of Dyfed*, deals essentially with Pwyll's exchange with Arawn, a king of the other world (Annwfn), and subsequently, the birth, loss, and restoration of his son Pryderi. That is a considerable simplification of the events recorded in the tale, and I stress the phrase "deals essentially"—I do not say that is what the tale is about. What the tale is about, I would venture, is the issue of the parentage of Pryderi and the joint issues of fertility in the land and among men.

Pryderi is a character of considerable importance in medieval Welsh tradition, though he does not figure largely in the Four Branches as a whole. He is certainly important enough to have a tale about his birth, and that is to be found in the First Branch. Gruffydd was insisting that the entire First Branch dealt with the issues of Pryderi's conception and birth, hence he had to posit an original version of the first part of the story that would be more directly relevant to the hero's birth. But I believe that it can be shown that his reconstruction—far from improving the version we have—in fact weakens the meaning of the tale.

The initial episode, consisting of columns 1 to 12.27 in Evans's edition[12] (pages 37–42 of my translation), tells how Pwyll met Arawn a king of Annwfn, and exchanged places with him in order to fight Arawn's other-worldly enemy. He successfully accomplished his mission and returned thence to his own kingdom, securing by his actions the everlasting friendship of Arawn. There are a number of literary themes adorning this basic plot, but they need not detain us here. The significant thing about the encounter and the exchange is that Pwyll and Arawn receive each other's form and shape, to the extent that none, either in Pwyll's mortal kingdom of Dyfed, or in Arawn's other world—not even Arawn's wife, with whom Pwyll sleeps every night for a year—knows that their chieftain is absent. Furthermore, at the end of this episode the text has it that, as a result of his successful year in Annwfn, Pwyll's title "Prince of Dyfed" fell out of use, and he was called "Pen Annwfn" (Lord of the other world) thenceforth.

The episode establishes that Arawn and Pwyll have each other's shapes and that Pwyll, formerly an earthly, mortal lord, now has a title equal to that of his other-worldly companion. In terms of the mediation of opposites or polarities, the mortal lives in the natural world with the title of the immortal from the supernatural world; Pwyll is now an anomalous character. It is important to note also that the circumstances in which the events of this episode take place are themselves anomalous or liminal. Pwyll is neither here nor there when he meets Arawn; he is lost. The initial encounter, as well as Pwyll's encounter with Hafgan, the otherworldly enemy, takes place neither on one day nor the next, but at night, at the boundary between days. It might at first seem strange to contemplate single combat at night, especially when a year's notice was given, but not, perhaps, when we consider the liminality of the event. Except for the sake of enrichment, there is no need to seek for any meaning in the first episode other than what we have considered; put simply, the events establish Pwyll's identity with the Head of the other world: Pwyll, Pen Annwfn.

We note that the cast of characters in this episode is very limited: only Pwyll, Arawn, and Hafgan. There is Arawn's wife, but she is given no name. Only one other female in these Four Branches is nameless, the wife of Teyrnon Twrf Liant; the reason for her anonymity seems clear to me, and I will offer it later in this essay. For the moment, let me venture to say that when a character has no real and separate identity in these tales, the character is anonymous. Thus the episode is really only about Pwyll, Arawn, and Hafgan. The first of these is a "mortal" who takes up residence in the other world; the second, an "immortal" who dwells temporarily in the natural world; the third a doomed "immortal." It will be seen that all three are anomalous figures. Furthermore, it is clear from the text that inhabitants of the other world cannot kill one another, and that that is why Pwyll is introduced there.

The usual device for conveying mortals into the otherworld is an animal (e.g., a pig in the tales of *Manawydan* and *Math*). Sometimes the animal is the object of a hunt, as when Pryderi and Manawydan pursue a gleaming white boar while out hunting.[13] In *Pwyll,* the other-worldly animals are coming towards Pwyll, not leading him on. That is, the other world is somewhat aggressively presenting itself to Pwyll, forcing the confrontation, as it were. It will be noticed that there are no special signals nor boundaries to indicate that the other world is at hand—only the colour of the animals. In both medieval Irish and Welsh tales the relationship between the two worlds scarcely—if ever—is articulated, and perhaps is even intentionally obscured. In this instance, Pwyll, hunting in the midst of his own realm, the seven cantrefs of Dyfed, meets a king whom he has never seen before. Arawn personally guides Pwyll to Annwfn, where Pwyll sees the most beautiful buildings he has ever seen, with the finest ornamentation and best-equipped household. The place seems to have been reached after only a very short while, and yet Pwyll registers no surprise at finding such a spot within easy reach of his own kingdom. It is safe to say that space-shifting is as common as shape-shifting in these tales, and that the former elicits no more reaction from the characters involved than does the latter. It would appear that the encounter between Pwyll and Arawn of Annwfn was carefully contrived by the latter, that he had arranged the meeting to make a contract with the mortal.

In his own previous encounters with his enemy, Arawn apparently has violated his own magical formula by giving Hafgan more than one blow. He instructs the mortal to give the opponent but a single blow, because "No matter how many more I would give him, he would attack me the next day as well as before" (38). An easy thing, one would think, for Arawn himself to give the single blow; clearly, it is not only the quantity that counts but the quality: the blow must be delivered by the liminal intruder. Furthermore, while Arawn's encounters seem to have been daily and continuous, the combat between Pwyll and Hafgan is to take place at night and on a single occasion.

Night-time is certainly an auspicious time in Celtic tradition. In *Pwyll* virtually all the events occur at one-year intervals, and since the only date mentioned in the tale is May eve, the beginning of Summer, the "light" half of the year, we may assume that all events in the tale occur then. Students of Celtic traditions know that in Irish the other end of the year, 1 November *(samhain)*, is the most portentous date. In a well-known passage, Caesar notes that the Celts believed they were descended from Dis Pater, and that therefore they measured time not from the day but from the night, that is, the cycle of time began with the dark half.[14] Indeed, in Welsh still the word for "week" is *wythnos*, literally "eight nights," and for "fortnight" *pythefnos* "fifteen nights." In Irish tradition, 1 November is the night when the doors to the other world lie open and there is unimpaired movement between the two worlds. Perhaps in Wales this notion somehow was reversed, so that the ominous period lay at the other end of the year. Whatever the reason may be, the text strongly implies that the events of the tale, in which there is considerable obscurity of the boundaries of the two worlds, took place at night and at one-year intervals. In Eliade's terms, we would say that the scenes are enacted only during sacred time and in sacred place.

The narrative stresses the fact that Pwyll and Arawn are interchangeable. Because of the title of the tale and because Pwyll is the character whose career we follow, we tend to discount the merger of the two characters. But from the time he enters Annwfn, Pwyll is called only "the man who was in Arawn's place," or some similar locution. When he has defeated Hafgan, he asks his nobles to discover who owes him allegiance. They answer that all do, "for there is no king over all of Annwfn except you" (40). By the following day, the two realms were in his power, that is, the realm of Hafgan and the realm of Arawn. And from then on Pwyll is *Pen Annwfn,* in spite of taking back his own shape and residing in Dyfed.

There are, then, three heads or kings of Annwfn, and they constitute a trinity that may be realigned as two sets of two with a common member. The two from the other world are incompatible, whereas one from the other world and one from the natural world are compatible. Arawn is the common member in the sets; he has shared Annwfn with another other-worldly king, and now he shares it with a mortal. The only difference between them is that one dwells thenceforth in the other world, the other in the natural world. The old alliance Arawn–Hafgan, an exclusively other-worldly relationship, is rejected and replaced by a new one, Arawn–Pwyll: "From that time on, they began to strengthen their friendship, and sent each other horses, hunting dogs, hawks, and treasures of the sort that each supposed would give pleasure to the other" (42). Such a realliance is resisted by Hafgan, who cries in anguish, "what right did you have to my death? I claimed nothing from you nor do I know any cause for you to kill me . . . " (40).

The encounter between Pwyll and Arawn is fraught with significance for the mortal's people, for it establishes communications between human society and the divine world, which in turn makes possible the acquisition of gifts and treasures of various kinds for human society. One of the gifts was swine. Pigs were a vitally important part of the domestic economy of the Celts, and it is not strange that they should have been provided with a divine origin; there is plenty of

Prolegomena to a Reading of the Mabinogi

evidence to show that they played an important role in the myth and religion of the Celts.[15] When he becomes king, the primary function of Pwyll's son Pryderi is to guard the treasures sent from the other world, and we shall see that, in the Fourth Branch, Pryderi loses his life for failing to keep the swine in his possession.

The opening episode of *Pwyll* is, I would suggest, part of the origin legends of the Welsh. It is concerned with the mediation of the two worlds, with bringing god to man and man to god. Just as man cannot do without gods, so gods are imperfect without man. The resolution is that the two are united by a kind of joint appointment: each partakes of both worlds. Pwyll establishes sovereignty in Annwfn, Arawn perfects the secular rule of Dyfed. In any story about Pwyll, this episode might have been adduced as a prelude, or, to borrow an important term from early Irish literary tradition, *fo-scél* "sub-tale." The *fo-scél* often establishes the identity of a principal character in the *prim-scél* "primary-tale." Alternatively, it may establish conditions relevant to setting, time, topography, or other details incidental to the main tale. Thus, as a prelude to the story about the marriage of Pwyll and the conception and birth of his son Pryderi, the storyteller might well have reminded his audience who Pwyll was and what his credentials were.

Let us turn now to the events surrounding the birth of Pryderi. They may be summarized as follows. Under magical circumstances, Pwyll encounters Rhiannon, who declares her love for him and apprises him of the existence of a rival. After an interlude in which the rival nearly succeeds in tricking Pwyll out of his bride, Pwyll and Rhiannon are married. After a period of time, the length of which distresses Pwyll's advisers, Rhiannon conceives a child and gives birth. The very night of his birth the child disappears mysteriously. In order to protect themselves from punishment, her ladies-in-waiting accuse her of destroying the child. Rhiannon is found guilty and is consequently compelled to remain beside the horseblock outside the court and to offer a horseback ride to visitors to the court and tell them her story, if she thought they did not already know it.

In the meantime, we learn of a neighbouring lord named Teyrnon. Teyrnon has a mare that foals every year, but the foals are lost. On this May eve he decides to discover the cause of his annual loss. As he watches, a demon attempts to steal the newly delivered foal; Teyrnon cuts off the monster's arm, then pursues the fleeing beast. When he returns to the house, he finds not only the foal he has rescued, but a baby boy. He and his wife (nameless) pretend they are the child's parents, until, hearing of the punishment of Rhiannon, they realize the identity of their charge and restore him to Pwyll and Rhiannon.

On the surface, then, the narrative recounts the marriage of Pwyll and Rhiannon, the conception and birth of Pryderi, and his loss and eventual restoration. But beneath the surface lies an infrastructure rich in details that provide numerous clues to the deeper meaning of those events. I examined some of it—the Adventure of the Boy and the Mare—in the Introduction to *The Mabinogi* (4–12); I give a summary of the argument here.

With very little difficulty, Rhiannon is to be equated with a goddess worshipped by the Celts of Gaul and, after the Roman conquest of Gaul, by the Romans themselves. Epona, whose name means "divine horse goddess," is attested in hundreds of statues and inscriptions on the continent, and was revered even in Rome. She is usually depicted mounted on a horse, surrounded by foals, sometimes with birds, sometimes holding a bag that has been taken to be a symbol of the fertility she represents. The horse on which she sits is usually depicted as being at an amble. Juvenal says images of her were to be seen in stables where asses were kept. One of her epithets is *regina.* The Rhiannon of our tale is first seen mounted on a horse that moves at an amble; even so, the horse cannot be overtaken by Pwyll's swiftest horses. When Pwyll is in danger of losing his betrothed, Rhiannon gives him a bag whose supply of food is unending. When her child is lost, she is punished by being forced to act like a beast of burden, specifically, a horse. In *Manawydan* she is punished similarly, being compelled to wear the collar of an ass. In the tale of *Branwen* the survivors of the battle in Ireland sojourn in the other world and are serenaded by the "birds of Rhiannon." In short, there is a considerable body of evidence that compels us to regard Rhiannon as a literary version of the horse goddess, Epona. Even her name derives from a

Celtic form meaning "divine queen," recalling Epona's Latin epithet, *regina*.

But, having established the connection between Rhiannon and the goddess Epona, we are still a long way from discovering meaning in the tale. It is a first step, and its methods are chiefly philology, archaeology, iconography, and epigraphy. For the rest we shall need some new tools.

In a *locus classicus* for the structural study of myth, Claude Lévi-Strauss has shown that the schemata of a tale must be read vertically, as one would read the melodic line and its contrapuntal apparatus in a musical score: "these sequences [i.e., narrative events] are organized, on planes at different levels (of abstraction), in accordance with schemata, which exist simultaneously, superimposed one upon another; just as a melody composed for several voices is held within bounds by constraints in two dimensions, first by its own melodic line which is horizontal, and second by the contrapuntal schemata (settings) which are vertical."[16] Thus are the events of *Pwyll* ordered. And where we find the same characters appearing again, we shall take the events to be part of the "contrapuntal schemata" of the myth. The present discussion, therefore, would be incomplete if we did not consider the Third Branch, *Manawydan*.

Manawydan is connected sequentially with *Branwen*, in that the story begins with a reference to the concluding events of the preceding tale. But the continuity is a temporal one only, for the story recounts events of a very different kind. Pryderi encourages his friend Manawydan son of Llŷr ("son of Sea") to return to Dyfed with him and consider marrying his mother, Rhiannon. Manawydan is at first disinclined to do so, but when he sees Rhiannon, he agrees. Thus, Manawydan becomes the stepfather of Pryderi, and the four of them, Manawydan and Rhiannon, and Pryderi and his wife Cigfa, celebrate conjointly the royal feast in the court at Arberth. At night, they go to the magical mound of Arberth, and as they are sitting there is a thunderous clatter followed by a descending mist. When the mist clears, they find themselves completely alone: "neither house, nor animal, nor smoke, nor fire, nor dwellings, only the court buildings, and those empty, deserted, desolate, without men or animals in them . . . " (77).

The four are content for a while to keep themselves by hunting and fishing, but then decide to go into England and earn their livings by practising crafts. Their work at making saddles, then shields, then shoes, is so successful that the other craftsmen conspire to kill them. Rather than fight, they move from place to place, finally giving up the enterprise and returning to Dyfed. There they commence hunting once again. On one of their expeditions they pursue a gleaming white boar who leads them cunningly to a magnificent fort. The boar and the dogs disappear into the fort, and when they do not return Pryderi goes after them. Inside, he sees a fountain atop a marble slab, and over the fountain a finely wrought gold basin secured by four chains that stretch beyond sight into the sky. Pryderi takes hold of the basin, is stuck fast, and loses his power of speech. Manawydan grows tired of waiting for his mate and returns home.

When Rhiannon sees that her son and the dogs have been lost, she chides Manawydan for his faithlessness and goes in search of Pryderi. She comes upon the fort, finds Pryderi, takes hold of the basin, and is stuck fast and rendered speechless. When night falls, there is a thunderous clatter and a mist; when it clears, the fort and its contents have vanished.

Cigfa, wife of Pryderi, and Manawydan are left alone and without the use of hunting dogs. Therefore, they decide to go to England and practice crafts. Manawydan plies his craft of shoemaking again, but the enterprise ends as before. The two return to Dyfed, bringing with them wheat. Manawydan sows three crofts. At harvest time, he discovers that the first croft has been ravaged: the stalks have been bent down and the grain gone. The next day brings the same results to the second croft. He decides to be more vigilant over the third croft, and goes out that night to keep watch. At midnight there is a great commotion as an enormous host of mice descends upon the field. With great difficulty, Manawydan manages to catch one of them, which turns out to be pregnant. He puts her in his glove, ties the top with a string, and returns home. The following day he proceeds to the mound of Arberth, intent on hanging the thieving mouse. A scholar, a priest, and a bishop in turn attempt to ransom the mouse, but Manawydan is adamant in his refusal. The bishop, in desperation, admits that he is Llwyd son of Cil Coed (?"forest recess, backwoods"), that the pregnant mouse is his wife, and the others members of her court. Ravaging the croft was a punishment, a revenge for the game of "badger-in-the-bag" played on Gwawl by Pwyll (in the First Branch). Manawydan releases the mouse in exchange for the freeing of Rhiannon and Pryderi, the restoration of the land, and the promise that Manawydan's present victory never be avenged on him nor on Rhiannon or Pryderi. During their incarceration, the punishment of the mother and son is described as follows: "The gate-hammers of my court were around Pryderi's neck, and the collars of asses after they had been hauling hay, were around Rhiannon's neck. Such was their prison" (87).

It is clear that the events of the story of *Manawydan* have little in common with those of the *Branwen* story, but a great deal in common with those of the First Branch, *Pwyll*. The paternity of Pryderi is at issue in both Branches, as is fertility in general. In *Pwyll*, Pryderi is the son of Rhiannon and Pwyll Pen Annwfn (it is significant that he is known now by his new title, which reflects his other-worldly nature). However, Pwyll's role in the generation of Pryderi is not at all clear. In the opening episode, the adventure of Pwyll, Hafgan, and Arawn, the chastity of Pwyll is emphasized. Although he has the most beautiful woman in the world to sleep with each night, he does not touch her. This fact surprises everyone, Arawn no less than his wife, and—no doubt—the audience. One may view this as contamination by the motif of The Chaste Friend/Brother, as some have, or even as a Christian overlay, although such a view would not be consistent with the overall treatment of traditional material by the scribes of medieval Wales.[17] Furthermore, after Pwyll and Rhiannon are wed, three years pass without issue to them. Pwyll's counsellors are understandably disturbed, and urge Pwyll to put away Rhiannon and take another wife that he might have an heir. His response to them is not a defence of Rhiannon; on the contrary, he says: "Be patient with *me* until the end of the year . . . " (50). When the child is born, Pwyll is not on hand, nor does he see the child before it disappears. Thus, Pwyll exhibits notoriously asexual and infertile characteristics— and he has no child until Pryderi is delivered to the court as a young boy.

At this point in the story, we are presented with another couple who also suffer from lack of fertility. Teyrnon's wife has never had a child. His mare is fertile, foaling every May eve—but the colts disappear. On this particular May eve, having decided to be vigilant, Teyrnon succeeds in providing both his mare and his wife with offspring. The woman, Teyrnon's wife, has no name and her pretended child has an alias. The superstructure appears to affirm the message of the substructure: the wife in Teyrnon's realm can have no name because she is a shadow of the child's real mother, Rhiannon. The boy, while he dwells in Teyrnon's realm, takes a name other than his "real"-world name. It is as though a substitute mother had to be found for Rhiannon while she gave simultaneous birth in her hippomorphic aspect, as the mare. Consider the characteristics of the principals:

RHIANNON: fertile, but her offspring disappear. Apparently this happens periodically, for Pwyll says to her critics 'I know she has children'—plural (51).
MARE: fertile, but her offspring disappear periodically.
PWYLL: chaste (? = infertile), apparently has no (? = cannot have) children.
TEYRNON: has never fathered children on his wife.

Both Pwyll and Teyrnon are custodians of a mare: Teyrnon literally, Pwyll by virtue of the punishment exacted upon Rhiannon, so that she is only a "pretend" horse. Meanwhile, her literal son has disappeared, only to reappear as the pretended son of Teyrnon and his wife. Teyrnon himself restores the boy to Pwyll, leaving his mare and his wife behind. Their arrival in Dyfed signals the end of Rhiannon's equine servitude. None will get on her back, and she is welcomed into the court among her own kind again. The structure of the sequences involved might be charted as follows:

Prolegomena to a Reading of the Mabinogi   211

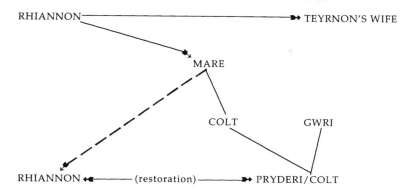

Reading the mythic schemata vertically, we might say the following. Rhiannon, partaking of both equine and human nature, must resolve the conflict between them before giving birth. The solution lies in separating the two natures (another joint appointment), bearing a colt on the one hand and a human child on the other. While the two are nurtured, Rhiannon partakes of both equine and human nature, both separately (in the realm of Teyrnon) and conjointly (in the realm of Pwyll). The crisis ends when the boy and the colt are united and both return to Rhiannon.

The tale of Manawydan adds some information to the schema and restates parts of it. Having become stepfather of Pryderi and husband of Rhiannon, his lack of aggressiveness causes him to lose them. In this respect he resembles Pwyll, whose lack of foresight and nonaggressiveness cause him nearly to lose Rhiannon twice. Furthermore, an external force has caused the land to lie barren and then plunders the crofts Manawydan has sown. In this respect, his plight is akin to Teyrnon's, whose newly born foals are stolen away by some mysterious aggressor. In closely similar language, Teyrnon and Manawydan at last decide to protect their interests and discover the cause of their losses: "'God's vengeance on me,' said he, 'if I do not find out what destruction is carrying off the colts: tonight is May eve'" (52); "'Shame on me,' he said, 'if I do not stand watch tonight, and whatever ravaged the other wheat will come to ravage this and I'll know what it is'" (82). As a result of his vigilance, Manawydan captures the mouse, which he puts in his glove, and, as though it were a bag, ties the top with a string. Later he ransoms this creature in the bag for the return of Pryderi and Rhiannon and the freeing of Dyfed from the enchantment upon it; the latter entails restoring the productivity and fertility of the land.

The narrative explains that the mouse's husband, Llwyd, was responsible for the enchantment, and that it had been done to avenge Llwyd's friend Gwawl, for having been the victim of "badger-in-the-bag" in *Pwyll*. This seems strange, for one of the conditions for the release of Gwawl on that occasion was that there "never be redress nor vengeance for it" (48). Let us return to that tale for a moment, and review the events.

At his wedding-feast, Pwyll carelessly but unwittingly granted Rhiannon's former suitor any wish. Naturally, Gwawl's wish was to have Rhiannon for his own wife. Rhiannon told Pwyll to agree since he had no choice, but to return at the end of a year on the occasion of her marriage-feast with Gwawl, and to have with him a bag that she would give him. Disguised as one of the suppliants, he was to ask as his boon from Gwawl that the bag be filled with food. It was a magical bag, of course, and could never be filled. Pwyll followed his instructions, and when Gwawl asked in desperation, "will the bag never be full?" Pwyll replied that it would not until a nobleman arose and said "enough has been put in," trampling the food in the bag at the same time. Gwawl arose to perform the act, but as he did so, Pwyll twisted the bag so that Gwawl went into it, whereupon Pwyll quickly tied the top with a string. At a signal from Pwyll, his men descended upon the court, and each in turn struck the bag asking, "what do we have here?" "A badger," replied the others, and that, we are told, was the origin of the game of "badger-in-the-bag." Pwyll finally called off the game and spared Gwawl in exchange for a promise that Gwawl would undertake to dispense gifts to suppliants and minstrels and a pledge that he would never seek redress or vengeance.

The similarities between this narrative sequence and the wheatcroft sequence in *Manawydan* are evident. The issue is food (prosperity) in each instance; the adversary is defeated and ends up in a bag with strings drawn. Each is released in exchange for pledges: no vengeance (both), provisions or productivity (both), and restoration (of Rhiannon to Pwyll;

of Rhiannon and Pryderi to Manawydan). The closeness of the two sequences is affirmed by the fact that Llwyd and Gwawl are friends. But we have to clear up at least one inconsistency; it seems improbable that a society governed so strictly by an honour code would permit vengeance for an act that was said explicitly to be unredressable. Indeed, if we read only horizontally the narrative is inconsistent. But if we read vertically, there is no inconsistency: the victory over the opponent who is confined in a bag may thus be seen to be motifs of which the episodes recounted in *Pwyll* and in *Manawydan* are multi-forms. The adversary so imprisoned is eventually ransomed in such a way that brings well-being and stability to the realm. At the moment he is captured, Gwawl is identical to a badger, an animal defined in Welsh as *pryf llwyd* "brownish-grey creature" (where *llwyd* means "brownish-grey").[18] At the moment she is captured, the pregnant mouse is, as it were, Mrs. *Llwyd*. There is an unabashed resemblance between the two animals at the moment they are imprisoned: both are animals (literally or functionally), both are in bags, one may be described as *llwyd*, the other actually so named.

It would be perverse to say, as critics were once accustomed to do, that the events we have been examining are one and the same event. But it is important to insist that they must be read vertically as well as horizontally or sequentially. Language and the verbal performance of it can only present material in a linear or horizontal way. But the structure of thought is ideogrammatic and is not restricted to linearity. In this respect, myth and poetry are diametrically opposed. In poetry, each lexical item is polysemic (potentially, at least), and each line, therefore, a complex of meanings reflecting the mathematical product of the potential meanings of each word in the line. Movement of meaning in poetry is from inside out; from a single utterance spring manifold meanings, and its very ambiguity constitutes at once its richness and its meaning. In myth, on the other hand, movement of meaning is from outside in. There is but one meaning, one message, and that derived from a complexity of utterances, manifold, as it were, to guarantee but a single meaning; a single message stated over and over again in a variety of ways to ensure that it will not be misconstrued. It is poetry that makes myth possible: that is, it is the ambiguity of language, its polysemic potential, that generates the necessity for repetition in order to ensure but a single interpretation for the myth. One might, of course, reverse the priorities and say that myth gives rise to poetry, that diversity of expression guarantees ideological exactness; uniformity of expression, therefore, obscures ideology and thus feeds creative imagination.

The method we have used here is founded on the principal of integrity of the narrative. We need not search for an *ur*-myth, nor need we assume that the text is corrupt or that the medieval redactor and his audience were ignorant of their traditions. The analysis attempted here shows that the First Branch and part of the Third Branch of the *Mabinogi* are concerned, among other things, with the birth of Pryderi and his loss and return, the latter events paralleled by loss and restoration of fertility in the land. Was Pryderi human or divine? Who was his father? Because Pryderi is a divine hero, his father was lord of the other world. In Celtic tradition, the Lord of the other world is pre-eminently the sea-god. When he mates with the Great Queen, he partakes of her characteristic shape, which is equine. Pryderi is a hero among mortal men, though his origins are divine; the narrative concerning his birth reflects, therefore, the natural and supernatural conditions attendant upon that event. He is at once son of the mortal Pwyll, Prince of Dyfed, who is also known as Lord of the Otherworld, the son of Teyrnon Twrf Liant ("Lord of the Tempestuous Sea"), who is the mare's consort, and the son of Manawydan son of Llyr ("Sea"). And he is the son of Rhiannon, Queen of Dyfed, whose equine nature is skilfully divided among several narrative sequences.

After his birth Pryderi disappears and his mother disappears from the royal couch of Dyfed (that is, as the Third Branch has it, Pryderi and his mother disappear from the human and mortal environment). Through the vigilance of Pryderi's father (Rhiannon's husband), the enemy who caused their disappearance is overcome and Pryderi and Rhiannon are restored. In the mythic tradition, these events are simultaneous and partake of the same schemata; in the narrative tradition, they cannot possibly occur at the same time and are, therefore, treated more or less sequentially.

Prolegomena to a Reading of the Mabinogi 215

This foreword to a reading of the tales is intended to show that meaning may be discovered by the application of methodologies not traditionally applied by Celtic scholars. It is not exhaustive and may not be conclusive, but it argues strongly for the integrity of the text, the only literary artefact we have of the expressive genius of the Celts of medieval Britain concerning their mythological traditions.

NOTES

1. See esp. 4–12. Subsequent references will be given parenthetically in the text.
2. Lévi-Strauss, "The Structural Study of Myth," 81–106.
3. *The Study of Celtic Literature* (reissued by Kennikat Press, 1970), 51.
4. One is reminded here to be sure, of Frank O'Conner's caveat regarding twelfth-century Irish scribal activity *vis-à-vis* secular material, that they went about their work "in a spirit of a small boy trying to make a bicycle from the wreck of a perambulator" (70). Very much to the point, however, is Susan Wittig's comment, following Jakobson and Bogatyrev, that "Community acceptance . . . is the major factor in deciding whether a piece of oral folk literature or popular literature will survive to the point where it may be recorded and brought into the realms of written literatures" (181).
5. For a useful discussion and summary, see Ó Cathasaigh, *The Heroic Biography of Cormac Mac Airt*, 1–8.
6. Gruffydd, *Rhiannon*, esp. 41–43.
7. Jones and Jones, ed. and trans., *The Mabinogion*, xv.
8. Gwyn Jones, "Prose Romances of Medieval Wales," 143.
9. Glyn E. Jones, "Early Prose: *The Mabinogi*," 196–199.
10. Gantz, trans., *The Mabinogion*, 13.
11. Some recently published scholarship indicates a healthy trend in the search for meaning in these stories. Bollard, "The Structure of the Four Branches of the Mabinogi" concludes that the author possessed a deep understanding of the materials which he used in his tales, and he illustrates the point by a thoroughgoing investigation of the themes of friendships, marriages, and feuds. I cannot accept the statement that "The friendship between Manawydan and Pryderi is the central element of the entire tale" (257), but Bollard argues his case well. Ó Coileáin's "A Thematic Study of the Tale *Pwyll Pendeuic Dyuet*" is rather too short to get the job done, but nevertheless makes some important contributions. His description of the tension that exists between theme and struc-

ture is especially good. It strikes me as an alternative way of accounting for what Lévi-Strauss describes as the schemata of narratives. The problem with Gantz's "Thematic Structure in the Four Branches of the Mabinogi" is that it reduces the four narratives to a series of arbitrary parallels, e.g., "Math punishes Gwydyon [sic] —Lleu punishes Goronwy [sic]," or again, "Rhiannon desires Pwyll— Gilvaethwy [sic] desires Goewin." The parallelism of such reductions is specious and contributes precious little to our search for meaning in the stories. Despite the title of the essay and his stated disagreement with those who see the *Mabinogi* as confused and incoherent, Gantz admits that "the plots of the Four Branches are marred by numerous inconsistencies and oversights" (247). Even so, it appears that at least the idea of structuralist criticism is making some headway in the study of our texts.

12. Evans, ed., *The White Book Mabinogion.*

13. For a good discussion of medieval literary conventions for bridging the gap between the worlds of reality and enchantment, see Green, "The Pathway to Adventure."

14. Caesar, *De Bello Gallico*, vi. 18.

15. See, e.g., Ross, *Pagan Celtic Britain*, 308–321.

16. Lévi-Strauss, "The Myth of Asdiwal," 17.

17. In Gruffydd's account, the storyteller found himself in trouble because the roles of the mortal and the Head of Annwfn had been reversed; he reconciled this by making Pwyll chaste, so that no son could be born in this section of the tale as a result of "normal marital relations in Annwvn" (*Rhiannon* 44–45).

18. *Geiriadur Pryfysgol Cymru*, s. v. broch.

11

Narrative Structure in Medieval Welsh Prose Tales

R.M. Jones

In attempting to map out the principal constituents of a structural analysis, we seem these days to be thinking of medieval traditional narrative from two main standpoints. On the one hand there is the generally acknowledged likelihood of there being chronological or diachronic *layers* of development, one period having added to the former period or periods, so that we may detect signs within the final version of former states of narrative, and hypothesise that within the tales we now read there are hidden traces of mythology and remnants of more primitive story structures that have now been overlayered by subsequent development. This material has been intermixed, and we need nowadays to use some sense of discrimination in identifying the various strands that have joined together to provide the present narrative. I shall call this relationship between overlaying states of being, now cohabiting the same tale, *vertical structure*.

Then, on the other hand, there is a linear or synchronic relationship between the beginning, the middle, and the end, i.e. in the way the tale has been strung together through temporal narrative succession or causality, quite apart from where the story-teller found the multifarious materials or motifs he utilised in building up his whole. This I shall call *horizontal structure,* and it will be the main subject of this discussion.

If one agrees that there are various levels of *vertical structure* in the prose tales, it may be advisable for the literary critic to identify as a first step and without overdue confusion what particular level of structure he is discussing at any given time. The deepest structure, one may presume, is mythological; the next is to do with narrative form, but is so fundamental as almost to be related in its elementary state to the mythological structure. (One might call this—adapting Saussurian terminology—"tongue" narrative structure); the next level, though still narrative structure, is more superficial and self-conscious and the product of the particular occasion; it lacks systematic significance *vis-à-vis* one's reactions to the fundaments of cognitive contrast that one finds at the second level and can be termed "expression" narrative structure; and fourthly, we have a related level of stylistic structures, which although seemingly deeprooted, is—as with all matters of style—inherently a surface phenomenon however ancient.[1]

Before proceeding, therefore, to discuss what will be on the whole a horizontal or synchronic analysis of medieval prose narrative, it is well to remind ourselves in this way that scholars have always been attracted by various *layers* that must have fallen into place as the tales were passed down the centuries, and that vertical or diachronic analyses (which must necessarily be more hypothetical) probing from one layer down to the next may be useful at least in locating at what particular stratum of development the structure we are discussing came into place, although the layers are never quite as tidily identifiable as some may wish. One may illustrate by referring to *Y Tair Rhamant.* As I see it, we can possibly refer here to four main layers, dealing with the fourth in an appendix and allowing for some give-and-take between each of them, locating narrative structure somewhere between mythological structure on the one hand and stylistic structure on the other.

A. Myth (not necessarily localised geographically): This corresponds to the type of mentality that eventually blossomed more obviously in *Pedair Cainc y Mabinogi.* It has been suggested[2] that for *Y Tair Rhamant* there may have been an overall mythological structure organising them into a triad, and possibly corresponding to the threefold offices of the leader—viz. Knowledge (Peredur), Battle and princely strength (Owain), Fruitfulness and riches (Geraint): this is, of course, the well-known Dumézilian analysis of one important mythological structure.[3]

Another unifying or linking mythological structure, probably later and more likely, suggested as appearing in each of these Three Romances and giving a similar organisation to each of them in turn is related to the idea of sovereignty; but this hypothesis overlaps into our next layer at B.(i) and will be touched on in more detail there.

There are, of course, other mythological elements that were referred to in their time by Rhŷs and others, which ostensibly belong to a profound international pattern but which most critics have been loth to discuss since the little mourned and ignominious setting of the sun gods. Besides the effect myth had, as we saw, in generally organising an overall structure, it is occasionally accepted that myth also appears in The Three Romances in frequent *occasional* elements, such as magic storms, gwŷr duon, magic rings, dwarfs, witches, and various Otherworld figures, both helpers and opponents, activating well-known motifs. This broad mythological layer is presumably pre-Christian, although the tales that evolved[4] within it continued on to at least about the eighth century.

B. (i) Chwedl Frutaidd (localised): the pre-Norman Caerllion period, *c*. 1060–1170. Now we may venture a possible geographical setting.

In historical times *c*. 1060–1170 one might imagine the story being revolutionarily transformed from Myth to Chwedl Frutaidd, if that had not already happened, as I suspect, during the main saga-period of the previous three centuries; and it may be at this late stage that what was originally a mythological structure of sovereignty was superimposed on the tales but with a Brutian narrative intention. We are now possibly at the Caerllion court of Caradog ap Gruffudd (d. 1081), lord of Gwynllwg and Gwent Uchaf who ruled from 1055–1081. Although hardly a "national" hero, he enkindled a great deal of local patriotism with his attack on Porth Ysgewin (Porth Sgiwed) in 1065[5] where Harold was building a royal residence for himself: later (1072) he would be asking for assistance from the Normans in his feud with Maredudd ab Owain; he defeated Rhys ab Owain in 1078 and conquered Morgannwg (from Cadwgan ap Meurig), and was to die at the Battle of Mynydd Carn in 1081.

One can imagine that his rule would be a suitable political context for taking hold of a group of mythological stories, and utilising them as Chwedlau Brutaidd, something like *Cyfranc Lludd and Llefelys* or *Breuddwyd Macsen* both of which may belong to the same literary flowering in Caerllion,[6] relating the tales to a particular location and using them meaningfully at a particular point in time of local patriotic fervour.[7] Perhaps, within this same Brutian context, at a time when hagiographers such as Caradog of Llancarfan were engrossed in devising saints' *Lives* and clerics at Llandaf forging claims to diocesan boundaries, the raw materials that Geoffrey (1090?–1155) would eventually use as he got on to this particular pseudo-historical bandwagon in his *Historia* 1136 also began to crystallise, again with Caerllion as centre.

Besides moving Arthur's court to Caerllion, the Brutian story-teller was possibly also responsible for relating on the basis of sovereignty the Knowledge tale to Peredur and Efrog (and it was during this period, possibly in a written version, that Efrog and Eliffer, the usual father of Peredur were confused), the Battle tale to Owain and Lleuddin[8] (whose name disappeared in the Welsh version but survived in the French as Laudine), and the Riches tale to *Gwerec and *(W)ened (who came out eventually as Erec and Enide in Chrétien). This Dumézilian interpretation is, however, very tentative. Historically, such a flourishing of the Brutian tales, which is basically pre-Norman, belongs to the vital interest in the golden age 383–633, that had also been reflected in the sagas, and may have been an attempt to bolster up Welsh morale on the borders of Wales at a time of social upheaval: it was still basically the age of "Brythonic nationalism,"[9] i.e. of *Armes Prydain*.

Caradog's father, Gruffudd, who died in 1055 and was the son of Rhydderch ab Iestyn[10] (d. 1033), was in conflict with Gruffudd ap Llywelyn (d. 1063); and we have some information about the latter's court poet. We know his name— Berddig; and we know that Gruffudd ap Llywelyn gave him lands free of rent in Is-Gwent in the middle of the 11th century.[11] Berddig would be quite possibly the sort of person who may have done the initial adaptation of the mythological materials.

Caerllion could have remained an important focus for these materials down to the days of Caradog's great grandson Hywel who ruled until 1175, who also housed a poet of whom we have some information, namely Meilyr (d. end of 1174).[12] I presume that the Arthurian tales of Caerllion were however already fairly mature by this time,[13] and even penetrating elsewhere; but Meilyr may well have given them an extra energetic redaction as he celebrated the quasi-historical characters with prophetic fervour,[14] and he even may have carried them to Margam.

B. (ii) Rhamant (again localised): the Monmouth Breton period, *c.* 1100–1200.

During this subsequent "Breton-Norman" period which overlapped B.(i), there may have been no important development from the structural point of view, although there was a dramatic development in style and atmosphere. There could however have been a slackening of the sovereignty theme, certainly; and as Patricia Williams suggested they would now be taken as tales of valour.[15] Possibly, amongst other things, as appropriate entertainment for the "neithior."[16] There would have been innumerable "influences" of course— manners, clothes, arms, knights, customs such as the tournament (instead of the "oed"), a few personal names such as Hywel fab Emyr Llydaw, Limwris and Luned,[17] with an occasional episode thrown in. Towards the end of this period the Breton name Gwerec would be replaced in the Welsh version by Geraint, the Cornish hero,[18] as the relationship (formerly strong) with Brittany had become from the Welsh point of view attenuated; Cornwall, once including the whole peninsula, was now chosen, as the crossing of water was still a definite element in the tale.[19] But the style could have already adopted its new style as early as about 1100 by a Welsh *cyfarwydd* who provided the base for both *Y Tair Rhamant* and Chrétien's adaptations, on the one hand "rhamant" and on the other "romance."

Monmouth was one of three most significant centres of Breton influence in Britain, Rievault (in Yorkshire) and

Cornwall being the other two—pointedly so as we remember the eminence given to both York and Cornwall in *Y Tair Rhamant*, and all three places would have a special interest in the Matter of Britain.[20] It is likely that in this area of Erging, where Breton, French and Welsh circulated, parallel versions of the romances were to be heard from bilingual *cyfarwyddiaid* and were mutually influential; there may have been a certain amount of stylistic development, which is of course important; but in the basic structure there is presumably no need to suppose any profound significant change.

There are a few historical points that may be mentioned as providing an appropriate context for this period.

Even *before* the Norman invasion there were important links between Brittany and this area. Both St. Gurthiern and St. Ninnoc of Quimperlé were of royal parentage in eastern Wales. St. Méen claimed descent from the royal family of Archenfield, and N.K. Chadwick says of him: "St. Méen, one of the earliest and best attested of the Breton founding saints, and traditionally a relative and follower of St. Samson was sent on a diplomatic mission which eventually resulted in the foundation of the greatest of all forest monasteries in Gaël in Brocéliande."[21]

Samson's importance is well-known; but Chadwick points out that he is said to have finally set out to Brittany from this same district of Erging, and makes an interesting point: "Samson's *Life* (chapter 26) relates that as he and his deacon were passing through a forest, an attack was made on Samson's deacon by a sorceress, armed with a trident. The story reads like an echo of the encounter of the hero Peredur in the Welsh romance with the Seven Witches of Gloucester of which Sir John Rhŷs has left us an illuminating study. Is our Breton story a story of the Welsh forest Border transferred to Brittany?"[22]

Sir J.E. Lloyd has summarised the early history of Monmouth, as outlined in *Lib. Land.* 276–278, like this: "The castle was built by Earl William, and, on the fall of the house of Breteuil and its adherents, given to 'gueithenauc,'[23] who became a monk and was succeeded, first by 'Randulf de Coliuil' and then by 'Willelmus filius Batrun.' The charters of Monmouth Priory corroborate this account in several particulars, showing that 'Wihenocus' became 'sancti Florentii monachus' and was succeeded by his nephew, William fitz Baderon (Cal. Doc. Fr. 406–407). William was the castellan and local magnate in 1086."[24]

In other words, having already taken a significant part in the colonisation of Brittany only a few centuries previously, this area was now to be garrisoned under Breton leadership and its priory to be occupied by Bretons. The latter was a Benedictine establishment (before 1086) as too were the priories at Chepstow (before 1071), y Fenni (1087–1100), Goldcliff (1113) and Llangiwa (before 1183).[25] The Breton connections of some of the products of this important centre are worthy of note, the main products being:

(1) *Historia Regum Britanniae*, Geoffrey of Monmouth 1130–1139. His Breton roots are well attested. (Tatlock, *The Legendary History of Britain*, 438–443; Roberts, "Sylwadau ar Sieffre o Fynwy a'r *Historia Regum Britanniae*," 128–129).[26]

(2) *De Situ Brecheniauc* on the basis of a manuscript before 1150: Miller, "Historicity and the Pedigrees of the Northcountrymen"; Bartrum, *Early Welsh Genealogical Tracts*, 14 ff., probably from Monmouth;[27] with other tracts *Progenies Keredic* and *Generatio s. Egweni* from Vespasian A xiv.

(3) The kalendar of *Vitae Sanctorum Wallensium* c. 1200 on an eighth-century framework (Harris, "The Kalendar of the *Vitae Sanctorum Wallensium*"), presumably used at Monmouth Priory (note particularly the reference to Saint Dochelinus—the Saint-Florent connection.)

(4) Saints' lives in Vespasian A xiv, *Vitae Sanctorum Britanniae et Genealogiae*, ed. Wade-Evans; c. 1200: the lives having been originally written about 1080–1180. It seems also to have been used liturgically at Monmouth.

Silas M. Harris points out the uniqueness of Monmouth amongst priories in its Welsh sympathies;[28] and from the point of view of Welsh literature it may have been *the* most important priory between 1080 and 1200. Most of the natural context one would expect from geographical references and cultural background seem to point to Monmouth and Erging as the most suitable environment for the redaction of the *Tair Rhamant*,[29] and we may some day be able to accumulate some odds and ends of internal evidence as pointing in the same direction, such as the reference to *ffawydd*,[30] or even dialectal idiosyncrasies.[31]

Apart from mythology,[32] the aspect of systematisation that has gained most attention from students of medieval Welsh narrative and by the Welsh Folk Museum at St. Fagan's has been the work carried out by what is called the Finnish school. Classification of stories into sub-genres or types was outlined, of course, in *Types of the Folktale*, Antti Aarne and Stith Thompson,[33] and an even more important work from the Welsh point of view was the *Motif-Index of Folk Literature*, Stith Thompson (followed by *A Handbook of Irish Folklore*, Seán O Suilleabháin and *Motif-Index of Early Irish Literature*, T.P. Cross). Subsequent criticism of this approach by structuralists such as Vladimir Propp and E. Meletinski, however, seems to have gone comparatively unnoticed in Wales: a significent exception is Stephen Matchek's MA dissertation.[34]

Whereas the former classification has led to unsystematic groupings of motifs, Propp's conclusion points to the principle that the sequence of functions is always identical, and that all fairy tales are of one type in regard to their structure. Brumond's refinement of this model (1966,1973) has introduced a more temporal orientation, which is closer to my own approach. Undoubtedly in the future, the sort of work being done on the poetics of fiction by descendants of the Propp school will prove of vital interest to students of Welsh medieval narrative, as too will such developments as Todorov's *Grammaire du Décaméron.* One is therefore tempted to survey some of the broad field of structuralism as it seems at the present moment, and suggest in what ways work by critics such as Gérard Genette can contribute to our understanding of the form of the *Mabinogion*.[35]

What I have decided to do however is much more elementary. I want to examine some of the horizontal structural presuppositions we tend to make at present and contrast them with the structural presuppositions[36] that were possibly made by the medieval storytellers, concluding that a sympathetic reading and a satisfactory reaction to the

Gestalt of a medieval tale is prejudiced unless we have examined what may have been the premises in the middle ages. Ideas of what constructed a whole in medieval times were somewhat different from our contemporary prejudices, and it seems to me that interference with a proper appreciation of medieval narrative can come from two directions—the presupposition that discriminating the vertical structure is a pre-essential for understanding the tale as it now is, and secondly that medieval storytellers and their audiences had the same attitudes to artistic unity as we have.

In reading the native medieval tales of Wales, one rather disconcerting point of structure has bothered modern critics. Professor Brynley F. Roberts rightly refers to this uneasiness in analysing *Breuddwyd Macsen:* "For modern readers the *Dream* is marred a little by a lack of unified structure as the author progresses beyond what may strike us as the end of his story."[37]

And the *Dream* is not the only culprit. Every single one of the three Arthurian romances contains something of this kind. R.S. Loomis complains of "an awkward appendage" in *Owain;*[38] "the only flaw," agrees Professor Roberts again regarding this romance "... unnecessary, perhaps because it is misplaced;"[39] and further, Jean Frappier complains, "The Welsh author . . . tacks on an episode corresponding to Chrétien's 'Pesme Aventure' but does not attempt to attach it to the main plot."[40]

The "irrelevant adventure at the Hedge of Mist"[41] in *Geraint* on the other hand, has been excused as duplication by Patricia Williams, and as providing a summary of the central theme of the tale.[42] But Nitze describes the episode as being a "footless addition."[43] Jean Frappier referring to the corresponding adventure in *Erec* says of it that it is "entered upon without any motivation except a sort of knightly dilettantism," although he attempts to apologise for it paradoxically, "its very superfluity may be considered its justification."[44]

Peredur, too, includes an appendage not unlike that found in *Owain* and *Geraint.* Says Dr. Goetinck: "Peredur's final battle with the Witches of Caer Loyw is similar in that it occurs after the final denouement. It is however, closely linked to the body of the romance by making the Witches of Caer Loyw responsible for the misfortunes of the hero's family."[45]

When we have a phenomenon as strikingly consistent as this, in tales which otherwise may be artistically pleasing, the irregularity from the modern point of view begins to take on a certain regularity from the medieval point of view. Turning to the *Pedair Cainc,* we are not at all surprised therefore in *Branwen* to recognise the "journey to London by way of Harddlech and Gwales as a separate episode in the narrative" as Professor Mac Cana has pointed out;[46] "then comes," he adds "a sort of epilogue to the story of the fight in Ireland. It is patently an addition or an afterthought."[47]

The structure of *Math,* again has a certain elegant balance up to the creation of Blodeuwedd from flowers. "This," says W.J. Gruffydd, "is the end of the main theme. The rest of the story... is concerned with the unfaithfulness of Blodeuwedd and her intrigue with a lover, Gronwy Pebr or Pevr."[48] In other words, we have the central points of development in the tale followed, for whatever reason, by another development, seemingly irrelevant from the point of view of coherent structure.

Now, Dr. Tony Hunt, in his discussion of the art of *Owain,* has drawn attention to the final *Ruhepunkt* that occurs after the last major action.[49] He explains its function as being a relaxation of the tension associated with the central theme. Whatever may have been the motive behind this structural phenomenon (and there can be a hundred-and-one explanations),[50] what I am concerned with at the moment is simply its existence, and more significantly a possible presupposition on the part of the medieval audience that it should be allowed to exist. The appendage—corresponding structurally to an *envoi* in the *ballade* and the *chant royal*—is an acceptable even an expected part of conventional structure.

The theory that accepts the *Ruhepunkt* as normal in medieval tales contrasts pointedly with the criticisms of modern scholars, and perhaps underlines the need to describe medieval narrative structure primarily on its own terms. At the same time, we are naturally concerned with modern presuppositions as they may have led us to read the medieval tales with a hardened structural attitude that may interfere with our enjoyment. In other words, our own structural expectations may mislead our interpretation of what the medieval storyteller himself *could* permit quite unconcernedly.[51]

If we are correct in assuming that a medieval listener would be more prepared to accept as structurally pleasing a tale containing what we might consider an irrelevant appendix, may it not equally be acceptable for a preamble or warming-up section (comparatively irrelevant from our point of view) to be included for a similar reason?

The First Branch of the *Mabinogi*, *Pwyll*, is obviously a combination of two main structural elements. It begins with a minor section relating the adventure of Pwyll in Annwfn, and his acquisition of the name Pwyll, lord of Annwfn. Then the story proceeds to the major section which consists of three consecutive movements:[52]

(1) Pwyll and Rhiannon meet and marry;
(2) Rhiannon gives birth to Pryderi, who is subsequently abducted from her bedside; and she is punished for this disappearance;
(3) Pryderi is restored to his parents.

For the modern reader the apparently pointless combination of the foregoing minor section with this main body of the tale serves simply to confuse. As Professor Jarman says, "Nid oes iddo ar yr wyneb unrhyw gysylltiad â'r rhannau o'r chwedl sy'n dilyn, ac eithrio ei fod yn esbonio teitl newydd Pwyll a ddefnyddir yn gyson o hyn ymlaen."[53] To a medieval reader or listener, however, were the convention of combining such sections common and expected, then he might well have automatically reacted to the narrative structure, analysing it or separating the seemingly anomalous section, and placing it mentally as an attached introduction that he did not insist should run smoothly into the rest.

Reading in this way, we accept a narrative structure that would seem formerly to have allowed different artistic criteria from those obtaining at present. This discussion, as you perceive, will be synchronic, in so far as that is feasible, and avoid on the one hand speculations about any possible stages of development that may or may not have led up to the present text, and on the other hand expressions of our overduly fashionable distaste that the author does not adopt an early twentieth-century regard for smoothness of narrative. We will consequently tend to omit terms such as "crude joinery" or "evolution," and deal more or less with the structure of the narrative as it is,[54] assuming that medieval attitudes towards structure could possibly be different from our own and coherence may have been sorted out more creatively by author and listeners when adopting a different attitude towards the juxtaposition of composite narrative elements. Even so, synchronic or not, one naturally may speculate on what effect the structure of the narrative may have had on the author and his audience at that time.

Up to this point, we have suggested a possible medieval convention that accepts an additional narrative tag preceding or following the main body of a tale. Let us now direct our attention to the main body of the tale itself. Frequent reference is made by diachronists to the phenomenon of duplication. They perceive a particular incident or character repeated, as it were pointlessly, within a short space within a tale, and conclude that the incompetent medieval craftsmen, who were stringing the story together from disparate flotsam and jetsam, had not amply realised that duplication had arisen because of the previous existence of different versions of the same *motif*. These story-telling nincompoops had crossed their wires. They had insisted on continuing on the same line even although they had already passed that way, repeating themselves because of some sort of narrative lethargy.

Thus, W.J. Gruffydd draws attention to the fact that both portions of *Pwyll* begin with the same introductory formula. "Arberth is named anew in the second portion as if it had not been named before, whereas, as *Pwyll* is now constituted, the explanation that it was the chief Court of Dyved had already been given." He concludes from this that the first portion of *Pwyll* must once have been an independent tale.[55]

Now, one *may* be quite content to accept that the two parts had actually once been independent tales and have no quarrel with the diachronic method as *one* academic approach. What has to be added, however, is that the actual material at hand is no longer in two completely independent parts, and that the formula of repetition is an acceptable technique of story-telling not necessarily derived from fortuitous combination.[56] Seán Ó Coileáin has taken this point further and argued that "what Gruffydd calls Part II is in fact a doublet of his Part I, and the reason for the duplication may be explained in terms of theme."[57]

A popular demonstration of such duplication, defined as an approximate or disguised repetition of a character or event, is the story of the feast in *Branwen*—first in Harlech, then in Gwales. The question is asked by Glyn E. Jones,[58] "Why, then does *Mabinogi Branwen* tell us of two feasts? The answer is, that the whole episode in the tale is based upon two variant versions of the story, two versions that are attested elsewhere."[59] One need not quarrel with that answer in order to insist on an additional structural reason *why* it should be acceptable to include the two, why the author used the two events traditionally available; and that is because duplication or dual contrast is an inherent *cynneddf,* one of the ways the mind has of managing materials, of bringing them within its artistic organisation, comparable to psalmic parallelism, *cynghanedd* and so on.

Gruffydd has dealt with the duplication of Rhiannon's wedding-feast, first with Pwyll and then a year later with Gwawl. He forms the hypothesis that "the original story . . . before the *myth* of Rhiannon had been joined to the fairy tale of the *Marriage of Pwyll and Rhiannon* contained only one wedding, that of Gwawl and Rhiannon."[60] He claims also: "the marriage of Pwyll and Rhiannon and her 'kidnapping' by the other-world were equally part of the original tradition, but they had entered it at widely different stages in time and development."[61]

I am certainly not always convinced by Gruffydd's hypotheses. But what particularly perturbs me here is the kind of attitude the reader can develop towards the narrative by making this particular approach. One can tend to be over-conscious of vertical incoherences and confusions, and too lightly receptive to the horizontal artistic form.

Gruffydd at one point in his study of Rhiannon makes a revealing suggestion: the author faced by duplication in his original material would in Gruffydd's view have tried to disown it, or rather to disguise it in some way. He relates the suffering in the story of Manawydan to the *Eustace* legend, and says: "the *Eustace* legend was *necessarily* in two parts, the wanderings and sufferings of the husband with his wife, and the wanderings of the wife and husband separately. This imposed on the *Manawydan* version a duplication which the author for all his artistry failed to conceal—the tribulations of Manawydan, Rhiannon, Pryderi and Cigva in the first part, and the tribulations of Manawydan and Cigva after losing the others in the second part."[62] Far from being anxious to conceal a duplication, a Formalist such as Shklovsky would consider foregrounding the formal literary device as an enhancement of a work of art:[63] it is an establishment of the fact that we are dealing with a special terrain of literary craftsmanship. "The reason for the inclusion of this doublet in *Manawydan* is at first sight obscure," Gruffydd continues, "since, as it stands, it has no bearing on the rest of the *Mabinogi*." However, whatever may have been what the author had in mind[64] regarding this incremental emphasis on the suffering, from a structural point of view the duplication or balancing of one incident with another, causes no obscurity whatsoever.

In dealing with the two births from Aranrhod in *Math* Gruffydd begins by conjecturing like this: "It would probably be too fanciful to see in this double birth an attempt to fuse the two birth versions already noticed, namely the one birth following on procreation by Gwydion, and the second, a magic birth, the result of stepping over the wand. In that case, the first birth, the normal one, would represent Gwydion's activity, and the second, the mysterious and abnormal birth, that of the magic wand. Such an explanation is not precluded, and it may even have been present in the mind of one of the redactors. . . . " We notice how loth he is to part with the hypothesis, however fanciful; then he adds most pertinently, "on the other hand, we have had ample evidence that the story of the twin birth was an essential feature of both the Irish and the Welsh stories."[65]

If we adopt the structural viewpoint, however, we tend to accept duplication as a normal device, although for Gruffydd it can occasionally be "extraordinary" and demand the most intricate reconstructions. For instance, wishing "to explain the extraordinary duplication of Goewin and Arianrhod," he promptly conjectures, "we take Goewin in the original version to be the name of the wife who, with the aid of Gilvaethwy her lover, transformed her husband into a succession of animals. The matter," he claims, "will be clearer

Narrative Structure in Medieval Welsh

if we put it in the form of summaries. We have seen that *Math* is a complex of two stories about Balor. These original stories may now be written thus . . . "[66] And he forthwith concocts a pair of tales to divide up the sources.

Such is the diachronic standpoint.

How do we view duplication (or doublets) from a synchronic and structural point of view?

Let me begin by referring to some examples, limiting myself to the *Pedair Cainc*.

In each of the Four Branches we have unconcealed—even highlighted—duplication of certain incidents or situations, as for instance when we noted the scene set for the first part of *Pwyll* with the sentence—"A threigylgweith yd oed yn Arberth, prif lys idaw," and subsequently the second part beginning "A threigylgweith yd oed yn Arberth, priflys idaw." In the second part of *Pwyll* we mentioned two feasts, the first for Pwyll and Rhiannon in the court of Hefeydd Hen, and the second for Gwawl and Rhiannon; all this being not unlike rhyme in verse. Likewise, as we have seen in *Branwen* we have two feasts, the one in Harlech lasting seven years, and the other in Gwales lasting eighty years. In *Manawydan* there are two visits to the bowl. First, when Pryderi, against Manawydan's advice, goes into the fortress and sees a golden bowl hanging by four chains over a marble rock. When he stands on the rock and seizes hold of the bowl, his hands cling to the bowl and his feet to the rock. Later his mother Rhiannon follows him to the fortress, and she likewise grabs hold of the bowl, with the same result. In the story of *Math* we hear of a double birth from Aranrhod, first of Dylan and secondly of "some small thing of her behind her" which eventually blossoms into a strapping lad.

Other similar duplicated incidents could be exemplified. But it is well to note a similar series of paired *characters*. In *Pwyll*, Arawn frenin Annwfn lends his wife to his corresponding character namely Pwyll. Nisien and Efnysien in *Branwen* are examples of characters bearing opposing characteristics, i.e. negative repetition, the one bearing peace and the other causing tumult and war. In *Manawydan* the narrative is supported by two pairs of characters, Pryderi and Cigfa on the one hand, Manawydan and Rhiannon on the other. The two consecutive footholders required by Math fab

Mathonwy, namely Goewin and Aranrhod, have an obviously duplicating function. As Gruffydd puts it: "The original foot-holder is *made into two*, Gwydion still pairing with Arianrhod and Gilvaethwy with Goewin."[67]

This binary method of developing narrative is something, one suggests, not very unexpectedly, that penetrates in the storyteller's craft down into his very style,[68] and relates to such balanced phraseology as "dyuot yn y uryt ac yn y uedwl" (*PKM* 1.3–4); "y llys a'r kyuoeth i'th uedyant" (4.2); "Ef a doeth makwyueit a gueisson ieueinc" (4.8); "guelei ef teulu ac yniueroed" (4.12–13); "dissymlaf gwreic a bonedigeidaf/i hannwyt a'y hymdidan" (4.21); and the whole of the paragraph: "Amser a doeth udunt e uynet e gyscu, ac y gyscu yd aethant, ef a'r urenhines. Y gyt ac yd aethant yn y guely ymchwelut e weneb at yr erchwyn a oruc ef, a'y geuyn attei hithau. O hynny hyt trannoeth, ny dywot ef wrthi hi un gair. Trannoeth, tirionwch ac ymdidan hygar a uu y ryngthunt. Peth bynnac o garueidrwyd a wei y rungthunt y dyd, ni bu unnos, hyt ym pen y ulwydyn amgen noc a uu y nos gyntaf" (4.26–5.5).

There is patently no need to labour this point, apart from mentioning that what we have in the balance of noun with noun or epithet with epithet, we also have in wider syntax as e.g. "wrth ual y guelych y guassanaeth yndi, yd adnabydy uoes y llys," (4.3–5); "y urenhines o'r neill parth idaw ef, a'r iarll, debygei ef, o'r parth arall" (4.17–19); and so on. From a structural point of view, we perceive here the simple and well-established practice of linking two elements, such as we have through juxtaposition phonologically in rhyme, assonance, cynghanedd and metre, or semantically in parallelism, irony, comparison and metaphor. The establishment of any relationship always commences with a binary connection, and the human mind (as Lévi-Strauss has enlarged upon in anthropology[69] and Jakobson in linguistics and poetics[70]) defines its objects through observation of duality. Herdan in the introduction to his *Type-token Mathematics* speaks of "Boole's algebraic law of duality as the fundamental law of thought, i.e. of *linguistic content*, and our principle of geometric duality in language as the fundamental law of *linguistic expression.*"[71]

What I am discussing now is of course very elementary and very basic. But it is so important to establish its fundamentality that I intend to make few extended quotations. First of all, Gerard Manley Hopkins, "The artificial part of poetry, perhaps we shall be right to say all artifice, reduces itself to the principle of parallelism, ranging from technical so-called parallelism of Hebrew poetry and the antiphons of Church music to the intricacy of Greek or Italian or English verse."[72] Secondly, Axel Olrik in his discussion of the "Epic Laws of Folk Narrative": "Another important principle of *Sage* composition is the *Law of Repetition*. . . . In literature, there are many means of producing emphasis, means other than repetition. For example, the dimensions and significance of something can be depicted by the degree and detail of the description of that particular object or event. In contrast, folk narrative lacks this fullbodied detail, for the most part, and its spare descriptions are all too brief to serve as an effective means of emphasis. For our traditional oral narrative, there is but one alternative: repetition. . . . Every time that a striking scene occurs in a narrative, and continuity permits, the scene is repeated."[73]

Duplication of incidents, or what Thurneysen calls "doublets," has been discussed for *Táin Bó Cúalnge* by Cecile O'Rahilly in the introduction (xvii–xx, xxx) to her edition of that work, although she explains the phenomenon as "merely an indication that the story had existed for a long period in transition."[74] Thurneysen too believed that repetition denotes interference by one version of a tale in a parallel version. Both Thurneysen and Cecile O'Rahilly conclude that inconsistencies and contradictions arising in the *Táin* stem from the conflation of two or more earlier versions, which can of course be true; but structuralism would make us wary of making the original narrator a person less conscious than he should be of consistency and not properly conscientious about ironing out all contradictions. That would seem to be an attitude more particularly prevalent in the nineteenth century and the first half of the twentieth, as too would be Windisch's conclusion that the *Táin* lacks the final welding of disparate parts into a great whole. In other words, a structural approach would be more tolerant—or perhaps understanding—towards doublets.

Further, another quotation from Olrik: "Whenever two people appear in the same role, both are depicted as being small and weak. In this type of close association, two people can evade the Law of Contrast and become subjugated instead to the *Law of Twins*.... The word 'twins' must be taken here in the broad sense. It can mean real twins—a sibling pair—or simply two people who appear together in the same role.... Beings of subordinate rank appear in duplicate.... If, however, the twins are elevated to major roles, then they will be subordinated to the Law of Contrast and, accordingly, will be pitted against one another ..."[75]

I have laboured this digression in order to emphasise that when we encounter duplication in a narrative, it may possibly be principally an inherent part of established narrative structure. We are not necessarily obliged to hunt after hypothetical incoherences due to muddle-headedness or primitive incompetence or even craftsmanlike combination of sources, although of course these may be an *additional* explanation.

We have in recent years been witnesses of what has been called a Copernican revolution in the study of medieval tales, a revolution noticed by numerous scholars. Instead of following Matthew Arnold, and surmising that the *Mabinogion* were odd bits of rubble left after "an older architecture, greater, cunninger, more majestical,"[76] we tend now to follow C.S. Lewis when he claimed that "the romance is the cathedral and the anthropological material the rubble that was used by the builders."[77] Followers of the Matthew Arnold approach, such as Gruffydd, (who also imitated his verse), looked away from our tales at something earlier and concealed, tales that were not (unfortunately) available, but the tales that should have been told; and they almost regretted the ruins that remained. We now try to examine the actual tales as they exist in their excellence, and attempt to reveal the artistry in constructing such narrative from whatever may have been the inherited materials. Both methods, I believe, are valid.

When we progress from duplication to triplication, surprisingly we find fewer suspicious storyologists seeking out pre-textual explanations for the repetition. Whereas binary structure enkindles all sorts of hypotheses, ternary structure is so obviously intentional, as if *three* were company, and *two* a crowd.[78]

I have attempted recently in *Llên Cymru* to discuss ternary structure. For the moment, I will just refer to it as something that seemed to me to have been a basic presupposition in the medieval concept of structure. What I am trying to get away from, however, is thinking of either simple or threefold repetition as merely a stylistic device. This it may be occasionally; but it certainly seems much more than that. It is, rather, a basic structure for combining diversity in unity, a way of thinking about and analysing reality, an Aristotelian framework for interpretation, a *form of being* within which narrative may exist; and it pre-exists (conditionally as it were) the composing of tales that image the episodes of myth, legend or folklore. It is a form that is found indiscriminately in a variety of tales, whatever may be the theme or the motivation.[79]

Professor Mac Cana has dealt with threefold repetition of an incident with modifications in *Fled Bricenn*,[80] as too has Cecile O'Rahilly for *Táin Bó Cúalnge*.[81] In the main body, i.e. the second section, of *Pwyll* as we have observed there are three movements each possessing a certain autonomy. So too the *Mabinogi* of *Branwen* has in its major section a threefold movement:

(1) *Branwen, Bendigeidfran, Matholwch in Britain:* Branwen and Matholwch meet and marry. Matholwch is insulted by Branwen's half-brother Efnisien.
(2) *Matholwch and Branwen in Ireland:* Matholwch punishes Branwen for the insult he has received.
(3) *Branwen, Bendigeidfran, Matholwch in Ireland:* Bendigeidfran, Branwen's brother, comes to Ireland to avenge Branwen. There is great carnage and numerous deaths including Bendigeidfran's and Branwen's.

The minor section dealing with the feasting of the seven survivors in Harlech and Gwales seems, as we have seen, to be something of an appendage.

The *Mabinogi* of *Manawydan* again has a three-fold movement with no minor section to "confuse" (as is said) the simplicity of development. This is possibly one of the reasons why the modern reader tends to express his admiration for the cohesion of structure in this tale. It is noteworthy that like *Pwyll* and *Branwen,* the tale of *Manawydan* begins with a marriage, rather in contrast with the romantic tales of more recent times: this is a matter of structure to which I shall return anon. This is how Glyn E. Jones has summarised its content:

(i) Manawydan fab Llŷr marries Rhiannon, Pryderi's mother.
(ii) Enchantment falls on Dyfed, and Manawydan and Pryderi spend a period in England. On their return to Dyfed, Pryderi and Rhiannon become entrapped in a magic fortress which vanishes.
(iii) Manawydan succeeds in lifting the enchantment and freeing Pryderi and Rhiannon.[82]

The *Mabinogi* of *Math* is the most complex of the Four Branches. But once again the simplest analysis of the tale will properly come up with three main sections (although admittedly it is easy to manufacture triads at will, if one is less than critical):

(1) *Math and his foot-holder:* Math can only live when his feet are on the lap of a virgin *troedawg* (except in war). His nephew Gilfaethwy falls in love with the virgin (Goewin), and with the help of his brother Gwydion arranges a war. While Math is away fighting, Gilfaethwy rapes Goewin. Math has to get another virgin, and tests Arianrhod by making her step over a wand. She gives birth (a) to Dylan eil Ton and (b) to "something" that appears eventually as a boy. Having completed this section, as Gruffydd says (*Math* 48): "Nothing more is said of Goewin, nor of a further attempt by Math to obtain a foot-holder."[83]
(2) *Arianrhod's three curses on Llew, and Gwydion's reaction to them:* The boy (b) is taken to the mother

Arianrhod who swears three destinies, (i) that he have no name unless she give it, (ii) that he have no arms unless she arm him, (iii) that he have no wife from among mortals. Gwydion by his trickery cracks the first two destinies, and then with the help of Math, he makes Llew a wife out of flowers.

(3) *The unfaithfulness of Blodeuwedd and her intrigue with Gronwy Pebr:* Although the main theme is completed, almost a third of the tale remains.

In the tale of *Breuddwyd Macsen* the ternary structure is even more striking. Professor Brynley Roberts describes it in this way: "It is made up of three similar sections, the dream journey and awakening, the search which re-enacts the dream with much less detail but where significant features are specifically called to mind by the messengers, and finally Maxen's journey to Caernarfon to meet his love."[84] Actually, the same journey is described three times, just as we have three visits to the Fountain and a ternary progression in *Owain*.[85]

What is now needed is a more detailed examination of the diversified means of threefold repetition that the *cyfarwydd* adopted in order to avoid monotony. Professor Mac Cana in a note already referred to ("An Instance of Modified Narrative Repetition in *Fled Bricrenn*"[86]) has examined a particular use of repetition "assimilated to the triadic form" and noted that the modifications may take the form of synonymous variants, morphological variants, syntactical variants, verbal extensions, and changes in word-order. One cannot but think of these variable repetitive resources as a structural phenomenon corresponding to the astonishing *stylistic* variations that Professor T.J. Morgan has pointed out as available to the professional storyteller.

We may safely conclude that all basic literary form, which has to contain diversity within unity, was inevitably structured on binary or ternary opposition.[87] Some of such structures (the central ones) are absolutely unconscious or sub-conscious, such as the choice between 1 plus 2 stresses or 2 plus 2 stresses for the *cywydd deuair hirion,* or the fact that *cynghanedd* is systematised in either two-part lines *(Llusg* and *Croes)* or three-part lines *(Sain* and *Traws),* or the internal structuring of stanzas in pairs such as the *cywydd deuair hirion* or triads such as the *englyn*. Obviously at a more superficial level, as with style for example, the contrast or repetition in pairs or triads may seem to be more arbitrary and a conscious matter of choice: but the level of frequency of this practice persuades one to surmise that there is a psychomechanical process much more fundamental and involving a deep-lying tendency to organise thought in simple-contrast of two mutually opposing or repeating positions, that can be then as a group contrasted once more, and only once more, with a single further position without abandoning the process of a subconscious (or unconscious) grasping of a unified contrast. Thus we discover, even at the level of style as in the organisation of character relationships or the repetitive development of incidents in plot, a marked tendency for all these structures to incline towards either binary or ternary groupings.[88]

So far, I have tried to touch on three aspects of narrative structure, viz. *Ruhepunkt* or the appendage (with a brief reference to the prefix), duplication, and three-fold development. I want now to mention a fourth characteristic that may easily be misconstrued by the modern reader, and to this I shall give the name "irrelevancies" or "asides." Gruffydd describes the medieval tolerance of such "irrelevancies" when he admits as a norm "that quite unrelated and extraneous themes may be introduced into the tale."

The modern reader tends to fuss first of all over *smoothness* of narrative. He makes the limited pre-supposition that the various "parts" of a story should be linked firmly and coherently.[89] His mind grasps the structure only in so far as it is organically related; and just as transplanted organs that are not of the right texture are refused by the body, so the modern taste refuses to accommodate a *complex* of portions that have not been tightly tied.[90]

A second, and just as crucial supposition as the *linking* of parts in his reading of structure, is that the very presence of any "irrelevancies" is anathema. Whereas a medieval author and his audience might have been quite prepared *en passant* to accept without undue emphasis a variety of subsidiary intrusions, the modern taste has some difficulty in responding favourably to minor irrelevant detail.

Thirdly, it is well for us to remember that the story-teller was working within the context of a much richer body of tales of which he may have expected his audience to be aware. In other words, he could have expected them to pick up light references or footnotes that were not centrally relevant to the movement of his tale. Professor Patrick K. Ford comments: "Sometimes the storyteller refers to lore outside the context of his narrative, lore that he knows but has chosen not to incorporate or elaborate; at the end of the Fourth Branch, for example, he says, 'and according to the lore (i.e. inherited tradition) he was lord of Gwynedd after that.'"[91]

In speaking of structure, therefore, we are faced with a problem of listening. And this problem is based on our presuppositions about the positive relationship of part to whole, whereas the medieval mind might have accepted a negative relationship as well. Our presuppositions are crucial in any attempts at evaluation: if we make absolute judgements regarding necessities of compilation that are not suitable for the medieval author, we are expecting him to produce a text that he did not intend. Thus, modern structural presuppositions favour the ironing out of irrelevancies. In reading diachronists, one tends to sense that irrelevancies have to be explained or excused. But studying these tales as they exist, one cannot but suspect that these so-called irrelevances or asides—dare I say sangiadau?—were an acceptable and normal part of narrative structure, even perhaps part of the unconscious craft.[92]

Let me note examples of what may be considered "irrelevancies" from the modern standpoint. In *Pwyll* we suddenly hear of an unheralded "earl:" "y urenhines o'r neill parth idaw ef, a'r iarll, debygei ef, o'r parth arall."(*PKM* 4.18) The "debygei ef" here reminds us of "Peri a wnaethont bedydyaw y mab, o'r bedyd a wneit yna:" (*PKM* 23.15) it is a consciousness of anachronism. W.J. Gruffydd asks desperately, "Where did this earl come from?"[93] And of course, he explains it offhand either as arising from an older version or from contamination with another tale; but, less ambitious than usual, he leaves it more or less unresolved.

Another point for which Gruffydd reserves the epithet "otiose" is the reference to the feast and provision already given to the retainers (*PKM* 15.22): this, says Gruffydd, is a "curious remark"[94] that necessitates an explanation which includes contamination from elsewhere. However, *Pwyll* simply bristles with such inconsistencies and irrelevancies. At one point Professor Jackson began a roll-call related to one section of the tale: "Who stole the child? What was this mysterious claw? Why did it steal Teyrnon's foals? How did it come to drop the child in Teyrnon's stable and what was it doing there anyway?"[95] None of these is answered. It seems obvious that either the demands of the medieval audience were different from ours, or that the storyteller had a different idea of what was permitted.

Branwen likewise provides us with a fair crop of similar red-herrings. Sometimes, however, the red-herrings are of our own cooking as when the motives of Efnysien (i.e. apart simply from his "cynneddf") are complained[96] of as being inadequately presented. Such discrepancies abound towards the end of the tale where the location of "Talebolyon" (*PKM* 34, 28; 45, 14) for instance is complained of as being interpolated.[97] "Mordwyd Tyllion"[98] and "Ysbydawt Urdaul Benn"[99] are both clear evidence of ambiguous remnants. And so on. None of these comments would I quarrel with; but it is important to note that they could be added to comfortably and bear evidence that such obscurities were not particularly abnormal.

Manawydan is less cursed with irrelevancies perhaps; but *Math* provides us again with a rich supply. Goewin[100] disappears in an unmodern way. Dylan eil Ton is not properly accounted for, and one has to resort to suspected missing onomastic tales to interpret words such as "peddyd" and "morynion."[101] Gruffydd asks, "Why could not Math live unless he had his feet in a virgin's lap? The story, as we have it, supplies no explanation of this strange *cynneddv*." Another difficulty regarding the foot-holder arises after the punishment extended over three years: "During this time Math was without a virgin foot-holder, which is in flat contradiction to the beginning of the tale. Likewise, there is no account of how he was supplied after Arianrhod was proved to have lost her virginity."[102] Now, the main point I am trying to make is this. All these discrepancies may not have troubled the medieval audience as they do the modern critic, and the storyteller himself seems able to accommodate them without the concern shown in later days.

In taking a structural approach and perhaps going to the extreme of assuming that every irregularity is deliberate and every inconsistency an artistic part of the medieval structure, we would be guilty of the same over-zealousness as found in the diachronic approach. There are undoubtedly certain examples of clumsiness that, had they been pointed out to the medieval author himself—such as the patching observed by Jackson in *Pwyll*—he would probably have muttered "Diolwch," though I also suspect he might have considered contradictory oral material as a not uncommon or unsalutary experience.[103] The diachronic explanation for such difficulties may, of course, as Jackson claimed "be found by the methods of comparative folktale study."[104] From the literary point of view, however, a lack of balance in our appreciation of the tales arises when the hunt for origins replaces the analysis of the material as it actually exists. The historical perspective does admittedly account for some shortcomings, if the present text is presented as one imperfect stage in the step by step evolution that has left an occasional vestigial organ. But the trouble with vestigial organs, such as the claws of a python or the cartilaginous rods of whales or man's appendix, is that someone eventually demonstrates their function and that they are not really vestigial. And at the moment, a number of the seeming examples of clumsiness formerly noted by critics in medieval tales are turning out to be part of an unsuspected pattern, as Bollard has demonstrated.[105]

The interpretation of inconsistencies in medieval narrative has led to some incredible conclusions; and I will certainly avoid claiming today that these inconsistencies were either deliberate or a natural part of narrative structure at the time. Whatever their motivation or their source may have been, they existed; and we should hardly try to avoid them or even to explain them away. Dr. Tony Hunt in an article discussing the textual relationship of *Li Chevaliers au Lion* and *Iarlles y Ffynnon*[106] was led to surmise that more rational and functionally indispensable use of motifs in the French where the Welsh text was more purposeless meant that the Welsh text, in its surviving form, had been influenced by Chrétien's version. Now, there must be numerous historical explanations for these differences: the Welsh text may have retained ancient so-called pointless features that were ironed out by Chrétien; or the Welsh surviving version may have lost some of the rationality that existed in a previous Welsh text; certainly there are numerous points (such as the retention of the name of the Iarlles—Laudine) where one can be relatively certain that the French text has retained ancient characteristics; and certainly, Chrétien occasionally though not always shows a tidier structural adeptness and much more frequently a more subtle psychological sense than the Welsh, apart from his many other virtues. But one could suppose that problematic features for the twentieth-century reader may not necessarily have seemed so puzzling or obtrusive to the twelfth-century listener, and probably the Welsh sense of form was at least as different from the French as prose from verse.

I want to move on to a fifth and final characteristic of medieval narrative structure, and to this I shall give the description "decentralised continuity."

The diachronic obsession builds up a resistance to accept a piece of narrative as it is, and inserts a presupposition regarding unity.[107] A synchronic idea of decentralised structure on the other hand would replace that artistic response with a different expectation, and acknowledge that at a particular time, when the tales were recorded, it could well have been aesthetically acceptable for each to have several centres of interest, numerous climaxes, and even a series of beginnings and endings. If we can rid ourselves then of diachronic yearnings, we can be free to examine the heterogeneous material before us, as it is, with a certain amount of aesthetic adjustment and ascertain what sort of structure seemed to be proper and satisfying at a particular point.

What I mean by decentralised or acentric continuity is what W.P. Ker has described, in discussing the *Song of Roland* as "separate scenes with no gradation or transition between them."[108] In trying to adapt Ker's generalisation on the *Song of Roland* to the Medieval Welsh tales as a whole, one would lose sight of the obvious inter-relationship of most scenes in the narrative. What I am arguing is that, seemingly, a medieval audience was more prepared to accept some sort of self-containment[109] in the various units forming the "flow of events." Syntactically we have frequently noticed the compulsive presence of connectives, alongside the distinct lack of *causal* connectives: this is reflected in the linking of narrative units, which may have a chronological sequence through juxtaposition, but by avoiding the subordination of a chain of events to a central climax, tends to suggest a certain equality of value in emphasis between the various parts of the tales. The events are linked by succession, not by coherently motivated causality. The scheme is there: there is a whole: but it is looser from the modern point of view than the cohesive continuity that, at least until the mid-twentieth century, most readers had expected from their story-tellers.

I have mentioned the fact that marriage can occur fairly early in a tale, even at the beginning. This is crucial in any structural presupposition. The modern romantic attitude expected marriage to provide a climax near the end of a tale. In three of the Four Branches, marriage, however, is placed near the beginning and provides a starting-point for development. In the Fourth Branch, although marriage is not at the commencement, when it occurs it does not imply a *finale*, any more than it does in the Three Romances—and a series of events flows from it. This fact leads one on to relate the decentralisation of continuity to a new approach to "climax." We do not of course deny that the value of medieval marriages was different, although perhaps not within its own context any the less; what we are emphasising is the structural location.

Although the medieval story-teller certainly places importance on what we would consider the kernel or centre-point of the event being described, the existence of a climax or organising-factor does not prevent him from moving on to an equally important new centre-point. A climax is not so important that it *may* not (necessarily) militate against the appearance of an equally significant climax.

This procession or decentralised structure, with "one marvellous event following swiftly upon the other" (as Glyn E. Jones puts it) is particularly obvious in the Three Romances, tales where the centre-points are scattered, decentralised, strung out, and reaches its ultimate extreme in *Breuddwyd Macsen*. J.K. Bollard has adapted Vinaver's theory of Interlace to the Four Branches; but its relevance for the Three Romances is of course even greater.[110] Vinaver argues,

"Lot made the all-important discovery that no single section of the ["Lancelot-Grail"] Cycle is self-contained: earlier or later adventures are recalled or announced, as the case may be, in any given part of the work. To achieve this the author, or authors, had recourse to a narrative device known to earlier writers, including Ovid, but never before used on so vast a scale, namely the device of interweaving a number of separate themes. . . . As C.S. Lewis puts it, 'there steals upon us unawares the conviction that . . . this is the sort of thing that goes on all the time, that it was going on before we arrived and will continue after we have left.' . . . Any theme can reappear after an interval so as to stretch the whole fabric still further until the reader loses every sense of limitation in time or space. . . . At the root of it all lies a highly developed sense of linear growth, and understanding of the great aesthetic possibilities of digression and recurrence, and the feeling of continuity and movement maintained throughout the vicissitudes of individual adventures."[111] From this viewpoint, one could surmise that the impression left on a medieval reader by the disjointed details of *Breuddwyd Rhonabwy* would be less incongruous than they are to us.

One would insist, however, in conclusion, that a synchronic structuralist approach should not be set up *in opposition* to a diachronic storyologist approach. It is rather, as I suggested at the beginning of this paper, as horizontal is to vertical. The one supplements the other, without invalidating it. When Gruffydd claims that "the first part of *Pwyll* can have *no meaning* unless we assume that the roles of the Lord of Dyved and the Head of Annwn have been reversed during the long developments of the *Mabinogi*,"[112] he is simply over-stating his case. Obviously, scholars may make storyologist, folkloric or mythological interpretations of these tales; but from a literary viewpoint, the text is as it is, and there is something of a challenge to respond to its own peculiar sort of complexity at least occasionally in a flexible and sympathetic manner within its own context of structural presuppositions as far as these can be analytically discerned.

APPENDIX (Stylistic Structure)

The structural and stylistic approaches have perhaps been most fruitful in the analysis of *formulae* a loose term (like "structure" itself) that I adopt here to imply a brief repeated device—be it the same combination of words or the same type of construction—used to represent a fairly regular or regular function in a tale. Professor Arwyn Watkins has drawn attention to the syntax of story-openings. I translate: "The placing of the subject at the head of the opening sentence as the narrator told his story was a declarative device used in the Medieval and the Early period. It would be a very effective way of gaining an audience's attention, first to the fact that the telling of a tale was about to begin, and secondly to the title of the tale intended. In other words, it was an additional item in the stylistic equipment at hand."[113] Similar ceremonial formulae could be discovered were we to examine the closing routine or "coda," which is a kind of rounding-off statement following the resolution of the plot.

Dr. Charles-Edwards in an examination of *Pwyll* has revealed "the existence of a set of rules governing the use of titles in dialogue and also determining the question of who should speak first."[114] He has given special attention to openings and modes of address. A further development of the analysis of dialogue (which would of course have been irrelevant to Dr. Charles-Edwards's analysis of honour and status) would include the methods of concluding conversation[115] as well as the rules for maintaining a give-and-take in the flow of discourse, such as giving the addressee options.[116] *Ymddiddanion* as a significant element in the tales have also received a certain amount of attention from both Professor A.O.H. Jarman[117] and Mr. Glyn E. Jones, as well as Mr. W. Lindsay Evans.[118]

Professor T.J. Morgan[119] has likewise drawn attention to a number of subtle syntactical points, such as the maintenance of diversity in narrative which is of necessity a succession of speech acts in the preterite.[120] Melville Richards's discussion[121] of the Araith, i.e. the multiplying of adjective runs and compound words, in the native tales was most suggestive and has been developed by J.K. Bollard.[122] But despite the high number of studies of copula constructions (and its possible usefulness for dating[123]) and countless studies of so-called abnormal sentences, the stylistic significance of these matters has hardly been touched upon.[124]

There still remain innumerable items of stylistic equipment in the armoury of the Welsh story-teller that need to be examined from the point of view of literary artistry, such as the conventional enumeration of names,[125] the use of the verbal-noun,[126] the postponal of the pronoun,[127] the use of the reduplicated auxiliary pronoun,[128] and numerous others.

Of what value can a rhythmic analysis of medieval Welsh prose narrative be? I have made a scattered survey of a number of paragraphs in the *Pedair Cainc* to try to discover what results are thrown up, and particularly to perceive whether certain impressions regarding the prose are defined more precisely or *pointed* by such an analysis.

The methodology I have adopted, rightly or wrongly, has been a slightly different approach from Dr. Sioned Davies of Cardiff,[129] although this in no wise suggests that her method, because its emphasis diverges from mine, is not eminently preferable. I have taken, rather, the familiar premise that rhythmic or other groups tend basically to cluster and contrast in twos or threes, and that we are dealing with prose and not with verse, and not necessarily in ruins. Here are the "sentences" therefore in the first paragraph of *Pwyll*, according to whether the rhythmic groups have two main stresses or three (*PKM* 1, 1–18): (1) 3,3; (2) 3,2,3,2; (3) 3,2; (4) 2,2,3,3; (5) 3,2,3,3; (6) 2,3,3,3; (7) 2,3,3,/2,2,3; (8) 3,2,/3,3,2,3; (9) 3,2,2,/3,2. Scanning this great variety of rhythmic form, a few characteristics are immediately obvious:

(i) The nature of the balance in the opening sentence:

> "Pŵyll, Pendéuic D'yuet,/ a oed yn árglwyd ar séith cantref D'yuet."

(ii) The quality of the swing in the *repetitive* rhythmic run in sentence six:

> "A chánu y górn/a déchreu dygýuor yr héla,/a chérdet yn ól y cwn, /ac ymgólli a'y gyd'ymdeithon."

i.e. attention being drawn to a run of three-beat groups, as it may elsewhere be drawn to a run of two-beat groups.

(iii) Attention is directed too to the precise point where there is rhythmic echo or repetition of an accented pattern as between sentences: (3), following a doublet in sentence (2), and (8)a:

> "Sef kýueir o'y gyúoeth a uynnei y héla,/Glýnn Cúch."
> "Ac ef a wélei lánnerch yn y cóet/o uáes guástat."

There are shadows of similar rhythmic repetition as between (6) and (7)a. A steady beat through rather regular repetition often tends to heighten the emotional force.

(iv) The variation of sentence-length is more specifically located by such a description as this as are the changes (or otherwise) of types of rhythmic groups within the sentences. Were we to make a more detailed rhythmic analysis, and use terms such as trochees which give us comparatively light endings, and spondee or amphibrach which tend to be heavier and give more of a feeling of finality, then the impression the ears sense would be made more precise on a number of further counts.

(v) It is interesting to notice the number of sentences in this particular paragraph-run that begin with a 3, 2 or a 2, 3 pattern, as if the author at this point has a framework for sentence-opening.

At the moment, there is far from agreement on a reliable and practically useful method of prose analysis. Readers, though only occasionally disagreeing on the location of stress, will feel quite strongly on the division into feet. Nevertheless, I would like to repeat this same excercise with a quite different paragraph (or rather run of sentences)—namely the famous passage in *Manawydan* describing the wasting of the land (*PKM* 51, 20–52,3): (1) 2,2/2,2/2,3,3; (2) 2,3; (3) 2,3,3/3,2,2,2/3,2,3/3,3,2.

(i) Sentence length, particularly in the remarkable third sentence is obviously an important element.

(ii) The monotonous repetition of double accent groups, almost to surfeit, particularly in the first sentence, but also in (3) though not so markedly, is another striking feature. Apart from this repetition, which provides a kind of balance between phrases, there is lack of balance as between sentences and within the individual sentences themselves.

(iii) There is rhythmic echo, not irrelevant from the semantic point of view, between sentence (2) and the beginning of sentence (3):

> "Ac yn ól y nyẃl,/llýma yn goleuháu pob llé."
> "A phán edrychýssant/y fórd y guélyn y préideu."

as too between sentence (1)c and sentence (3)a:

> "llyma gáwat o nýwl/yn dýuot hýt na chánhoed/yr ún ohónunt wy y gílid."
> "A phán edrychýssant/y fórd y guélyn y préideu,/a'r anréitheu a'r kyuánhed kyn no hyñny."

One would be foolish as yet to be dogmatic regarding any of these conclusions. One may add that in this broad arena in Welsh prose, we find, as usual, Saunders Lewis having already led a skirmish or two, particularly regarding the *cursus* of sentence endings, albeit in Renaissance Prose. And, as there has been a slight enkindling of interest recently in the transition between Medieval Welsh Prose and the Prose of the Renaissance, no doubt when such a study develops, we shall hear more about the *cursus* of Medieval Prose too and other characteristics of its rhythm from a contrastive point of view.

Another aspect of rhythm not mentioned here is the presence and proportion of non-accented syllables, a profusion of them providing lightness and seeming less authoritative. An analysis of this kind may, it seems to me, serve to sharpen the response of the senses, though I doubt whether it is the proper path to follow in hypothesising diachronically on whether an earlier version of the *Pedair Cainc* included a greater share of verse interludes than at present, in the form of *englynion*, a not unlikely possibility, but hardly to be proved by this method.

NOTES

1. At this highest (i.e. latest) archaeological layer, one would come across—in the Romances for instance—contemporary references to clothes, manners, fashionable (particularly Norman-French) preferences such as blonde hair or clean-shaven features, arms and methods of fighting, buildings, food fads, "religion" and the social hierarchy.

2. Rees, *Ceinciau'r Mabinogi*, 52 ff.

3. The idea has been mainly developed by Goetinck, *Peredur: A Study of Welsh Tradition in the Grail Legends*; "Historia Peredur"; and "Sofraniaeth yn y tair rhamant"; and criticised by Lovecy, "The Celtic Sovereignty Theme and the Structure of *Peredur*." See also, Rees, *Ceinciau'r Mabinogi*, 42. Dr. Jenny Rowland in her PhD dissertation, Wales, *A Study of the Saga Englynion*, 1982, has suggested a sovereignty theme for Canu Heledd, as too for the poets of the princes has Andrews, "Rhai Agweddau ar Sofraniaeth yng Ngherddi'r Gogynfeirdd," where other examples of the sovereignty theme, such as *Breuddwyd Macsen* and *Manawydan* are touched upon, 23–30. McKenna has dealt with "The Theme of Sovereignty in *Pwyll*." This is how Bromwich, in *Trioedd Ynys Prydein*, describes the theme of *Geraint*: "I believe that indications have survived in the story of *Erec-Gereint* which suggest that this was ultimately based on a narrative ... in which the hero ... was mated to a heroine who represented the tribal goddess of the land he conquered" (348): compare, Mac Cana, "Aspects of the Theme of King and Goddess in Irish Literature," esp. 76–114, 356–483; Máille, "Medb Chruachna," 129 ff; O'Rahilly, "On the Origin of the Names *Érainn*

and *Ériu"*; Bromwich, "The Celtic Inheritance of Medieval Literature," 213–214, and in "Dwy Chwedl a Thair Rhamant," 167–169.

4. There are numerous relevant discussions, e.g. Ross, *Pagan Celtic Britain*, 24, 29–30, 38, 137. For suggestions on mythological structure sometimes critical of the Dumézilian approach see Littleton, *The New Comparative Mythology*, and Gray, "Cath Maige Tuired: Myth and Structure'" (1–24). Besides mythology, structuralists such as Lévi-Strauss have also opened out a number of related fields in anthropology that are of relevance in studying medieval prose narrative.

5. Lloyd, *A History of Wales* II, 372–373, 377.

6. The fact that this was the most Romanised area in Wales, with Julian and Aaron having been martyred here, and a Christian chapel belonging to the Sub-Roman period having been found at Caerwent seems still to have had some significance in its identity. Gwent would provide a most suitable location to present the Macsen connections with Brittany, Chadwick, *The Colonization of Brittany from Celtic Britain*, 258–259. For the Gwentian connections of Macsen, see Wade-Evans, "The Llancarfn Chronicles," 163. Caerllion, together with Caernarfon and Caerfyrddin are named as forts built for Elen (I. Williams, ed., *Breuddwyd Maxen*, 9,9). And it was from Caerllion that Macsen set out on his victorious conquest towards Rome (*Breuddwyd Maxen*, 10, 4–9). As Brewer and Jones demonstrate, "Popular Tale Motifs and Historical Tradition in *Breudwyt Maxen*," and the fact is particularly significant in light of the Breton connections at Caerllion—"traditions about the Roman Helena have become attached to another Elen, the daughter of Eudaf... a sister of Cynan. Cynan,... is none other than the Conan Meriadoc of Geoffrey, the Dumnonian leader regarded in one strand in Welsh historical tradition as the founder of Brittany. In the *Dream of Maxen*, thererore, it would appear that one has the bringing together, within a 'Falling in Love through a Dream' tale, of the two reputed leaders of the colonization of Brittany, Cynan and Maxen... " (27). For the Breton connections with Maxen, see Fleuriot, *Les Origines de la Bretagne*, 110–123, 259. Andrews, in "Rhai Agweddau ar Sofraniaeth yng Ngherddi'r Gogynfeirdd," has suggested parallels between *Y Tair Rhamant* and *Breuddwyd Macsen* besides some of the tales related by Geoffrey, as too have Bromwich, "Dwy Chwedl a Thair Rhamant," 155, and Goetinck, *Peredur*, 181. Bowen, *The Settlements of the Celtic Saints in Wales* has located the Maxen Wledig cult in this area, 21–22, 36; and there are connections between Elen's genealogy and Dyfnaint, (Bromwich, *Trioedd Ynys Prydein*, 342, 357); Pearce, "The Traditions of the Royal King-List of Dumnonia," 130, 134–135, 139; Pringle, "The Kings of Demetia," 70 ff; and Chadwick, *The Colonization of Brittany from*

Celtic Britain, believes that there were oral traditions about Maximus within Geoffrey's hearing. The great saint of this area was Dyfrig, the great-great-grandson of Maxen, (see Wade-Evans, "Brychan Brycheiniog," 13). I had it from Wade-Evans that he would have revised the scheme in"The Llancarfn Chronicles," 163, adding Iddon II son of Ynyr Gwent son of Carata150c (son of Gurcant Maur), and deleted Meuric, Athrwys, and Morgan Mwynfawr as well as Tewdric (the Tintern martyr); further adding Teitfall son of Idnerth (brother to Nynnio). The link between Wales and the splendour of Rome would have appealed to a Caerllion audience.

The Geoffrey of Monmouth context for *Cyfranc Lludd a Llefelys* need not be laboured, compare Brynley F. Roberts's edition, Dublin, 1975, xi–xxxix: this, of course, does not prove any certain relationship between the tale and Geoffrey's geographical situation; but it is usual to recognise some connection between Geoffrey and these two tales, though they are independent (e.g. Bromwich, "Dwy Chwedl a Thair Rhamant," 143). Marie de France also seems to have vital links with the Caerwent/Caerllion/Caerdydd area: see Bullock-Davies, *Professional Interpreters and The Matter of Britain,* 14–15.

7. A late eleventh-century poem already refers to the tale of *Cyfranc Lludd a Llefelys,* therefore pre-dating Geoffrey.

8. Bartrum,*Welsh Genealogies,* I, 11.

9. Britannia was displaced by Gualia and Cambria in some ways about the twelfth century: Wade-Evans,*Vitae Sanctorum Britanniae,* vii, n. 4, although this is a bold generalisation.

10. Rhydderch ab Iestyn (1023–1033) king of Deheubarth
|
Gruffudd d. 1055 (opposed by Gr. ap Llewelyn)
|
Caradog d. 1081 (ruled 1055–1081)
|
Owain (ruled from 1081)
|
Morgan d. 1158   Iorwerth o Wynllwg (ruled Caerllion
                                          1158–1171,1173–1175)
                |
       Owain d. 1172   Hywel, ruled with Iorwerth
                          until1175;established
                          Llantarnam in 1179; i.e.
                          Caerllion, a Cistercian
                          branch of Ystrad Fflur.

11. E.G. Jones, "Llythyrau Lewis Morris at William Vaughan, Corsygedol," 13; Lloyd, *A History of Wales,* II, 372. On the question of an author for The Three Romances, Bromwich has some valuable suggestions in "Dwy Chwedl a Thair Rhamant," 169–172.

12. It is interesting to note that even in the second half of the fifteenth century a similar interest continued in these parts, Trahaearn ab Ieuan ap Madog of Pen-rhos Fwrdios near Caerllion possessing a Welsh copy of the Greal.

13. It is not unlikely that Arthurian sagas grew and matured particularly between c. 700–1000, and possibly were known to the Normans who settled in Herefordshire before 1066: Lloyd, *A History of Wales*, II, 363; I. Williams ed., *Pedeir Keinc y Mabinogi*, xxxiv. On the basis of the Triads (I. Williams, ed., *Canu Llywarch Hen*, xci) one could suppose them pre 1050–1100.

14. Gruffydd, "Meilyr Brydydd a Meilyr Awenydd," 313–316; Lloyd *A History of Wales*, II, 546 n. 50. Iolo Morganwg was the first to suggest that the court of Caerllion-ar-Wysg provided the basis for medieval Welsh prose: Ms. Llanover C.71, National Library of Wales (13158A), 133–135.

15. P. Williams, "Y Gwrthdaro Rhwng Serch a Milwraieth yn y Tair Rhamant," 49. Of the Three Romances the only one that succeed in leaving an impressive ideal for the noblemen in subsequent years was *Owain* which not only provided the image of Owain as Iarll y Cawg, Iarll y Ffynnon, Iarll yr Og (e.g. Gwaith Wiliam Llŷn, Roy Stephens, Ph.D. Wales, 1983, 49.37; 93.23; 7.92; 3.73) but also Luned as the ideal lady (ibid 66.59; 140.93; 143.77).

16. In "Posidonius's Celtic Parasites," J.E.C. Williams says: "Until comparatively recent times, even in Europe, marriage involved not only the union of two persons, the man and the woman united in marriage, but also the association of the two families and two circles of kinsmen"(334).

17. I am not so convinced as formerly, "Y Rhamantau Cymraeg a'u Cysylltiad a'r Rhamantau Ffrangeg," that Luned comes from the French. It is generally conceded that *Le Lai de Désiré* and *Yvain* come from a common source (Ahlström, Arthur Brown, Loomis), 217. The name Désiré(e) is an exact translation of Eluned, and Jean-Claude Lozachmeur's attempt, *La Genèse de la légende d'Yvain*, II, 16 ff to relate "Désiré" to a Breton variant of Yvain, viz. Ionet or Ivonet is not nearly so convincing. The prefix *El-* (great, many) is of course well-testified in personal names, Elgi, Elfan, Elgan (Thomas, "Enwau Afonydd a'r Olddodiad-Wy," 30), and may as an unaccented initial vowel have been lost by this time: Pierce, *The Place-names of Dinas Powys Hundred*, 17, 51, 261–262, Lecwith, Ligwg, Lywlod, Lai, Liddon, Luggy Brook, Leri.

As regards the tournament, the step from serious single combat to more "playful" combat is not a big one, particularly in the Romances; and single combat amongst the Celts was witnessed in Classical times as Diodorus, based on Poseidonios, mentions "When the armies are drawn up in battle-array they are wont to advance before the battle-line and to challenge the bravest of their opponents to single combat, at the same time brandishing before them their arms so as to terrify their foe." (Tierney, "The Celts and the Classical Authors," 32). B. Jones makes a different interpretation, "Rotunda Tabula neu Dwrneimant yn Nefyn yn 1284," 23–29.

18. According to Pearce, "The Cornish Element in Arthurian Tradition," one should look for the context of the Black Book Geraint poem in South-east Wales, 154.

19. The "market" interest from Cornwall may have been significant, as in the case of Geoffrey (Ditmas, "Geoffrey of Monmouth and the Breton Families in Cornwall," 451–461.); Roberts, "The Treatment of Personal Names in Early Welsh Versions of *Historia Regum Brittaniae*," 276n, 277, 287.

20. Constance Bullock-Davies, *Marie de France and South Wales*, Wales PhD dissertation, 1963, 153–155, 348, 350, 358, 361–365, 408, 436; Stenton, *The First Century of English Feudalism: 1066–1166*.

21. Chadwick, *The Colonization of Brittany from Celtic Britain*, 277–278; compare De La Broderie, *Histore de Bretagne*, i, 423 n. 3. This would explain one possible link of interest between Erging and Bro Erech (Bro Weroc, named after Waroch II, c. 577–594) who acquired Vannes in 579 and ravaged the Frankish territory as far as Rennes, giving his name to the romance hero of *Erec et Enide*. Fleuriot, *Les Origines de la Bretagne*, draws attention to the South Glamorgan connections of Paul, Teliau, and Leonor, the Gwent connections of Malo, and the Erging connections of Méen and Tudual, 215. Fifth century Erging is described by Fenn, "The Age of the Saints," in these terms: "Missionaries as well as traders made their way to Wales where the main centre of their activities seem to have been in Erging . . . the centre of a network of Roman roads leading to all parts of England and Wales. . . . The centre of this missionary activity was Hentland whose fame should equal that of St. Paulinus's *Ty Gwyn* and St. Illtud's *Llanilltud Fawr* in the chronicles of the Welsh Church" (2–3).

22. Chadwick, *The Colonization of Brittany from Celtic Britain*, 297; Lloyd, *A History of Wales*, II, 396n; 444–445; Stenton, *English Feudalism*, 24, 25, 28n; Goetinck, "Historia Peredur," 143.

23. The Breton Gwethenoc, Guidhenoc, Guienoc, Wethenoc, Wihenoc.

24. Lloyd, *A History of Wales*, II, 276–278.

25. Knowles, *Medieval Religious Houses: England and Wales*, 58–93. Further to the Breton connections of this area, see Roberts, "Sylwadau ar Sieffre o Fynwy a'r *Historia Regum Britanniae*," 128.

26. I tend to see what is sometimes referred to as "Geoffrey's mythmaking" as part of the well-established activity in the border area (from Clwyd to Casgwent) and including many of the sagas, that attempted to bolster morale at a time of peril.

27. Miller makes a relevant point in "Historicity and the Pedigrees of the Northcountrymen": "The admission of this group of purely secular people into a predominantly ecclesiastical and Latin document presumably demonstrates pressure from venacular literature at some time before 1150" (258).

28. Harris, "The Kalendar of the *Vitae Sanctorum Wallensium*," 21. Of the saints' lives Wade-Evans omits a Life of St. Teilo by Galfriaus, two lives of St. Dyfrig, a Life of St. Clydog, a life of St. Maedóc and the navigation of St. Brendan. For further discussion of *VSB* see "Presidential Address: 'Vespasian A XIV'"; Emanuel, "An Analysis of the Composition of the 'Vita Cadoci'"; and particularly Hughes, *Celtic Britain in the Early Middle Ages*, 53 ff. Also omitted in *VSB* were the Kalendar, the Old Cornish glossary, and *De primo situ Landauentis ecclesiae*.

29. The change from *Gwerec (Erec) to Geraint of Cornwall raises the question of the Cornish interest at Monmouth. In the Monmouth priory was copied the first "dictionary" of Cornish, about 600 years before the next vocabulary followed it— Vocabularium Cornicum (E.T. Graves, "The Old Cornish Vocabulary, PhD," Columbia, 1962); Jackson, *Language and History in Early Britain*, 60–61; I. Williams, "Vocabularium Cornicum." Geoffrey's interest in the Bretons of Cornwall is now manifest. (Ditmas, "A reappraisal of Geoffrey of Monmouth's allusions to Cornwall"). The significance of the peninsula of south-west Britain as the natural bridge between the Monmouth area and Brittany is well-attested: Bowen, *Saints, Seaways, and Settlements in the Celtic Lands*, 38–39, 106–108. See too, Pearce, "The Cornish Element in Arthurian Tradition," 145–163.

30. *Owain* refers to "gwascwyn du telediw, a chyfrwy fawyd arnaw." Gwent and Erging were the main Welsh areas for *ffawydd*, the only ones where it grew naturally. (Linnard, *Trees in the Law of Hywel*, 10–12; Caer Ffawydd = Hereford; Kirby, "British Dynastic History in the Pre-Viking Peiod," 87–88; Bromwich, *Trioedd Ynys Prydein*, 236.)

31. Apart from the well-known suggestions about the abnormal sentence-form some particular words such as *llewa* (bwyta, yfed), *gwers* (ysbaid o amser), *pawin* (paun), *diarchenu*. Versus, G.J. Williams, *Agweddau ar Hanes Dysg Gymraeg*, 220, though one presumes a lost manuscript for "llewa."

32. Where structural considerations have recently been paramount: see Lévi-Strauss, "The Structural Study of Myth," 105; Ford, Introduction to *The Mabinogi and Other Medieval Welsh Tales*.

33. Translation of Antti Aarne, *Verzeichnis der Märchentypen*, Helsinki, 1911. There have been various studies adapting this

methodology to tales of Welsh interest as for instance type 400, "The Man on a Quest for His Lost Wife" to the "Le Chevalier au Lion" corresponding to *Owain* by Claude Luttrell.

34. Stephen Matchek, "Aspects of Structure and Folklore in 'Culhwch and Olwen,'" MA dissertation, Wales, 1975, particularly 20–32; see also, Bollard, "The Structure of the Four Branches of the Mabinogi" and DPhil dissertation 1983, Oxford by Sioned M. Davies; Marx, "Observations sur le structure du roman gallois de Peredur," 88–108.

35. The contribution of stylistics to our understanding of the internal structure of prose narrative is of course considerable; see the Appendix to this paper.

36. Compare Ryding, *Structure in Medieval Narrative*.

37. Roberts, "Tales and Romances," 213. In *Trioedd Ynys Prydein*, Bromwich says: "Buasai'n well petai'r stori wedi dod i ben gyda phriodas Maxen ac Elen. Dim ond *disjecta membra* o hen draddodiadau sy'n dilyn yn yr ail ran" (146). In *Breuddwyd Maxen*, Williams comments, "Ar ôl priodi Maxen ac Elen, ni chawn gan yr ysgrifennydd hwn ond dyrnaid ddidrefn o draddodiadau" (viii).

38. Loomis, *Arthurian Tradition & Chrétien de Troyes*, 321.

39. Roberts, "Tales and Romances," 231.

40. Frappier, "Chrétien de Troyes," 182; Lozachmeur discusses this appendix in *La Genése de la légende d'Yvain*, II, 140.

41. Roberts, "Tales and Romances," 229.

42. P. Williams, "Y Gwrthdaro Rhwng Serch a Milwriaeth yn y Tair Rhamant," 56.

43. Nitze, "The Romance of Erec, Son of Loc," 472. Gaston Paris is even more abrasive, "Il est assurément impossible d'imaginer quelque chose de plus absurde, de plus incohérent et en même temps de moins intéressant que ce récit" (154).

44. Frappier, "Chrétien de Troyes," 167.

45. Geotinck, *Peredur*, 153.

46. Mac Cana, *Branwen Daughter of Llŷr*, 150.

47. Mac Cana, *Branwen Daughter of Llŷr*, 15. Mac Cana's suggestions are discussed by Glyn E. Jones in "Y Wledd in Harlech ac yng Ngwales ym Mabinogi *Branwen*," 381.

48. Gruffydd, *Math vab Mathonwy*, 49.

49. Hunt, "The Art of *Iarlles y Ffynnawn* and the European Volksmärchen," 118.

50. Even such as a "medieval" *encore:* a reaction by the storyteller to the disappointed groans of his listeners, as they realise the story is drawing to a close.

51. The effect of particular presuppositions is reflected in Ford's remark in *The Mabinogi:* "This eclectic theory of the composition of the *Mabinogi*, that is, that each Branch represents a collec-

tion of more or less related lore . . . offers an explanation of why the quality of the redactor's work is so high within individual sections and episodes, and why continuity between these sections is often lacking or poor" (4).

52. Compare Glyn E. Jones, "Early Prose: *The Mabinogi*," 191.

53. Jarman, "Pedair Cainc y Mabinogi," 89.

54. Thus following McKenna in her discussion of "The Theme of Sovereignty in *Pwyll*." Looking for "the coherence it might have held for that contemporary audience" (35).

55. Gruffydd, *Rhiannon*, 23.

56. Olrik, "Epic Laws of Folk Narrative," "Every time that a striking scene occurs in a narrative, and continuity permits, the scene is repeated" (133).

57. Ó Coileáin, "A Thematic Study of the Tale *Pwyll Pendeuic Dyuet*," 78.

58. G.E. Jones, "Early Prose: *The Mabinogi*," 194–195.

59. This answer is more suitable for the question, "Where did the *Mabinogi* get the material for two feasts? i.e.what was available?" Compare "Y Wledd yn Harlech ac yng Ngwales ym Mabinogi Branwen," Jones, 380–386 for further discussion.

60. Gruffydd, *Rhiannon*, 53.

61. Gruffydd, *Rhiannon*, 52.

62. Gruffydd, *Rhiannon*, 75.

63. Jakobson maintains: "Sur tous les niveaux du langage l'essence de l'artifice poétique consiste en retours périodiques." (quoted in *Roman Jakobson*, ed. Armstrong and Van Schroneveld, 479). Compare, Bann and Bowlt, eds., *Russian Formalism*, 34.

64. The psycho-mechanic view, which I have tried to develop elsewhere, would claim that the profoundest literary forms are inevitably unconscious; or, as Genette puts it in *Figures I*, "La littérature—comme toute autre activité de l'esprit—repose sur des conventions que, sauf exceptions, elle ignore. Il ne s'agit que de les mettre en évidence" (258).

65. Gruffydd, *Math vab Mathonwy*, 227.

66. Gruffydd, *Math vab Mathonwy*, 318. Doublets abound in other tales, such as *Culhwch*, as when Ysbaddaden demands first the tusk of the boar of Ysgithrwyn Pen Beidd to shave his beard, and later notes the comb and shears between the ears of Twrch Trwyth; similarly with the duplicating of the story of Eidoel fab Aer by Mabon fab Modron.

67. Gruffydd, *Math vab Mathonwy*, 137. In *The Mabinogi*, Ford aptly maintains, "The punishment of Math's nephews, then, may be structurally significant, and but a repetition of the underlying theme of the whole tale. As Lévi-Strauss says, 'repetition has as its function to make the structure of the myth apparent'" (13).

68. Henry, "Culhwch and Olwen—Some Aspects of Style and Structure," has an interesting discussion of the two-stress phrase in "Culhwch and Olwen," 32. I would tend to revise his stress analysis or the description of Olwen in this way, seeing in it a variation between the two-stress and the three-stress phrase such as we have in the cywydd deuair hirion, the triban, mesur carol and tri thrawiad: Evans and Jones, *Llfyr Gwyn Rhydderch*, col. 475–476 "Ae dyúot hítheu/achámse sídan/flámgoch amdánei.// a górdtorch rúdeur/am ymýnwgyl y uórwyn.// A merérit gwérthuawr ýndi/a rúd gémmeu.// Oed melýnach y fénn/no blódeu y bánadyl.//Oed gwýnnach ychnáwd/no dístrych y dónn//Oed gwýnnach y fálueu ae byssed/no chanáwon gódrwyth/o blíth man gráyan/fynhawn fynhónus//Na gólwc hébawc mút/na gólwc gwálch trimut/ nýd oed ólwc tégach/nór éidi.//No brónn álarch gwýnn/ oed gwýnach y dẃy uron.//Oed kóchach y déu rud nor fion.// y sáwl ae gwélei/kyflawn uydei oe sérch.//Pédeir meillónen gwýnnyon/a dýuei yny hól/mýnyd élhei.//Ac am hýnny y gélwit hi ólwen.// Henry adds regarding another passage, "Parallel phrases with similar stressing are linked by repetition and characterized by alliteration and occasional rhyme" (34). Here one hears a pattern of similar syntax, syllable structure and stress. It is interesting that on the whole the author tends to follow the principle enunciated by Morris-Jones, *Cerdd Dafod*, 269: "Ni ddylai fod mwy na dwy sillaf ddiacen, neu wan, gyda'i gilydd yn unman, oddieithr yn unig lle bo un o flaen gorffwysfa neu raniad llinell, a dwy ar ei hôl." There are two other points that may be developed sometime: (a) The grouping of "uwchcorfannau," be they two-stressed or three-stressed, into runs each run ending with a double line. Each grouping into a run seems to be patterned. (b) The variation and contrasting between "cytbwys ddiacen"—"Ae dyuot hitheu"/"anghytbwys ddisgynedig"—"Oed melynach y fenn"/ "anghytbwys ddyrchafedig"—"o blith man grayan"/and the absence of "cytbwys acennog" seems to merit attention. We will return to the question of rhythm in the appendix.

69. Jakobson and Lévi-Strauss, "Les Chats de Charles Baudelaire," 1. Sherwood in "Viktor Shklovsky and the Development of Early Formalist Theory on Prose Literature," says, "The various types of stepped construction—repetition, rhyme, tautology, tautological parallelism, psychological parallelism, retarding, epic repetition, story ritual and peripeteia are termed by Shklovsky devices of syughetnost (i.e. "embodiment of plot"), an invented word. Taking the particular case of parallelism, Shklovsky noted that Veselovsky had made a distinction between psychological parallelism and rhythmical or tautological parallelism; the first of these was supposed to be an echo of primitive totemism, and the second arose from the exigencies of metre in particular languages;

the formulae of psychological parallelism, Veselovsky noted, sometimes 'sink' into the other type" (34).

70. Jakobson, *Questions de poétique*, 234–279.
71. Herdan, *Type-token Mathematics*, 17.
72. Quoted in *Roman Jakobson*, ed. Armstrong and Van Schooneveld, 59.
73. Olrick, "Epic Laws of Folk Narrative," 132–133. A contrast in narrative structure of some significance is made by Bremond when he suggests that all macro-sequences are either of improvement or of deterioration. Thus in *Owain* the "sept grandes articulations du récit" mentioned by Lozachmeur can be re-grouped first as an improvement movement from a lack of a wife through "la conquête du bonheur" to "le mariage du héros et de sa dame"; then the equilibrium is disturbed by "le départ" deteriorating through "la crise" to "la folie du héros." Finally commencing from the rock bottom stage the hero moves forward again through "la reconquête du bonheur" to "la réconciliation des amants." I have elsewhere related the pattern of descent to the mode of tragedy and the ascent pattern to the mode of comedy, the one leading to mortification and the other to invigoration: "Y Moddau Llenyddol 1 a 2," i.e. the two basic modes of narrative progress.
74. O'Rahilly returns to discuss the matter in "Repetition: A Narrative Device in TBC," 67–74 in light of Professor Mac Cana's discussion in a previous volume.
75. Olrick, "Epic Laws of Folk Narrative," 135–136.
76. Arnold, *On the Study of Celtic Literature*, 51.
77. Lewis, "The Anthropological Approach," 224.
78. Thomson, in *Branwen Uerch Lyr*, suggests that the triadic groupings are used to lend historical authority as well as dramatic force, xlv.
79. Olrik, "Epic Laws of Folk Narrative," "In hundreds of thousands of folk traditions, three is the highest number with which one deals. . . . Three is the maximum number of men and objects which occur in traditional narrative"(133). For bibliographical references to ternary structure, see Rees, *Ceinciau'r Mabinogi*, 33, 37–40, 45, 51.
80. Mac Cana, "An Instance of Modified Narrative Repetition in *Fled Bricrenn*," 168–172.
81. O'Rahilly, "Repetition: A Narrative Device in TBC," 67–74. Bremond in his "La logique des possibles narratifs," posits three logical stages for any normal narrative structure: (1) potentiality, (2) process of actualisation (3) outcome 60-76.
82. Glyn E. Jones, "Early Prose: *The Mabinogi*," 191–192; Gruffydd, *Math vab Mathonwy*, makes the same three-part analysis, 326–327.

83. Ford, *The Mabinogi*, who recognises three sections approximately corresponding to those described above, adds: "The initial episode, which tells of the love of Gilfaethwy for Goewin and the ruse by which he rapes her, bears no apparent relation to the rest of the story" (89).

84. Roberts, "Tales and Romances," 210.

85. Hunt, "The Art of *Iarlles y Ffynnawn* and the European Volksmärchen," has dealt extensively with the triads of plot-structure in *Owain:* compare comments by Roberts, "Owein *Neu* Iarlles y Ffynon," 128.

86. Mac Cana, "An Instance of Modified Narrative Repetition in *Fled Bricrenn*," 168–172.

87. One cannot but be as yet dissatisfied with the unsystematic results of the analysis of prose narrative as contrasted with metrics and grammar, although the Dumézilian approach is an advance on the Finnish school. For me, a system is a configuration of relationships, a purposeful contrast of two or three identifiable elements that takes its place meaningfully within a hierarchy of other systems; and we are as yet only fumbling towards the recognition of systems in narrative. For a contrast between the two schools favouring the Dumézilian approach, see Rees, "Modern Evaluations of Celtic Narrative Tradition." Though not a Dumézilian, my own preference is systematic.

88. Rees's important (though almost secret) study, *Ceinciau'r Mabinogi*, sees the *Pedair Cainc* as a ternary structure with each of the original three branches belonging to each of the three regions of Wales—Dyfed (Pwyll, with Manawydan), Powys (Branwen—the family of Llŷr and Brân), Gwynedd (Math—The Dôn family). No new family is introduced in the "*Trydedd Gainc*"which runs on from the Second Branch but is linked narratively with the First. He argues for a Dumézilian interpretation of the three—Knowledge (Gwynedd), War (Powys), Fruitfulness and Crafts (Dyfed). Numerous other scholars, such as Anwyl "The Four Branches of the Mabinogi," 281, have seen in the *Pedair Cainc* a similar ternary structure.

89. Poor linking in *Peredur* has been criticized by Marx, *Nouvelles Recherches sur la Littérature Arthurienne*, 124; Marx,"Observations sur la structure du roman gallois de Peredur," 90.

90. Albeit Bollard has made a valid point regarding "interlacing:" "The Structure of the Four Branches of the Mabinogi," 250 ff. This has been developed cogently for *Peredur* by Ceridwen Lloyd-Morgan, "Narrative Structure in *Peredur*," 221–231.

91. Ford, *The Mabinogi*, 3. Bromwich also refers to these wider references, "Traddodiad Llafar y Chwedlau," 46–64.

92. I am not suggesting that they were used with deliberation to energise rhythm, create tension or contrast or make ironic asides, as "sangiadau" often may have been, although I do suggest that they were such a normal part of the flow of narrative, that (in the same way as "sangiadau") they were taken in the author's stride. They can also feasibly be explained in their own way by folklorist and storyologist.

93. Gruffydd, *Rhiannon*, 45.

94. Gruffydd, *Rhiannon*, 52.

95. Jackson, *The International Popular Tale and Early Welsh Tradition*.

96. Gruffydd, *Rhiannon*, 62.

97. Mac Cana, *Branwen Daughter of Llyr*, 157.

98. Gruffydd, *Rhiannon*, 62; Mac Cana, *The Mabinogi*.

99. Mac Cana, *Branwen Daughter of Llyr*, 144–145.

100. Gruffydd, *Math vab Mathonwy*, 50.

101. Gruffydd, *Math vab Mathonwy*, 339; Gruffydd, *Rhiannon*, 7–8.

102. Gruffydd, *Math Vab Mathonwy*, 50.

103. Gruffydd notes in *Rhiannon:* "Rhiannon insists that 'his own name would fit him best' (i.e. Pryderi's) *before* that name had been made known" (57).

104. Jackson's method has been criticised by McKenna, "The Theme of Sovereignty in *Pwyll*," "Attention to international popular motifs involved an analytical method whose end result is fragmentation of each tale into its component parts"(36).

105. Compare Ford, *The Mabinogi,* "What the opening episode does quite clearly is establish Pwyll's Otherworldly connections and account for the fact that he was, mortal Prince of Dyfed or not, a head or lord of the Otherworld. From that point on, the story proceeds in a linear way . . . "(36).

106. Hunt, "Some observations on the Textual Relationship of Li Chevaliers au Lion and Iarlles y Ffynnawn."

107. Dr. Ceridwen Lloyd-Morgan who has made one of the most enlightened contributions to the study of medieval narrative structure, "Narrative Structure in *Peredur,*" has argued against the false premise that a text must have a "unity in the Aristotelian or post-Aristotelian sense, that is, that the story must have a linear progression or sequence of events, a clear narrative thread that proceeds from the exposition through to the conclusion, when the action is satisfactorily resolved, whilst any subsidiary narrative threads contribute directly to the main one"(189).

108. Ker, *Epic and Romance,* 290.

109. Vinaver in an excellent discussion of this point, *The Rise of Romance,* after quoting Ker, goes on to quote Gaston Paris, again on

"Roland:" "une suite d'explosions successives, toujours arrêtées court et toujours reprenant avec soudaineté" (5).
110. Although as Lloyd-Morgan mentions in "Narrative Structure in *Peredur*," interlacing is "far more common in Continental romances than in Middle Welsh narrative" (221).
111. Vinaver, *The Rise of Romance*, 71, 76, 92.
112. Gruffydd, *Rhiannon*, 41. Perhaps the proper method for reading would be to accept the situation as it is, with no reversal of roles; then if a reversal is obvious, one should take it, first, as deliberate; only if it could *not* have been deliberate, should one interpret a confusion.

NOTES: APPENDIX

113. Watkins, T. Arwyn. "Trefn yn y Frawddeg Gymraeg." *SC* 12–13 (1977–1978): 394.
114. Charles-Edwards, "Honour and Status in Some Irish and Welsh Prose Tales." Useful discussion is Schegloff, "Sequencing in Conversational Openings," *Directions in Sociolinguistics*, eds., John J. Gumperz and Dell Hymes, New York, 1972.
115. Emanuel A. Schegloff and Harvey Sacks, "Opening up Closings," *Semiotica* 8 (1973): 290–337.
116. Harvey Sacks, Emanuel A. Schegloff, and Gail Jefferson, "A Simplest Systematics for the Organization of Turn-Taking for Conversation," *Language* 50 (1974): 696–735.
117. Jarman, "Pedair Cainc y Mabinogi," 133–138.
118. G.E. Jones, "Early Prose: *The Mabinogi*" 200–201; compare "Astudiaeth o Gelfyddyd Ymddiddan mewn Llenyddiaeth Gymraeg hyd at ddiwedd y bedwaredd ganrif ar ddeg," MA dissertation, W.L. Evans, Wales, 1956. This was the subject of a paper by Dr. Ann G. Martin, "Features of Dialogue in the Stories of the Mabinogion," presented at the 7th International Congress of Celtic Studies, Oxford, 1983.
119. Morgan, *Ysgirfau Llenyddol*, 163–174.
120. Compare Hamburger, *The Logic of Literature*, on literary tense; Wolfson, "The Conversational Historical Present Alternation," deals with tense in conversation.
121. *Breudwyt Ronabwy*, Richards, xix–xxiii; *Llenyddiaeth Cymru 1450–1600*, W.J. Gruffydd, Lerpwl, 1922, 64–67; *Llenyddiaeth Cymru 1540–1660*, W.J. Gruffydd, Wrecsam, 1926, 100; *Chwedleu Seith Doethon Rufein*, H. Lewis, Wrecsam, 1925, 25; *Y Bardd Cwsg a'i Gefndir*, G. Thomas, Caerdydd, 1971, 274–287; *Meistri'r Canrifoedd*, Saunders Lewis, Caerdydd, 1973, 211–212; and Dr. Bromwich's comments in "Dwy Chwedl a Thair Rhamant," 154.

122. "Traddodiad a Dychan yn 'Breuddwyd Rhonabwy,'" J.K. Bollard, *Llên Cymru,* 13 (1980–1981): 155–163. The "list," as a rhetorical ingredient in the *Araith* style, is of obviously structural importance in *Culhwch* with the *anoethau*; but elsewhere it is more of a grand embellishment, as e.g. in *Geraint* (*Y Tair Rhamant,* ed. Bobi Jones, Aberystwyth, 1960, 97, 11–15; 98, 3–6; 98, 9–11; 99, 23–25; 100, 22–26; 101, 18–24; 103, 26–27; 116, 13–15; 121, 10–18.) It corresponds to the "spectacle" in film terms.

123. Watkins, Arwyn, and Proinsias Mac Cana. "Cystrawennau'r Cyplad mewn Hen Gymraeg." *BBCS* 18 (1958–1960): 1–25.

124. The main steps in the discussion are "Y Ferf a'r Testun," Lewis, *ZCP* 17 (1927), 107–110; "Safle'r Ferf," Henry Lewis, *BBCS* 4 (1928): 149–152; *Datblygiad yr Iaith Gymraeg,* Henry Lewis, Caerdydd, 1931, 111–119; *Cystrawen y Frawddeg Gymraeg,* Melville Richards, Caerdydd, 1938, 99–109; "Y Frawddeg Gymysg," Melville Richards, *BBCS* 10 (1940): 105–115; "The Sentence in Welsh," Henry Lewis, *Proceedings of the British Academy,* 28 (1942): 259–280; *Gramadeg Cymraeg Canol,* D.S. Evans, Caerdydd, 1951, 93–95; *Y Treigladau a'u Cystrawen,* T.J. Morgan, Caerdydd, 1952, 368–377; *Pwyll Pendeuic Dyuet,* R.L. Thomson, xxii–xxvii; *Ystorya Bown De Hamtwn,* Morgan Watkin, Caerdydd, 1958, clxvii–clxxii; *Branwen Uerch Lyr,* Derick S. Thomson, xv–xix; "The Sentence in Early Modern Welsh," D.S. Evans, *BBCS* 22 (1968): 311–337; "Concord in Middle Welsh," D.S. Evans, *SC* 6 (1971): 42–56; "On Celtic Wordorder and the Welsh 'Abnormal' Sentence," Proinsias Mac Cana, *Ériu* 24 (1973): 90–120; "Questions about Early Welsh Literature," Kenneth Jackson, *SC* 8/9 (1973–1974): 3–5; "Trefn yn y Frawddeg Gymraeg," T.A. Watkins, *SC* 12/13 (1977–1978): 367–395; "Y Frawddeg Gymysg a'r Frawddeg Dro," E.I. Rowlands, *BBCS* 28 (1979): 218–222; "Notes on the 'Abnormal' Sentence," Proinsias Mac Cana *SC* 14/15 (1979–1980): 174–187; "Sylwadau Pellach ar Gystrawennau'r Frawddeg Gymysg a'r Frawddeg Dro," E.I. Rowlands, *BBCS* 29 (1980): 674–680. One consideration that may be relevant to the discussion is the phenomenon of "Internal Plural" (see *Number and Inner Space,* W.H. Hirtle, Quebec, 1982, where differences between such sentences as "The woods is on fire./The woods are on fire." are discussed) and the fact that with some of the plural nouns taking singular verbs in Medieval Welsh one is thinking of a grouping. Could there not therefore have been a semantic distinction between the morphemes of "Gwyr a aeth . . . " and "Gwyr a gryssyassant," as between "The committee is sure" and "The committee are sure"?

125. *Branwen Uerch Lyr,* D.S. Thomson, xlv; "Traddodiad a Dychan yn *Breuddwyd Rhonabwy,*" J.K. Bollard, *Llên Cymru* 13 (1980–1981): 160–162.

126. "Y Berfenw," Henry Lewis, *BBCS* 4 (1928): 179–189; "Defnydd Cynddelw Brydydd Mawr o'r Berfenw," *BBCS* 6 (1932): 16–23; "Braslun o Gystrawen y Berfenw," T.J. Morgan, *BBCS* 9 (1938): 195–215; *Tafod y Llenor*, R. M. Jones, Caerdydd, 1974, 229–231.

127. "Gohirio'r Rhagenw mewn Cymraeg Canol," Emrys Evans, *BBCS* 21 (1965): 141–145.

128. "Y Rhagenw Ategol Dwbl Mewn Cymraeg Canol," Emrys Evans, *BBCS* 18 (1968): 173–176.

129. Whose Oxford doctoral dissertation (1983) I did not have an opportunity of studying before preparing this paper.

IV

Thematic Interpretations

12

Thematic Structure in the Four Branches of the Mabinogi

Jeffrey Gantz

Inasmuch as Celtic scholars have tended to feel that the Four Branches of the *Mabinogi* (the first four tales of the *Mabinogion*) are devoid of both theme and structure, this article's title is not as innocuous as it might seem. The following comment by Kenneth Jackson is, in fact, distressingly representative: "But if there is one thing on which most students of the *Mabinogion* are agreed, it is that the plots of the Four Branches, to mention no others, are extraordinarily confused and incoherent, so much so that there has been a wide divergence of opinion as to how some of these plots are to be explained and even what they really are."[1] It is true that the plots of the Four Branches are marred by numerous inconsistencies and oversights; nonetheless, this article will attempt to demonstrate that these same Four Branches, in their present form, possess a greater degree of logic and coherence than has heretofore been acknowledged—specifically, that a systematic arrangement of parallel and antithetical sequences creates from the *Mabinogi* a single matrix, and that this matrix generates the work's central theme.[2]

For those who are not familiar with the *Mabinogi*, these four Welsh stories, based largely upon myth and folklore, survive in two manuscripts of the fourteenth century, though the tales are certainly older than that. These manuscripts identify the quartet as a unit; this has created something of a problem for scholars, inasmuch as no unifying elements are immediately apparent. Even the meaning of the title *Mabinogi* (singular, not plural) is in doubt;[3] and, while some have argued that the hero Pryderi was once the central figure of these tales, it is clear that he does not serve that function in the *Mabinogi* in its present form.[4] This is a vexing problem, but it does not affect my argument, which concerns *structural* rather than *narrative* unity. How this structural unity came into being is likewise unclear. While the stories of the *Mabinogion* developed over an extended period of time, a single redactor appears to have taken the Four Branches in hand; however, the extent to which he refashioned them is a matter for conjecture. Fortunately, that problem need not concern us here. In what follows, I will restrict myself to describing the structural properties of the text; the readers may form their own opinions as to the degree to which these properties are the conscious creation of the redactor.

In outline, the structure of the *Mabinogi* is readily apparent: of the four stories, the first and third *(Pwyll* and *Manawydan)* are set in the south of Wales, while the second and fourth *(Branwen* and *Math)* are set in the north. This alternation is more than just ornamental or geographical. *Branwen* and *Math* embody a world close to that of the Irish sagas: fierce, heroic, primitive; *Pwyll* and *Manawydan* are infused with a sense of gentility and graciousness that reflects the south's closer contact with Norman chivalry. In these southern Branches not one person is killed (though some are wounded); in *Branwen* Gwern is destroyed by fire, Evnissyen dies in the cauldron of rebirth, Brân is poisoned by an arrow, Branwen succumbs to a broken heart, and virtually the entire population of Ireland and Britain is wiped out in battle. In *Math,* moreover, Pryderi and Goronwy are killed, while Gwydyon, Gilvaethwy, Lleu and Blodeuedd are all changed into diverse birds and animals; and another great battle claims men from both north and south Wales. It should surprise no one to learn that *Pwyll* and *Manawydan* conclude upon notes of rejoicing, while *Branwen* and *Math* are, to say the least, equivocal in their final statements.

Thematic Structure

But this technique of developing a theme through contrasting or complementary sequences is employed in detail as well as in outline—that is, each Branch can be seen in terms of one or more parallel sequences. Similar structural motifs form a network of parallels and contrasts among the different Branches, thereby contributing further to the unity and cogency of the *Mabinogi*. I shall consider the individual sequences first.

Pwyll Lord of Dyved comprises three distinct parts, of which the third contributes to the narrative but not to the structure. The first section—*Pwyll I*—offers its own contrasting sequence: Pwyll's initial greed in appropriating Arawn's stag is set against his subsequent good sense in following Arawn's instructions as to the fight with Havgan, and against his subsequent self-sacrifice in refusing Arawn's wife. In that Pwyll redeems his mistake (selfishness) both in contrast (good judgement) and in kind (generosity), he demonstrates his essential goodness; in that his just reward—Rhiannon—arrives only at the beginning of *Pwyll II*, the first two sections of the tale (as narratives completely independent) create a structural interlock.

But the most striking parallel lies between these two sections, for the development of *Pwyll II* is very similar to that of *Pwyll I*.

Pwyll I	*Pwyll II*
1 Pwyll meets Arawn.	Pwyll meets Rhiannon.
2 Pwyll takes Arawn's stag.	Pwyll gives Rhiannon to Gwawl.
3 Journey to Arawn's court.	Journey to Rhiannon's court.
4 Pwyll refuses Arawn's wife.	Pwyll beats Gwawl in the bag.
5 Mercy to Havgan.	Mercy to Gwawl.
6 Friendship with Arawn.	Marriage with Rhiannon.

In each case, Pwyll has to redeem an initial blunder. The contrast at 2 is suggestive of the way in which these sections complement each other: in poaching Arawn's stag Pwyll is too greedy, but in offering Gwawl anything in his possession (Gwawl chooses Rhiannon) he is too generous. Pwyll does show good sense in carrying out the instructions of Arawn and Rhiannon; however, whereas in *Pwyll I* unnecessary greed gives way to unexpected generosity, in *Pwyll II* misplaced generosity gives way to unnecessary cruelty. This is apparent from the irony at 4: Pwyll's seeming cruel indifference to Arawn's wife is really a kindness to Arawn, while his beating of Gwawl, far from being a harmless diversion, is the catalyst that brings about the misfortunes of *Manawydan* (and on a structural level those of *Pwyll III* as well). Thus, *Pwyll II* resembles *Pwyll I* even to the extent that neither section is complete within itself. The relationship of *Pwyll III* to this framework is tenuous, though the abduction of Pryderi and the accusations levelled against Rhiannon may be seen as structural consequences of Gwawl's beating. Teirnon's generosity in returning the boy to his parents restates the concluding motifs of *Pwyll I*: good-will, sacrifice, friendship.

In *Branwen Daughter of Llŷr* these same themes appear; but the development is very different: good faith is answered by treachery, and generosity by greed. The plot involves a double agreement made by the kings of Ireland and Britain; as in *Pwyll* the sequences are expounded consecutively:

1 Mallolwch gives his horses into Brân's care.   Brân gives Branwen into Mallolwch's care.
2 Evnissyen mistreats the horses.   Mallolwch mistreats Branwen.
3 Mallolwch demands compensation.   Brân demands compensation.
4 Brân offers horses, reparation.   Mallolwch offers kingship.
5 Mallolwch overruled by Irish.   Brân overruled by Evnissyen.

As in *Pwyll*, these sequences interlock: the refusal of the Irish to remain content with their compensation takes the form of mistreating Branwen, so that the climax of the first section also serves as the initial episode of the second. But, in contrast to *Pwyll*, the predominant motif here is self-interest: the tale has hardly begun when we are introduced to the disenfranchised stepbrother whose frustration triggers all the selfishness and vindictiveness of the tale.[5]

The first section is rife with parallels and contrasts to the First Branch. Brân, for example, is as generous as Pwyll in offering to make peace on Mallolwch's terms, especially as he is only indirectly responsible for the breach-causing insult. Brân's conduct also recalls Pwyll's foolishness at the first wedding banquet; for in giving a potential enemy the cauldron of rebirth he allows his generosity to override his judgement. On the other side, Mallolwch emerges as irresolute and avaricious: instead of demanding an explanation for the injury done to his horses—the natural course—he stalks off to his ships; later, in council, he and his advisers accept Brân's offer of restitution only out of fear (entirely justified) that they might disgrace themselves by asking for more. Even then he is not content but must sulk in his tent—or rather, in Brân's tent, where everyone can see; and it takes a further show of generosity on Brân's part to cheer him. Compare the conclusion of *Pwyll I*, where the mutual generosity and good-will of Pwyll and Arawn make them fast friends.

The conclusion of this first section echoes that of *Pwyll II*: Branwen also is accorded a joyful welcome by the inhabitants of her new land, and she also presents her husband's nobles with lavish gifts. But there is a contrast; for, while Rhiannon was barren for two years, Branwen presents Mallolwch with a son after only one. Note the contrast in the respective husbands' reactions: Pwyll, though with no child and under pressure from his nobles, stands firmly by Rhiannon; but Mallolwch, with no cause whatever for complaint, wavers and ultimately condemns Branwen to the kitchen. And the quarrel has broader ramifications: at the end of *Pwyll I* there is a strong bond of friendship between Annwvyn and Dyved; but at the beginning of the second section of *Branwen* Mallolwch has interdicted all communication with Britain.

The contrasts persist through the second section. Earlier, Brân had sent messengers after Mallolwch in hopes of making restitution; now, Mallolwch runs away from Brân in hopes of avoiding the same, and he offers terms only when there is no alternative. Just as Evnissyen had earlier maimed the guiltless horses of Mallolwch, so now he dispatches the Irishmen treacherously concealed within the house of peace, a development symptomatic of the darker character of the second section. And, just as Mallolwch had punished Bronwen for Evnissyen's cruelty, so Evnissyen punishes Gwern for Mallolwch's treachery. Evnissyen's subsequent self-sacrifice (another theme from *Pwyll*) overcomes the destructive power of the cauldron of rebirth, but it cannot stop the fighting and dying; moreover, the themes of treachery and death are developed in simultaneous occurrences in Britain, where Casswallawn kills the seven men left behind and usurps Brân's throne. The yearning idealism of the final episode is characteristically Celtic, and yet so is the company's return to the real world: the timeless otherworld of eternal feasting is only a temporary haven; for from the reality of sorrow and suffering there is no permanent escape.

In structure *Manawydan Son of Llŷr* is by far the simplest of the Four Branches—indeed its peculiar opening suggests that it may have replaced an earlier story. Still, there is one set of parallel events:

1 Rhiannon and Pryderi enter Llwyd's stronghold.	The ladies of Llwyd's court raid Manawydan's wheatfield.
2 Llwyd captures Rhiannon and Pryderi.	Manawydan captures Llwyd's wife.
3 Llwyd returns his prisoners.	Manawydan returns his prisoner.

Actually, the tale is nearly half over before this pattern begins to assert itself. In the meantime Manawydan's good sense is contrasted with his companions' rash actions and superficial concerns. In each of the English towns where their business competitors plot against them, Pryderi and Kigva want to fight; but Manawydan always prudently insists that they move on. In the last of these towns Kigva complains that shoemaking is neither clean nor honourable; but Manawydan has the sense to see that there is no shame in good craftsmanship. The lack of caution shown by Pryderi (not unlike his father) and Rhiannon in entering Llwyd's stronghold is set against Manawydan's circumspection; the latter shows goodwill by waiting for Pryderi until dusk, and good sense by not following him in. And, while Kigva fears that Manawydan may disgrace himself by handling the mouse, Manawydan is wise enough to perceive that his prisoner is no ordinary creature, and bold enough to persist in his course, despite the social and financial pressures brought against him by the succession of clergymen.

The bargaining between Manawydan and Llwyd recalls that between Rhiannon and Gwawl in *Pwyll II;* but Manawydan is both shrewder and more generous. Having secured the release of Rhiannon and Pryderi, he insists on what Pwyll overlooked: assurance that there will be no revenge; on the other hand, he is content wlth what is fair, and having achieved his goal he willingly returns Llwyd's wife, thus bringing the *Pwyll–Manawydan* sequence to a happy and harmonious end.

Like *Pwyll, Math Son of Mathonwy* falls into three distinct sections; but they are more complex and thematically better integrated than those of the First Branch. *Math* can be read as a minor-key version of *Pwyll,* for while it treats the same themes, and even embodies comparable plots, it exposes a dark and frightening aspect of human nature. The events of *Math II* and *III* parallel those of *Math I:*

Math I	*Math II* and *III*
1 Gwydyon deprives Goewin of her honour.	Aranrhod deprives Lleu of name and weapons.
2 Gwydyon deprives Math of Goewin as footholder.	Goronwy deprives Lleu of Blodeuedd, his wife.
3 Gwydyon kills Pryderi.	Goronwy "kills" Lleu.
4 Math punishes Gwydyon.	Lleu punishes Goronwy.

Lleu is Gwydyon's nephew and heir, so that the pattern of lust and betrayal that Gwydyon initiates in *Math I* is brought back to him in *Math II* and *III*. *Math I* actually presents two themes: Gilvaethwy's desire for Goewin, and Gwydyon's perfidy in extracting the swine of Annwvyn from Pryderi; and the second theme has a counter-subject in the short-sighted greed that induces Pryderi to facilitate the execution of Gwydyon's plan. Growing in intensity and violence, these themes culminate in the rape of Goewin and the death of Pryderi and of many others. Math's choice of punishment is as appropriate as it is bizarre: the nephews are victimised by their own lust, each one suffering the fate that he inflicted on Goewin. In this sense, *Math I* is a self-contained unit. Evil has been returned for evil; and the story, while disappointing as a narrative (the nephews take no action to protect themselves from Goewin's confession), is structurally complete and satisfying.

Math II and *III*, however, go on to show that evil, once perpetrated, tends to perpetuate itself. The three episodes of

Math II echo *Math I:* as Gwydyon has inflicted evil, so Lleu suffers it; and as Gwydyon has deprived Goewin of her honour, so Aranrhod attempts to deprive Lleu of his by denying him both name and weapons. In procuring these for his nephew, Gwydyon effects a partial compensation, just as Math has partially compensated Goewin by making her his wife; and he seems to find a loophole in the third curse (that Lleu should have no wife of the earth) as well—a loophole that proves as illusory as the one he had shown Pryderi. For as Gwydyon's treatment of Goewin was inhuman, so Lleu is granted only a non-human wife; and though Blodeuedd may have a flower's beauty, her feelings reflect a flower's impermanence. Goewin cannot be a virgin again: therefore Lleu is fated not to have a real woman for a wife. *Math II* ends on a deceptively triumphant note; and it may be significant that Blodeuedd never speaks for herself.

Math III further parallels *Math I*. As Gwydyon killed Pryderi, so Goronwy seems to kill Lleu. As Blodeuedd is created in part from the flowers of the oak, it is appropriate that Gwydyon should find Lleu (in eagle form) perched in an oak; and as Gwydyon had professed a desire to feed upon the swine of Pryderi, so a sow feeds upon Lleu's rotting flesh. Like *Math I*, *Math II* and *III* are self-contained in that fitting punishments are meted out: the deceitful Blodeuedd is transformed into an owl, a bird that hides by day and hunts by night, while Goronwy is made to expose himself to the spear that he cast at Lleu. He is mean enough to ask his retinue to take his place, and they are mean enough to refuse; then he asks leave to protect himself with a stone, claiming that Blodeuedd led him on; but, as this is patently untrue, the stone avails him nothing. The conclusion is somewhat ambivalent: Lleu regains his lands and rules prosperously thereafter, but he has no wife, and presumably never will.

Thus, each story of the *Mabinogi* possesses its own unique structural pattern, in which themes develop out of the sequences of parallels and contrasts. But, while the narratives of these tales are largely independent of each other, their structures interlock. In the broadest sense, *Pwyll* and *Manawydan* balance *Branwen* and *Math;* we have also seen that many motifs from the First Branch reappear (in inverted form) in the Second. But there are more extended correspon-

Thematic Structure

dences. *Manawydan*, for example, is presented as a narrative continuation of *Branwen*, but in fact it completes the structural framework of Pwyll:

Cause	Effect
1 Pwyll wrongs Arawn.	Arawn rebukes Pwyll.
2 Pwyll overcomes Havgan.	Arawn and Pwyll become friends.
3 Pwyll refuses Arawn's wife.	Rhiannon accepts Pwyll.
4 Gwawl outwits Pwyll.	Rhiannon goes to Gwawl.
5 Pwyll outwits Gwawl.	Rhiannon returns to Pwyll.
6 Pwyll beats Gwawl in the bag.	Llwyd captures Rhiannon.
7 Manawydan captures Llwyd's wife.	Llwyd frees Rhiannon.
8 Manawydan frees Llwyd's wife.	Peace.

Such a sequence requires no comment. The thematic unity of the Four Branches is, moreover, underlined by two parallel sequences linking *Pwyll* and *Math*. The first of these connects *Pwyll II* with *Math I*:

Pwyll II	Math I
1 Rhiannon desires Pwyll.	Gilvaethwy desires Goewin.
2 Rhiannon and Pwyll meet.	Gilvaethwy and Gwydyon plot.
3 Gwawl becomes an obstacle.	Math becomes an obstacle.
4 Pwyll tricks Gwawl, ties him in a bag, beats him.	Gwydyon tricks Math and Pryderi, kills Pryderi.
5 Pwyll marries Rhiannon.	Gilvaethwy rapes Goewin.
6 Pryderi is born.	Lleu is born.
7 Pryderi suffers because of Pwyll's misdeed.	Lleu suffers because of Gwydyon's misdeeds.

(In the first column, 7 is added from *Manawydan*; in the second, 6 and 7 are added from *Math II* and *III*, in each case to complete the sequence.) The differences are striking. Wishing to marry Pwyll, Rhiannon confronts him directly; in the corresponding episode of *Math I*, Gilvaethwy does not approach Goewin but plots with his brother instead.[6] The disparity between Pwyll's insensitivity and Gwydyon's disregard for human life accounts for Pryderi's relatively slight misfortunes as compared to those of Lleu. (Pryderi's troubles in *Math* are another matter, the result of his own thoughtlessness and greed.) The antithesis at 5 requires no comment.

In the same way, *Math III*, a darker version of *Pwyll I*, ties the opening and closing episodes of the Four Branches together:

Pwyll I	*Math III*
1 Pwyll goes hunting.	Goronwy goes hunting.
2 Arawn offers Pwyll his wife.	Goronwy takes Lleu's wife.
3 Pwyll refuses Arawn's wife.	Goronwy sleeps with Lleu's wife.
4 Pwyll overcomes Havgan.	Goronwy "kills" Lleu.
5 Pwyll rules Arawn's land.	Goronwy rules Lleu's land.
6 Pwyll returns.	Lleu returns.
7 Pwyll surrenders Arawn's wife and land.	Goronwy is compelled to surrender wife and land.
8 Arawn and his wife reunited.	Lleu and his wife estranged.
9 Pwyll and Arawn become friends.	Lleu kills Goronwy.

Whereas Pwyll is the ideal guest, Goronwy makes love to Blodeuedd (without Lleu's knowledge), plots with her to kill her husband, and, that seemingly accomplished, appropriates his host's land. *Math III* does not refute *Pwyll I*, but it does act as a counterweight: extremes of selfless and of selfish action are set at either end of the Four Branches.

The theme generated by this structure should now be apparent. In a sense, the structure is the theme; for, as alternating tales balance and sequences parallel each other, so the world of the Four Branches is an ideally just one in which good begets good, evil evil. Simple as this idea is in principle (though far removed from the heroic world of earlier Celtic literature), it is amply underlined by the great variety of statement and development that forms the structural framework of the *Mabinogi*.

NOTES

1. Jackson, *The International Popular Tale and Early Welsh Tradition*, 124–125.
2. I have used Ifor Williams, ed., *Pedeir Keinc y Mabinogi*, 1930, Cardiff: University of Wales Press, 1964.

3. See I. Williams, ed., *Pedeir Keinc y Mabinogi*, xlv–xlvi (in his introduction, written in Welsh); also Rachel Bromwich, "The Character of Early Welsh Tradition."

4. See I. Williams, ed., *Pedeir Keinc y Mabinogi*, xlix; see also Gruffydd, *Rhiannon*, 10–19.

5. In her fantasy *The Children of Llŷr* (New York: Ballantine 1971) Evangeline Walton provides an imaginative and compelling expansion of the Llŷr–Penarddun–Eurosswydd triangle.

6. Contrast the direct approach of Phaidra in Euripides' *Hippolytos*, or that of Ailill in the Irish tale *Tochmarc Étaíne* (The Wooing of Étaín). Like Gilvaethwy, Ailill is wasting away for a woman, but he conceals the cause of his grief and will not betray his unlawful desire.

13

The Role of Myth and Tradition in *The Four Branches of the Mabinogi*

J.K. Bollard

One of the difficulties in discussing myth and tradition in the Four Branches of the *Mabinogi* is that of determining what we mean by myth and tradition. For this chapter a rather simplified distinction between them should suffice, and we can begin by defining *myth* as a body of lore or narrative about gods and demigods and defining *tradition* as a body of lore or narrative about real or legendary figures who do not have the status of gods or other supernatural beings. In essence this is a distinction expressed more elegantly by W.J. Gruffydd in 1913: "Mythology is the legend of the gods, and legend is the mythology of men."[1]

The problems begin, of course, when we recognize that, especially after a new religious pantheon displaces the old, figures who were once gods lose some of their divine stature. And conversely, legendary and historical figures can acquire attributes and capabilities beyond those of the ordinary mortal. The interpretation of the *Mabinogi* is difficult partly because we are dealing with a number of these more or less intermediate figures.

However, there is a broader sense of *myth* which is relevant to our study of the *Mabinogi* and that is the view of myth as those tales and poems through which a society is able to examine the fundamental elements of its own structure. In the conclusion to an earlier article on the interlaced pattern of the *Mabinogi* I stated that

> the author has created a world in which all actions are relevant to the structure of society within that world, and by implication, the ideals and the very straightforward code of conduct which underlie these actions become relevant in the somewhat less controllable world of the author and his audience.[2]

The more I read and study the *Mabinogi* the more I am convinced not only that this is true but that it is the core which imbues the whole with meaning, especially for a medieval audience more familiar than we with both their own world and the literary conventions of their own time.

The *Mabinogi* is set in a non-Christian milieu and it is obvious from the text that the author or redactor was conscious of this fact. But neither author nor scribe feels obliged to include a disclaimer such as the Latin colophon to the Book of Leinster version of the *Táin Bó Cúailnge:*

> Sed ego qui scripsi hanc historiam aut uerius fabulam quibusdam fidem in hac historia aut fabula non accommodo. Quaedam enim ibi sunt praest(r)igia demonum, quaedam autem figmenta poetica, quaedam similia uero, quaedam non, quaedam ad delectationem stultorum.
>
> I who have copied down this story, or more accurately fantasy, do not credit the details of the story, or fantasy. Some things in it are devilish lies, and some poetical figments; some seem possible and others not; some are for the enjoyment of idiots.[3]

On the contrary, the author of the *Mabinogi* has minimized the non-Christian elements of the tales and within his version of these obviously ancient stories he presents a *Weltanschauung* and an ethos which is of great import and relevance to his contemporary audience and which is not inconsistent with the Judaeo-Christian ethical system within

The Role of Myth and Tradition

which the audience lives. In the course of this paper I hope to illustrate some of the ways in which the author has fused the two types of myth defined above into a consistent and enduring work of art. Another of the things I want to examine is the apparent conflict in the different ways we have chosen or discovered of looking at and analyzing the Four Branches. In this context we would do well to keep in mind Oscar Wilde's dictum that "Diversity of opinion about a work of art shows that the work is new, complex, and vital."[4]

One of the great puzzles of *Mabinogi* criticism is that on the one hand there is almost unanimous agreement that someone at a late stage in the development of the *Mabinogi* was a master of Welsh prose to be reckoned among the best, while on the other hand many faults of construction or characterization are often remarked upon, although (and this is a crucial point) there is frequently disagreement among critics as to what is faulty. Some remarks by Professor J.R.R. Tolkien in reference to the author of *Beowulf* are applicable here:

> It is, one would have said, improbable that such a man would write more than three thousand lines (wrought to a high finish) on matter that is really not worth serious attention. . . . Or that he should in the selection of his material, in the choice of what to put forward, what to keep subordinate "upon the outer edges," have shown a puerile simplicity much below the level of the characters he himself draws. . . . Any theory that will at least allow us to believe that what he did was of design and that for that design there is a defence that may still have force, would seem more probable.[5]

In other words, if we agree that the author of the *Mabinogi* was highly skilled then we should also recognize the possibility, at least, that his work may have a coherent and subtle structure just as it has a coherent and subtle style.

This may be as good a place as any to touch briefly on what is meant here by the "author" of the *Mabinogi*. I use the word *author*, for want of a better term, to mean the person or persons who put the *Mabinogi* into much the form in which it has come down to us. Thus, "author" may be a blanket term for a series of storytellers, revisers, and scribes, but if so I am willing to go back in that series no further than the earliest point (now unknown to us) at which the basic four stories which we refer to as *Pwyll, Branwen, Manawydan,* and *Math* were brought together in essentially the form that we have them now. Beyond that we reach a level of conjecture at which the notion of author is meaningless. Merely for the sake of variation I also similarly use such terms as redactor and storyteller.

In my earlier paper on the structure of the Four Branches it was suggested, taking the lead most notably from Professor Eugène Vinaver, that if we set aside our predilections for an Aristotelian structure of narrative as being composed with a beginning, a middle, and an end we may be able to perceive a different set of structural principles.[6] An apt analogy for the structure which emerges is interlaced art work in which threads of textile (or text) repeatedly come to the fore and recede, eventually creating a design which can be perceived as a whole, and which often looks deceptively simple until it is scrutinized in detail. Now, there is no doubt that each of the Four Branches is constructed as a series of episodes arranged basically in chronological order and that there is a perceptible chronological order to the Four Branches taken as a unit. But the overriding principle through which the *meaning* of the *Mabinogi* is revealed is that of structural and especially thematic juxtaposition and interlace. The events of one episode are made clear by comparison with other similar but different episodes. The cues to this comparison are often verbal similarities and repetitions, not to mention a few explicit textual cross-references. Viewing the *Mabinogi* from this perspective, I believe, allows us to perceive much of the narrative and artistic unity of the work.

As twentieth-century critics it would seem that we are duty bound to ask a number of questions of a work of art, such as How is it constructed? What does it mean? and Where does it come from? If these three questions are asked it is my opinion that they should be asked only in that order, insofar as is possible. To begin, as many have done, with the question "Where does it come from?" before determining the coherence of the work itself means that we run the risk of damaging its vital organs as we dissect it, with the result that when we put it back together again it is no longer a living work of art. The discovery of meaning is dependent to a large degree on an understanding of the structure of a work, although, to be sure, a knowledge of origins is often invaluable in elucidating details. In the case of the *Mabinogi* meaning lies in the behaviour of the characters and in the choices they make, though like all great artists the author of the *Mabinogi* was acutely aware that right and wrong may be matters of degree and are not always easily distinguishable. In a tale in which magic and fantasy are prominent, good and evil, right and wrong may be made to stand out in stark relief but the ultimate lessons to be learned are as applicable in the mundane world of the twelfth century (or even the twentieth) as they are in the timeless realms of story set on the boundaries of the Otherworld. Tolkien expresses this very clearly in *The Lord of the Rings,* a work in which he embedded much of his considered thinking and learning about the functions of narrative:

> . . . said Eomer. "It is hard to be sure of anything among so many marvels. The world is all grown strange. Elf and Dwarf in company walk in our daily fields; and folk speak with the Lady of the Wood and yet live. . . . How shall a man judge what to do in such times?"
> "As he ever has judged," said Aragorn. "Good and ill have not changed since yesteryear; nor are they one thing among Elves and Dwarves and another among Men. It is man's part to discern them, as much in the Golden Wood as in his own house."[7]

Issues of human choice occur repeatedly throughout the Four Branches as the predominant overriding theme. The themes of Friendship, Marriage, and Feud discussed in my earlier article are but the specific elements which make the tales relevant (and interesting) to eleventh- and twelfth-century audiences.

If we accept that there is a structural and thematic coherence to the *Mabinogi,* either as I have outlined it or according to some other demonstrable and workable pattern, our task becomes easier, for we are thereby constrained within the boundaries of that basic construct. It is, perhaps, a worthwhile task to try to reconstruct some earlier version of the tale, but every step we take which goes beyond these boundaries or violates the structure of the tale leads us into conjecture and away from the practice of objective literary criticism designed to help us understand the work itself.

For some time now, especially under the influence of the theories of W.J. Gruffydd, we have concentrated our attention on the Scylla and Charybdis of sources and analogues, and, failing to perceive the narrative coherence of the *Mabinogi*, we have led ourselves into some unclear or perhaps even fallacious thinking. For example, let us take a brief look at the character of Pwyll and some analyses of it.

Many critics seem to have centered their search for the meaning of the First Branch around the author's statement, "y diffygywys y enw ef ar Pwyll, Pendeuic Dyuet, ac y gelwit Pwyll Penn Annuwyn o hynny allan" (*PKM* 8; "His name, Pwyll Prince of Dyfed, fell out of use, and he was called Pwyll Head of Annwn from that time forth").[8] From this statement critics have concluded, contrary to the evidence of the text itself, that Pwyll was in origin an otherworld figure. Proinsias Mac Cana states in his book *Celtic Mythology*:

> Since . . . Annwn is a traditional name for the otherworld, it has been assumed that Pwyll was originally a deity. His name means literally "wisdom," an apt title for the all-knowing god of the otherworld.[9]

The arguments which W.J. Gruffydd brings forth in *Rhiannon* to establish Pwyll's divinity or otherworldliness require several shifts of identity beyond the one made clear in the text and they also require a considerable reorganization of the story itself, leaving us with one of his elaborately structured but rather precarious theories bearing little resemblance to the text.[10]

In "Some Popular Motifs in Early Welsh Tradition" Kenneth Jackson betrays a degree of indecisiveness about Pwyll. First he states:

> Now, it is generally believed, and probably rightly, that Pwyll himself represents a mythological be-

ing too, in fact another lord of the Otherworld, as his title "Chief of the Otherworld" and other evidence shows.[11]

Jackson goes on to observe that "nevertheless the First Branch of the *Mabinogi* treats him as a purely human being when the story begins."[12] But then he states, "Of course, his character as an Otherworld god would doubtless be primary, and very much older than this invention, but it is quite natural that a tale might grow up that he was originally a human being who later became a god."[13]

The striking thing about Jackson's argument is that he then goes on to present quite convincing evidence that the first part of *Pwyll* is an example of the motif of an otherworld figure seeking, indeed requiring, the aid of a mortal in battle. This is completely consistent with the events recounted in *Pwyll* and it is difficult to see a need to postulate an otherworld origin for Pwyll himself. Since the tale states that Pwyll was Lord of Dyfed and since the parallels which Jackson gives us for a mortal aiding an otherworld king support the reading of the text, the application of Ockham's razor suggests strongly that we should accept Pwyll's mortality.

So far as I know, no one has yet pointed out in this context that Pwyll does, indeed, die. In the second part of the tale his men themselves express their apprehension that Pwyll will die without an heir: "'Nyt byth,' heb wynt, 'y perhey di'" (*PKM* 19; "'Not forever,' said they, 'will you last'"). Later, talking to Teyrnon, Pwyll makes reference to his own mortality:

"Y rof i a Duw," heb y Pwyll, "tra parhawyf i, mi a'th kynhalyaf, a thi a'th kyuoeth, tra allwyf kynnhal y meu uy hun." (*PKM* 26)

"Between me and God," said Pwyll, "while I last I shall maintain you, you and your possessions, so long as I am able to maintain my own."

And finally, in the conclusion to the First Branch we are told unequivocally: "Uelly y treulyssant blwydyn a blwydyned, yny doeth teruyn ar hoedyl Pwyll Penn Annwn, ac y bu uarw" (*PKM* 27; "Thus they spent years and years, until there came an end to the life of Pwyll Head of Annwn, and he died"). Thus, Pwyll's mortality is an important element not only in the first part of the tale, in which he is enlisted to help Arawn, but also in the second part, in which his inevitable death is a significant factor in the motivation of the final episodes.

The first part of *Pwyll*, therefore, is not *primarily* the story of how Pwyll came to be called Pen Annwn, though that is indeed one of the things which happens. Structurally speaking, it is the story of how there came to be a friendship between Dyfed and Annwn—a friendship which has considerable implications some years later in the events recounted in the Fourth Branch. In thematic terms, as I have shown elsewhere, it is a careful examination of various aspects of the nature of friendship itself.[14]

As a means of getting into a specific discussion of other mythological and traditional elements in the *Mabinogi* I should like to respond to some objections which my reading of the *Mabinogi* has occasioned, for obviously our conception of the unity (or lack of unity) in the Four Branches will have considerable bearing on how we understand the work itself, on how we perceive the workings of traditional elements in the tale, and on the extent to which we allow ourselves to postulate earlier redactions.

It is rare that one's work is both commented on so favourably and criticized so graciously as was mine in Professor Mac Cana's short book *The Mabinogi*. In that book Mac Cana outlines the differences between the synchronic and diachronic approaches to the study of the *Mabinogi* and he sets out what he sees as their strengths and weaknesses. He remarks that "a . . . snag in the synchronic approach adopted by Bollard is that it tends to understate the breaks and inconsistencies which are quite frequent in the text."[15] As a general reply to this statement I would simply say that the breaks and inconsistencies in the *Mabinogi* are neither as frequent nor as troublesome as some critics believe. The approach to the *Mabinogi* which I have taken is, I admit, one that pays considerable attention to the strengths of the work, but it is primarily through a recognition of the compositional method adopted by the author that we are able to perceive the meaning of the surviving text. Some critics have seen breaks in the tale at precisely those points at which the tale

The Role of Myth and Tradition

refuses to conform to one or another of the various theories of origin.

Let us take as an example the episode which Mac Cana adduces to illustrate the above remark—the story of the stealing of Rhiannon's child. He summarizes Kenneth Jackson's analysis of this part of *Pwyll*, and I agree with this analysis insofar as I believe Jackson is right in seeing a conflation of three widely used motifs—the Calumniated Wife, the Monster Hand, and the Congenital Animal. Where I disagree with Jackson is in his conception of the *Mabinogi* as the result of contamination and disintegration. One of the most notable and exciting aspects of widely known international motifs is that in the hands of a skilled narrator they can be combined, rearranged, and adapted in any number of ways to suit the storyteller's purposes. The language which Jackson uses, however, betrays a different notion of development and composition. Postulating an original Monster Hand tale he remarks: "This original tale was, I suggest, *badly broken up* and altered by the later introduction of the other two motifs"; first the Congenital Animal motif was interjected, and "Then came the third stage in the *disintegration* of the tale," the interpolation of the Calumniated Wife theme, more specifically, the motif of the woman charged with eating her own child.[16] He then goes on to conclude:

> It was the *clumsy patching* at this stage of the tale, consequent on the *violent* introduction of the Calumniated Wife, which has left it *practically unintelligible* in its present form. Who stole the child? What was this mysterious claw? Why did it steal Teyrnon's foals? How did it come to drop the child in Teyrnon's stable and what was it doing there anyway? These are some of the questions which arise when we first read *Pwyll*, and the tale provides no answers—the answers are only to be found by the methods of comparative folktale study.[17]

Professor Mac Cana states, "By contrast Mr Bollard brushes these difficulties aside as so many 'details.'"[18] The questions which Jackson asks of the tale at this point, however, seem to add to the sense of confusion and give more stress to these details than does the author himself. Some answers to these questions can indeed be found by the study of comparative folklore, but within the context of the tale the questions and even the answers found by folklorists are not entirely relevant. Nor are all of Jackson's questions entirely unanswerable in the context of the tale itself. For example, the author does not choose to tell who stole the child until it is implied by the appearance of the claw in a subsequent episode that the monster was somehow involved in the matter. It is part of the author's style that the audience sleeps through the stealing of the child, as it were, along with the women set to watch:

> Gwylat a wnaethont wynteu dalym o'r nos, ac yn hynny eisswys, kyn hanner nos, kyscu a wnaeth pawb ohonunt, a thu a'r pylgeint deffroi. (*PKM* 20)

> They watched for a portion of the night, but nevertheless, before midnight, every one of them fell asleep and awoke towards dawn.

When we do learn about the claw the author does not concern himself with identifying it; indeed, its owner never becomes more than a *twrwf mawr*, a "great commotion" (*PKM* 22). It had come to steal Teyrnon's foal as, presumably, it had done each year in the past, and it dropped the child at the door either because of its wound or perhaps because it had intended to leave the child in any case. More than this the author does not tell us and we must give him the benefit of the doubt at least in this instance, because the very fact that we never learn more about this strange occurrence heightens the power and wonder of the tale. Thus, while the author uses the tradition of the Monster Hand, it is not the monster with which he is ultimately concerned, but the relations between the characters of the tale, in this instance between Pwyll, Rhiannon, Teyrnon, and the men and women of the court.

Although a medieval audience had no Stith Thompson *Motif-Index*, we do have the evidence of the triads that some form of classification of tradition was engaged in and we also have the evidence of similar episodes and incidents in different tales that variation in motif and theme would be under-

The Role of Myth and Tradition

stood by the audience. Thus a contemporary audience may have needed no explanation of the origin of the mysterious claw, for other similar tales may have been known. Even if there were no other coexistent Monster Hand tales the surviving examples of strange incidents recurring on *nos galan Mai* (May Day eve), such as the scream heard annually in *Lludd a Llefelys* and the fight each year between Gwythyr ap Greidawl and Gwyn ap Nudd in *Culhwch ac Olwen* suggest that a medieval audience would understand the repeated stealing of Teyrnon's foals and the appearance of the claw as additional examples of those mysterious events which, in tales at least, have a tendency to happen at such times.

Thus it is possible to recognize the great skill with which the author has combined the themes of the Calumniated Wife, the Monster Hand, and the Congenital Animal. He has integrated them into a complex of incidents demonstrating some basic moral lessons about truth, faithfulness, and humility, especially in his portrayals of the characters of Rhiannon and Teyrnon. The use of familiar traditional elements makes it easier for the audience to apprehend the significance or meaning of the tale.

A further drawback which Mac Cana sees to my synchronic approach to the *Mabinogi* is "the danger . . . that one is prone to find what one sets out to look for."[19] For example, my article comments on the author's subtle portrayal of the relationship between Pwyll and Rhiannon and suggests that one of the elements of this characterization is the fact that Rhiannon has kept her position of honour in the court at Pwyll's side "for at his arrival Teyrnon is given a place of honour between them."[20] Mac Cana objects to this on the grounds that "some might see this as a pardonable inconsistency, explicable by the conventional manner in which court seating arrangements are described in these texts or simply by the fact that the Calumniated Wife theme has been interpolated into an earlier and more conventional setting."[21]

Given the tightly knit structure of the First Branch, however, it is unwise to postulate an error or slip resulting from the uneasy interpolation of this theme into some hypothetical earlier version. I would like to suggest that it is precisely because of the stylized nature of the statement "Sef ual yd eistedyssont, Teirnon y rwg Pwyll a Riannon" (*PKM* 25;

"This is how they sat—Teyrnon between Pwyll and Rhiannon") that it has broader implications for our reading of the tale. First of all, to dispel any lingering doubts about the very real significance of the order of seating in medieval Wales and elsewhere, let us remind ourselves of a passage in the Red Book version of *Brut y Tywysogyon* reporting an event which took place during the very time the manuscript tradition of the *Mabinogi* was apparently getting under way. In the entry for the year 1176 we read:

> In that year, in Lent, a council assembled in London to confirm the laws of the churches there before a cardinal from Rome, who had come thither for that purpose. And after trouble had been bred between the archbishop of Canterbury and the archbishop of York, the council was thrown into confusion. For on the first day of the council the archbishop of York had occupied the seat of the chair on the right-hand side of the cardinal, where the archbishop of Canterbury had a right and was wont to sit. And the following day, when they came before the cardinal, after disputing about their rights in the presence of the whole court, those behind the archbishop of York came and overturned his chair, so that the archbishop's back was on the floor and the chair on top of him and they upon him trampling him with their feet and striking him with their fists, so that it was with difficulty that the archbishop escaped thence alive.[22]

To a chronicler who does not go out of his way to report events outside of Wales this was clearly an occasion of note.

The narrative statements of the order of seating found especially in the first two Branches of the *Mabinogi* and in the three Welsh romances serve several functions. They are, of course, statements which evoke vivid visual images, thus enlivening the story. They also provide clues as to the status of the characters concerned, and the above anecdote from the chronicles indicates that such outward manifestations of status were important. In the *Mabinogi* in particular these statements also provide clues to the structure and development of the narrative. In the description of Pwyll's arrival in Annwn we read:

> ac eisted a wnaethant ual hynn—y urenhines o'r
> neill parth idaw ef, a'r iarll, debygei ef, o'r parth
> arall. (*PKM* 4)
>
> and they sat like this—the queen on one side of
> him, and the earl, he supposed, on the other side.

This sentence demonstrates clearly that, as Arawn had promised, the disguise of Pwyll is absolute, for we see him sitting in the king's place observing and learning the usage of the court. We might also point out that Pwyll recognizes the *iarll* as such specifically because of the order of the seating.

The next two examples of the seating statement occur at the two wedding feasts held for Rhiannon. At the first feast we are told:

> Sef ual yd eistedyssont, Heueyd Hen ar neill law
> Pwyll, a Riannon o'r parth arall idaw; y am hynny
> pawb ual y bei y enryded. (*PKM* 13)
>
> This is how they sat, Hefeydd the Old on one side
> of Pwyll, and Rhiannon on the other side of him;
> after that, each according to his honour.

Here we see Pwyll sitting in the highest seat and the wedding feast proceeding according to plan. However, the wedding is interrupted and Gwawl is promised to Rhiannon in a year's time. At the second feast note that there is no seating statement made until after Gwawl is tricked out of marrying Rhiannon and he leaves for his own land. Straightaway everyone goes in to dinner and we read:

> ac ual yd eistedyssant ulwydyn o'r nos honno, yd
> eistedwys paub y nos [honno]. (*PKM* 18)
>
> and as they sat a year from that night, each one sat
> that night.

From this we can see that the events resume at the place they were interrupted a year earlier. In the Second Branch the account of Branwen's interrupted wedding feast is framed by a very similar pair of statements.[23]

The structural and thematic significance of these examples suggests that the fourth instance in *Pwyll* may also function similarly. The audience is aware that Rhiannon is innocent of the charges for which she is being punished and the text makes it clear that the members of Pwyll's court also believe her to be innocent:

> Sef a wnaeth Teirnon Twryf Uliant, o achaws y douot a gawssei, ymwarandaw am y chwedyl, ac amouyn yn lut ymdanaw yny gigleu gan lawer o luossogrwyd, o'r a delei y'r llys, mynychu cwynaw truanet damwein Riannon, a'y phoen. (*PKM* 24)
>
> Teyrnon Twryf Liant, because of the find he had made, listened to the news and asked about it continually until he heard from many of the multitude who came to the court repeated complaining of Rhiannon's sad fate and punishment.

Earlier in the story Pwyll's counsellors tried to make Pwyll take another wife. After Rhiannon is accused, these noblemen again come to ask him to leave his wife, and among other things Pwyll replies: "Nyt yscaraf a hi" (*PKM* 21; "I will not separate from her"). The later statement of the seating order made upon Teyrnon's arrival makes it clear that Pwyll has indeed kept Rhiannon with him and that she has kept her place of honour in the court as his wife, in contrast to the treatment of Branwen in the Second Branch. A structural indication that Rhiannon's inclusion in the seating formula is not inadvertent is provided by the fact that she takes part in the subsequent conversation. Thus, this reference to the seating contributes to the subtle balance which the author achieves in his handling of the accusation, punishment, and vindication of Rhiannon.

I have laboured this point because I believe that such close reading of the text reveals the narrative methods of the author and demonstrates how he manages to infuse his telling with significance without ever faltering in the grace and liveliness of his style. As I pointed out in my earlier article there are a number of similarities and contrasts between the weddings and unjustified punishments of Rhiannon and Branwen.[24] The skill with which the author presents these two tales in relation to each other raises another question about the extent to which he may have reshaped the materials which came to him in order to fit the pattern of the *Mabinogi* as he saw it. For instance, the variant tradition of Branwen's punishment recorded in the triad of the *Teir Gvith Baluawt Ynys Prydein* (Three Harmful Blows of the Island of Britain) has been noted by others:

> Vn onadunt a drevis Matholwch Vydel ar Vranwen verch Lyr.[25]
>
> One of them Matholwch the Irishman struck upon Branwen daughter of Llŷr.

In the *Mabinogi*, of course, the punishment is inflicted on Branwen by the butcher rather than by Matholwch himself. This serves to increase the pathos of Branwen's situation but it also heightens the contrast with the story of Rhiannon in the First Branch. Whether this is a change introduced by the author of the *Mabinogi* is ultimately unknowable but the circumstances are suggestive.

In terms of its structure and continuity the story of *Branwen* has been more severely criticized than have the remaining three Branches. For instance, W.J. Gruffydd said of the tale that "the outstanding characteristic of *Branwen* is the excessively large number of 'loose ends' in the narrative and a vast amount of incoherence and confusion."[26] Professor Mac Cana, who has commented most extensively on the Second Branch states that "the tale itself is a collage of disparate materials marked by discontinuity and lack of internal development."[27] I should like, therefore, to point out some of the unifying elements of this tale and briefly discuss their significance.

Some time ago I was struck by the number of times that the word *cyngor* "counsel, council" occurs in the tale. There are no less than twelve incidents in this relatively short story in which *cyngor* is used, sometimes three or four times, or in which the giving of advice is an important element. Looking at these instances a fairly simple pattern emerges: Bendigeidfran gets good advice from his counsellors and Matholwch, for the most part, gets bad advice from his. This is not simply a pro-Welsh bias betraying itself; it is of considerable relevance to our comprehension of the structure and meaning of the tale. A list of the councils in the tale is very nearly a summary of the whole story up to the return of the survivors to Wales.

In the beginning a marriage is proposed "y ymrwymaw ynys y Kedeirn ac Iwerdon y gyt, ual y bydynt gadarnach" (*PKM* 30; "in order to bind together the Island of the Mighty and Ireland, so they might be stronger"). From the moment that Efnisien takes umbrage and vents his rage on Matholwch's horses, however, the tale moves inexorably towards the final catastrophe which destroys the population of Ireland and which gives but a Pyrrhic victory to the few Welsh survivors. The movement towards the unavoidable battle is set out in increments by detailing the negotiations between the Welsh and the Irish, recounting the advice which the noblemen of each court give to their respective kings. We have already seen in the First Branch how Pwyll responds to the advice of his counsellors with utmost care and how his deliberate judiciousness provides for a minimum of personal and social upset until finally the truth is revealed. In *Branwen* this theme is examined in much greater detail and is brought to a level of profound significance to the audience of the *Mabinogi*. Throughout the story there are repeated efforts by Bendigeidfran to establish or restore peace. Matholwch, too, seems interested in maintaining peace with the Island of the Mighty, yet he is prevailed upon by his fosterbrothers and counsellors to carry on a feud which had already been settled in specifically enumerated legal terms, with the not insignificant augmentation of a magic cauldron included to seal the alliance.

In my earlier article I discussed the feud theme in the *Mabinogi*; it is clear that the bloodfeud presented a serious problem in Wales as it did in other societies based on a heroic model. However, the series of events recounted in *Branwen* is significant in that it goes beyond the boundaries of the clan or *cenedl*. The negotiations are carried out at the medieval equivalent of the diplomatic level and indeed the final result is the almost total destruction of two countries, for not only is Ireland depopulated, but practically the entire Welsh army is destroyed and upon their return to Britain the survivors find that the throne has been usurped by Caswallawn. The constant alternation of peace and strife and of good counsel and bad in *Branwen* provides the narrative and thematic coherence for much of the tale. This use of alternation also contributes to an ever-increasing dynamic tension throughout the story which is not relieved until the fury of the final battle breaks loose.

At a pragmatic level the examples of good and bad counsel in the tale can be seen to provide models from which obvious lessons can be drawn; however, the significance of the tale goes beyond this mundane or moralistic aspect. The story becomes a study in the relationship between a king and his country. In this context it is significant to note that the noun *dygyuor* "muster" and the corresponding verb *dygyuoryaw* occur fairly frequently in connection with instances of *cyngor*. Sometimes the people gather to make demands of their king and at other times the king summons his people. *Branwen* can be seen, then, as a tale which probes a very crucial aspect of the structure of the social machinery available in that culture to prevent war and as such it is a mythic paradigm of that all-important facet of society. The fact that the story ends in disaster heightens the mythic function of the tale, for it provides the audience with an archetypal example of a kind of cultural failure which must have seemed endemic.

While a brief respite from grief is shared by the audience during the account of the elysian sojourn in Harddlech and in Gwales, the end of the Second Branch is largely a tale of further woe and loss; the loss felt by those at the *Ysbydawt Urdawl Benn*, "The Assembly of the Wondrous Head," when the charm is broken has often been remarked as one of the most touching and effective passages in the *Mabinogi*. A brief review of the various direct and implied references to the triads in the tale will show how the author's world-view extends beyond the story itself. The triads cited in the Second Branch place some of the characters and events into the broader narrative and historical tradition. In addition to this, however, there is a thematic relevance to these triads which helps us to understand the thematic concerns of the tale.

Although there is no direct reference to the triad of the *Tri Chynweissyat*, "The Three Stewards," in the tale, the occurrence of the name of Caradawc mab Bran in the Peniarth

16 version of the triad is of some importance to the study of *Branwen:*

> Tri Chynweissyat Enys Prydein:
> Caradavc mab Bran,
> a C(h)aurdaf mab Karadauc,
> Ac Ewein mab Maxen Wledic.

Rachel Bromwich has suggested that "it may be significant that each of the three *cynweissieid* named in the triad could be described as the son of a father more famous in Welsh tradition than himself."[28] We have no story about Caurdaf mab Karadawc but the various stories concerning the son of Maxen Wledic are suggestive. The Red Book version of triad 35, "Three Levies that departed from this Island," includes "And the second [army] went with Elen of the Hosts and Maxen Wledic to Llychlyn: and they never returned to this Island."[29] In the Orosian account of Maximus we learn that the emperor left his son Victor as emperor over the Gauls. Victor was slain and a certain Eugenius, a name perhaps to be equated with *Owein*, was set up as emperor.[30] A garbled memory of this may account for later traditions of Owein uab Maxen Wledic and these traditions seem consistent with the story of *Branwen* in which a Welsh host leaves the island and only seven return. I should like to suggest here the possibility that the triad refers to stories of three sons whose fathers led armies from Britain never to return.

Unfortunately, no early version of the triad of the "Three people who broke their hearts from bewilderment" has survived, but at least two of the three members of this triad are referred to in early sources—Cradawc in *Branwen* and Ffaraon Dandde in the independent versions of *Lludd a Llefelys*. Dr. Bromwich further suggests that Moses Williams was not far off the mark with his inclusion of Branwen in his version of this triad.[31] We might point out also that there is in *Branwen* an implied contrast or comparison between the stories of Branwen and Cradawc, whose hearts broke from sorrow or bewilderment, and that of Efnisien, whose heart burst as he destroyed the magic cauldron in repentance for the destruction he had caused.

The reference to the burial and subsequent exhumation of Bendigeidfran's head as one of the *Tri Matgud* (Three

The Role of Myth and Tradition

Fortunate Concealments) and the *Tri Anfad Datgud* (Three Unfortunate Disclosures) provides a link with a famous and perhaps later tradition of disaster coming to the Island of Britain for, as the Red Book version of the triad states, "And Arthur disclosed the head of Bendigeidfran from the White Hill since it did not seem right to him that this island be kept by the strength of anyone but his own."[32] A further link to early historical tradition is provided by the account of Caswallawn's seizure of the crown of London. The version of Caswallawn's accession given in *Brut y Brenhinedd* contains a passage in Avarwy's letter to Caesar which expresses Avarwy's discontent in terms different from those given in Geoffrey of Monmouth's *Historia Regum Britanniae*. Referring to Caswallawn, Avarwy writes, "Y mae ym digyuoythi ynneu o'm kyuoeth weithion, a mynneu a dylywn kystal ac ef o ynys Brydein" "he is despoiling me of my possession now, and I have as good a right as he to the island of Britain."[33] There was a tradition, therefore, that Caswallawn usurped the throne from his nephew or nephews and it would appear that a version of this tradition is embedded in the Second Branch of the *Mabinogi*.

The final triadic reference in *Branwen* is also to a triad of catastrophe, the *Teir Gvith Balvawt Ynys Brydein*, "Three Harmful Blows of the Island of Britain."[34] Matholwch's punishment of Branwen occasioned the destruction of Ireland and much of the Island of the Mighty. Gwenhwyfach's blow struck upon Gwenhwyfar resulted, we are told, in Arthur's final battle at Camlan. And thirdly, Golydan Vard struck down Cadwaladr Vendigeit, the hope of Wales whose return is prophesied in *Armes Prydein*. Thus the Second Branch is a story which deals consistently with a vision of society which is doomed to a series of losses and catastrophes within both the accepted historical tradition of the time and the mythological tradition which provides the culture with a reflection of itself. The triads in *Branwen* help to highlight these thematic implications and for the modern reader they provide evidence external to the text itself that such themes were familiar to a medieval Welsh audience or at least to a storyteller with a working knowledge of *Trioedd Ynys Prydein*.

The narrative method of the *Mabinogi*, drawing heavily on thematic and structural interlace and on direct and implied cross-reference, allows (perhaps even requires) us to compare its parts with one another. In a given reading or recitation of the whole, however, this is not accomplished by the literal turning back of pages or the juxtaposing of widely separated passages for comparative purposes. That is the *modus operandi* of the modern literary critic. The reader or listener experiences the *Mabinogi* as a linear continuum through time and the comparative aspects of the work make themselves felt as an increasingly complex body of information accrues and colours our understanding of events as we come to them and incorporate them into the whole. The above discussion of *cyngor* "council, counsel" in *Branwen* is, therefore, incomplete without taking into account the workings of this minor theme in the other three Branches. From one perspective we can see the use of *cyngor* throughout the *Mabinogi* simply as a reflection of reality, insofar as that is how decisions are often made in both life and literature. From a more literary perspective, however, we have been able to see that a closer look at this theme in *Branwen* reveals some of the underlying literary and cultural significance of the tale. This is compounded and enriched by extending our examination to the whole of the *Mabinogi*, although a brief return to this theme in the first part of *Math* will have to suffice here as a demonstration.

The first reference to *cyngor* in *Math* comes when Gwydion calls his eleven companions together after Pryderi's refusal to present them with the gift of swine. At this council Gwydion prepares the trickery that he has planned. Magic stallions and hounds are all very interesting and make for a visually colourful tale; however, this midnight council serves a more important purpose as a reminder that the real goal of Gwydion's quest is to start a war. Gwydion, at least, could have been neither surprised nor disappointed at Pryderi's initial refusal to give them the swine. The moral issues at stake in Gwydion's behaviour affect the entire country and the stage is finally set when Pryderi in turn takes counsel with his men and agrees to trade the swine for Gwydion's ephemeral horses, dogs, and paraphernalia.

When the chase is on and battle is imminent Math, too, takes counsel about where to engage Pryderi's army, and the geographic detail and planning of strategy must have struck

The Role of Myth and Tradition

a note of realism in an audience whose lives were filled with war and some of whom must have been familiar with the very places named. After returning home from this disastrous war and after dealing with the treachery of Gwydion and Gilfaethwy, Math also takes counsel about selecting a new footholder. On a narrative level this prepares the way for the rest of the tale, leading to the birth of Lleu and the humiliation of Aranrhod. But there is a deeper significance to this reference to the selection of the virgin footholder necessary for Math's survival. As we noted in the discussion of *Branwen*, much of that story examines the relationship between a king and his country. The same is true in *Math*. Math's remarkable necessity for a virgin footholder is undoubtedly a reflection of his magical, mythological, and mysterious origins. In the context of the *Mabinogi*, however, it portrays quite directly and starkly the fact that the welfare of the country is closely tied to the welfare of the king, not just in his judicial and military functions as ruler but in his very person. This becomes more clear when we note that Math's debility (if it is such) prevents him from personally going on a *cylch* or circuit of the land. This custom has a twofold function in that on the one hand it provides the king and his aristocracy with the tangible necessities for their survival and on the other hand it provides the people with firsthand evidence of the power and character of their king and of his abilities to rule, to judge, and to defend them from their enemies. In the *Mabinogi* Math's own forcefulness, wisdom, and good counsel enable him to prevent such total destruction or even disappearance of the country which we find in the Second and Third Branches, though great loss is also suffered in the Fourth Branch.

One brief anecdote will perhaps illustrate that such thematic pressures do indeed make themselves felt to the audience of the *Mabinogi*. In the spring of 1982 I inflicted upon the members of my car-sharing pool a reading of the Four Branches (in English) on our way to and from work, partly to while away the time with "pleasant tales and storytelling" and partly to see what response it would receive. Upon finishing the Fourth Branch, one of the listeners directed a comment towards the moment at which Gronw Bebyr asks:

> "Wy gwyrda kywir, a'm teulu, a'm brodyr maeth,
> a oes ohonawch chwi, a gymero yr ergyt drossof?"
> "Nac oes, dioer," heb wynt. (*PKM* 92)
>
> "My trusty noblemen and my warband and my fosterbrothers, is there one of you who will take the blow for me?" "God knows, there is not," said they.

The response to this was to the effect that "I like the way the author didn't say, 'And so they took counsel and this is what they decided. . . . ' They just said 'Oh, no! Not us!'" This demonstrates fairly clearly that the narrative method of repetition and interlaced cross-reference does indeed work, even for an audience hearing the tale for the first time.

One critical method which has been used in the study of the origins and development of the *Mabinogi* and which I should like to touch upon before ending is the isolation of various events or episodes which seem to have an independent structure. It has been said about a number of incidents in the Four Branches that they each form an independent story which is not closely connected to the tale around it. For instance, Professors Gruffydd and Jarman have commented that the Mice in the Corn episode and the first part of *Pwyll*, respectively, have little connection with the rest of the *Mabinogi*.[35] It is occasionally remarked that each such episode could be extracted and related independently as a coherent short tale. There are two basic problems with this assumption, however. On the one hand, if an episode is taken out of its context it may at first glance seem to form a complete coherent tale, but closer analysis often reveals that some key motivation has been lost and more questions would need to be asked than before we isolated it. This is the case with the Mice in the Corn episode. First of all, some character relationships would have to be changed, otherwise we would have to account for Manawydan living with someone else's wife. This is no great problem; perhaps we could just change the names. But we would also have to explain how a noblemen of the stature necessary to account for Cigfa's repeated rebukes comes to be doing his own farming without any help. Thus we already require the sort of explanation that is given earlier in the Third Branch—the enchantment of Dyfed.

Assuming that we overcome these problems we must still find an explanation for things at the end. Why should all these enchanted mice be raiding someone's cornfield? The explanation of Llwyd uab Cil Coed, of course, provides not only the motivation for this episode but the resolution to earlier episodes in the *Mabinogi* as well. Thus, to tell the story of the Mice in the Corn independently requires considerable change in the episode itself, especially in the crucial matter of motivation. In essence, it becomes a different story, for in a narrative style which is so blatantly episodic, as is much medieval narrative (and certainly the *Mabinogi*), this question of motivation is of utmost importance.

We might also look at this question of independent episodes from the opposite perspective. If we extract an episode from the *Mabinogi* what are we left with? Without the Mice in the Corn in the Third Branch we would be left without any resolution to the tale and we would never learn what happened to Pryderi and Rhiannon. A slightly trickier case is presented by the account of Pwyll's year in Annwn. This section of the First Branch can indeed be presented as a separate narrative leaving no loose ends. But then, what is the *Mabinogi* without it? At the purely structural level, in the Fourth Branch Gwydion would have to find some other excuse for sending Math off to war. Thus there is a strong motivational link between the First and the Fourth Branches and the further thematic comparison of events in these two Branches is also considerably revealing in our attempts to understand the *Mabinogi* as a whole.[36] In the Second Branch the Iron House episode, which is manifestly a story within a story, could indeed be extracted and told on its own, though we might be left wondering where Llassar and his wife escaped to and what was the significance of the cauldron he carried with him. At the same time not much would seem to be missing in terms of narrative structure if the Second Branch does not contain this account. However, it is again in terms of its thematic implications that this story has significance to the tale around it, for the ruse of the Iron House devised by the Irish parallels the ruse designed to trap Bendigeidfran inside a building.

A basic compositional method drawn heavily upon by the author of the *Mabinogi* is the weaving together of such seemingly independent episodes, stories, and traditions. In this chapter I have tried to show that some of the thematic threads which run throughout the resulting tightly knit structure are concerns of great social significance to the audience. It is primarily this consistent thematic undercurrent which unifies the Four Branches and which lifts the whole into the realm of cultural myth. It is not surprising that the author draws on traditional stories ultimately derived from earlier primary Celtic mythology, for these are his cultural "deposits" about which David Jones wrote: "You use the things that are yours to use because they happen to be lying about the place or site or lying within the orbit of your 'tradition.'"[37] What is striking in the *Mabinogi* is the consummate skill with which the author adapts these materials, creating a revitalized myth infused with a vision and a moral code to meet the contemporary needs of his audience, a myth in terms of which it could examine and evaluate its own society. This is, of course, one of the recognized roles of mythology. It is also an important function of a work of literature, and the *Mabinogi* is both myth and literature.

NOTES

A version of this chapter was read at a meeting of the Cylch Trafod Rhyddiaith at Jesus College, Oxford, in May 1981 and some additions to it are based on remarks read at the 1982 meeting of the Celtic Studies Association of North America. I would especially like to thank the Jingo Foundation for financial assistance which enabled me to attend these meetings.

1. Gruffydd, "The Mabinogion," 46.
2. Bollard, "The Structure of the Four Branches of the Mabinogi," 276.
3. O'Rahilly, ed., *Táin Bó Cúalnge from the Book of Leinster*, 136; Kinsella, trans., *The Táin*, 238.
4. Wilde, "Preface," *The Picture of Dorian Gray*.
5. Tolkien, "Beowulf: The Monsters and the Critics," 61.
6. Bollard, "The Structure of the Four Branches of the Mabinogi," 250–253.
7. Tolkien, *The Two Towers*, 40–41.
8. I. Williams, ed., *Pedeir Keinc y Mabinogi*. Cardiff: University of Wales Press, 1951. Hereafter cited in the text as *PKM*.

The Role of Myth and Tradition

9. Mac Cana, *Celtic Mythology*, 80.
10. Gruffydd, *Rhiannon*.
11. Jackson, "Some Popular Motifs in Early Welsh Tradition," 84.
12. Jackson, "Some Popular Motifs," 84.
13. Jackson, "Some Popular Motifs," 84.
14. Bollard, "The Structure of the Four Branches of the Mabinogi," 253–256.
15. Mac Cana, *The Mabinogi*, 36.
16. Jackson, *The International Popular Tale and Early Welsh Tradition*, 92.
17. Jackson, *The International Popular Tale*, 93; my emphasis throughout the paragraph.
18. Mac Cana, *The Mabinogi*, 37.
19. Mac Cana, *The Mabinogi*, 37.
20. Bollard, "The Structure of the Four Branches of the Mabinogi," 265.
21. Mac Cana, *The Mabinogi*, 37.
22. T. Jones, ed. and trans., *Brut y Tywysogyon or The Chronicle of the Princes, Red Book of Hergest Version*, 166–167.
23. "Sef ual yd eistedyssant, brenhin Ynys y Kedeirn, a Manawydan uab Llŷr o'r neill parth idaw, a Matholwch o'r parth arall, a Branwen uerch Lyr gyt ac ynteu" (*PKM* 31; "This is how they sat, the king of the Island of the Mighty, with Manawydan son of Llŷr on one side of him, and Matholwch on the other side, and Branwen daughter of Llŷr together with him"); "Ac ual y dechreuyssant eisted ar dechreu y wled, yd eistedyssant yna" (*PKM* 34; "And as they began sitting at the beginning of the feast, they sat then").
24. Bollard, "The Structure of the Four Branches of the Mabinogi," 263–266.
25. Bromwich, *Trioedd Ynys Prydein: The Welsh Triads*, triad 53, 144, with addendum on 538–539.
26. Quoted in Mac Cana, *The Mabinogi*, 41.
27. Mac Cana, *The Mabinogi*, 56.
28. Bromwich, *Trioedd Ynys Prydein*, triad 13, 23–24.
29. Bromwich, *Trioedd Ynys Prydein*, 77.
30. Bromwich, *Trioedd Ynys Prydein*, 478.
31. Bromwich, *Trioedd Ynys Prydein*, triad 95, 226.
32. Bromwich, *Trioedd Ynys Prydein*, triad 37R, 89.
33. Parry, ed., *Brut y Brenhinedd*, 76; my translation.
34. Bromwich, *Trioedd Ynys Prydein*, triad 53, 144.
35. Gruffydd, *Rhiannon*, 71; Jarman, "Pedair Cainc y Mabinogi," 89.

36. See Bollard, "The Structure of the Four Branches of the Mabinogi," 269–270
37. D. Jones, *The Anathemata,* 34.

14

The Theme of Sovereignty in *Pwyll*

Catherine A. McKenna

Although it is generally agreed that *Pedair Cainc y Mabinogi* is a highly literary work, most studies have been devoted to reconstructing coherent narratives which can be regarded as the original, and implicitly the correct, forms of the stories, or to explaining, by reference to oral traditional processes, their development out of a jumble of originally separate themes and motifs. The first approach sees the *Mabinogi*, or at least each of its Branches, as a unified whole of which we see but the distorted shadow on the wall of the cave. The second sees it as a patchwork whole, and is more interested in examining the seams which traverse it than in describing the design thereby created. While both approaches have yielded valuable insight into the *Mabinogi* and underlying Celtic traditions, both leave us, finally, with an uncomfortably contradictory view of the author of the text as we have it. He appears to have been, on one hand, a master of fine prose, especially of dialogue, and a connoisseur of courtly manners, and on the other, a man who did not understand the stories he was recounting but who dutifully recorded, to the best of his limited ability, ancient and fragmentary Welsh traditions. Perhaps we must ultimately come to terms with this portrait of the artist, but perhaps a re-examination of the Four Branches which assumes that the text is in some sense coherent, whatever its relations to its origins, might yield a less paradoxical understanding. Such a re-examination would assume that the text was intended to be read as meaningful narrative by an audience which did not consist entirely of antiquarians or literary archaeologists and would look for the coherence it might have held for that contemporary audience. So examined, it is possible to regard the First Branch as a story about the growth to full and effective lordship over Dyfed of its protagonist, Pwyll, and as a mirror and exhortation for medieval Welsh princes.

The reconstructive approach to *Mabinogi* criticism is, of course, best exemplified by the work of W.J. Gruffydd, who regarded the Four Branches as the story of the hero Pryderi. The First Branch, he contended, comprises Pryderi's *compert* or birth story and a version of the tale of his abduction by Otherworld forces. He saw the Second Branch, *Branwen,* as a tale of Pryderi's greatest exploit, which he understood to have been, originally, an expedition to Annwfn to seize the cauldron of resurrection. He read *Manawydan* as a version of the "rape of Pryderi" alternative to the second part of *Pwyll* and *Math* as Pryderi's *aided* or death tale.[1]

In the original form of the First Branch, as Gruffydd would have it, a mortal stole an Otherworld woman from her Otherworld lover, who pursued her and begot upon her the child Pryderi, whom he subsequently abducted to the Otherworld.[2] This interpretation involved considerable violence to the text, for Gruffydd arrived at it by separating Pwyll from the title he bears at the beginning of the story, "Pendefig Dyfed," and making of him two separate characters, the Otherworld king Pwyll Pen Annwfn and the mortal chieftain or "Pendefig Dyfed" whose role is actually played in the text by Arawn, mistakenly identified there as himself a king of Annwfn. Further, according to Gruffydd, Pwyll the lord of Annwfn fathered Pryderi upon Rhiannon, the Otherworld bride of the mortal chieftain with whom he had exchanged forms. Yet according to the text, Pwyll remained chaste in his relationship with Arawn's wife—a circumstance whose dramatic and humorous implications are explored with great skill.

Gruffydd supported his reconstruction of *Pwyll* by reference to Irish tales which he saw as analogues of the original story, and the method he thereby introduced into *Mabinogi* scholarship has been a very fruitful one. It is the method of

Proinsias Mac Cana's excellent study of the Second Branch[3] and essentially the method of Kenneth Jackson's criticism of Gruffydd's work as well. Professor Jackson examined the *Mabinogi* in relation not only to Irish literary analogues but to international tale types and motifs as well. He demonstrated that reconstruction of the Annwfn section of *Pwyll* to make Pryderi a son of Pwyll and Arawn's wife conceived during that period is unnecessary, since the motifs of exchanging shapes, the chaste friend, and the vicarious duel had been joined in international popular tradition before the *Mabinogi* as we have it was composed. In his view, this complex of motifs was adapted by a storyteller for use in a Welsh narrative tradition according to which Pwyll went to the Otherworld to fight Arawn's enemy on his behalf.[4] He showed further that Gruffydd's identification of Pwyll as the original Otherworld king and Arawn as properly a mortal is equally unnecessary, since the motif of the mortal warrior assisting the Otherworld king in battle appears in several Irish sagas.[5]

Jackson's work on the *Mabinogi* led criticism in several directions simultaneously. His revision of Gruffydd's reading of the Annwfn episode suggested the possibility of reading the text as a consciously crafted narrative, valid in itself and not merely a puzzle from which a hypothetical lost original might be reconstructed. At the same time, his attention to international popular motifs involved an analytical method whose end result is fragmentation of each tale into its component parts.

Subsequent work on the Four Branches has tended to develop Jackson's analytical methods of criticism and Gruffydd's archaeological interest in uncovering by such analysis Celtic mythic traditions, although a recent article by Seán Ó Coileáin attempts to synthesize Jackson's analysis of *Pwyll* into a comprehensive thematic explanation of the tale.[6] He reads *Pwyll* as Pryderi's birth tale, and explains the Rhiannon section as a functional doublet of the Annwfn section necessitated by the deflection of the story from its narrative goal—the birth—which occurs when the motif of the chaste friend is introduced. The Teyrnon section in turn is a doublet of part of the Rhiannon section, which is deflected by introduction of the Calumniated Wife theme. However, while Ó Coileáin reads *Pwyll* as a unified tale, his interest is primarily in the processes by which its separate parts are joined and only secondarily in the nature of the whole thereby created. Furthermore, he is not concerned with the question of why the birth story of Pryderi should have been of interest to a late eleventh- or twelfth-century audience, but with the developmental processes which forged it.

With few other exceptions, recent criticism has tended to focus on the underlying mythic nature of material in the Four Branches, but has avoided the temptation to reconstruct lost originals of the tales. Proinsias Mac Cana approached the text in this fashion in *Celtic Mythology*,[7] and so more recently has Patrick Ford, who describes the *Mabinogi* as "an extensive collection of more or less related adventures, related sufficiently for them to be metaphorically conceived as branches," each consisting of "episodes of related lore *(cyfarwydd)* and adventures *(cyfrangau)*."[8] Study of the mythic material in the Four Branches has indeed proven fruitful; in regard to *Pwyll* its most valuable discovery has been the relationship of Rhiannon to the continental Epona and other equine divinities of Celtic tradition.[9] However, as much as such scholarship contributes to our understanding of the Four Branches, it does not in and of itself define the nature of the text for us at all.

Such definition ought properly to begin, as has been generally recognized, with an understanding of the term *mabinogi*. Many interpretations have been put forward over the years,[10] of which the most recent and the most closely argued is that of Eric Hamp. Professor Hamp interprets the term as meaning "the collective material pertaining to Maponos,"[11] thus associating the Four Branches with the "divine youth" whose cult is attested archaeologically in Britain and Gaul. This analysis offers strong support for the view of the *Mabinogi* as mythology. Whether we read the Four Branches, with Professor Ford, as a "collection of more or less related adventures" grounded in the mythology of Maponos or as four separate but individually unified tales dealing with discrete aspects of a mythic tradition,[12] it seems clear that their redactor had some notion of the material he was recounting as traditional mythic material, regardless of the confusion over ancient traditions which may have caused him to drop the thread of his narrative occasionally. Survival of the term *mabinogi* is very difficult to explain otherwise.

Nevertheless, to claim, tentatively, for the redactor of the Four Branches an awareness of the nature of his received material is not, necessarily, to understand his intention in composing the text. Despite general agreement on the presence of mythological tradition in the *Mabinogi,* there are some scholars who regard the preservation of this material as the sole or primary purpose of the text and others who see the mythology as a material rather than a formal cause, that is, as the narrative matter out of which the redactor consciously formed a different literary artefact.

It is to the former group, of course, that W.J. Gruffydd belonged. While he regarded the *Mabinogi* as a conscious work of art never very well known in Wales,[13] he believed it to be a reworking of traditional material into, figuratively speaking, "one sentence with only one subject and one main verb,"[14] a sentence about the hero Pryderi. *Pwyll,* in his view, is Pryderi's birth story and explains how it is "that Pryderi is said to have succeeded his father as Lord of Dyfed when he was notoriously the son of the Head of Annwvn. The question was answered by making the Lord of Dyfed and the Head of Annwvn into *one* person under *two* names."[15]

Jackson regards the text as the studied work of a courtly entertainer of antiquarian bent "who 'revived' this body of tales which had been out of fashion for so long that it was capable of being made fashionable and interesting once again . . . but he was not able clearly to restore the thread of the tales where this had been lost."[16] Like Gruffydd, he focuses on the traditional nature of *Pwyll,* a tale which may have originated as an explanation of how Pwyll became the Head of Annwfn,[17] and he accounts for its literary redaction by reference to the traditional, antiquarian inclinations of the Celtic peoples. Seán Ó Coileáin's recent analysis of *Pwyll* supports Jackson's view by demonstrating, very persuasively, that the structure of the tale might very well reflect development in the oral tradition.[18] Although Ó Coileáin reads the tale as a *compert,* or birth story, and attributes the breaking and twisting of its narrative threads to its oral history, rather than to the inability of the antiquarian redactor to restore lost material, he implicitly regards the tale as traditional narrative preserved for tradition's sake. Brynley Roberts holds a similar view.[19]

Patrick Ford goes a step further than other scholars of this school and claims that the redactor of the Four Branches not only recounted ancient mythic traditions but to some extent understood them. The First Branch, for example,

> appears to confront the problem of the failure of the horse-goddess to guarantee fertility and generate a hero (at the anthropomorphic level) and a foal (at the hippomorphic level). For that failure, she is punished by being reduced to the function of beast of burden . . . . The story is successfully resolved . . . in that the hero and foal are restored and so is Rhiannon to her proper role as consort of the king and guarantor of fertility.[20]

Among those who credit the author with rhetorical intentions beyond the preservation of ancient mythic tradition is Proinsias Mac Cana, who has himself contributed a great deal to our recovery of that tradition from the text. Jackson describes the *Mabinogi* as "the product of the study rather than the mead-hall,"[21] and Mac Cana concurs, picturing the redactor as "a cleric, learned in Latin and reasonably well informed, if not professionally expert in vernacular literature."[22] But he believes further that the redactor has exalted the virtues of the study, rather than the battlefield, in his literary treatment of traditional oral material. "In his narrative and use of character," Mac Cana contends, "particularly in the case of Manawydan, he subtly conveys a scale of values which, by implication, he commends to the practice of contemporary society. For the exaggerated and impulsive ideals of heroic tradition . . . he projects the more Christian and more practical virtues of patience and compromise."[23] For Mac Cana, as for D. Myrddin Lloyd, it is the character of Manawydan, who does not appear in the First Branch, whom the author has chosen to voice his own attitudes; in connection with the First Branch, however, it is noteworthy that "good sense" is Manawydan's outstanding virtue, a virtue whose Welsh name is *pwyll*.[24] Mac Cana's reading of the Four Branches is supported by a close study of the First Branch, which shows the tale to be concerned with Pwyll's growth to effective sovereignty through the development and exercise of his wisdom and good sense.[25]

Obviously, any attempt to define the rhetorical intentions of the redactor of the Four Branches must begin with a description of the audience he was addressing. Chronologically, that audience seems to have belonged to the last half of the eleventh century or the first quarter of the twelfth. Sir Ifor Williams argued that the text was composed *c.* 1060 (*PKM* xli),[26] but recent scholarship has called into question the possibility of making such a precise determination on the basis of available evidence, and Professor Mac Cana and Dr. T.M. Charles-Edwards have concurred that composition may have occurred as late as 1120.[27]

Socially, of course, the original audience of the Four Branches may be taken to have been an aristocratic one. This is attested by the preoccupation of the tales with the activities of kings and lords, as well as by what is known about the circumstances in which literature was produced, in medieval Celtic and in early medieval European society generally. The Four Branches draw upon a tradition of native learning. In *Pwyll* this tradition manifests itself in a concern with specific geographical and genealogical data. Pwyll holds court in Arberth, *prif lys idaw,* whence he sets forth on the hunting expedition to Glyn Cuch via Pen Llwyn Diarwya which culminates in his meeting with Arawn. It is from Arberth, too, that Pwyll sets out on the after-dinner walk which leads him, ultimately, to his meeting with Rhiannon. It is at Presseleu that Pwyll meets with *gwyr y wlat* in the third year of his marriage to discuss Rhiannon's barrenness. Teyrnon is lord of Gwent Is Coed, and it is thence that he and his wife travel to Arberth in Dyfed to return Pwyll's son to him. Finally, at the end of the story, Pryderi's expansion of his realm is detailed quite specifically: he ultimately rules not only the seven cantrefs of Dyfed, but also the three cantrefs of Ystrad Tywi and the four cantrefs of Ceredigion, collectively known as the seven cantrefs of Seisyllwch. The redactor's interest in genealogy is clearest in his description of Pryderi's bride as Cigfa daughter of Gwyn Gohoyw son of Gloyw Gwallt Llydan son of Casnar Wledig *o dyledogyon yr ynys hon.*

The redactor's interest in Welsh lore is even more apparent in the other Branches—in his onomastic stories about places with the element *moch* in their names in *Math,* for example, and in the explicit references to *Trioedd Ynys Prydain*, which appear in all of the stories except *Pwyll*. Yet, even in the First Branch his approach to his material is a learned one, although he only once allows his knowledge to slow the pace of his narrative. That one occasion is his indulgence of the Celtic penchant for onomastic material in the story of the naming of Pryderi:

> "Y rof i a Duw," heb y Riannon, "oed escor uym pryder im, pei gwir hynny." "Arlwydes," heb y Pendaran Dyuet, "da yd enweist dy uab, Pryderi." ... "Yawnahaf yw hynny," heb y Pwyll, "kymryt enw y mab y wrth geir a dywot y uam, pann gauas llawen chwedyl y wrthaw." (*PKM* 26)

All of this geographical, genealogical, and onomastic lore suggests an educated audience, interested in more than a satisfying series of adventures; it suggests an audience in court or monastery. That the original audience was more likely a courtly than a monastic one is suggested by the interest which the tales take in courtly life and manners.

In *Pwyll*, for example, considerable space is devoted to descriptions of hunting and feasting, the major peacetime activities of aristocratic life. The redactor enjoys, too, the details of courtly conversation among noblemen of various ranks and among aristocratic ladies and gentlemen.

In Pwyll's first adventure, his meeting with Arawn in the wood, the redactor observes the scene with the eyes and ears of an experienced huntsman:

> Ac ual y byd yn ymwrandaw a llef yr erchwys, ef a glywei llef erchwys arall, ac nid oedynt unllef, a hynny yn dyuot yn erbyn y erchwys ef. (*PKM* 1)

He not only hears the difference in vocal quality between the two packs of hounds, but visualizes very precisely the rapid sequence of events which ensues:

> Ac ef a welei lannerch yn y coet o uaes guastat; ac ual yd oed y erchwys ef yn ymgael ac ystlys y lannerch, ef a welei carw o ulaen yr erchwys arall. A pharth a pherued y lannerch, llyma yr erchwys

> a oed yn y ol yn ymordiwes ac ef, ac yn y uwrw y'r
> llawr. (*PKM* 1)

Later on in the tale, in the episode of Pwyll's meeting with Rhiannon, the redactor demonstrates an aristocratic feeling for specific details of horsemanship. The first of Pwyll's men to pursue the mysterious horsewoman who rides past the Gorsedd Arberth waits until he reaches open, level ground *(maestir guastat)* and then shows his horse the spurs *(ef a dangosses yr ysparduneu y'r march)*. He knows enough to give up the chase, however, when he feels his horse failing in speed *(pan wybu ef ar y uarch pallu y bedestric)* (*PKM* 10). In the second attempt to overtake Rhiannon, the rider is said to give the horse its head, or more literally, to release it from the reins *(ellwg y uarch a oruc wrth auwyneu)* (*PKM* 11).

The redactor is equally familiar with the pleasures of the hall and the protocol of courtly life. He paints a vivid picture of the appointments of Arawn's court, with its beautifully adorned sleeping quarters, halls, and chambers *(hundyeu ac yneuadeu ac ysteuyll a'r addurn teccaf a welsei neb o adeiladeu)*, its golden vessels and royal jewels *(eur llestri a theyrn dlysseu)*. He describes Pwyll's being assisted out of his hunting garments and into a robe of gold-embroidered silk, young lads or squires *(makwyueit a gueisson ieueinc)* performing the menial chore of pulling his boots off, before two knights *(deu uarchauc)* array him in his feasting robe. He attends to such details of the feast as washing before the meal *(e ymolchi yd aethant)* and seating arrangements *(y urenhines o'r neill parth idaw ef, a'r iarll, debygei ef, o'r parth arall)*. And he praises the pleasures of courtly life: hunting *(hela)*, conversation *(ymdidan)*, food *(bwyt)*, drink *(llynn)*, song *(cerdeu)*, affection *(carueidrwyd)*, and carousal *(cyuedach)* (*PKM* 4–5).

Similar detail enlivens the accounts of the two feasts at the court of Hyfaidd Hen, Rhiannon's father. At the second of these, after being released from the bag in which he has been trapped, Gwawl quickly recovers his dignity: his first thought is of a bath:

> briwedic wyf i, a chymriw mawr a geueis, ac
> ennein yssyd reit ymi, ac i ymdeith yd af i, gan
> dy gannyat ti. (*PKM* 18)

Courtly interests are evident in other dialogues as well. Pwyll's first interchange with Arawn centres at first on the identification of social status, so that the privileges and obligations of each party with respect to the other may be determined:

> "A unben," heb ef, "mi a wnn pwy wytti ac ny chyuarchaf i well it." "Ie," heb ef, "ac atuyd y mae arnat o anryded ual nas dylyei."

Arawn explains that it is, rather, Pwyll's discourtesy in seizing the stag for himself which explains his coldness. Pwyll then offers to pay compensation, *vrth ual y bo dy anryded, ac ny wnn i pwy wytti*. Arawn announces that he is a crowned king *(brenhin corunawc)*, which Pwyll is not. In his response, Pwyll addresses Arawn as *arglwyd*, a form of address suitable to his newly revealed status. Hitherto, Pwyll and Arawn have been addressing each other as *unbenn* (PKM 2).[28]

At the conclusion of the tale, the privileges and obligations of social rank and relationship are again the main concern of the dialogue between Pwyll and Teyrnon. They comment on Pryderi's obligation to remember and recompense the foster parents of his infancy. Pwyll in his gratitude promises to support Teyrnon in his lordship over Gwent Is Coed, but the main bond is between the foster father and the child himself: *iawnach yw idaw dy gynnhal nogyt y mi* (PKM 26).

The general atmosphere of courtliness in Pwyll, then, reveals itself under close scrutiny as a real and reasonably specific knowledge of and interest in the ways of the court. This fact suggests that it was for a secular court, rather than a monastic audience, that the redaction of the First Branch was originally intended.

Before proceeding further with an examination of the aristocratic concern which most fundamentally informs the tale, that is, the nature of effective sovereignty, it would be well to consider briefly the historical situation of Welsh princes during the period when the text was composed (*c.* 1060–1120). The beginning of that period was marked by the considerable statesmanship of Gruffudd ap Llywelyn, who

Sovereignty in Pwyll

united all Wales under his rule from 1055 until he was defeated and killed by Earl Harold of Wessex in 1063. He accomplished the unification of Wales and successful resistance to English incursion by virtue of birth, victory in battle, and judicious alliance. He was the son of Llywelyn ap Seisyll, ruler of Gwynedd, and of Angharad, daughter of Maredudd ap Owain of Deheubarth and descendant of the great kings of tradition, Rhodri Mawr and Hywel Dda. Such ancestry lent a certain legitimacy and considerable emotional appeal to his gradual armed conquest of Deheubarth after his accession to the throne of Gwynedd in 1039. Meanwhile, his successful maintenance of the Welsh border against the English was facilitated by his alliance with Aelfgar, who was from 1057 the Earl of Mercia. This alliance was cemented by Gruffudd's marriage to Aelfgar's daughter Ealdgyth. Gruffudd's reign revived in Wales on the eve of the Norman invasion a spirit of ardent nationalism; yet interestingly, tradition has it that he began his life as a weak and lazy youth, and only shortly before his accession to the throne of Gwynedd began to develop lordly virtues.[29] It would be a mistake, of course, to make too much of such traditions, since the theme of the unpromising youth is known to attach itself to the stories of legendary heroes of mythic, fictitious, and historical origin. Whether or not this story is based in fact in Gruffudd's case, however, it is certainly true that his reign was a great one in the history of medieval Wales.

During the remainder of the period, of course, the major concern of Welsh political leadership was the Norman attempt to subjugate Wales. This period produced several outstanding princes in the persons of Gruffudd ap Cynan, Rhys ap Tewdwr, Gruffudd ap Rhys, and Bleddyn ap Cynfyn. Gruffudd ap Cynan, born in Ireland of a Welsh father and a Dublin Norse mother, devoted his young manhood to recovering the throne of Gwynedd, which had been held by his grandfather. This goal he had accomplished, with the help of various Irish and Scandinavian allies, by 1081. Subsequently, during the period 1094–1114, he was able to expand the borders of Gwynedd by recovering territory from the Normans, and although he was compelled in 1114 to do homage to Henry I, the strength of Gwynedd was maintained during the rest of his reign by his sons. Gruffudd ap Cynan

(d. 1137) was not only a militarily strong prince, but one with whom was associated a renaissance of the arts in Wales.[30] The *Historia Gruffud Vab Kenan*,[31] the only biography in medieval Welsh literature, tells us that Gruffudd brought poets and musicians from Ireland to his court in Gwynedd. The biography is neither contemporary, having been composed *c.* 1162–1170, nor unbiased, since it is highly eulogistic, but the tradition of Gruffudd's interest in the arts was strong enough that a sixteenth-century codification of *eisteddfod* regulations was attributed to him. Whether or not such traditions have an historical foundation, it is certain that it is with Gruffudd's reign that the work of Meilyr Brydydd, the earliest of the *Gogynfeirdd* whose name has come down to us, is associated. Whether as a result of Gruffudd's encouragement or by sheer coincidence, his reign marked the beginning of an outpouring of bardic poetry which continued through the end of Welsh independence in the thirteenth century.

A third notable prince of the period was Rhys ap Tewdwr of Deheubarth (*c.* 1078–1093), who maintained authority over southern Wales despite some opposition from other Welsh princes. He seems to have accomplished this by force of arms, by alliance with Gruffudd ap Cynan, and by compact with William. Most of Deheubarth fell to the Normans soon after Rhys's death, but his son Gruffudd ap Rhys (d. 1137) led in 1116 a rising against the Normans and their Welsh allies which, although its successes were very minor, rekindled for a time the courage and hope of South Wales. Gruffudd eventually established an acceptable relationship with Henry I; furthermore, although he received little assistance to his rebellion from Gruffudd ap Cynan of Gwynedd, he established a connection between the two royal houses by marrying Gruffudd ap Cynan's daughter Gwenllian, upon whom he fathered the lord Rhys, one of the greatest Welsh princes of the late twelfth century.[32]

Finally, mention may be made of Bleddyn ap Cynfyn of Powys (d. 1075), a prince whose military achievements in maintaining his realm against Welsh opposition and Norman incursion were modest but respectable, and a prince singled out for praise by the *Brut y Tywysogion.* He is described there as "support of the wise, the glory and cornerstone of the Church . . . terrible in war, but in peace beloved." And he is

Sovereignty in Pwyll 315

one of very few Welsh princes known to have introduced reforms into the legal code attributed to Hywel Dda.[33]

Scholars have speculated about relationships between some of these princes and the composition of the Four Branches. Ifor Williams, for example, suggested that the text was composed during the reign of Gruffudd ap Llywelyn, when the unification of Wales under one prince would have facilitated the exchange of narrative traditions among bards and story tellers from different parts of Wales (*PKM* xl–xli).[34] Without going so far as to identify a particular prince as patron of the text of *Pedair Cainc y Mabinogi*, however, one may certainly say of the period that it was one in which strong rulers were absolutely essential to the survival of Wales, whose political and cultural identity was threatened with Norman conquest. It was a period, too, which produced several such princes, men worthy of the supportive service of literary artists, able to offer them patronage, and in several cases associated by tradition with support of the peaceful arts.

Given the historical situation of the Welsh princes during the period 1060–1120 and the aristocratic preoccupations of the redactor of *Pwyll*, I would suggest that it was in a princely court that the text was composed. Further, I would suggest that the redactor's intention was not only to record or reweave archaic traditions to create a courtly entertainment, but also to compose a tale which would describe and praise the traditional virtues of Celtic sovereignty, as well as some newer political virtues, thus fulfilling a function similar to that of contemporary bardic poetry, which was both eulogistic and exhortatory.

Welsh bardic poetry often associates its subject with great heroes and rulers of the past, both by explicit reference and by the use of traditional diction, epithets, and forms which echo earlier panegyrics. In his *molawd* to Owain Gwynedd (d. 1170), for example, Cynddelw Brydydd Mawr calls his patron,

> hil cadyr Cadell Hiryell hiryein ar beryg
> koelyg.[35]

Cynddelw thus associates the twelfth-century prince Owain with his legendary ancestors, Coel Hen, fifth-century king of northern Britain, and Cadell son of Rhodri Mawr, a late-ninth-century prince. Elsewhere, lamenting the death of Madog ap Maredudd of Powys (d. 1160), he terms this prince

rut ongyr bran vab llyr lledyeith.[36]

Here he associates his late patron with the king of Britain in the Second Branch of the *Mabinogi*.

The conventions of bardic poetry had clearly accustomed the Welsh princes to thinking of themselves as reflections of legendary heroes. Thus, a prince for whom the text of the *Mabinogi* was composed would have been predisposed to see himself mirrored in the story of Pwyll, the legendary lord of Dyfed.[37] In this model of lordship he would have seen heroism, justice, and promotion of the land's fertility and prosperity—three qualities associated throughout Celtic tradition with effective sovereignty. The redactor's concern with these qualities is apparent in the nature of the mythic material he employs, in the structure, whether received or original, of that material, and in the prose style of the tale. He devotes all three aspects of his narrative art to creating, despite the significant element of the magical and fantastic in Pwyll's adventures, a very human model of effective sovereignty. Pwyll is a figure who enters into full and successful lordship only as a result of meeting a series of challenges, successfully passing a series of tests, and gradually acquiring wisdom *(pwyll)*, which he conspicuously lacks at the tale's beginning. Unlike legendary heroes as they are presented in bardic verse, Pwyll is a fairly comic, and thus accessible, figure. In him a medieval Welsh prince could see not only an image of good lordship, but an image too of inept humanity, struggling successfully to achieve full sovereignty not so much through battlefield heroics and unlimited munificence as through the exercise of less spectacular but more practical virtues—humility, prudence, judicious wisdom, and self-restraint. Hence the tale of the lord of Dyfed would serve not only as an implicitly flattering catalogue of princely virtues but also as an exhortation to similar achievement in the challenging circumstances of contemporary Wales.

The theme of sovereignty is implicit in the traditional material which the redactor of *Pwyll* chose as the basis for his tales. This may help to explain why he chose it, although it is by no means certain that he understood, in the eleventh or twelfth century, the implications which scholars have articulated for us in the twentieth. The core of the sovereignty theme in *Pwyll* is the figure of Rhiannon. Her name has been analysed as Rīgantonā, or "great divine queen," and as such she may be identified with the goddess of sovereignty so important to Celtic tradition, the goddess whose hand must be won by any aspirant to kingship. Further evidence for the identification of Rhiannon with the goddess of sovereignty, who appears under many names in Celtic tradition, lies in her equine associations: she initially appears to Pwyll riding on a horse; the birth and abduction of her son are associated with the birth and abduction of a foal; and her punishment for the suspected murder of her child is to fulfill the function of a horse as beast of burden. These features link her to the Gaulish goddess Epona, to other Celtic equine divinities, and to the equine aspects of some Celtic and other Indo-European rites of inauguration to kingship.[38] In addition, Rhiannon behaves, in her manifestation of supernatural power, her independent strong-mindedness in choosing a husband, and her superior wisdom, like other manifestations of the sovereignty goddess such as the Irish Medb.

Proinsias Mac Cana's detailed study of the goddess of sovereignty in Irish tradition[39] explores some dozen different versions of the story of her union with the rightful king of the land. He demonstrates the importance of the sovereignty goddess in Irish literature from the earliest times down to the present and shows that she appears in historical texts as late as the eleventh century. Perhaps most importantly, he shows that the theme "was one of which the early Irish story-teller understood the implications and, moreover, was one which he would not hesitate to attach to characters, be they historical or unhistorical, which literature and tradition set in the seventh century."[40] That ancient mythical implications of sovereignty stories, because of the continuity of tradition, were understood by eleventh-century Irish writers lends credence to the notion, advanced by Professor Ford, that the myths reflected in *Pwyll* "were very much alive and that the story-teller was very much aware of them,"[41] in eleventh- or twelfth-century Wales. Unfortunately, it is impossible to trace the Welsh sovereignty tradition as Mac Cana has traced the Irish because of the lack of surviving Welsh narrative significantly earlier than the Four Branches. Professor Mac Cana himself believes that

> by the eleventh or twelfth century in Wales the knowledge and understanding of native mythology, even among the learned poets, was patchy and unsystematic, but nevertheless, as in a much later period in Ireland, certain basic concepts seem to have survived the social system which had generated them, and of these the myth of the goddess of sovereignty and of the sacred marriage, the *hieros gamos,* was one of the most permanent and productive.[42]

In support of his claim for the tenacity of such traditions he cites the symbolic marriage between her son Richard and the legendary patron of the region, Ste. Valery, which Eleanor of Aquitaine arranged in conjunction with Richard's installation as Duke of Aquitaine.[43]

The salient features of the sovereignty myth which are pertinent to the tale of *Pwyll* are as follows. First, the aspiring ruler at once reveals himself as the rightful king and claims his kingship by union with the goddess of sovereignty. Professor Binchy recognizes that a symbolic mating, "destined to bring fertility to man and beast in his reign," was an essential feature of early Irish inauguration rites.[44] In Irish myth, according to Mac Cana, the two main elements of the theme are the feast or libation which the goddess offers to her kingly spouse and their sexual union.[45] In *Pwyll*, it is Rhiannon who provides the wedding feast, both on the occasion when Gwawl attempts to claim her from the unwary Pwyll and a year later, when Pwyll wins her back. She emphasizes this in her response to Gwawl's demand, on the first occasion, for *yr arlwy a'r darmerth yssyd ymma (PKM* 14). She answers that,

> am y wled a'r darpar yssyd yma, hwnnw a rodeis
> i y wyr Dyuet ac y'r teulu, a'r yniueroed yssyd
> ymma. Hwnnw nit eidawaf y rodi y neb. *(PKM* 15)

Concerning the second element of the marriage theme, the narrator tells us that *y'r ystauell yd aeth Pwyll a Riannon, a*

Sovereignty in Pwyll 319

threulaw y nos honno drwy digriuwch a llonydwch (*PKM* 18). He is discreet, but explicit.

A second pertinent feature of Celtic sovereignty tales, according to Mac Cana's analysis, is that the goddess not only marries the rightful king but is "the mother of such a king and the ancestress of a royal line."[46] It is possible to understand in these terms the fact that the tale of Pwyll concludes with the restoration of Pryderi to his natural parents and with the reassuring information that Pryderi grew into a noble manhood and succeeded Pwyll as the prosperous and beloved lord of Dyfed, whose borders he expanded through conquest, and that he in turn married (*PKM* 27). The tale's concern with Pwyll's effective sovereignty demands that it conclude with the securing of continuity to his royal line.

A third common feature of sovereignty tales is the theme of the goddess's changing her form or condition when without her proper spouse and king. This theme, which is in origin closely related to a belief that the fertility and prosperity of the land depend upon true and rightful kingship, takes various forms in Celtic tradition. Sovereignty may appear as an aged hag who is transformed into a beautiful young woman upon sexual acceptance by the rightful king, as a madwoman whom he restores to sanity by sexual intercourse, or as a princess reared among peasants and restored to her proper dignity through a royal marriage.[47] A fourth variant, in which Sovereignty appears in the form of a white hart and must be disenchanted by the rightful king, appears to have been common in Breton tradition.[48] Rhiannon undergoes none of these transformations, but she does suffer a tremendous loss of queenly dignity when she is compelled to wait by the horse-block near the gate of the court and to bear to the court any guest or stranger who will permit her to carry him. Although her change in status is not associated directly with the loss of her rightful spouse, it is the result of the loss of her child, the rightful heir to the kingship who is himself, as has been seen, integral to the sovereignty myth. Furthermore, her restoration to dignity, while it is the result of her vindication when the child is found, coincides with Pryderi's refusal to be carried, in which is implicit a recognition of her true nature. To her offer he replies, *"aet a'y mynho,... nyt af i"* (*PKM* 25). Moreover, Rhiannon's suffering is at least loosely related to a separation from her spouse, for it is a penance imposed on her by Pwyll to appease those who demand that he divorce her for her supposed crime (*PKM* 21). Her marriage to Pwyll is disrupted and threatened until Pryderi is restored. Rhiannon's suffering has roots in international popular tradition[49] and in history,[50] but it is appropriate to a Celtic sovereignty tale as well. The redactor may have understood this and other features of the myth that he incorporated into his tale, although the felicitous conjunction of mythic traditions about sovereignty and rhetorical emphasis on princely virtues may be a coincidence of which he was unaware.

It is not only in its treatment of the figure of Rhiannon that the tale deals with the theme of sovereignty, but also in its narrative structure and use of dialogue. The composition reflects conscious rhetorical intention, whatever may be true of the content.

In the first section of the tale, Pwyll meets Arawn king of Annwfn, exchanges shapes with him for a year, fights and defeats Arawn's enemy Hafgan, and returns to his own realm. The most obvious result of this sequence is that Pwyll is established as a champion among warriors. He defeats Hafgan quickly and dramatically, and in the traditional manner of Celtic heroes: although Pwyll and Hafgan fight on horseback rather than from chariots or on foot, like CúChulainn, they do meet in single combat in the middle of a ford (*PKM* 5). It does not diminish Pywll's achievement that Hafgan's death depends upon his refusing to administer a second blow, which he does only at Arawn's behest; victory in battle by force of arms is his none the less.

The magnitude of this victory is measured by its result: Pwyll is now *brenhin ar holl Annwuyn*, and his might is so great that

> dechreu guereskynn y wlat. Ac erbyn hanner dyd drannoeth, yd oed yn y uedyant y dwy dyrnas.
> (*PKM* 6)

It is primarily his achievement in battle which wins Pwyll the title *Pen Annwfn:*

Sovereignty in Pwyll

> Ac o achaws i drigiant ef y ulwydyn honno yn Annwuyn, a gwledychu o honaw yno mor lwydannus, a dwyn y dwy dyrnas yn un drwy y dewred ef a'y uilwraeth, y diffygywys y enw ef ar Pwyll, Pendeuic Dyuet, ac y gelwit Pwyll Penn Annwuyn o hynny allan. (*PKM* 8)

By demonstrating his valour and prowess in battle, Pwyll gives proof of his ability to protect and defend, the first and foremost quality required of a king and the attribute most praised by Welsh bards.[51]

The significance of the victory over an Otherworld enemy seems not to have escaped the redactor. Dramatically, it is after his combat with Hafgan that Pwyll first addresses the men of Annwfn directly:

> Vy ngwyrda innheu ... kymerwch ych kyuarwyd, a gwybydwch pwy a dylyo bot yn wyr ymi. (*PKM* 6)

When the nobles reply that Pwyll is now king over the whole of Annwfn and entitled to claim the homage of all, he answers with a kingly dignity which he has had no previous opportunity to reveal:

> Ie ... a del yn waredauc, iawn yw y gymryt. Ar ny del yn uuyd, kymmeller o nerth cledyueu. (*PKM* 6)

The testing of Pwyll's valour, from which he emerges a greater ruler than he had been previously, stems directly from an action on his part which reveals him to be seriously deficient in qualities of great importance to a ruler. After Pwyll has driven Arawn's hunting dogs away from the stag they have felled, in favour of his own animals, Arawn accuses Pwyll of *anwybot* and *ansyberwyt* (ignorance and discourtesy) (*PKM* 2). Medieval Welsh law prescribed that a certain period of time, amounting to several hours, must elapse before a stag which had been felled by the king or his huntsman might be claimed by whoever held the land.[52] Pwyll, of course, violates this law when he so precipitously seizes the quarry of a crowned king. He does so, in all likelihood, in the belief that there is no greater lord than he in the region and that he has, consequently, first hunting rights. He violates the law out of ignorance and rashness rather than malice, but he breaks it none the less, as is indicated by the use of the legal term *carennydd* to denote the state of amity with Arawn which he seeks to restore (*PKM* 2–3).[53] Hence, Pwyll's achievement in Annwfn is directly related to the error which takes him there. He is guilty of an overweening pride in his own sovereignty; consequently, he must not only compensate the victim of his rashness but must also undergo a trial of an aspect of that sovereignty, a trial which both tests and increases his kingliness, winning for him the title *Pen Annwfn.*

One further feature of this first section of the tale, whose main concern is with the proof of Pwyll's valour, may be mentioned. Despite the approval which is accorded to Pwyll for lordly prowess, the redactor clearly advocates prudence and self-restraint to counterbalance the aggression which Pwyll channels into martial activity, as is clear in the treatment of the chaste friend motif. Considerable attention is devoted to the beauty of Arawn's wife, who is *yn deccaf gwreic o'r a welsei neb,* and to her graciousness: she is *dissymlaf gwreic a bendigeidaf i hannwyt a'y hymdidan* (*PKM* 4). There are *tirionwch ac ymdidan hygar* (*PKM* 5) between her and Pwyll by day. Yet, the text emphasizes, every night for a year,

> Y gyt ac yd aethant yn y guely ymchwelut e weneb at yr erchwyn a oruc ef, a'y geuyn attei hitheu. O hynny hyt trannoeth ny dywot ef wrthi un geir.
> (*PKM* 4–5)

Both Arawn and his wife marvel at the chastity of Pwyll, which had not been required of him, but both regard it approvingly as a mark of the strong friendship between the two men. Arawn thinks,

> Oy a Arglwyd Duw. . . cadarn a ungwr y gydymdeithas a diffleeis, a geueis i yn gedymdeith.
> (*PKM* 7)

His wife, meanwhile, observes that

> gauael gadarn a geueist ar gedymdeith yn herwyd
> ymlad a frouedigaeth y gorff, a chadw kywirdeb
> wrthyt titheu. (*PKM* 7-8)

Her language makes it explicit that Pwyll has been tested successfully not only with respect to martial prowess against enemies but with respect to sacrifice and keeping of faith with allies as well. Significantly, it is after the revelation of Pwyll's chastity that the narrator comments on the strong and productive alliance between Pwyll and Arawn which obtained thenceforth:

> Ac o hynny allan, dechreu cadarnhau
> kedymdeithas y ryngthunt, ac anuon o pop un y
> gilid meirch a milgwn a hebogeu a fob gyfryw
> dlws, o'r a debygei bob un digrifhau medwl y gilid
> o honaw. (*PKM* 8)

However, the first successful test of Pwyll's royal mettle gives rise to another, for upon his return to Dyfed, his men observe concerning their governance during the preceding year that

> ny bu gystal dy wybot; ny buost gyn hygaret guas
> ditheu; ny bu gyn hawsset gennyt titheu treulaw
> dy da, ny bu well dy dosparth eiroet no'r ulwydyn
> honn. (*PKM* 8)

Having successfully challenged Pwyll to prove his royal might in arms, Arawn has now set a standard of justice, generosity, and beneficence which Pwyll must match. Like heroism in battle, these are princely qualities much praised in bardic eulogy.[54] The second section of the tale concerns itself with Pwyll's further growth towards full sovereignty through the development of these virtues. He assures his men that he will not deprive them of the governance (*arglwydiaeth*) they have had from Arawn, but the section of the tale dealing with the courtship of Rhiannon shows that he has much to learn about the virtues of a sovereign.

Pwyll demonstrates his lack of discernment (*gwybot* or *dosparth* or *pwyll*) from the time of Rhiannon's first appearance. Although he acknowledges on the first day that the failure of his servant to overtake her on horseback betokens some magic meaning *(ryw ystyr hut)* (*PKM* 10), it is not until the third day, when he himself is unable to overtake her, that he adopts the more appropriate course of asking her to stop. As he does so often, the redactor underscores the point, that is, Pwyll's foolishness, in dialogue. Rhiannon responds, *"Arhoaf yn llawen . . . ac oed llessach y'r march, pei ass archut yr meityn"* (*PKM* 12).

Although his belated discernment in dealing with the mysterious horsewoman wins him a vision of Rhiannon's face unveiled and her offer of her hand in marriage (*PKM* 12–13), Pwyll still has a great deal to learn. In his first encounter with the rival suitor Gwawl, Pwyll fails to temper lordly generosity with prudence, and he makes the rash promise that *"Pa arch bynnac a erchych di ymi, hyt y gallwyf y gaffael, itti y byd."* Again, Rhiannon, who is herself the boon which Gwawl claims, judges Pwyll unhesitatingly: *"ny bu uuscrellach gwr ar y ssynnwyr e hun nog ry uuost ti"* (*PKM* 14).

However, although he has not yet achieved full sovereignty, Pwyll is the chosen mate of the sovereignty figure, and she provides him with a ruse by means of which he may reclaim his bride.[55] Having learned his lesson, Pwyll is then able, albeit only with the further counsel of Rhiannon and Hyfaidd, to moderate lordly munificence with prudence and discernment. He frees Gwawl from the bag in which he has trapped him only when he has taken sureties for Gwawl's pledge to refrain from seeking compensation or vengeance (*PKM* 17–18).

In the second part of the tale, Pwyll achieves the wisdom which his name reflects, and so it ends, appropriately, with the consummation of his marriage to the sovereignty figure and a celebration of his lordly generosity, especially towards courtly entertainers:

> Ef a gyuodes Pwyll y uynyd, a pheri dodi gostec, y erchi y holl eircheit a cherdoryon dangos, a menegi udunt y llonydit pawb o honunt wrth y uod a'y uympwy; a hynny a wnaethpwyd. Y wled honno a dreulwyt, ac ny ommedwyt neb tra barhaud. (*PKM* 18–19)

At this point in the tale, it remains to Pwyll to prove and achieve his sovereignty in one further regard. The consummation of the marriage at the conclusion of the preceding section naturally raises the question of its fertility. It has been seen that giving birth to a future ruler was a function of the sovereignty figure in Celtic narratives about her. It is known too that fertility of the land was dependent in Celtic thought on the "truth" of the prince and magically related to his own potency. Hence the fertility of the royal marriage is not only a dynastic necessity but also a measure of the rightfulness of the reign.[56] The importance of the king's fertility is also reflected in the concern with lineage of medieval Welsh bards.[57]

For Pwyll, this final achievement of full sovereignty is impeded first by Rhiannon's failure to give birth to a son until nearly three years have passed and then by the mysterious abduction of the boy and the accusation of murder against Rhiannon. Throughout, Pwyll acts in accordance with the wisdom he has acquired. He refuses at first to divorce his wife for barrenness because they have been married so short a time, but he promises to submit to the counsel of his men after an allotted period passes (*PKM* 19–20). When the child disappears, he refuses again to divorce Rhiannon, but agrees because of the evidence against her that she should be punished:

> Nyt oed achaws ganthunt wy y erchi y mi yscar
> a'm gwreic namyn na bydei plant idi. Plant a wnn
> i y uot idi hi. Ac nyt yscaraf a hi. O gwnaeth hitheu
> gam, kymeret y phenyt amdanaw. (*PKM* 20)

This judicious wisdom, however, does not solve the problem of Pwyll's fertility. The tale requires the restoration of the child for its completion.

The focus of the tale shifts to Teyrnon, who has been Pwyll's "man" (*gwr*) or vassal (*PKM* 24), and his wife, who find and raise the boy. When they hear the story of Pwyll's loss and recognize the child, they are motivated to return him by anticipation of the fruits of beneficent sovereignty which they will reap (*PKM* 25). Thus it is through the strength and righteousness of his reign that Pwyll achieves the restoration of his heir and the proof of the fertility of his marriage, just as it is through the glory of his earlier career that he wins the love and guidance of Rhiannon.

At the conclusion of the tale, Pwyll and his son have achieved full sovereignty over Dyfed, but that sovereignty has been won in a series of trials and lessons through which Pwyll develops from a rash and foolish fellow into a powerful, prudent, prosperous, and well-connected lord. There can be no doubt that the tale is woven of fragments of myth, international and Celtic narrative motifs, and pedantic lore. Yet this material has been consciously worked into a coherent tale about what an eleventh- or twelfth-century Welsh prince should be—brave, generous, just, and of noble lineage, like the ideal prince of the bards, but prudent and self-restrained as well. He must be able to augment the traditional virtues with skill in making useful political and marital alliances, as were men like Gruffudd ap Llywelyn, Gruffudd ap Cynan, Rhys ap Tewdwr, and Gruffudd ap Rhys.

NOTES

An earlier version was presented to the Celtic Discussion Group of the Modern Language Association of America at its annual meeting in New York on 28 December 1978.

1. Gruffydd, *Rhiannon*, 11.
2. Gruffydd, *Rhiannon*, 12–13.
3. Mac Cana, *Branwen Daughter of Llŷr*.
4. Jackson, *The International Popular Tale and Early Welsh Tradition*, 82–83.
5. Jackson, "Some Popular Motifs in Early Welsh Tradition," 84.
6. Ó Coileáin, "A Thematic Study of the Tale *Pwyll Pendeuic Dyuet*," 78–82.
7. Mac Cana, *Celtic Mythology*, 75–83.
8. Ford, *The Mabinogi and Other Medieval Welsh Tales*, 3–4. Brinley Rees has explored the *Mabinogi* in terms of Dumézilian tripartation in *Ceinciau'r Mabinogi*; I am grateful to Professor D. Ellis Evans for bringing this work to my attention. Eric Hamp, too, has examined the Indo-European background of the tales, in his lecture for the opening of the Centre for Advanced Welsh and

Celtic Studies at the University College of Wales, Aberystwyth, on 18 July 1979.

9. See, e.g., Ford, *The Mabinogi*, 4–10; Charles-Edwards, "Native Political Organisation and the Origin of MW *brenhin*," 40.

10. These are reviewed by Eric P. Hamp in "Mabinogi," 243.

11. Hamp, "Mabinogi," 247.

12. Such a view of the Four Branches is fundamental, of course, to Gruffydd's analysis of the collection. It is implicit, too, in studies which regard the tales as distinguished by the divine families which provide the main characters for each, but united in being traditional narratives about the most ancient gods or ancestors remembered in various parts of Wales. Such studies include Edward Anwyl's "The Four Branches of the *Mabinogi*," and Rachel Bromwich's "The Character of Early Welsh Tradition," 103–104. Brinley Rees and Eric Hamp, on the other hand, view the *Mabinogi* as a single body of myth reflecting the tripartition of divine and social functions perceived by Georges Dumézil in Indo-European myth and society. Both see each of the Branches as particularly concerned with one of these functions, although they disagree in the conclusions they draw concerning the places of *Pwyll* and *Branwen* in the tripartite scheme. See Rees, *Ceinciau'r Mabinogi*, 12–16.

13. Gruffydd, *Rhiannon*, 4–5.

14. Gruffydd, "Mabon vab Madron," 131.

15. Gruffydd, *Rhiannon*, 33.

16. Jackson, *The International Popular Tale*, 126.

17. Jackson, "Some Popular Motifs," 84.

18. Ó Coileáin, "A Thematic Study of the Tale *Pwyll Pendeuic Dyuet*," 82.

19. Roberts, "Tales and Romances," 206.

20. Ford, *The Mabinogi*, 13.

21. Jackson, *The International Popular Tale*, 130.

22. Mac Cana, *The Mabinogi*, 60.

23. Mac Cana, *The Mabinogi*, 60.

24. The word is used in this sense in early poetry. See, e.g., Ifor Williams, ed., *Canu Llywarch Hen*, 91.

25. Another scholar who has examined the *Mabinogi* for authorial intentions is Bollard, in "The Structure of the Four Branches of the Mabinogi." In Bollard's view, the author develops three main themes in the Four Branches—friendships, marriages, and feuds. Through these themes, which are interlaced through the four tales, the author explores "the modes of personal conduct which are necessary for society to survive and progress" (252). See further Gantz's idiosyncratic reading "Thematic Structure in the Four Branches of the Mabinogi."

26. Ifor Williams, ed., *Pedeir Keinc y Mabinogi*. Caerdydd: Gwasg Prifysgol Cymru, 1964, xli. Hereafter cited in the text as *PKM*.

27. Charles-Edwards, "The Date of the Four Branches of the *Mabinogi*," 298.

28. The use of dialogue to explore the issue of "relative status" in *Pwyll* is examined in detail in Charles-Edwards, "Honour and Status in Some Irish and Welsh Prose Tales." This illuminating disscusion of the protocol of greetings and of terms of addresses provides further evidence of the aristocratic preoccupations of *Pwyll*. I am grateful to Professors D. Ellis Evans and Eric Hamp for bringing this article to my attention.

29. Lloyd, *A History of Wales from the Earliest Times to the Edwardian Conquest*, 358–371. Hereafter cited as *HW*.

30. Lloyd, *HW* II., 379 ff.

31. Evans, *Historia Gruffud Vab Kenan*.

32. Lloyd, *HW* II., 392 ff.

33. Lloyd, *HW* II., 377.

34. It has been observed, however, that such freedom of movement was probably the privilege of men of letters at all times. See, e.g., Thomson, *Pwyll Pendeuic Dyuet*, xvi, and Charles-Edwards, "The Date of the Four Branches of the Mabinogi," 268. Nevertheless, the Deheubarth connections of Gruffudd ap Llywelyn's mother and his own *de facto* authority there might have rendered him particularly receptive to stories about lords of Dyfed as well of Gwynedd. He would be able to identify with Pwyll and Manawydan as well as with Math, and the description of Brân as *brenhin coronawc ar yr ynys hon* (*PKM* 29) might have been taken as a hyperbolic compliment to the extent of his authority in Wales. References to authority over *Prydain*, rather than the *Cymry* alone, appear in *gogynfeirdd* poetry. See Andrews, "Rhai Agweddau ar Sofraniaeth yng Ngherddi'r Gogynfeirdd," 25–26. Gruffudd himself is described as *brenhin y brytanyeid*. See Jones, ed., *Brut y Tywysogyon or the Chronicle of the Princes; Red Book of Hergest Version*, 26. Bleddyn ap Cynfyn (28) and other, earlier kings are accorded similar titles. I believe that a case can indeed be made for redaction of the *Mabinogi* at Gruffudd's court, although without greater precision in the dating of the text it is of course impossible to make a confident judgement on this issue.

35. Morris-Jones, et al., *Llawysgrif Hendregadredd*, 84.

36. Morris-Jones, et al., *Llawysgrif Hendregadredd*, 118. On the use of legendary figures by the *gogynfeirdd* in genealogy and metaphorical description, see further Lloyd, *Rhai Agweddau ar Ddysg y Gogynfierdd*, 4–10. Although the earliest extant *gogynfeirdd* poetry of known authorship (c. 1137) is later than the *terminus ad quem*

which has been established for the text of the *Mabinogi* (c. 1120), there is evidence for a continuity of tradition in bardic eulogy from the time of Aneirin and Taliesin to that of the *gogynfeirdd*, as well as evidence that *gogynfeirdd* poetry properly speaking was being composed as early as c. 1081. See J.E.C. Williams, "Beirdd y Tywysogion: Arolwg," 12–14; Gruffydd, "A Poem in Praise of Cuhelyn Fardd," 198–209. Consequently, it seems valid to make these comparisons between the poetry and the *Mabinogi*.

37. It may be significant that Pwyll himself is not *brenhin*, but *arglwyd* or *pendeuic*. Perhaps this reflects the historical situation of the twelfth century, for which the Bruts employ the title *brenhin* only three times. In the laws, however, *arglwyd* and *brenhin* are often interchangeable, although the use of *arglwyd* may be a thirteenth-century development. See Jenkins, "Kings, Lords and Princes: The Nomenclature of Authority in Thirteenth-Century Wales," 451–661, and cf. n. 42, above.

38. See Ford, *The Mabinogi*, 8–10.

39. Mac Cana, "Aspects of the Theme of King and Goddess in Irish Literature."

40. Mac Cana, "Aspects of the Theme of King and Goddess in Irish Literature," Part 2, 357.

41. Ford, *The Mabinogi*, 13.

42. Mac Cana, *The Mabinogi*, 116. Andrews sees evidence for the survival of the myth of the *hieros gamos* in the *gogynfeirdd* formula *Prydein priawd* and its variants ("Rhai Agweddau ar Sofraniaeth," 26–27). It is not clear to me, however, that the term has the sense of "spouse" in the poetry as Andrews suggests, rather than that of "owner" or "holder."

43. Mac Cana, *The Mabinogi*, 116.

44. Binchy, *Celtic and Anglo-Saxon Kingship*, 11. Andrews believes that the idea of relationship between true sovereignty and the fertility of the land may survive in some *gogynfeirdd marwnadau* that describe the land as wasted by the death of the sovereign ("Rhai Agweddau ar Sofraniaeth," 28–29); she acknowledges, however, the possibility that such imagery is influenced rather by the Christian eschatological tradition of Judgment Day signs, and the role of this *topos* in classical elegy also needs further examination. See Matonis, "Gruffudd ap yr Ynad Coch's Elegy on the Last Llywelyn."

45. Mac Cana, "Aspects of the Theme of King and Goddess in Early Irish Literature," Part 1, 85–86. Mac Cana also points out that these two elements do not receive equal emphasis in all stories and, further, that Irish *fess* (or *feis*) means both a "feast" and a "sleeping (with)."

46. Mac Cana, "Aspects of the Theme of King and Goddess in Early Irish Literature," Part 1, 88.

47. For Irish examples of each type, see Mac Cana, "Aspects of the Theme of King and Goddess in Early Irish Literature," Part 3, 64 ff.

48. Bromwich, "The Celtic Inheritance of Medieval Literature," 214.

49. See Jackson, *The International Popular Tale*, 94 ff.

50. See Roberts, "Penyd Rhiannon," 325–327.

51. See Binchy, *Celtic and Anglo-Saxon Kingship*, 17 and *passim*, on the importance of valour as a kingly attribute. In bardic poetry, Gwalchmai ap Meilyr's description of Owain Gwynedd as "dreic mon mor drud y eissylud yn aer" (14), Morris-Jones, et al., *Llawysgrif Hendregadredd*, is typical. Bravery, generosity, and lineage are the princely qualities most praised by the *gogynfeirdd*; see Jane Ann Cousins, "Moliant Beirdd gyda Sylw Arbennig i Waith y Gogynfeirdd," MA thesis, University of Wales, Swansea, 1978, 37–85. I am grateful to Professor D. Ellis Evans for bringing this thesis to my attention.

52. Wiliam, ed., *Llyfr Iowerth*, 136.

53. On *carennydd*, see Charles-Edwards, "The Date of the Four Branches of the *Mabinogi*," 278. Elsewhere, Charles-Edwards defines the legal issue involved in this incident somewhat differently ("Honour and Status in Some Irish and Welsh Prose Tales," 124–125); it is clear, however, that Pwyll's seizure of the stag is a legal infraction.

54. For example, in his *marwnad* for Llywelyn ap Gruffudd, Bleddyn Fardd called that prince

> gwr gwaewrut gwr prut uegys priaf
> gwr gwiw yn urenhin uyddin ualchaf
> gwr hylwyt y glod gwr haelaf am dreul
> hyd yr gertei yr heul yr hwyl bellaf
>
> (Morris-Jones, *Llawysgrlf Hendregadredd*, 66).

55. An interesting feature of the ensuing *broch yng nghod* episode is Rhiannon's bag of unlimited capacity. This appears to belong to the class of Celtic vessels of plenty and associate her, as sovereignty goddess, with the fertility of the land.

56. See Binchy, *Celtic and Anglo-Saxon Kingship*, 9 ff.

57. Gwalchmai ap Meilyr, for example, often opens his poems of praise with a reference to lineage: *Ardwyreafy hael o hil gruffut; Ardwyreaf hael o hil yago Ardwyreaf hael o hil rodri* (Morris-Jones, et al., *Llawysgrif Hendregadredd*, 12–13).

15

Gwydion and Aranrhod: Crossing the Borders of Gender in *Math*

Roberta L. Valente

The lives of the men and women of the first three Branches of the *Mabinogi* are sometimes made bitter by tribulation, but it is in the retributive exchanges between Gwydion and Aranrhod in the Fourth Branch that we see how the failure of individuals to live up to appropriate codes of behavior can alienate them from their social group. Math, Goewin, and Lleu act within the traditional limits of legal codes, but Gwydion and Aranrhod, in challenging each other, evade the gender roles which convention demands of them. Gwydion, who should have some responsibility for the protection of the women in his kinship group, not only violates this trust when he rapes Goewin and continuously shames Aranrhod—he also manifests a female function—fertility—which no man ought to possess. Aranrhod, his equally unconventional sister, refuses to accept the limitations of socially determined female behavior when she denies the proof and punishment of her fertility, so that both attempt to cross borders of behavior to which they should have no access.

All the Branches of the *Mabinogi* illustrate in some way the codes which must be obeyed to maintain the social order, as well as the kinds of reparation which are owed if a character willfully goes against the rules of society,[1] but in the Fourth Branch, in the two episodes concerning both Gwydion and Aranrhod, the discussion of correct behavior and reparation is subordinated to a narrative showing individual will prevailing over custom. Interestingly, the primary issue over which Gwydion and Aranrhod battle is fertility, a function traditionally ascribed to women. Three legal violations related to this function occur in the Fourth Branch: a rape, a false claim of virginity, and an adultery. In each case, the codes prohibiting these crimes are meant to protect the social group from undesirable manifestations of fertility. And each legal violation is linked in the narrative to either Gwydion or Aranrhod and their actions which are inappropriate to their gender.

Before I begin to look at particular events concerning these two unusual siblings, I would like to consider the ways in which men's and women's responsibilities are defined in the whole of the *Mabinogi*—in preparation for a discussion of the significance of behavior that crosses the socially and legally defined borders of gender.

Men in the *Mabinogi* are described in terms of the titles which indicate their status in their own lands. What we also learn about rank in the first three Branches is that it does not necessarily divide men from each other. Even though Pwyll, the Lord of Dyfed, is of lesser rank than Arawn, the King of Annwfn, the two can evolve a relationship which is based on the obligations of friendship rather than the divisions of hierarchy. In the Second Branch, Bendigeidfran's title of *brenhin coronawc* places him above his brothers, but the description of his kinship ties with the group who sit around him also suggests the obligations he shares with his kin. When a man is without status, as Manawydan is in the beginning of the Third Branch, the first order of business in the narrative is to establish him securely in a position which will give him honor and a sense of affectionate obligation to his friend Pryderi.

This emphasis on titles reminds us of the men's role as protectors of their people—and the women nearest them. In the world of the *Mabinogi*, most women are defined through their fathers, husbands, or brothers. This is in keeping with medieval Welsh law, as Morfydd Owen has demonstrated: a woman's position in society was as a dependent of her nearest male kin. In terms of compensatory payments for insult or injury, a woman's worth was valued at half her brother's; and when she married, her worth dropped to a third of her husband's. Events reflecting on her honor were answerable by her male kin—her husband, if she were married.[2]

In a literary work like the *Mabinogi*, the descriptions of these types of relationships are in keeping with the essence of medieval Welsh law. Most of the women of the Four Branches live under the protection of their male kin and are named according to their relationships to these men: Rhiannon, the daughter of Hefeydd Hen, comes from the house of her father to court Pwyll, and the closing lines of the First Branch define Cigfa as the wife of Pryderi and the daughter of Gwynn Gohoyw. Arawn's, Teyrnon's, and Llwyd ap Cil Coed's wives are known to us only through their husbands' names, while Branwen, whom we know as the daughter of Llŷr, is better protected by her brothers than her husband.

For the most part, the men of the *Mabinogi* enact their obligations to their women as willingly as they prove their loyalty to men. Pwyll must protect Arawn's wife from insult at the same time that he compensates the insult he had unwittingly offered the King of Annwfn. Though he might, in Arawn's form—and by Arawn's own offer[3]—sleep with Arawn's queen, Pwyll also concerns himself with Arawn's wife's sense of honor; he sleeps with her chastely to avoid causing her the kind of insult the laws prohibit.[4] Bendigeidfran, of course, is responsible for Branwen's protection when Matholwch, who should be her protector as her husband and king, insults her unjustly. Even in the Third Branch, the issue of woman's need for a protector emerges in the discussion between Cigfa and Manawydan, after Pryderi and Rhiannon have been whisked away by magic.

> Pann welas Kicua, uerch Gwyn Gloew, gwreic Pryderi, nat oed yn y llys namyn hi a Manawydan, drygyruerth a wnaeth hyt nat oed well genti y byw no'y marw. Sef a wnaeth Manawydan, edrych ar hynny. "Dioer," heb ef, "cam yd wyt arnaw, os rac uy ouyn i y drygyruerthy di. Mi a rodaf Duw

> y uach it, na weleisti gedymdeith gywirach noc y
> keffy di ui, tra uynho Duw it uot uelly. Y rof a
> Duw, bei et uwni yn dechreu uy ieuengtit, mi a
> gadwn gywirdeb wrth Pryderi, ac yrot titheu mi
> a'y cadwn; ac na uit un ouyn arnat," heb ef. "E
> rof a Duw," heb ef, "titheu a gey y gedymdeithas
> a uynych y genhyf i, herwyd uyg gallu i, tra welho
> Duw yn bot yn y dihirwch hwnn a'r goual." (*PKM*
> 57)

Cigfa's lament functions as a preface to a cooperative negotiation between a woman concerned for her protection and a man who is willing to enact his obligatory role. This passage begins by naming Cigfa and, significantly, her relationships with her earlier protectors, her father and husband. At this point in her life, Cigfa's *naud* or protection should come from her husband, as would her honor and status, but Pryderi has mysteriously disappeared and might well be dead. Legally, a woman who has no near male kin must rely on the lord of the land to protect her,[5] and in this situation Manawydan is the only man in sight who might qualify in this respect. Manawydan's words are meant not only to comfort Cigfa, but to make the strongest possible contract of protection with her.

Though the female characters of the *Mabinogi* rely on their male kin for protection, we cannot say that they are entirely helpless, any more than we can say that the men of the *Mabinogi* always live up to their obligations. Challenges to those aspects of life which concern women most closely—fertility and protection from shame—inspire responses from the women of the *Mabinogi* (and no woman reacts more vehemently in this respect than Aranrhod) which can range from the entertaining to the dramatic. Legally, a woman's fertility has positive significance in her social group if she gives birth in a legitimate relationship, helping to ensure the continued stability and honor of her husband and her people; but if she gives birth under circumstances which prohibit her from having any kind of sexual exprience, she causes shame for herself and her kin.[6]

Fertility also operates on a mythological level in the Four Branches, a substratum which occasionally emerges in the text. We know that, in a number of medieval Celtic tales, woman's maternal function is metaphorically linked with the fertility of the land—and thus with goddesses associated with the land—suggesting that her ability to give birth is a divine gift,[7] a creative, female power which men like Gwydion and Math emulate in the Fourth Branch. But the divine aspect of fertility is counterbalanced by mortal experience. Suffering accompanies the bearing of children in the stories of Rhiannon, Branwen, and Aranrhod, the three mothers in these tales.[8] Rhiannon is first under threat of divorce for not having given birth, and then she is accused of murdering her child.[9] Branwen gives birth without any trouble, but she suffers the agony of seeing her own brother throw Gwern to his death on the fire, setting off the war that destroys two islands. Aranrhod is manipulated by her brother into demonstrating her fertility publicly, and he fosters the product of her female power to her everlasting shame. In terms of a discussion of the unconventional behavior of Gwydion and Aranrhod, we find that the focus of their problems is fertility, which comes as no surprise, since fertility is a significant issue in most of the stories in which the women in the *Mabinogi* appear.

We expect a story of unconventional behavior to have unconventional personalities in it, and the Fourth Branch satisfies us in this respect. Gwydion and Aranrhod, brother and sister, are extraordinary types in contrast with the rest of the characters of the *Mabinogi*. Though Gwydion is of the real world, the Island of the Mighty, he possesses magical powers which link him with the Otherworld. He is also a remarkable storyteller—"goreu kyuarwyd yn y byt oed"(*PKM* 69)—but he does not use his skill to entertain, as a bard should, rather he employs it to distract those whom he wishes to trick—like Pryderi or his own sister, Aranrhod. His duplicity is one of the first things we notice about him; he is so intent on setting things up in his own way that he is careless of the obligations he owes others as a man in a closely knit social group. He helps Gilfaethwy, his brother, but he is assisting him in the crime of rape, and he does so by instigating a devastating war. He cares for Lleu, but it is at the cost of humiliating his sister again and again, in violation of his fraternal obligations. He is not a man who protects the members of his social group from dishonor, nor does he show respect for the obligations which he owes his lord and uncle, Math; indeed, he is often the instigator of the acts which cause shame or suffering.

His atypical socialization is reinforced by a particular ability he manifests, one which usually belongs to women, not men: the creation of new life. In each of the three main sections of the Fourth Branch, Gwydion seems to "give birth," either as the victim or wielder of magic. In the first part, he and Gilfaethwy are changed into animals as punishment for their own bestial behavior and alternately give birth to three animal-children. In the story of the testing of Aranrhod's virginity and its repercussions, the birthing process is more symbolic, as he takes up the generative role his sister spurns. And in the last section, with the help of his magician-uncle, Math, Gwydion truly and consciously usurps the female power of fertility in the creation of Blodeuedd.

Aranrhod is a fair match for her conniving brother, as willful a creature as he is. Like him, she can use her speech in powerful ways—and she uses that power to curse her son. Even though Gwydion manages to twist her own words to circumvent the first two curses she places on Lleu, he cannot manipulate his sister into participating in the breaking of the last curse. We are reminded again of her strength in the link between her name and the name of her fortress, Caer Aranrhod, a naming which suggests her independent power on two levels. In terms of the narrative style of the Four Branches, this reminds us of the traditional manner in which the men in the Four Branches are named. On the level of a mythological substratum, this naming reminds us of the powerful goddesses who give their names to the lands with which they are connected.[10] She is never named in relation to a man who might be her protector, suggesting her independence from conventional rules of female behavior. And unlike any other woman in the Four Branches, she really commits a violation for which she should be punished, but she walks away from her shame—as well as abandoning the responsibilities she has to the proof of her shameful fertility.

Gwydion is the character through whom the various episodes of the Fourth Branch are woven together. He functions as the "villain" in the story, in the sense that Vladimir Propp used the word: *not* as the embodiment of evil, but rather as a catalyzing agent whose meetings with other characters precipitate the crises which must be resolved by the end of the tale;[11] in this role, he treats most of the other characters as accomplices to or victims of his machinations. The exception is Aranrhod, who resists his efforts to effect control over certain intimate areas of her life. She functions as his female foil: her denial of both her sexual experience and her responsibilities as mother instigates a number of crises in the sections of the text which deal with the life of Lleu.

Gwydion and Gilfaethwy's act of rape is not only a serious violation of Goewin's honor,[12] but is also an insult to the honor of Math, her lord and her protector.[13] Additionally, this rape is tantamount to a threat to Math's life, since he cannot live without placing both his feet in the lap of a virgin.[14] In this sense, Gwydion is not as careful of his obligations to his kin and his people as the other men of the *Mabinogi* are, since he puts the desires of an individual, his lust-filled brother, Gilfaethwy, above the security of the social group when he risks war with Dyfed. The brothers' punishment is the most interesting aspect of this part of the Fourth Branch, for they both take on a function which is inappropriate to their human gender.

The punishment is symbolic rather than a realistic reflection of the laws: Math strikes them with his rod (a symbol which links this passage to Goewin's rape and, later, Aranrhod's test of virginity), so that the two brothers are three times turned into a male/female pair of animals and they alternate giving birth in each of these transformations. The law texts tell us that a rapist was obligated to make compensatory payments to both the victimized woman and the king, but according to one code, if a man rapes a woman who is alone and without protection, and he is unable to offer material compensation, then he may be castrated.[15] Math's enchantment symbolically suggests this kind of punishment, since both men are, in the process of being changed into female animals, emasculated. Their unconventional fertility is emphasized in this story when Math tells them that their punishment shames them for each of them has borne a child to the other.[16] It is as though the Lord of Gwynedd has chosen this punishment to teach them the vulnerability of the female role when men are unconcerned with the codes that protect women. In suffering this punishment, Gwydion has crossed a gender border, a change which causes him shame and a change which he undergoes unwillingly. In the next episode, he will parallel the experience of this punishment, when he crosses a gender border again. Here he will take on a female function willingly, using that function to cause Aranrhod shame: he will initiate the process whereby she commits a punishable violation, and he will use the illusion of fertility to attempt to punish her for that violation.

In literary terms, the rape of Goewin motivates the introduction of Aranrhod into the Fourth Branch, as Math must find a new virgin to serve as footbearer. Gwydion offers his sister as a candidate, suggesting that he has some responsibility for or knowledge of his sister's status in this area. This makes sense, since a young woman's virginity was in the care of her kin. Math asks her if she is a maiden, and she answers rather ambiguously: "Ny wnn i amgen no'm bot" (*PKM* 77).[17] The evasiveness of Aranrhod's reply recalls Gwydion's duplicity in the previous episode when he tricks both Math and Pryderi into war. The inexactness of her words forces Math to make a more specific test of her virgin status. He tells her to step over his "hutlath" or magic rod (the symbolism of this gesture is fairly striking, an image which recalls the violation of Goewin), and she does, dropping a yellow-haired boychild. Aranrhod then makes for the door, but before she can exit, she drops a small something, "ryw bethan ohonei" (*PKM* 77), which Gwydion snatches up before anyone has seen it.

Presumably, Aranrhod would have known her true status, so her answer to Math takes on the quality of a lie, a denial of her sexual experience. A false claim of virginity before marriage was a legal violation, and though Math is not intending to marry Aranrhod, his dependence on the veracity of her claim is as urgent as that of any bridegroom.[18] Aranrhod's quick exit out the door is a second denial, a rejection of the proof of her fertility. It is Math who must recognize the existence of the first child and name him, for it is clear that Aranrhod will not take responsibility for the fruit of her experience. The only woman in the *Mabinogi* having no defined obligatory bonds to any man, Aranrhod illustrates an unconventional image of fertile woman. She is not punished by any man when her illicit fertility is proven, but neither does any man take her part when she accuses her brother of causing her humiliation. Instead, she goes off alone to her own retreat, Caer Aranrhod. In a sense, she functions as her own protector.

Gwydion not only violates his sister's protection by exposing her to shame, but he nurtures it by taking over the care of the small "thing" which she abandons in the doorway. He wraps it in "llen o bali" (a kind of cloth which reminds us of another child whose birth led to the mother's humiliation—Gwri/Pryderi), and he hides it in a chest at the foot of his bed: "y mywn llaw gist is traed y wely" (*PKM* 77). The "small thing," which is not identified as a child, as the first boy was, is a kind of premature baby, and Gwydion, by putting it in the chest, has put it back in a womb-like place. The success of this unusual action is manifest when, some time later, Gwydion becomes aware of its presence again.

> Val yd oed Wydyon diwarnawt yn y wely, ac yn deffroi, ef a glywei diaspat yn y gist is y draet. Kyny bei uchel hi, kyuuch oed ac y kigleu ef. Sef a oruc ynteu, kyuodi yn gyflym, ac agori y gist. Ac ual y hegyr, ef a welei uab bychan yn rwyuaw y ureicheu o blyc y llen, ac yn y guascaru. Ac ef a gymerth y mab y rwng y dwylaw ac a gyrchwys y dref ac ef, lle y gwydat bot gwreic a bronneu genti. Ac ymobryn a wnaeth a'r wreic ueithryn y mab.
> (*PKM* 78)

Gwydion takes over the maternal process which Aranrhod has fled, and the description of the child's emergence from the chest is a caricature of a mother's experience. Gwydion is awakened by an awareness of the child's presence at the other end of the bed and opens the chest/womb. The image of a child pushing its way out of a fold in the sheet is a fairly clear imitation of a real birth. The phrase "o blyc y llen" reminds us again of women's sexual experience and fertility; it stylistically echoes two other phrases used in reference to women who must be protected from illicit sexual activity: the description of the proper resting place for Math's feet,

"Ymlyc croth morwyn" (*PKM* 67), the virgin Goewin's lap; and a phrase Arawn's wife uses when she comments on the lack of sexual activity between herself and the disguised Lord of Dyfed "yn nyblyc yn dillat guely" (*PKM* 7). In this scene, Gwydion essentially gives birth to the child, and like a good mother, cradles it in his arms and finds it a satisfactory wetnurse.

The next events show us how Gwydion and Aranrhod fight over the fate of the child which has been "born" to both of them.

When Gwydion presents his sister with a prodigiously matured four-year-old son, the two siblings engage in a word-play which demonstrates both their anger and their intransigence. As long as Gwydion continues to nurture the child, taking on an inappropriately maternal role, Aranrhod will continue violating her obligations as a real mother to evade the shame her false claim has provoked. She says to her brother angrily:

> "Oy a wr, ba doi arnat ti, uyg kywilydaw i, a dilyt uyg kywilyd, a'y gadw yn gyhyt a hynn?" (*PKM* 78)

Aranrhod's words have a double meaning: she refers to her shame in the abstract, a shame for which she has never been punished, but she also refers to her son in the noun "kywilyd," indicating that her attitude towards maternity has not yet changed. In the terms of the literary structure of this Branch, this expression of Aranrhod's anger is necessary to explain why she will later try to keep her son, the living proof of the shame, from a normal existence by denying him a name, arms, and a human wife. She, like her brother, intends to use him as the tangible symbol of *their* battle.

Gwydion, in his retort to her challenge, puns as cleverly:

> "Ony byd arnat ti gywilyd uwy no meithryn o honaf i uab kystal a hwnn, ys bychan a beth uyd dy gywilyd di." (*PKM* 78–79)

He tries to goad her into admitting her maternal function by telling her he has played the female role better than she has. His words too have a double meaning: the small thing which she dropped before fleeing her test is recalled in his phrase "ys bychan a beth uyd dy gywilyd di."

This exchange instigates Aranrhod's first curse—that the child will not have a name unless he gets it from her.[19] Gwydion's wrathful reply unambiguously charges Aranrhod with the legal violation for which she has not been officially punished yet:

> "A thitheu," heb ef, "yr hwnn yd wyt ti [i.e., a *gwreic*], ac auar arnat am na'th elwir y uorwyn, ni'th elwir bellach byth yn uorwyn." (*PKM* 79)

For the child to survive, Aranrhod must recognize it, but no ordinary means will induce her to obey; it is only through magic that Gwydion can get Aranrhod to fulfill her obligations, and even then, Gwydion succeeds only because Aranrhod is involuntarily deceived. The man and the boy set themselves up in magical disguise, stitching shoes outside Aranrhod's *caer*; when she approaches the two false shoemakers at their work, she watches their actions and inadvertently names Lleu,[20] through the kind of word-play we have already seen in the exchanges between this brother and sister. This manipulative success incites Aranrhod's wrath again, for now the child has a name which he can pass on, creating the potential, as J.K. Bollard has noted, for Lleu's "possibly perpetuating the memory of her shame even in future generations."[21] She swears a destiny on the boy again, that he will never bear arms until she herself arms him.[22]

The child needs a name and arms to take his place as a man in this society, so Aranrhod is not only denying her socially defined role in rejecting him, but she is also threatening the boy's ability to fulfill his obligations as a man. By refusing the child a name, Aranrhod unmaternally attempts to sever him from a relationship with herself or anyone, for that matter, since names are so closely connected with identification in a kinship bond. By denying him arms, Aranrhod cuts him off from the tools which will allow him to serve as a protector and gain lasting fame as a warrior.

To evade this unpleasant destiny, Gwydion must once again create the illusion of war through magic duplicity, as he did before to deceive Pryderi and Math; he magically creates an attacking navy. The irony of this trick is that his sister unwittingly performs her obligations to her child—and does so gladly, "yn llawen" (*PKM* 82)—because she is forced to demand protection from men. Her rage when the fleet disappears instigates her last curse—that Lleu will never have a wife of the race which is now on earth.[23] This destiny is phrased slightly differently, protecting Aranrhod from any further trickery. She simply says he will never have a wife, making no reference to her own agency in fulfilling this destiny. This is not a direct denial or rejection; she returns to her earlier policy of evasion, but this time she leaves no loose ends for Gwydion to pick up and twist to her disadvantage.

This signals the end of the competition between the siblings. In one sense, she has won the battle, for Gwydion will never punish her again with the proof of an illicit fertility which can only cause her shame, but in another sense, it is Gwydion who has won, for he will overcome her last prohibition without her assistance, taking on the female power of creation one more time, to "give birth" to Blodeuedd. But even this manifestation of masculine fertility fails, for the new woman is as willful as the old one was and Gwydion's gift to Lleu instigates the process of yet another legal violation, the adultery of Blodeuedd and Gronw. Gwydion may be able to nurture and shape a real boy into a chieftain, but he cannot succeed entirely at directing a woman, even one who is of his own making. Crossing the borders of gender functions in the Fourth Branch leads to legal violations, and men and women who refuse to recognize their roles bring shame to themselves or insult those close to them. The closing sentences of the Fourth Branch tell us that Lleu wins his lands back, becoming a prosperous chieftain and eventually the Lord of Dyfed, a successful portrait, but one which is missing something. Looking back, we see that the First Branch closes with a marriage, the Second Branch ends with a bizarre but successful story of fertility, and the third tells us of the restoration of a husband and wife to their respective mates, all descriptions of cooperative couplings of men and women. As though to dramatize the hopelessness of male/female conflict through ironic understatement, the Fourth Branch ends with the image of a man alone.

NOTES

1. Owen, "Shame and Reparation; Woman's Place in the Kin," 58; Bollard, "The Structure of the Four Branches of the Mabinogi," 252; Rees, *Ceinciau'r Mabinogi*, 15.
2. Iorwerth 46.1–2, Jenkins and Owen, 165. Her *galanas*, if she were unmarried, was half the value of her brother's; her *sarhaed* was half the value of her brother's *sarhaed* but it would drop to a third of her husband's after marriage.
3. " . . . mi . . . a rodaf y wreic deccaf a weleist eiroet y gyscu gyt a thi beunoeth" (3). Ifor Williams, ed., *Pedeir Keinc y Mabinogi*. 1964. Caerdydd: Gwasg Prifysgol Cymru, 1982. Hereafter cited in the text as *PKM*.
4. "O teyr ford e serheyr e urenhines; o torry e naud, neu o'y tharau, neu o grybdyllau peth o'y llau." Iorwerth 110 1–10, quoted by Owen,"Shame and Reparation," 46. See also: Charles-Edwards, "Nau Kynywedi Teithiauc," 35, for the terms defining the deception of a woman in a sexual context.
5. "[T]he lord is clearly the guardian of all those women not *sui juris*. . . . i.e. not in the *mundium* or wardship of her husband, father or other male agnate; or he is regarded as enjoying a species of *mundium* over all his vassals" (125). Walters, "The European Context of the Welsh Law of Matrimonial Property."
6. See in Jenkins and Owen, eds., *The Welsh Law of Women*: Charles-Edwards, 30–37; Owen, 51; Davies, 106–108. See also: Davies, "Buchedd a Moes y Cymry," 176.
7. The quantity of articles and books dealing with this topic are too numerous to list in their entirety here, but those dealing with the female fertility function and its link to one-time divinity in the *Mabinogi* are: Gruffydd, *Rhiannon: an inquiry into the origins of the First and Third Branches of the Mabinogi;* Ross, *Pagan Celtic Britain;* Mac Cana, *Celtic Mythology,* and *The Mabinogi;* Roberts, "Penyd Rhiannon," 325–327; Ford, *The Mabinogi*, 13; McKenna, "The Theme of Sovereignty in *Pwyll*," 35–52. In the case of a character like Rhiannon, the connection between Otherworld magic and her fertility function is fairly clear. When she first appears on Gorsedd Arberth, the place of wonders, the supernatural ability of her horse to evade Pwyll and his servants tells us that she has access to magic, and later, the monstrous claw which steals her newborn child reasserts the connection between fertility and magic.

8. These are the women identified in the expression "tryded prif rieni yn yr ynys hon" (*PKM* 30–31). The only other demonstrably fertile woman in the *Mabinogi* is Llwyd ap Cil Coed's wife. Her pregnancy has an unfortunate effect as well: Llwyd's magically planned revenge fails, since Manawydan can catch her and hold her hostage, forcing Llwyd to redeem her with Rhiannon and Pryderi.

9. Teyrnon's wife is presented as a positive foil to Rhiannon and her problems of fertility: Rhiannon is fertile, but loses her child after birth, while Teyrnon's wife is barren, but adopts a newly born child; Rhiannon cannot raise her child, but Teyrnon's wife can raise a boy who grows larger and more skilled than any other children of his age; Rhiannon cannot refute the charge of murder (and by extension, of her own infertility) because her husband will not take her part against the conspiracy of her serving-women, but Teyrnon's wife creates the illusion of fertility with her husband's approval when she and her serving-women agree to conspire together. The other women who have no children (by either natural or adoptive means) are Arawn's wife, Cigfa, Goewin, and Blodeuedd. All of these women are involved in triangular relationships (whether voluntarily or not), and it may be that the discussion of the interactions with more than one man makes it too complicated to deal with their powers of fertility in addition to the resolution of interpersonal problems.

10. This connection is very clearly developed in Irish legend. See: O'Rahilly, "On the Origin of the Names Érainn and Ériu," 7–28; Ross, *Pagan Celtic Britain*, 204–205, 209, 218–219, 229–233. Aranrhod's divine aspects have been discussed in: O'Rahilly, *Early Irish History and Mythology;* Bromwich, *Trioedd Ynys Prydein*, 277; Ross, *Pagan Celtic Britain*, 227; Bowen, "Great-Bladdered Medb: Mythology and Invention in the *Táin Bó Cuailgne*," 14–34.

11. *Morphology of the Folktale*, 21.

12. "[T]he most extreme violation a girl might suffer was the forcible termination of her virginity by rape. . . . The offensiveness of the action of rape and the dishonour that it brings is acknowledged in the exaction of *sarhaed* or *wynebwerth* which is paid to the girl" (49), Owen, "Shame and Reparation." See also: Jenkins, "Property Interests in the Classical Welsh Law of Women," 86–88. The relevant passages are printed in Jenkins and Owen, eds., *The Welsh Law of Women:* Cyfnerth 73.13c–22; Latin Redaction A 52.35–41; Iorwerth 50.1–5, 54.4–6.

13. "The last payment exacted as compensation for rape is the *dirwy* payable to the king. In the Iorwerth text this is specified as being twelve kine but elsewhere in terms which make it virtually identical with the king's *sarhaed*; according to these texts it con-

sists either of a silver rod, a golden plate and cup or of the silver rod alone. [Owen cites here: *Welsh Medieval Law*, Wade-Evans, ed., 92.10; *The Laws of Hywel Dda (The Book of Blegywryd)*, 63.23; Latin Redaction A 52.39 in Jenkins and Owen.] The implication of this rule is that the safe keeping of virgins lay within the king's *nawdd* or protection" (49), Owen, "Shame and Reparation."

14. "Ac yn yr oes honno Math uab Mathonwy ny bydei uyw, namyn tra uei y deudroet ymlyc croth morwyn, onyt kynwryf ryuel a'y llesteirei" (*PKM* 67).

15. Peniarth 37, 72.16, in Jenkins and Owen, *The Welsh Law of Women*, 143.

16. "a chywilyd mawr a gawssawch, bot plant o bob un o honawch o'y gilid" (*PKM* 76–77).

17. See also: McAll,"The Normal Paradigms of a Woman's Life," 9; Owen, "Shame and Reparation," 48; Jenkins, "Property Interests in the Classical Welsh Law of Women," 77.

18. The woman who falsely asserts her virginity and is found out is called a *twyllforwyn*. See especially: McAll, "The Normal Paradigms of a Woman's Life," 9; Charles-Edwards, "Nau Kynywedi Teithiauc," 34.

19. "'Ie,' heb hi, 'mi a dynghaf dyghet idaw, na chaffo enw yny caffo y genhyf i'" (*PKM* 79).

20. This incident reminds us of another mother, Rhiannon, who fulfills her responsibilities willingly, though she is suspected of not having done so. Like Aranrhod, she names her child inadvertently through her exclaimation of surprise; and the significant word is picked out by a man, just as Aranrhod's words are picked out by Gwydion, as a formal process of naming.

21. Bollard, "The Structure of the Four Branches of the Mabinogi," 268.

22. "'Ie,' heb hi, 'minheu a dyghaf dyghet y'r mab hwnn, na chaffo arueu byth yny gwiscof i ymdanaw'" (*PKM* 81).

23. "'A mi a dynghaf dynghet idaw,' heb hi, 'na chaffo wreic uyth, o'r genedyl yssyd ar y dayar honn yr awr honn'" (*PKM* 83).

16

Inheritance and Lordship in *Math*

C.W. Sullivan III

The female characters in the Four Branches of the *Mabinogi* have always received their share of critical attention and, I suspect, audience appreciation. In fact, a number of major studies have been given titles which include or are comprised solely of women's names: Gruffydd's *Rhiannon* and Mac Cana's *Branwen* are but the most obvious cases in point. And while there has been no doubt about the prominence of women in these narratives, there has been much speculation concerning their natures and roles—especially as those roles might reflect on the Celtic cultures from which these narratives sprang. Recent studies by McKenna and Valente, for example, have focused on women as important determiners of lordship in *Pwyll* and on female/male gender conflicts in *Math* respectively, and both critics use historical and sociological as well as literary evidence to support their arguments.[1] Building upon their articles, as well as on additional evidence and analysis, it is possible to suggest a reading of *Math* in which the struggle between Gwydion and Aranrhod is not only a gender struggle, which it certainly is, but is also an inheritance struggle wherein matrilineal inheritance traditions conflict with patrilineal inheritance traditions. The bequest or legacy in this case is not property, as such, but the Lordship of Gwynedd; and in the course of *Math*, that Lordship, passed on to Math and from Math to Gwydion according to matrilineal inheritance traditions, becomes Lleu's in a process through which the matrilineal system of inheritance is essentially displaced by a patrilineal system.

If *Math* does depict a matrilineal-to-patrilineal shift, it would certainly be reflecting a similar shift in Celtic cultural history. There is a long-established consensus regarding the presence of matrilineal elements in early Celtic society, elements which the Celts may have taken over from the Picts. In *The Celts*, Nora K. Chadwick comments that when the Pictish kings "married and had families, their sons did not succeed them," that their "system must have entailed a way of life quite different from what we understand, and it probably goes back to something very old," and that the "organization of the royal family seems to have been at times matrilocal as well as matrilinear, but not matriarchal."[2] Elsewhere, she mentions that "Bede was aware of succession through the female as a living custom among the Picts in his day."[3] And Jean Markale suggests that the Celts "stood halfway between these [matrilineal Picts] and the patriarchal Indo-European societies other than their own."[4]

Celtic inheritance and naming traditions, some of which can be traced into the twentieth century, also suggest the existence of a matrilineal society at some historical point. As Jan Filip notes, "Traces of matriarchal rights are observable in illegitimate offspring, who took the name of their mother. Irish law actually bound illegitimate children to their mother and accorded them civil rights."[5] T. Gwynn Jones, referring to John Rhŷs's late nineteenth-century collections of folklore as well as to his own twentieth-century research, reports "the habit . . . of wives not taking their husbands' family names" and of the woman's having "the privilege of naming the firstborn, if a male, after her own family."[6] Inheritance, and especially succession to kingship, shows similar traces of a matrilineal influence. Chadwick remarks that in all the "Celtic countries tribal kingship was in theory open to every adult male member of the royal line whose great-grandfather or nearest ascendant had been king," that in the "laws of Hywel Dda the right to nominate his successor is assigned to the king. The successor may be his son or his brother or his paternal nephew," and that in Dalriada, "kings were succeeded, not by their sons directly, but by their brothers in the first instance, and then by their nephews."[7] In "Sons and Mothers: Family Politics in the Early Middle Ages," Pauline Stafford examines the various situations in which a vacant British regional throne was contested for by the several widows of the recently deceased king who had married and divorced a number of women in turn, each woman acting for her own son and each asserting a legitimate claim "because the rules of primogeniture were not yet fully established."[8] At the very least, these naming and inheritance traditions show patrilineal succession to have been less than the established way; at most, these traditions suggest a continuing, if fading, influence from an older, matrilineal tradition.

The continuing influence of matrilineal traditions is most clearly illustrated in the laws and customs regarding marriage. Various critics have suggested that marriage was a relatively late socio-cultural development, for as M. Esther Harding notes, "primitive people [were] by no means all convinced that the man plays any very important part in reproduction."[9] Women, thus, were the primary ones connected with the sacred fertility process at that early stage and were, therefore, the determiners of lineage and inheritance. When men became aware of their own role in the reproductive process and began to want increasing authority in matters of lineage and inheritance, marriage as a legal and moral institution was developed; but the previously important status of women—especially women in the Celtic countries— affected that development and gave women rights which, according to Peter Beresford Ellis and Jean Markale, among others, "would have been envied by their Roman sisters."[10]

In the Celtic countries, especially Ireland and Wales, marriage was a very complex institution in which women had certain specified rights into recorded medieval history and well beyond.[11] According to Nora K. Chadwick and Myles Dillon, "In Ireland . . . there were various forms of marriage. Ten classes are recognized in the law tract on marriage, of which only nine are explained. The first three are regular marriages. . . . The others are temporary unions."[12] Comparing a thirteenth-century Welsh list to its eighth-century Irish counterpart, T.M. Charles-Edwards remarks that the "existence of the Welsh list suggests that in many respects the Welsh law of women resembled the Irish until the gradual progress of Christian ideas on marriage caused a fundamental transformation." However, Charles-Edwards continues, "even in the thirteenth century this transformation was still very incomplete, as the law on *ysgar* demonstrates."[13] Several scholars have suggested, however, that it is difficult to assess previous Celtic culture from these thirteenth-century laws for several reasons, not the least of which are that they exhibit at least some Norman influence and that their language, especially in the descriptions of situations which illustrate the laws, contains formulaic structures and traditional literary devices also found in fictional narratives.[14]

Ysgar, which would have been translated then as "parting," not as "divorce," points to the single most impressive right of Celtic women, the right to divorce almost equal with that of the Celtic man. Marriage and divorce, especially within the several recognized temporary unions, were relatively simple matters, and divorce did not automatically reflect badly on either party; moreover, in these divorces, "the man and the woman were treated with absolute equality."[15] And this "ease with which marital union was concluded and the almost equal ease with which it was dissolved," continues R.R. Davies, goes a long way in explaining the "apparently cavalier attitude toward so-called illegitimate offspring."[16] To complicate matters still further, there is substantial evidence to suggest that concubinage was legally recognized and that there may well have been arrangements which we would now term polygamy and polyandry.[17]

In the third volume of his *Masks of God* tetralogy, *Occidental Mythology*, Joseph Campbell argues that the "third function of a mythology is to support the current social order, to integrate the individual organically with his group."[18] That certainly seems to have been true of Celtic mythology in regard to the social status of women, for the Celtic myths, like the myth systems of a number of western European culture groups, contain strong female figures suggesting, if not explicitly illustrating, a strong matrilinear configuration. Marija Gimbutas maintains that the "masculine world is that of the Indo-Europeans, which did not develop in Old Europe but was superimposed upon it. Two entirely different sets of mythical images met. Symbols of the masculine group replaced the images of Old Europe."[19] Old European culture, according to Gimbutas, was "matrifocal, probably matrilinear, agricultural, sedentary, egalitarian, and peaceful" as opposed to the culture of the Indo-Europeans which was "patriarchal, stratified, pastoral, mobile, and war-orientated."[20] Old Europe, she maintains, "was savagely destroyed by the patriarchal element and it never recovered, but its legacy lingered in the substratum which nurtured further European cultural development."[21]

This conquest moved from east to west with the migration of the Indo-Europeans, and the mythologies of western Europe reflect that geographical progression. In the Greek narratives, Zeus is a dominant patriarchal figure while Hera, perhaps a formerly powerful matrilineal goddess, is now his wife and clearly his subordinate. Among the Germans and especially the Scandinavians, the takeover was somewhat less complete. Odin and the Aesir still compete with Frigg and the Vanir; and Thor, called Odin's eldest son, actually has strong ties with the Vanir.[22] The Celtic myths, the farthest west, also have the most obviously matrilineal aspects, especially in the stories of the Tuatha dé Danann and the Children of Dôn. Danu/Dôn is the head of the pantheon and a female figure through whom lineage is traced, and Beli is not her husband, but her consort—a second-in-command designation.

In *Pagan Celtic Britain*, Anne Ross comments that "Although divine couples do figure in the epigraphy and iconography of Roman Britain, no divine couple having names apparently exclusive to Britain has so far come to light. Divine pairs having names in Britain are also known from Gaul, and even these are not numerous. The implication here ... is that these are imports, either in the immediately pre-Roman period, or during the Roman occupation."[23] This interpretation supports not only the east-to-west progression of the patriarchal conquest, but also the belief that, in the Celtic countries, a goddess was at the head of the pantheon. And discussing various local goddesses and fairy queens, Proinsias Mac Cana asserts, "The significant point is that in these instances the ruler of the supernatural realm is a goddess rather than a god, precisely as in those early Irish tales which represent the otherworld as 'The Land of Women.' It is evidently an old tradition and one which proved remarkably tenacious, and it seems to confirm that the notion of a great goddess who was the mother of the gods is a basic element of insular Celtic mythology. One consequence of this priority is that the goddess often assumes a dominant role vis-à-vis her male partners."[24] Another result, according to Ross, is that "we are confronted with the obvious belief that, over and above the mother goddesses who were concerned with the well-being of humanity and of their own limited localities where they were propitiated, there were even more powerful mothers, the nurturers of the gods themselves."[25] With such strong female figures in the myths, it is not surprising that there are similar strong female leaders in Celtic legend (Medhbh) and history (Boadicea) as well.

This focus on the female aspect is, of course, also a focus on fertility; and that fertility, like the goddess, is bound up in and with inheritance and kingship in the Celtic countries. In "Aspects of the Theme of King and Goddess in Irish Literature," Mac Cana notes that "it was only through [marriage and/or] sexual union with the territorial goddess of Ireland or her provinces that legal title to the kingship might be won."[26] In *Celtic Mythology,* he argues that "the Irish, and indeed the Celtic, goddess is primarily concerned with the prosperity of the land: its fertility, its animal life, and (when it is conceived as a political unit) its security against external forces."[27] And the *Mabinogi,* he suggests, is about "strongly delineated" female figures. "Rhiannon, Aranrhod, and Blodeuwedd are all in their different ways strong and assertive characters that lend themselves to dramatic treatment. In some ways they recall the noble women whom the poets of *amour courtois* purported to serve as their slaves or vassals, but it is more simple to take them for what they are: literary reflexes of the Celtic goddess in some of her many aspects."[28]

As W.J. Gruffydd was the first extensively to delineate, however, *Math* is not a mythological document nor, for that matter, is it a socio-cultural or historical document. But it does contain all of those elements—and more. According to Mac Cana, "However much mythology the Four Branches contains, it is not a mythological document in the primary sense: it is a literary construct which makes use of mythological, and other, materials. Its author is not a mythographer conscientiously recording the traditions of the gods for their own sake, but a gifted writer shaping the shattered remains of a mythology to his own literary ends."[29] In the past two decades, several critics have tried to suggest what those ends might have been. For example, J.K. Bollard believes that the "overriding theme" of the Four Branches is choice; Elizabeth Hanson-Smith interprets *Pwyll* as a tale about the restoration of the wasteland and being a good ruler; Catherine McKenna, also focusing on *Pwyll*, sees sovereignty (lordship) and being a good ruler as the main theme; and for Roberta Valente, a gender struggle between Gwydion and Aranrhod is the dominant theme in *Math*.[30] The implicit suggestion to be drawn from these analyses, and others, is that the author of the Four Branches was, indeed, using mythological materials, and others from such sources as legend and history, for his own literary ends, ends which may be, at least in part, social and political.

My reading of the Fourth Branch builds especially upon McKenna's and on Valente's; *Math* is about lordship, certainly, but it is a lordship bound up in a matrilineal-to-patrilineal inheritance shift in which Gwydion and Aranrhod are the primary antagonists and in which Gwydion is the pivotal figure between Math, who inherits matrilineally, and Lleu, who inherits patrilineally. As Gruffydd remarks, all Four Branches exhibit some traces of a matrilineal inheritance pattern. "One of the distinguishing marks of the Four Branches is the great prominence given to the social position of nephew and niece. It is due, of course, to the existence of some form of inheritance other than the usual one of the son succeeding his father; there is little doubt that the state of society denoted by this form of inheritance was matriarchal, where the position of son and daughter was occupied by nephew and niece."[31] The number of rulers (Pwyll and Arawn in the First Branch; Brân, Matholwch and Beli in the Second Branch; Caswallawn and Pryderi in the Third Branch; and Math and Pryderi in the Fourth Branch) and the number of inheritors or potential inheritors of lordship (Pryderi in the First Branch; Gwern, Caradawg, and Caswallawn in the Second Branch; Manawydan in the Third Branch; and Gwydion and Lleu in the Fourth Branch) who are primary and secondary figures in the narratives support the interpretation that lordship and inheritance are at least important topics, if not the central focus, in all of the Four Branches.[32]

After a brief explanation of which geographical areas Math and Pryderi rule, the Fourth Branch establishes a matrilineal basis for Math's lordship:

> Ac yn yr oes honno Math uab Mathonwy ny bydei uyw, namyn tra uei y deudroet ymlyc croth morwyn, onyt kynwryf ryuel a'y llesteirei. (*PKM* 67) [33]

As Rachel Bromwich points out in *Trioedd Ynys Prydein*, we can not be certain "whether *Mathonwy* denotes the name of Math's father or mother." It may, she continues, be "matronymic . . . since there are indications in the *Mabinogi* that the dynasty to which Math belonged was regarded as matrilinear. . . . Thus Math may have been supposed to have inherited the rule of Gwynedd through his mother, as he in turn is succeeded by the sister's son *(Lleu)* of his sister's son *(Gwydion)*. In these circumstances a matronymic might be expected, such as we find in fact that Gwydion receives: he is known invariably as *vab Dôn*." [34]

Math's name, however, is only one aspect of the matrilineal nature of his lordship; the position of his feet in the lap of a virgin suggests a Fisher King motif and thereby a connection to the fertility goddess and the fertility of the land. As Mac Cana notes, Math had to have his feet in Goewin's lap "because she embodied the vital and undiminished source of fertility with which he must maintain constant and harmonious contact so as to ensure the fruitful discharge of his royal function"[35]—except when war prevented him. Gimbutas (above) identified war as a characteristic of patriarchal societies; and so although Math's primary identification at this early stage of the Fourth Branch is predominantly with the matrilineal and fertility aspects of his lordship, there is already a patriarchal note echoing the patriarchal aspects of the earlier Branches as well, perhaps, as presaging the patriarchal and patrilineal aspects which are to come.

In the first major section of the Fourth Branch, two essentially patriarchal episodes occur. The first is Gilfaethwy's rape of Goewin which is arranged, if not actually participated in, by Gwydion. In the Greek myths, rape is one of the ways through which the invading patriarchal gods dominate the resident female goddesses, and contemporary psychologists have quite convincingly shown that rape is not a sexual act but an act of power or domination. Gilfaethwy may have expected Goewin to couple with him willingly, but when she chose not to do so, he forced himself on her in an act of physical male power. The second patriarchal episode is the war between Gwynedd and Dyfed, also arranged by Gwydion. The primary reason for this war, according to the Fourth Branch, is to get Math away from Caer Dathyl so that Gilfaethwy could approach Goewin; but war is also a patriarchal activity, and Gwydion is arranging for Gwynedd to dominate Dyfed at the same time as he is arranging for Gilfaethwy to dominate Goewin. Gwydion has power, both magical and political, and he uses it to achieve recognizably male, patriarchal ends.

The conflict between Gwydion and Pryderi, or, in a larger sense, between Gwynedd and Dyfed, is more than merely a traditional Celtic livestock raid which has, as its hidden agenda, the rape of Goewin, and the contrasts between the two men and their respective societies underscore the emerging themes of lordship and inheritance. First, Gwydion stands to inherit the lordship of Gwynedd from Math in the matrilineal tradition, but Pryderi has already inherited the lordship of Dyfed from his father in a patrilineal tradition. The people of Gwynedd, therefore, live in a matrilineal society; whereas, the people of Dyfed are patrilineal.[36] That two such different culture groups might have existed side-by-side in Wales at one time is certainly possible. As Mac Cana notes, "the south-eastern corner [of Wales] has stood somewhat apart from the rest of what was later to become Wales, looking outward rather than inwards and, by the same token, providing a gateway to external influence.... In the eleventh and twelfth centuries it brought together Welshmen and Normans in what was evidently a fruitful [literary] union." The cultural differences between the two areas of Wales, Mac Cana continues, "persisted from prehistoric times down to the Middle Ages."[37]

This geographical and cultural division certainly seems to have been important to the version of the Four Branches which has come down to us. According to Jeffrey Gantz, "*Branwen* and *Math* embody a world close to that of the Irish sagas: fierce, heroic, primitive; *Pwyll* and *Manawydan* are infused with a sense of gentility and graciousness that reflects the south's closer contact with Norman chivalry."[38] Rachel Bromwich accounts for this duality by suggesting that the person who wrote down the Four Branches was probably "a South Wales *cyfarwydd* [who] wished at the same time to do honour to his hero Pryderi, and to bring together stories from the other parts of Wales which he recognized as belonging to a certain class: that is, the stories which comprised the oldest traditions of his people, and of which the actors, though in his mind they represented the remote forbears of his race, were in fact the ancient deities of the Celts. In this way, the North Welsh tales of *Math* and *Branwen* were incorporated into the cycle of Pryderi."[39] It is not incidental, then, that *Branwen* and *Math* are more matrilineal and *Pwyll* and *Manawydan* are more patrilineal; it is a result of geography and of the east-to-west movement of the patriarchal and patrilineal traditions.

The Four Branches and presumably ancient Wales, however, are not the only places in which matrilineal and patrilineal societies exist side-by-side. According to Carmelo Lisón-Tolosana's research, such a situation can be found in the Galicia region of Spain, a region which shows a considerable degree of cultural homogeneity and which also sees itself as significantly different from the rest of Spain. In the mountains, the eldest son (or daughter if there is no son) inherits two-thirds of the total estate but is responsible for any unmarried younger siblings; on the plains, the eldest may receive one-third with the rest divided among the others. "Another pattern of inheritance predominates among the fishing villages and valleys near the sea. Here a daughter, not necessarily the eldest, is the one who inherits." In those regions where the primary heir is male, Lisón-Tolosana continues, "the transmission of rights is patrilineal . . . and the residence is patrivirilocal;" but where the primary heir is female, "the transmission of rights is matrilineal . . . and the residence is matriuxorilocal."[40] The Galicia region of Spain was widely settled by the Celts and, according to some legends, was the original home of "an aristocratic warrior group . . . whose colonising had as thorough an effect upon Ireland as the Roman conquest had on Britain."[41] Moreover, that such a situation currently exists in Spain suggests that it certainly could have existed in Wales, especially given the similar geographical/cultural division of the regions. In addition, the raiding, warfare, conquest and exchange of hostages would have given patrilineal ideas, among others, an opportunity to move into Gwynedd.

Gwydion's display of power is only partially successful, however, for while he has conquered Dyfed and satisfied Gilfaethwy, he has also cost his country many men, dishonoured an important woman, and left his lord without a footholder. When Goewin reports the rape to Math, he speaks of *her* dishonour, "Mi a baraf iawn y ti yn gyntaf." But when he punishes Gwydion and Gilfaethwy, Math speaks generally of *his* dishonour, "ay y wneuthur iawn ymi y doethauch chwi?" and specifically of the loss of Gwynedd's men and of the death of Pryderi (*PKM* 74). But for Gwydion to commit errors and suffer some punishment for them at this stage in his career is not without precedent in the *Mabinogi*. As McKenna comments, Pwyll makes mistakes in the First Branch—chasing Arawn's dogs away from the stag that they have brought down and rashly promising Gwawl any boon he asks, for example; but she argues that these situations, and others, including the restitution he makes or the punishment he suffers, are also learning experiences for Pwyll which will make him a better ruler of Dyfed.[42]

Punishing Gwydion and Gilfaethwy by turning them into animals and having each of them bear at least one offspring seems symbolically appropriate in a number of ways. First, if they have acted like beasts, they are now experiencing beasthood, and the punishment fits the crime. Second, if they have offended a representative of the goddess and fertility, they are now experiencing both the male and female aspects of fertility first hand. This is the first time Gwydion actually adopts the female generative role in the Fourth Branch, and it will not be the last. And third, the animals into which Gwydion and Gilfaethwy are changed (deer to boar to wolf) are certainly increasingly powerful and predatory, and symbolically, perhaps, increasingly male and patriarchal.

The next major episode, the testing of Aranrhod, is the point at which the shift from matrilineal inheritance to patrilineal inheritance takes an important step. Goewin can no longer be Math's footholder (and even though Math makes her his wife, she disappears from the narrative at that point). Gwydion suggests his sister, Math's niece, Aranrhod, as Goewin's replacement, but when Math tests her virginity by making her step over his wand or rod, an obvious symbol of male power, she gives birth to a yellow-haired baby boy.[43] As she heads for the door, she leaves behind something else which Gwydion scoops up, wraps in silk, and hides in a chest at the foot of his bed. Later, Gwydion hears a cry from the chest and opens it to find a baby boy inside. Gwydion has accomplished two things here. He has effectively separated Math from the goddess's representative, Goewin, the female fertility figure, and he has begun to become, himself, the male representative of the generative power in the story; he has eliminated Goewin's role and is on the way to taking over Aranrhod's role. The baby which Gwydion "gives birth to" and will now raise could have, as Aranrhod's biological son and Gwydion's nephew, inherited the lordship of Gwynedd in the traditional matrilineal pattern; now, as Gwydion's "son," he can inherit from Gwydion in the emerging patrilinear pattern as well.

But Lleu is also Gwydion's son in the biological sense. According to W.J. Gruffydd, Gwydion is so named in an older version of the story; moreover, Gruffydd argues, Sir John Rhŷs assumes that Lleu's paternity is so obvious that it needs no explanation or discussion. Thus, Lleu's "father is not specifically mentioned, but it is certain that he was Gwydion."[44] Moreover, when Gwydion presents the boy to Aranrhod, each refers to him as the other's son. Gwydion tells her, "Y mab hwnn, mab y ti yw," and then she asks Gwydion directly, "Pwy enw dy uab dy?" (*PKM* 78–79). That such a relationship could produce a hero and future ruler is not unknown among the mythologies and legends of the northern European peoples. In a discussion of the possibly incestuous relationship between Conchobhar and Deichtine, his sister, Marie-Louise Sjoestedt notes, "In this way there

Inheritance and Lordship in Math

appears in the myth, beside the motif of divine origin, the motif of incestuous origin, which was also sacred and is of frequent occurrence in the heroic sagas."[45] If incest may not be the issue here, and therefore the cause of Aranrhod's shame as several critics have argued, then inherited power and status certainly could be. Because she has lost her chance to become Math's footholder and because Gwydion now has Lleu in a father-son (rather than an uncle-nephew) relationship, Aranrhod has lost virtually all of her opportunities for power and status; and in the next section of the Fourth Branch, she will lose the rest.

In raising the child he now has, Gwydion completes his taking over of Aranrhod's role as mother and nurturer. His first task, finding the baby a wet nurse, is one that Aranrhod herself might have done in the time period of the narrative, and Gwydion completes that task with relative ease. The next series of tasks—getting the child a name, arms, and a wife—are increasingly difficult and increasingly important. As it is the child's mother who should name him and arm him, Gwydion takes him to Aranrhod. She, feeling that Gwydion has shamed her and that the child is a part of that shame, refuses to name him. Gwydion, however, tricks her into doing so, and the child is named Lleu Llaw Gyffes. Aranrhod next refuses to arm him. Gwydion tricks her into that as well, and she then curses Lleu to have no wife from a race of people now on the earth. Aranrhod, after her unsuccessful attempts to stop Gwydion by withholding a mother's rights from her son, departs from the narrative, all of her social power and status taken over by Gwydion. To circumvent Aranrhod's last curse, Math and Gwydion create, from flowers, Blodeuedd, the most beautiful of maidens, to be Lleu's wife. Gwydion then asks Math for territory so that Lleu has land to rule and live on; and Math gives him an excellent holding for a young man, Cantref Dunoding. With his participation in this series of acts, Gwydion completes his role as nurturer and adds to it the role of creator; he has become the generative power, controlling creation.

Valente maintains that Gwydion "gives birth" three times: as an animal, to Aranrhod's baby (symbolically), and with Math, "truly and consciously [usurping] the female power of fertility," to Blodeuedd.[46] But there is still one more generative episode, and it is in that episode that Gwydion finalizes not only his generative role, but also the patriarchal nature of that generative role. When he finds the wounded Lleu in eagle form, from which worms and rotten flesh are falling, he sings him down from the tree and touches him with his rod/wand. The rod is, again, the obvious symbol of male generative power, but singing Lleu down from the tree is "creation by mouth," a familiar type of creation among patriarchal mythologies whether it is an actual speaking creation, in which something is named and then exists, or a more sympathetic form of creation, in which, for example, a god might use his own breath, sweat, or tears to bring something to life.[47] Gwydion is now acting alone, without Math's help, as sole life force.

But Blodeuedd's faithlessness with Gronw Bebyr is more than just the occasion for Lleu's death and rebirth episode; it, too, has its patriarchal overtones. Markale suggests that Blodeuedd's affair with Gronw is not just "an egotistical whim" nor the "banal adultery of a woman dissatisfied," but the "vital assertion of woman seeking control of her personality and freedom to use her intelligence (reason) and her emotions (instinct) as she wishes."[48] And Mac Cana suggests that Blodeuedd "is the Celtic goddess in her role of *femme fatale*."[49] Her assertion is short-lived, however, for Gwydion discovers the deception, restores Lleu to life, and helps him regain Cantref Dunoding. Blodeuedd, like Goewin and Aranrhod before her, is no match for Gwydion; the female power is defeated by the male. In addition, the sundering of Lleu and Blodeuedd's marriage is a negation or rejection of the sacred ritual (referred to by Mac Cana and McKenna, above) in which marriage to and/or sexual union with the goddess secured the fertility of the land and legitimized the claimant's kingship or sovereignty.

Finally, Gwydion proves his power and his control by changing Blodeuedd into an owl and leaving Gronw Bebyr to Lleu. Gwydion deals with the aspect of the situation for which he, in the creation of Blodeuedd, was directly responsible; and Lleu takes the revenge on Gronw to which he is entitled and reclaims his land:

> Ynteu Llew Llaw Gyffes a oreskynnwys eilweith y
> wlat, ac y gwledychwys yn llwydanhus. A herwyd
> y dyweit y kyuarwydyt, ef a uu arglwyd wedy
> hynny ar Wyned. (*PKM* 92)

Valente suggests that something is missing here. "As though to dramatize the hopelessness of male/female conflict through ironic understatement, the Fourth Branch ends with the image of a man alone."[50] The image of a man alone may, in fact, be just what the author intended. In the course of the Fourth Branch, the women have been eliminated and their roles taken over by men. Goewin, as footholder and as fertility figure, and Aranrhod, as mother and as generative figure, are no longer necessary; Gwydion has taken over their roles and their power. And the ultimate manifestation of Gwydion's triumph is that Lleu does not inherit the lordship of Gwynedd in a matrilineal tradition as Gwydion's sister's son, as had Gwydion and Math before him, but in a patrilineal tradition, as Gwydion's son. Rather than an "ironic understatement," he is a triumphant patriarchal and patrilineal ruler whose rule is a prosperous one.

If the Fourth Branch presents a matrilineal system giving way to a patrilineal system, as I suggest, that would place the *Mabinogi* in accord with other heroic and epic literatures which conclude with a changed or changing world. At the end of *Beowulf*, we are told that a heroic age is over for the Geats and that bad times are on the way; and the Homeric poems, which center on the heroic exploits of Achilles in the *Iliad*, conclude, in the *Odyssey*, with Odysseus's most unheroic slaughter of the suitors—the hero having given way to the trickster, the heroic age to the political. Moreover, a patrilineal triumph to a series of stories which began with Rhiannon's telling Pwyll how to court her, how to wed her, and how to win her back from Gwawl is compatible with what we know of the cultural change from matrilineality to patrilineality which took place as the post-Celtic Indo-Europeans moved westward across Europe.

There is no doubt about the matrilineal aspects of the Celtic cultural matrix through which these narratives descended before being written down in the form available to us today, and at least some of the matrilineal aspects of those narratives have been recognized for almost a century. *Math* begins with a traditional fertility scene in which a matrilineal king cannot live (and presumably the land will not be fertile and prosper) without his footholder and ends with a companionless patrilineal lord ruling prosperously; and the Four Branches as a whole take the reader from an initially dominant Rhiannon in *Pwyll* to a raped Goewin, a displaced Aranrhod, and a transformed Blodeuedd (who had had no free will or choice in her marriage) in *Math*.[51]

Math is certainly a tale about a gender conflict in which the main adversaries are Gwydion and Aranrhod, but the conflict is about lordship and the inheritance traditions through which one attains lordship. Ultimately, Gwydion is the pivotal figure about whom his society changes from matrilineal inheritance to patrilineal inheritance as he makes his nephew his son and his son his successor. Lleu's position is the stronger for being able to claim lordship in both traditions, but the absence of women (and Lleu's prosperous rule) at the end of the Fourth Branch symbolizes both Gwydion's victory and the establishment of patrilineal lordship in Gwynedd.

NOTES

Some of the research for this article was completed at the National Library of Wales and the Hugh Owen Library of the University College of Wales, Aberystwyth, on grants from East Carolina University and the Southern Regional Education Board.

    1. In "The Theme of Sovereignty in *Pwyll*," Catherine A. McKenna, drawing on the recent scholarship assessing the *Mabinogi* as a unified work and on Proinsias Mac Cana's "Aspects of the Theme of King and Goddess in Irish Literature," reads the First Branch as a "coherent tale about what an eleventh- or twelfth-century Welsh prince should be—brave, generous, just, and of noble lineage, like the ideal prince of the bards, but prudent and self-restrained as well" (52). Roberta Valente, in "Gwydion and Aranrhod: crossing the borders of gender in *Math*," examines the conflicts between Gwydion and Aranrhod and suggests that each is attempting to take over the other's gender role with Gwydion

Inheritance and Lordship in Math

"taking on the female power of creation" in a triumph over his sister which is also a violation of traditional and legal norms that leaves Lleu "a prosperous chieftain and eventually Lord of Dyfed [sic]" but "a man alone" (9).

2. Chadwick, *The Celts*, 118. It is important to note the distinction between matriarchal and matrilineal, here. While there has been much assertion by Robert Graves and others (see Filip, note 5) of a matriarchal Celtic culture, there is little solid evidence for such an interpretation; the evidence for a matrilineal society, on the other hand, is certainly there.

3. Chadwick, *Celtic Britain*, 82.

4. Markale, *The Women of the Celts*, 16–17.

5. Filip, *Celtic Civilization and Its Heritage*, 94. Here, Filip speaks of matriarchal rights which could just as well be termed matrilineal rights.

6. T.G. Jones, *Welsh Folklore and Folk-Custom*, 185–186. Jones comments that even after the "introduction of surnames, it was the general custom for wives to retain their own" (186). See also: Rhŷs, *Celtic Folklore: Welsh and Manx*, 76–77.

7. Chadwick, *Celtic Britain*, 81–82.

8. Stafford, "Sons and Mothers: Family Politics in the Early Middle Ages," 82. Concerning more everyday inheritance situations, Anne Ross notes: "According to ancient Irish law, a daughter was permitted to inherit when there was no son" (*Everyday Life of the Pagan Celts*, 113). Concerning women's status in general, Peter Beresford Ellis remarks that women "could rule as chieftains on their own merits. The status of women and their social prominence has been found remarkable by many scholars" (*Celtic Inheritance*, 20). See also: Markale, *The Women of the Celts*, 253.

9. Harding, *Women's Mysteries*, 23. See also: Gimbutas, *The Goddesses and Gods of Old Europe;* Walker, *The Woman's Encyclopedia of Myths and Secrets*, especially 585–597.

10. Ellis, *Celtic Inheritance*, 20; Markale, *The Women of The Celts* 16–17; Chadwick, *The Celts*, 115.

11. In *"Besom Wedding* in the Ceiriog Valley," W. Rhys Jones describes a wedding in which a birch broom is set slantwise in the doorway of a house for a young man and woman to jump over in the presence of witnesses. A successful leap by each constituted a marriage ceremony. By jumping backwards over the broom, within the first year, they could end the marriage and both be free to marry again. Jones collected his material in 1919 and 1920, and he speculates that "the besom wedding lingered in the Ceiriog Valley as late as the year 1840" (156).

12. Chadwick and Dillon, *The Celtic Realms*, 27. In "The Normal Paradigms of a Woman's Life in the Irish and Welsh Law

Texts," McAll discusses the "various categories of wife that a girl was liable to become," 11–18.

13. Charles-Edwards, "Nau Kynywed Teithiauc," 39. See also: Ross, *Everyday Life of the Pagan Celts,* 112.

14. Chadwick and Dillon, *The Celtic Realms,* 135; Davies, "The Status of Women and the Practice of Marriage in Late-Medieval Wales," 94.

15. Markale, *The Women of the Celts,* 35. See also: Ross, *Everyday Life of the Pagan Celts,* 113.

16. Davies, "The Status of Women and the Practice of Marriage in Late-Medieval Wales," 106.

17. Ellis, *Celtic Inheritance,* 21; Ross, *Everyday Life of the Pagan Celts,* 113; Chadwick and Dillon,*The Celtic Realms,* 132; Markale, *The Women of the Celts,* 36.

18. Campbell, *Occidental Mythology,* 520.

19. Gimbutas, *The Goddesses and Gods of Old Europe,* 238.

20. Gimbutas, *The Goddesses and Gods of Old Europe,* 9.

21. Gimbutas, *The Goddesses and Gods of Old Europe,* 238.

22. Davidson, *Gods and Myths of Northern Europe,* 80–84.

23. Ross, *Pagan Celtic Britain,* 210.

24. Mac Cana, *Celtic Mythology,* 86.

25. Ross, *Pagan Celtic Britain,* 230. In *Celtic Mythology,* Mac Cana remarks that the "divine people, the Tuatha Dé, were reputed to be the family or descendants of the goddess Danu, as the Welsh gods were said to be issued from Dôn (or the Indian from Aditi), and Wales, like Gaul, had its 'great mother,' *Modron*" (85–86).

26. Mac Cana, "Aspects of the Theme of King and Goddess in Irish Literature," Part 3, 60.

27. Mac Cana, *Celtic Mythology,* 92.

28. Mac Cana, *The Mabinogi,* 57.

29. Mac Cana, *The Mabinogi,* 54.

30. Bollard,"The Role of Myth and Tradition in *The Four Branches of the Mabinogi*"; Hanson-Smith, "*Pwyll Prince of Dyfed:* the narrative structure"; McKenna, "The Theme of Sovereignty in *Pwyll*"; and Valente, "Gwydion and Aranrhod." See also: Bollard, "The Structure of The Four Branches of the Mabinogi"; Ford, "Prolegomena to a Reading of the *Mabinogi:* 'Pwyll' and 'Manawydan'"; and Ó Coileáin, "A Thematic Study of the Tale *Pwyll Pendeuic Dyuet.*"

31. Gruffydd, *Math vab Mathonwy,* 94. Gruffydd could just as easily (and perhaps more accurately) use the term matrilineal where he uses matriarchal.

32. For additional comments on the importance of lordship to the audience of *Math,* see Hanson-Smith, "*Pwyll Prince of Dyfed:* the narrative structure," and McKenna, "The Theme of Sovereignty in *Pwyll.*"

33. Ifor Williams, ed., *Pedeir Keinc y Mabinogi*. 1964. Caerdydd: Gwasq Prifysgol Cymru, 1982. Hereafter cited in the text as *PKM*.

34. Bromwich, *Trioedd Ynys Prydein*, 448.

35. Mac Cana, *Celtic Mythology*, 72.

36. In her novel, *The Island of the Mighty* (1930; New York: Ballantine Books, Inc., 1970), based on the Fourth Branch of the *Mabinogi*, Evangeline Walton makes the matrilineal culture of the people of Gwynedd a major aspect of her story and suggests that the people of Gwynedd are of the "old tribes" while the people of Dyfed are of the "new tribes." She includes an *apologia* for this speculation which, she says, she based on some hints in John Rhŷs, *Celtic Folklore: Welsh and Manx*, and John Rhŷs and David Brynmor-Jones, *The Welsh People*.

37. Mac Cana, *The Mabinogi*, 15, 17.

38. Gantz, "Thematic Structure in the Four Branches of the Mabinogi," 247.

39. Bromwich, "The Character of Early Welsh Tradition," 104.

40. Lisón-Tolosana, "The Ethics of Inheritance," 305–307.

41. Delaney, *The Celts*, 48. Delaney also suggests that the people in Galicia continue to celebrate themselves and sell themselves to tourists as Celts, 199. See also: Cunliffe, *The Celtic World*, 130, 140; Herm, *The Celts*, 166–167; Mac Cana, *Celtic Mythology*, 25, 61.

42. McKenna, "The Theme of Sovereignty in *Pwyll*," 49–52.

43. In *The Women of the Celts*, Markale suggests that the "word *morwyn* obviously meant one thing for Aranrhod and another for Math and Gwydion. For her it signified 'free young girl, outside all male constraints,' namely woman defined according to the criteria of a gynaecocratic society; for Aranrhod is still the image of the ancient goddess of female-orientated structures. But for Math and Gwydion, the representatives of the new patriarchal system, the term denotes only physical virginity" (130).

44. Gruffydd, *Math vab Mathonwy*, 136–138.

45. Sjoestedt, *Gods and Heroes of the Celts*, 60. See also: Gruffydd, *Math vab Mathonwy*, 134–135. In addition to his conception and birth, Lleu's rapid rate of growth also identifies him (as it did Gwri/Pryderi in *Pwyll*) as a traditional hero.

46. Valente, "Gwydion and Aranrhod," 5.

47. Campbell, *Occidental Mythology*, 157. For general discussion of the shift from matriarchal creation to patriarchal creation see: Merlin Stone, *When God Was a Woman*, 219–223; and Barbara Walker, *The Woman's Encyclopedia of Myths and Secrets*, 183–186.

48. Markale, *Women of the Celts*, 172.

49. Mac Cana, *The Mabinogi*, 58–59.

50. Valente, "Gwydion and Aranrhod," 9.

51. It is tempting to see the combined defeats of Goewin, Aranrhod, and Blodeuedd as a defeat of the Triple Goddess; but the three as we find them in the Fourth Branch do not conform to the mother, wife, lover configuration traditional with the Triple Goddess.

Works Cited

Abbreviations:

BBCS — *Bulletin of the Board of Celtic Studies*
CMCS — *Cambridge Medieval Celtic Studies*
EC — *Études celtiques*
LC — *Llên Cymru*
NLWJ — *National Library of Wales Journal*
SC — *Studia Celtica*
THSC — *Transactions of the Honourable Society of Cymmrodorion*
WLW — *The Welsh Law of Women.* Ed. Daffydd Jenkins and Morfydd E. Owen. Cardiff, 1980
ZCP — *Zeitschrift für celtische Philologie*

Aarne, Antti. *Verzcichnis der Marchentypen.* Helsinki, 1911.
_____, and Stith Thompson. *The Types of the Folktale: A Classification and Bibliography.* 2nd rev. ed. Helsinki, 1961.
Anderson, Alan O. and Marjorie O. Anderson, trans. and eds. *Adamnán's Life of Columba.* London: 1961.
Andrews, Elizabeth. *Ulster Folklore.* London, 1913.
Andrews, Rhian. "Rhai Agweddau ar Sofraniaeth yng Ngherddi'r Gogynfeirdd." *BBCS* 27 (1976): 23–30.
Anwyl, Edward. "The Four Branches of the *Mabinogi.*" *ZCP* 1 (1897): 277–293; 2 (1899): 124–133; 3 (1901): 123–134.
Armstrong, D., and C.H. Van Schroneveld, eds. *Roman Jakobson.* Lisse, 1977.
Arnold, Matthew. *On the Study of Celtic Literature.* London, 1910.
Auvergne, William of. *De Universo,* II, iii, 23, quoted in Lynn Thorndike, *A History of Magical and Experimental Science,* II, 236. New York, 1923.

Bann, Stephen, and John E. Bowlt, eds. *Russian Formalism*. Edinburgh, 1973.
Bar, F. "Le Mabinogi de Pwyll, Prince of Dyvet et la Légende d'Amis et Amile." *Romania* 68 (1944): 168–172.
Barbulesçu, Cornelius. "The Maiden without Hands: AT 706 in Romania." *Studies in East European Folk Narrative*. Ed. Linda Dégh. 319–367. Bloomington, 1978.
Bartrum, Peter C. *Early Welsh Genealogical Tracts*. Cardiff, 1966.
_____. *Welsh Genealogies*. I. Cardiff, 1976
Basile, Giambattista. Day 3, Tale ii. "La Bella dalle Mani Mozze." *Il Pentamerone, La Fiaba delle Fiabe*. Trans. Benedetto Croce. Bari, 1925.
Battaglia, Salvatore, ed. Tale iv. *Il Pecarone di Ser Giovanni Fiorentino e Due Racconti Anonimi del Trecento*. Milan, 1944.
Baugh, Albert C., and Thomas Cable. *A History of the English Language*. 3rd ed. Englewood Cliffs, NJ, 1978.
Bede. *Historia Ecclesiastica*. Ed. Charles Plummer. Oxford, 1896.
Bergin, Osborn J. "White Red-eared Cows." *Ériu* 14 (1946): 170.
Bessborough, Earl of. *Lady Charlotte Schreiber*. London, 1952.
_____, ed. *The Diaries of Lady Charlotte Guest*. London, 1950.
Best, Richard I., and Osborn J. Bergin, eds. *Lebor na hUidre*. Dublin, 1929.
_____, Osborn J. Bergin, and M.A. O'Brien, eds. *The Book of Leinster*. Dublin, 1965.
_____, and R. Thurneyson, eds. *The Oldest Fragments of the Senchas Már*. Dublin, 1931.
Binchy, Daniel A. *Celtic and Anglo-Saxon Kingship*. Oxford, 1970.
_____. "The Saga of Fergus Mac Léti." *Ériu* 16 (1952): 33–48
_____. "St. Patrick and His Biographers." *Studia Hibernica* 2 (1962): 7–173.
_____, ed. *Críth Gablach*. Dublin, 1941.
Bloch, M. *Feudal Society*. London, 1961.
Bowen, Charles. "Great-Bladdered Medb: Mythology and Invention in the *Táin Bó Cuailgne*. " *Erie Ireland* 10.4 (1975): 14–34.
Bowen, Emrys G. *Saints, Seaways, and Settlements in the Celtic Lands*. Cardiff, 1969.
_____. *The Settlements of the Celtic Saints in Wales*. Cardiff, 1954.
Bowen, Geraint, ed. *Y Traddodiad Rhyddiaith yn yr Oesau Canol*. Llandysul, 1974.
Bremond, Claude. "La Logique des possibles narratifs." *Communications* 8 (1966): 60–76.
Brewer, George W., and Bedwyr L. Jones. "Popular Tale Motifs and Historical Tradition in *Breudwyt Maxen*." *Medium Aevum* 44 (1975): 23–30
Briggs, Katherine. *A Dictionary of British Folk-Tales in the English Language*. London, 1970.

Bromwich, Rachel. *Aspects of the Poetry of Dafydd ap Gwilym.* Cardiff, 1986.
_____. "Celtic Dynastic Themes and the Breton Lays." *EC* 9 (1960-1961): 439-474.
_____. "The Celtic Inheritance of Medieval Literature." *Modern Language Quarterly* 26 (1965): 203-227.
_____. "The Character of Early Welsh Tradition." *Studies in Early British History.* Ed. H. Munro Chadwick, et al. 83-136. Cambridge, 1954.
_____. "Cyfeiriadau Dafydd ap Gwilym at Chwedl a Rhamant." *Ysgrifau Beirniadol* 12 (1982): 57-76.
_____. "Dwy Chwedl a Thair Rhamant." *Y Traddodiad Rhyddiaith yn yr Oesau Canol.* Ed. Geraint Bowen. 143-175. Llandysul, 1974.
_____. *Matthew Arnold and Celtic Literature, A Retrospect: 1865-1965.* Oxford, 1965.
_____. "Traddodiad Llafar y Chwedlau." *Y Traddodiad Rhyddiaith yn yr Oesau Canol.* Ed. Geraint Bowen. 46-64. Llandysul, 1974.
_____. "TRIOEDD YNYS PRYDAIN: The *Myvyrian* 'Third Series.'" I. *THSC* (1968): 299-338.
_____. "TRIOEDD YNYS PRYDAIN: The *Myvyrain* 'Third Series.'" II. *THSC* (1969): 127-156.
_____. *Trioedd Ynys Prydein.* 1961. 2nd ed. Cardiff, 1978.
_____. *Trioedd Ynys Prydain in Welsh Literature and Scholarship.* Cardiff, 1969.
Bruce, J.D. *Le Morte Arthur.* 1888. Oxford, 1959.
Bruford, Alan. *Gaelic Folk-Tales and Mediaeval Romances: A Study in Early Modern Irish "Romantic Tales" and Their Oral Derivatives.* Dublin, 1969.
Bullock-Davies, Constance. *Professional Interpreters and the Matter of Britain.* Cardiff, 1966.
Burton, R.F. "Two Sisters Who Envied Their Cadette." *Supplemental Nights to the Book of One Thousand Nights and a Night.* 6 vols. 491-510. London, 1886-1888.
Cambrensis, Geraldus. "Topographia Hibernica." *Giraldi Cambrensis Opera.* Ed. J.F. Dimock. Rolls Series: Book I, Chapters xxxiv-xl. London, 1867.
Campbell, J.F. *Popular Tales of the West Highlands.* 4 vols. 1860-1862. London, 1983.
Campbell, Joseph. *Occidental Mythology.* Vol. 3: *The Masks of God.* 1964. New York, 1970.
Carr, Glenda. *William Owen Pughe.* Caerdydd, 1983.
Carson, Angela. "The Structure and Meaning of The 'Dream of Rhonabwy.'" *Philological Quarterly* 53 (1974): 289-303.
Chadwick, Nora. "The Borderland of the Spirit World in Early European Literature." *Trivium* 2 (1967): 17-36.

_____. *Celtic Britain*. London, 1963.
_____. *The Celts*. 1970. New York, 1979.
_____. *The Colonization of Brittany from Celtic Britain*. Oxford, 1965.
_____, and Myles Dillon. *The Celtic Realms*. 1967. London, 1973.
Charles-Edwards, T.M. "Honour and Status in Some Irish and Welsh Prose Tales." *Ériu* 29 (1978): 123–141.
_____. "Native Political Organisation and the Origin of MW *brenhin*." *Antiquitates Indogermanicae*. Ed. Manfred Mayrhofer, et al. 35–45. Innsbruck, 1974.
_____. "Nau Kynywedi Teithiauc." *WLW*. 23–39.
_____. "Some Celtic Kinship Terms." *BBCS* 24 (1970–1972): 105–122.
Chaucer, Geoffrey. *The Works of Geoffrey Chaucer*. Ed. F. N. Robinson. Boston, 1957.
Child, Francis James, ed. *The English and Scottish Popular Ballads*. 1882–1888. New York, 1965.
Clarkeson, Atelia, and Gilbert Cross, eds. *World Folktales*. New York, 1980.
Cox, Marian. *An Introduction to Folklore*. London, 1904.
Cronne, Henry A., and R.H.C. David, eds. Introduction. *Regesta Regum Anglo-Normannorum*. III. Oxford, 1967.
Cross, Tom Peete. *Motif-Index of Early Irish Literature*. Bloomington, 1952.
Crossley-Holland, Kevin. *Folk-Tales from Great Britain*. New York, 1985.
Cunliffe, Barry. *The Celtic World*. London, 1979.
Cutt, Nancy, and W. Towrie Cutt. *The Hogboon of Hell*. London, 1979.
d'Ancona, Alessandro. "Rappresentazione di Santa Uliva." *Sacre rappresentazioni dei secoli*. 3 vols. Florence, 1872.
Davidson, H.R. Ellis. *Gods and Myths of Northern Europe*. Baltimore, 1964.
Davies, John. *Bywyd a Gwaith Moses Williams*. Caerdydd, 1937.
Davies, R.R. "Buchedd a Moes y Cymry." *The Welsh History Review* 12.2 (1984): 155–179.
_____. "The Status of Women and the Practice of Marriage in Late-Medieval Wales." *WLW*. 93–114.
_____. "The Survival of the Bloodfeud in Medieval Wales." *History* 54 (1969): 338–357.
Delaney, Frank. *The Celts*. London, 1968.
Denholm-Young, N. "The Tournament in the Thirteenth Century." *Studies in Medieval History Presented to Powicke*. 240–268. Oxford, 1948.
Ditmas, E.M.R. "Geoffrey of Monmouth and the Breton Families in Cornwall." *Welsh History Review* 6 (1973): 451–461.

_____. "A Re-appraisal of Geoffrey of Monmouth's Allusions to Cornwall." *Speculum* 48 (1973): 510–524.
Douglas, Mary. *Purity and Danger: An Analysis of Concepts of Pollution and Taboo.* London, 1970.
Ellis, Peter Beresford. *Celtic Inheritance.* London, 1985.
Ellis, T.P. "Legal References, Terms and Conceptions in the 'Mabinogion.'" *Y Cymmrodor* 39 (1928): 86–148.
_____. *Welsh Tribal Law and Custom in the Middle Ages.* 2 vols. Oxford, 1926.
Emanuel, Hywel D. "An Analysis of the Composition of the 'Vita Cadoci.'" *NLWJ* 7 (1952): 217–227.
_____. *The Latin Texts of the Welsh Laws.* Cardiff, 1967.
Evans, D. Silvan, ed. *Celtic Remains.* London, 1878.
Evans, D. Simon. *Historia Gruffud Vab Kenan.* Cardiff, 1977.
Evans, J. Gwenogvryn, ed. *The Black Book of Carmarthen.* Pwllheli, 1906.
_____, ed. *The Book of Taliesin.* Llanbedrog, 1910.
_____, ed. *The White Book Mabinogion.* Pwllheli, 1907.
_____, and R.M. Jones, eds. *Llyfr Gwyn Rhydderch.* Caerdydd, 1973.
_____, and John Rhŷs, eds. *The Text of the Book of Llan Dav.* Oxford, 1893.
Evans, Leslie Wynne. *Education in Industrial Wales 1700–1900.* Cardiff, 1971.
Evans, Theophilus. *Drych y Prif Oesoedd: Y Rhan Gyntaf* (argraffiad 1740). Ed. David Thomas. Caerdydd, 1955.
Fenn, R.W.D. "The Age of the Saints." *A History of the Church in Wales.* Ed. David Walker. 1–23. Pennarth, 1976.
Filip, Jan. *Celtic Civilization and Its Heritage.* Prague, 1960.
Fleuriot, Leon. *Les Origines de la Bretagne.* Paris, 1982.
Florentinus, Joannus. *Novella della Figlia del Re di Dacia.* Ed. Allessandro Wesselofski, Pisa, 1806.
Ford, Patrick K. *The Mabinogi and Other Medieval Welsh Tales.* Berkeley, 1977.
_____. "On the Significance of Some Arthurian Names in Early Welsh." *BBCS* 30 (1983–1984): 268–273.
Frappier, Jean. "Chrétien de Troyes." *Arthurian Literature in the Middle Ages.* Ed. R. S. Loomis. 157–192. Oxford, 1959.
Fraser, Maxwell. "The Halls of Pembrokeshire, Ancestors of Benjamin Hall, Afterwards Lord Llanover of Llanover and Abercarn." *NLWJ* 12 (1961–1962): 1–17.
_____. "Lady Llanover and Her Circle." *THSC* (1968): 170–196.
_____. "The Waddingtons of Llanover. 1791–1805." *NLWJ* 11 (1959–1960): 285–329.
_____. "Young Mr. and Mrs. Hall. 1823–1830." *NLWJ* 13 (1963–1964): 29–47.

Friedman, Albert B. ed., *The Viking Book of Folk-Ballads of the English-Speaking World*. New York, 1956.
Ganshof, F.L. *Feudalism*. 3rd ed. London, 1964.
Gantz, Jeffrey, ed., *The Mabinogion*. Harmondsworth, UK, 1976.
Genette, G. *Figures I*. Paris, 1966.
Gimbutas, Marija. *Goddesses and Gods of Old Europe*. 1974. Berkeley, 1982.
Glob, Peter V. *The Bog People*. Trans. Rupert Brice-Mitford. 1969. Ithaca, NY, 1988.
Glover, Richard. "English Warfare in 1066." *English Historical Review* 67 (1952): 1–18.
Goetinck, Glenys. "Historia Peredur." *LC* 6 (1960–1961): 138–153.
_____. *Peredur: A Study of Welsh Tradition in the Grail Legends*. Cardiff, 1975.
_____. "Sofraniaeth yn y tair rhamant." *LC* 8 (1964–1965): 168–182.
Gomme, G.L. *Folklore as an Historical Science*.1908. Detroit, 1968.
Gourvil, Francis. *Theodore Hersart de la Villemarqué et la "Barzaz-Briez."* Rennes, 1960.
Gower, John. "The Tale of Constance." *Confessio Amantis*. Ed. R.A. Peck. New York, 1968.
Gray, Elizabeth. "Cath Maige Tuired: Myth and Structure (1–24)." *Eigse* 18 (1981): 183–209.
Green, D.H. "The Pathway to Adventure." *Viator* 8 (1977): 145–188.
Greene, David. "Miscellanea." *Celtica* 4 (1958): 44–47.
Gruffydd, R. Geraint. *Celtic Studies in Wales*. Cardiff, 1963.
_____. "Meilyr Brydydd a Meilyr Awenydd." *Barn* 213 (1980): 313–316.
_____. "A Poem in Praise of Cuhelyn Fardd." *SC* 10–11 (1975–1976): 198–209.
_____, and Brynley F. Roberts. "Rhiannon Gyda Theyrnon Yng Ngwent." *LC* 13 (1980–1981): 289–291.
Gryffydd, W.J. *Folklore and Myth in the Mabinogion*. Cardiff, 1958.
_____. "The Mabinogion." *THSC* (1912–1913): 14–80.
_____. "Mabon ab Modron." *Revue Celtique* 33 (1912): 452–461.
_____. "Mabon vab Madron." *Y Cymmrodor* 42 (1931): 129–147.
_____. *Math vab Mathonwy*. Cardiff, 1928.
_____. *Rhiannon: An Inquiry into the Origins of the First and Third Branches of the Mabinogi*. Cardiff, 1953.
Hamburger, Kate. *The Logic of Literature*. Trans. Marilynn J. Rose. Bloomington, 1973.
Hamp, Eric. "Early Welsh Names, Suffixes, and Phonology." *Proceedings of the 9th International Congress of Onomastic Sciences*. Ed. H. Draye. 266–272. Louvain, 1969.
_____. "Mabinogi." *THSC* (1974–1975): 243–249.

Harder, Bernard D. "Cradle of the Gods: Birth of the Hero in Medieval Narrative." *University of Windsor Review* 10.1 (1974): 45–54.

Harding, M. Esther. *Women's Mysteries*. 1955. London, 1971.

Harris, Silas. "The Kalendar of the *Vitae Sanctorum Wallensium*." *Journal of the Historical Society of the Church in Wales* 3 (1953): 3–53.

Heffernan, Thomas J. "An Analysis of the Narrative Motifs in the Legend of St. Eustace." *Medievalia et Humanistica* NS 6 (1975): 63–89.

Hennessy, W.M., ed. *Chronicon Scotorum*. London, 1866.

Henry, P.L. "Culhwch and Olwen—Some Aspects of Style and Structure." *SC* 3 (1968): 30–38.

Herdan, G. *Type-token Mathematics*. 'S-Gravenhage, 1960.

Herm, Gerhard. *The Celts*. London, 1976.

Hollister, C. Warren. *Anglo-Saxon Military Institutions*. Oxford, 1962.

Hughes, Kathleen. *Celtic Britain in the Early Middle Ages*. Woodbridge, Suffolk, 1980.

———. "Introduction." *A History of Medieval Ireland*. Ed. A.J. Otway-Ruthven. 1–33. London, 1968.

Hunt, Tony. "The Art of *Iarlles y Ffynnawn* and the European Volksmärchen." *SC* 8–9 (1973–1974): 107–120.

———. "Some Observations on the Textual Relationships of Li Chevaliers au Lion and Iarlles y Ffynnawn." *ZCP* 33 (1974): 93–113.

Imbriani, Vittorio, coll. and ed. *La Novellaja Fiorentina, Fiabe e Novelline*. Livorno, 1877.

Jackson, Kenneth H. *Early Welsh Gnomic Poems*. 1935. Cardiff, 1961.

———. *The International Popular Tale and Early Welsh Tradition*. Cardiff, 1961.

———. *Language and History in Early Britain*. 1953. Edinburgh, 1983.

———. *The Oldest Irish Tradition: A Window on the Iron Age*. Cambridge, 1964.

———. "Some Popular Motifs in Early Welsh Tradition." *EC* 11 (1964–1965): 83–99.

———. "*Varia*: II. Gildas and the Names of the British Princes." *CMCS* 3 (1982): 30–40.

Jakobson, Roman. *Questions de poétique*. Paris, 1973.

———, and Claude Lévi-Strauss. "Les Chats de Charles Baudelaire." *L'homme, revue francaise d'anthropologie* 2 (1962): 5–21.

Jarman, A.O.H. "Mabinogi Branwen: Crynodeb o Ddadansoddiad W.J. Gruffydd." *LC* 4 (1957): 129–134.

———. "Pedair Cainc y Mabinogi." *Y Traddodiad Rhyddiaith yn yr Oesau Canol*. Ed. G. Bowen. 83–142. Llandysul, 1974.

_____, and Gwilym Rees Hughes, eds. *A Guide to Welsh Literature*. Swansea, 1976.

Jenkins, Dafydd. "Lords, Kings, and Princes: The Nomenclature of Authority in Thirteenth-Century Wales." *BBCS* 26 (1974–1976): 451–461.

_____. "Property Interests in the Classical Welsh Law of Women." *WLW*. 69–92.

Jenkins, R.T., and H.M. Ramage. *History of the Honourable Society of Cymmrodorion*. London, 1951.

Johnson, Charles, and Henry A. Cronne, eds. Introduction. *Regesta Regum Anglo-Normannorum*. II. Oxford, 1956.

Johnston, Arthur. *Enchanted Ground: The Study of Medieval Romance in the Eighteenth Century*. London, 1964.

_____. "William Owen-Pughe and the Mabinogion." *NLWJ* 10 (1958): 323–328.

Jones, Bedwyr Lewis. "Bedd-Branwen—the Literary Evidence." *Transactions of the Anglesey Antiquarian Society* (1966): 32–37.

_____. "Rotunda Tabula neu Dwrneimant yn Nefyn yn 1284." *Trafodion Cymdeithas Hanes Sir Gaernarfon* 34 (1973): 23–29.

_____. *Yr Hen Bersoniaid Llengar*. Gwasg yr Eglwys yng Nghymru, 1963.

Jones, David. *The Anathemata*. London, 1953.

Jones, Emyr Gwynne. "Llythrau Lewis Morris at William Vaughan, Corsygedol." *LC* 10 (1968–1969): 3–58.

Jones, Glyn E. "Early Prose: The *Mabinogi*." *A Guide to Welsh Literature*. Vol. I. Ed. A.O.H. Jarman and Gwilym Rees Hughes. 189–202. Swansea, 1976.

_____. "Y Wledd yn Harlech ac yng Ngwales ym Mabinogi Branwen." *BBCS* 25(1972–1974): 380–386.

Jones, Gwyn. "The Prose Romances in Medieval Wales." *Wales through the Ages*. Vol. I. Ed. Arthur J. Roderick. 138–144. Llandybie, 1959.

_____, and Thomas Jones, ed. and trans. *The Mabinogion*. London, 1949.

Jones, R.M. *Highlights in Welsh Literature: Talks with a Prince*. Wales, 1969.

_____. "Moddau Llenyddol (1)." *Y Traethodydd* 579 (1981): 93–104.

_____. "Moddau Llenyddol (2): Tywyll Heno." *Y Traethodydd* 580 (1981): 149–158.

_____. "Y Rhamantau Cymraeg a'u Cysylltiad â'r Rhamantau Ffrangeg." *LC* 4 (1957): 208–225.

Jones, T. Gwynn. *Welsh Folklore and Folk-Custom*. 1930. Totowa, NJ, 1979.

Jones, Thomas. "Rhieni." *BBCS* 9 (1938): 131–133.

_____, ed. *Brut y Tywysogion* (Peniarth MS. 20 version). Cardiff, 1941.

_____, ed. and trans. *Brut y Tywysogyon or the Chronicle of Princes; Red Book of Hergest Version*. 1955. Cardiff, 1973
Jones, W. Rhys. "Besom Wedding in the Ceiriog Valley." *Folk-Lore* 39 (1928): 149–166.
Kelly, Fergus, ed. and trans. *Audacht Morainn*. Dublin, 1976.
Kennedy, Patrick. *Legendary Fictions of the Irish Celts*. 1886. Detroit, 1968.
Ker, W.P. *Epic and Romance*. London, 1896.
Kinsella, Thomas, trans. *The Táin*. Oxford, 1970.
Kirby, D.P. "British Dynastic History in the Pre-Viking Period." *BBCS* 27 (1976–1978): 81–115.
Klaeber, F., ed. *Beowulf*. Boston, 1950.
Knott, Eleanor, ed. *Togail Bruidne Da Derga*. Dublin, 1963.
Knowles, David. *Medieval Religious Houses: England and Wales*. London, 1957.
Koch, John T. "A Welsh Window on the Iron Age: Manawydan, Mandubracios." *CMCS* 14 (Winter 1987): 17–52.
La Broderie, Arthur de. *Histoire de Bretagne*. Mayenne, 1922.
Leodhas, Sorche Nic. *Heather and Broom*. New York, 1960.
Lévi-Strauss, Claude. "The Myth of Asdiwal." *The Structural Study of Myth and Totemism*. Ed. Edmund Leach. 1–47. London, 1967.
_____. "The Structural Study of Myth." *Myth: A Symposium*. Ed. Thomas A. Sebeok. 81–106. Bloomington, 1958.
Lewis, C.S. "The Anthropological Approach." *English and Medieval Studies Presented to J.R.R. Tolkien on the Occasion of His Seventieth Birthday*. Eds. Norman Davis and C.L.Wrenn. 219–230. London, 1962.
Lewis, H., ed. *Brut Dingestow*. Cardiff, 1942.
Lewis, Saunders. "Branwen." *Ysgrifau Beirniadol* 5 (1970): 30–43.
_____. "Manawydan Fab Llyr." *Y Traethodydd* 532 (1969): 137–142.
_____. "Math fab Mathonwy." *Y Traethodydd* 533 (1969): 185–202.
_____. "Pwyll Pen Annwfn." *LC* 9 (1967): 230–233.
_____. "The Tradition of Taliesin." *THSC* (1968): 293–298.
Leyerle, John. "The Interlace Structure of Beowulf." *University of Toronto Quarterly* 38 (1967–1968):1–17.
Lhuyd, Edward. *Archaeologia Britannica*. Oxford, 1707.
Lieberman, F., ed. *Die Gresetze der Aryelsachsen*. Halle, 1903–1916.
Linnard, William. *Trees in the Law of Hywel*. Aberystwyth, 1979.
Lisón-Tolosana, Carmelo. "The Ethics of Inheritance." *Mediterranean Family Structures*. Ed. J.G. Peristiany. 305–315. Cambridge, 1976.
Littleton, C. Scott. *The New Comparative Mythology*. Berkeley, 1973.
Lloyd, D. Myrddin. *Rhai Agweddau ar Ddysg y Gogynfeirdd*. Cardiff, 1977.
Lloyd, J.E. *A History of Wales from the Earliest Times to the Edwardian Conquest*. 2 vols. 1911. London, 1939.

Lloyd-Jones, J. *Geirfa Barddoniaeth Gynnar Gymraeg.* Cardiff, 1931.
Lloyd-Morgan, Ceridwen. "Narrative Structure in *Peredur.*" *ZCP* 38 (1981): 187–231.
Loomis, R.S. *Arthurian Tradition and Chrétien de Troyes.* New York, 1949.
_____. "Pioneers of Arthurian Scholarship." *Bibliographical Bulletin of the International Arthurian Society* XVI (1964): 95–106.
Lot, Ferdinand. *Étude sur le Lancelot en Prose.* 1918. Paris, 1954.
Lovecy, I.C. "The Celtic Sovereignty Theme and the Structure of *Peredur.*" *SC* 12–13 (1977–1978): 133–146.
Lozachmeur, Jean-Claude. *La Genèse de la légende d'Yvain.* II. Rennes, 1981.
Luttrell, Claude. "From Traditional Tale to Arthurian Romance: 'Le Chevalier au Lion.'" *Nottingham Medieval Studies* 22 (1978): 36–57.
Mac Airt, S., ed. *The Annals of Innisfallen.* Dublin, 1951.
Mac Cana, Proinsias. "Aspects of the Theme of King and Goddess in Irish Literature." *EC* 7 (1955–1956): 76–114, 356–413 and 8 (1958): 59–65.
_____. *Branwen, Daughter of Llŷr: A Study of the Irish Affinities.* Cardiff, 1958.
_____. *Celtic Mythology.* 1970. Rushden, UK, 1983.
_____. "An Instance of Modified Narrative Repetition in *Fled Bricrenn.*" *Ériu* 28 (1977): 168–172.
_____. *The Mabinogi.* Cardiff, 1977.
MacCulloch, John Arnott. "Celtic Mythology." *The Mythology of All Races.* Ed. Louis Herbert Gray. Vol. 3: *Celtic, Slavic.* John A. MacCulloch and Jan Machal. 5–213. Boston, 1918.
_____. *The Religion of the Ancient Celts.* Edinburgh, 1911.
_____, and Jan Marchal. *The Mythology of All Races.* Ed. Louis Herbert Gray. Vol. 3: *Celtic, Slavic.* Boston, 1918.
Mackenzie, Donald. *Scottish Folklore and Folk-Life.* London, 1935.
Magnusson, Magnus, and Hermann Palsson, trans. *Njal's Saga.* London, 1967.
Máille, Tomas Ó. "Medb Chruachna." *ZCP* 17 (1927–1928): 129–146.
Markale, Jean. *The Women of the Celts.* London, 1975.
Marx, Jean. *Nouvelles Recherches sur la Litterature Arthurienne.* Paris, 1965.
_____. "Observations sur le structure du roman gallois de Peredur." *EC* 10 (1962–1963): 88–108.
Matonis, Ann T.E. "The Rhetorical Patterns in *Marwnad LLewelyn ap Gruffydd* by Gruffudd ap yr Ynad Coch." *SC* 14–15 (1979–1980): 188–192.
Matthews, Caitlin. *Mabon and the Mysteries of Britain.* London, 1987.

Maxwell, Gavin. *Seals of the World*. Liverpool, 1967.
McAll, Christopher. "The Normal Paradigms of a Woman's Life in the Irish and Welsh Law Texts." *WLW*. 7–22.
Meid, W. *Tain Bó Fraích*. Dublin, 1967.
Meyer, Kuno. *Líadain and Cuirithir*. London, 1902.
_____. "Mitteilungen aus irischen Handschriften." *ZCP* 13 (1921): 3–30.
Miller, M. "Historicity and the Pedigrees of the Northcountrymen." *BBCS* 26 (1974–1976): 255–280.
Morgan, T.J. *Ysgrifau Llenyddol*. Llundain, 1951.
Morris, Lewis. *Celtic Remains*. Ed. D. Silvan Evans. London, 1878.
Morris-Jones, John. *Cerdd Dafod*. Rhydychen, 1925.
_____. "Taliesin." *Y Cymmrodor* 28 (1918): 1–290.
_____, Rhiannon Morris-Jones, and T.H. Parry-Williams. *Llawysgrif Hendregadredd*. Cardiff, 1933.
Murphy, Gerard. *Saga and Myth in Ancient Ireland*. Dublin, 1955.
Nelson, Lynn H. *The Normans in South Wales, 1070–1171*. Austin, 1966.
Nennius. *Historia Brittonumn*. Ed. T.H. Mommsen. Berlin, 1888.
Newell, Venetia. "The Jew as Witch." *The Witch Figure*. Ed. Venetia Newell. 95–124. London, 1968.
Nitze, William A. "The Romance of Erec, Son of Loc." *Modern Philology* 11 (1914): 445–489.
Nutt, Alfred. The Mabinogion *Translated by Lady Charlotte Guest, with Notes by A. Nutt*. London, 1904.
O'Brien, M.A., ed. *Corpus Genealogiarum Hiberniae*. Dublin, 1962.
Ó Cathasaigh, Tomás. *The Heroic Biography of Corman Mac Airt*. Dublin, 1977.
O'Connor, Frank. *The Backward Look*. London, 1967.
Olrick, Axel. "Epic Laws of Folk Narrative." *The Study of Folklore*. Ed. Alan Dundes. 129–141. Englewood Cliffs, 1965.
O'Rahilly, Cecile. "Repetition: A Narrative Device in TBC." *Ériu* 30 (1979): 67–74.
_____, trans. and ed. *Táin Bó Cúalnge*. Dublin, 1967.
_____, trans. and ed. *Táin Bó Cúalnge from the Book of Leinster*. Dublin, 1970.
O'Rahilly, T.F. *Early Irish History and Mythology*. Dublin, 1946.
_____. "Notes, Mainly Etymological." *Ériu* 13 (1942): 144–219.
_____. "On the Origin of the Names Érainn and Ériu." *Ériu* 14 (1943): 7–28.
_____. "Some Fermoy Place Names." *Ériu* 12 (1938): 254–256.
O Suilleabháin, Séan. *A Handbook of Irish Folklore*. Dublin, 1942.
O'Sullivan, Sean. *The Folklore of Ireland*. New York, 1974.
_____, ed. and trans. *Folktales of Ireland*. Chicago, 1966.
Otway-Ruthven, A.J. *A History of Medieval Ireland*. London, 1968.

Owen, Morfydd. "Shame and Reparation: Woman's Place in the Kin." *WLW*. 40–68.
Paris, Gaston. "*Erec and Enide*" *Romania* 20 (1891): 148–166.
Parry, John J., ed. *Brut y Brenhinedd*. Cambridge, 1937.
Parry, Thomas. *Gwaith Dafydd ap Gwilym*. Caerdydd, 1961.
_____. *Hanes Llenyddiaeth Gymraeg hyd 1900*. Cardiff, 1944.
Pearce, Susan. "The Cornish Element in the Arthurian Tradition." *Folklore* 85 (1974): 145–163.
_____. "The Traditions of the Royal King-List of Dumnonia." *THSC* (1971): 128–139.
Phillimore, Egerton G.B. "A Fragment from Hengwrt MS. No 202." *Y Cymmrodor* 7 (1886): 89–154.
Phillips, D. Rhys. *Lady Charlotte Guest and the Mabinogion*. Carmarthen, 1921.
Pierce, Gwynedd O. *The Place-names of Dinas Powys Hundred*. Cardiff, 1968.
Poole, A.L. *Doomsday Book to Magna Carta, 1087–1216*. Oxford, 1951.
"Presidential Address: 'Vespasian A XIV.'" The Lord Bishop of Swansea and Brecon. *Archaeologia Cambrensis* 101 (1951): 91–105.
Pringle, K.D. "The Kings of Demetia, I." *THSC* (1970): 70–76.
Propp, Valdimir. *The Morphology of the Folktale*. 2nd ed. Austin, 1970.
Protter, Eric, and Nancy Protter, eds. *Celtic Folk and Fairy Tales*. New York, 1966.
Rees, Alwyn D. "Modern Evaluations of Celtic Narrative Tradition." *Proceedings of the Second International Congress of Celtic Studies*. Ed. Henry Lewis. 31–61. Dublin, 1963.
Rees, Brinley. "Apair fris, ni fil inge cethri flathemna and . . . " *BBCS* 29 (1980–1982): 686–689.
_____. *Ceinciau'r Mabinogi*. Bangor, 1975.
Reiss, Edmund. "The Welsh Versions of Geoffrey of Monmouth's *Historia*." *The Welsh History Review* 4 (1968–1969): 97–127.
Renan, Ernest. "The Poetry of the Celtic Races." 1854. *Literary and Philosophical Essays*. Ed. Charles W. Eliot. 143–191. New York, 1910.
Rhŷs, John. *Celtic Folklore: Welsh and Manx*. 2 vols. 1901. London, 1980.
_____. *Lectures on the Origin and Growth of Religion as Illustrated by Celtic Heathendom*. The Hibbert Lectures: 1886. 1898. New York, 1979.
_____, and David Brynmor Jones. *The Welsh People*. 3rd. ed. London, 1902.
_____, and J. Gwenogvryn Evans, eds. *The Red Book of Hergest*. Oxford, 1890.

_____, and J. Gwenogvryn Evans, eds. *The Text of the Mabinogion from the Red Book of Hergest*. Oxford, 1887.
Richards, Melville, ed. *Breudwyt Ronabwy*. Cardiff, 1948.
_____, ed. *The Laws of Hywel Dda*. Cardiff: 1954.
Rickert, Edith, ed. *The Romance of Emaré*. Early English Text Society, extra series, 99. London, 1906.
Roberts, Brynley. "From Traditional Tale to Literary Story: Middle Welsh Prose Narratives." *The Craft of Fiction: Essays in Medieval Poetics*. Ed. Leigh Arrathoon. 211–230. Rochester, MI, 1984.
_____. "Historical Writing." *A Guide to Welsh Literature*. Ed. A.O.H. Jarman and Gwilym Rees Hughes. 244–247. Swansea, 1976.
_____. "Oral Tradition and Welsh Literature: A Description and Survey." *Oral Tradition* 3 (1988): 61–87.
_____. "Owein *Neu* Iarlles y Ffynon." *Ysgrifau Beirniadol* 10 (1977): 124–143.
_____. "Penyd Rhiannon." *BBCS* 23 (1968–1970): 325–327.
_____. "Sylwadau ar Sieffre o Fynwy a'r *Historia Regum Britanniae*. *LC* 12 (1973): 127–145
_____. "Tales and Romances." *A Guide to Welsh Literature*. Ed. A.O.H. Jarman and Gwilym Rees Hughes. 203–243. Swansea, 1976.
_____. "The Treatment of Personal Names in the Early Welsh Versions of *Historia Regum Britanniae*." *BBCS* 25 (1972–1974): 274–290.
_____, ed. *Brut y Brenhinedd*. Dublin, 1971.
_____, ed. *Cyfranc Lludd a Llefelys*. Dublin, 1975.
Roberts, Rhiannon F. "Y Dr. John Davies O Fallwyd." *LC* 2 (1952–1953): 97–109.
Ross, Anne. *Everyday Life of the Pagan Celts*. London, 1970.
_____. *Pagan Celtic Britain*. London, 1967.
Ryding, William. W. *Structure in Medieval Narrative*. The Hague, 1971.
Salter, H.E. *Medieval Oxford*. Oxford, 1936.
Sargent, Helen Child, and George Lyman Kittredge, eds. *English and Scottish Popular Ballads*. Boston, 1904.
Schlauch, Margaret. *Chaucer's Constance and Accused Queens*. New York, 1929.
Sheppard-Jones, Elisabeth. *Scottish Legendary Tales*. Edinburgh, 1962.
Sherwood, Richard. "Viktor Shklovsky and the Development of Early Formalist Theory on Prose Literature." *Russian Formalism*. Eds. Stephen Bann and John. E. Bowlt. 26–40. Edinburgh, 1973.
Sims-Williams, Patrick. "The Evidence for Vernacular Irish Literary Influence on Early Mediaeval Welsh Literature." *Ireland in Early Mediaeval Europe: Studies in Memory of Kathleen Hughes*.

Ed. Dorothy Whitelock. Rosamond McKitterick, and David Dumville. 235–257. Cambridge, 1982.

———. "The Riddling Treatment of the 'Watchman Device' in *Branwen* and *Togail Bruidne Da Derga*." *SC* 12–13 (1977–1978): 83–117.

———. "The Significance of the Irish Personal Names in *Culhwch ac Olwen*." *BBCS* 29 (1980–1982): 600–620.

Sjoestedt, Marie-Louise. *Gods and Heroes of the Celts*. Trans. Myles Dillon. 1940. London, 1949.

Skeat, W. *AElfric's Lives of Saints*. II. 1881. London,1966.

Slover, Clark. "Early Literary Channels between Britain and Ireland." *Studies in English* 6 (1926): 5–52.

Stafford, Pauline. "Sons and Mothers: Family Politics in the Early Middle Ages." *Medieval Women*. Ed. Derek Baker. 79–100. Oxford, 1978.

Stenton, Frank M. *Anglo-Saxon England*. 2nd ed. Oxford, 1947.

———. *The First Century of English Feudalism: 1066–1166*. Oxford, 1932.

Stevenson, W.H., ed. *Asser's Life of King Edward*. 2nd ed. Oxford, 1959.

Stone, Merlin. *When God Was a Woman*. 1976. New York, 1978.

Strachan, J., and J.G. O'Keeffe, eds. *Táin Bó Cúailnge*. Dublin, 1912.

Stubbs, W., ed. *The Chronicle of the Reigns of Henry II and Richard I Commonly Known as Benedict of Peterborough*. London, 1867.

Suchier, Hermann. "La Fille Sans Mains." *Romania* 30 (1901): 519–538.

Tatlock, J.S.P. *The Legendary History of Britain*. Berkeley, 1950.

Thomas, Mair Elvet. *Afiaith yng Ngwent*. Caerdydd, 1978.

Thomas, R.J. "Enwau Afonydd a'r Olddodiad-Wy." *BBCS* 8 (1937): 27–43.

———, ed. *Geiriadur Prifysgol Cymru*. Cardiff, 1950.

Thompson, Stith. *Motif-Index of Folk-Literature*. 1932–1936. Rev ed. 6 vols. Bloomington, 1955–1958.

———. *The Folktale*. New York, 1946.

Thomson, David. *The People of the Sea*. London, 1954.

Thomson, Derick S., ed. *Branwen Uerch Lyr*. Dublin, 1961.

Thomson, R.L., ed. *Pwyll Pendeuic Dyuet*. Dublin, 1957.

Thurnysen, R. "Aus dem irischen Recht II." *ZCP* (15 1925): 238–276.

———. *Cóic Conara Fugill*. Berlin, 1926.

Tierney, James. "The Celtic Ethnography of Posidonius." *Proceedings of the Royal Irish Academy* 60 (1960): 189–275.

———. "The Celts and the Classical Authors." *The Celts*. Ed. Joseph Raftery. 23–33. Cork, 1964.

Works Cited

Tolkien, J.R.R. "Beowulf: The Monsters and the Critics." *An Anthology of Beowulf Criticism*. Ed. Lewis E. Nicholson. 1936. 51–103. Notre Dame, 1963.
_____. *The Two Towers*. Boston, 1965.
Vandelli, Giuseppe, ed. *I Reali di Francia di Andrea da Barberino*. 2 vols. Book 2; chapters 42, 49, and 52–53. Bologna, 1900.
Vinaver, Eugène. *Form and Meaning in Medieval Romance*. Cambridge, 1966.
_____. *The Rise of Romance*. Oxford, 1971.
_____, ed. *Malory: Works*. 2nd ed. Oxford, 1967.
Wade-Evans, Arthur W. "Brychan Brycheiniog." *Transactions of the Brecknock Society* 1 (1928–1929): 13.
_____. "The Llancarfan Charters." *Archaeologia Cambrensis* 87 (1932): 151–165.
_____. *Vitae Sanctorum Britanniae*. Cardiff, 1944.
_____, ed. *Welsh Medieval Law*. Oxford, 1909.
Walker, Barbara. *The Woman's Encyclopedia of Myths and Secrets*. New York, 1983.
Walters, D.B. "The European Context of the Welsh Law of Matrimonial Property." *WLW*. 115–131.
Watkins, Arwyn, and Proinsias Mac Cana. "Cystrawennau'r Cyplad mewn Hen Gymraeg." *BBCS* 18 (1958–1960): 1–25.
Wats, William, ed., *Vitae Duorum Offarum*. London, 1775.
Welsh, Andrew. "The Traditional Narrative Motifs of *The Four Branches of the Mabinogi*." *CMCS* 15 (Summer 1988): 51–62.
_____. "Traditional Tales and the Harmonizing of Story in *Pwyll Pendeuic Dyuet*." *CMCS* 17 (Summer 1989): 15–41.
Whitelock, D., ed. *English Historical Documents*. I. London, 1955.
Wilde, Oscar. *The Picture of Dorian Gray*. London, 1891.
Wiliam, Aled Rhys, ed. *Llyfr Iorwerth*. Cardiff, 1960.
Williams, G.J. *Agweddau ar Hanes Dysg Gymraeg*. Caerdydd, 1969.
_____, and E.J. Jones, eds. *Gramadegau'r Penceirddiaid*. Caerdydd, 1934.
Williams, Ifor. "Hen Chwedlau." *THSC* (1946–1947): 28–58.
_____. *Lectures on Early Welsh Poetry*. Dublin, 1944.
_____. "Trystan ac Esyllt." *BBCS* 5 (1930): 115–129.
_____. "Vocabularium Cornicum." *BBCS* 11 (1941–1943): 1–12, 92–100.
_____, ed. *Armes Prydein*. Cardiff, 1955.
_____, ed. *Breuddwyd Maxen*. Bangor, 1908.
_____, ed. *Canu Aneirin*. 1938. Caerdydd, 1961.
_____, ed. *Canu Llywarch Hen*. 1935. 2nd ed. Cardiff, 1953.
_____, ed. *Cyfranc Lludd a Llevelys*. Bangor, 1910.
_____, ed. *Pedeir Keinc Y Mabinogi*. 1930. Caerdydd, 1982.
_____, ed. *The Poems of Taliesin*. Dublin, 1968.

Williams, J.E. Caerwyn. "Beirdd y Tywysogion: Arolwg." *LC* 11 (1970): 3–94.

―――. "Posidonius's Celtic Parasites." *SC* 14–15 (1979–1980): 313–343.

Williams, Patricia. "Y Gwrthdaro Rhwng Serch a Milwriaeth yn y Tair Rhamant." *Ysgrifau Beirniadol* 12 (1982): 40–56.

Williams, S.J., and J.E. Powell, eds. *Llyfr Blegywryd*. Caerdydd, 1961.

Wilson, Barbara Ker. *Scottish Folk-Tales and Legends*. London, 1954.

Wittig, Susan. *Stylistic and Narrative Structures in the Middle English Romances*. Austin, 1978.

Wolfson, Nell. "The Conversational Historical Present Alteration." *Language* 55 (1979): 168–82.

Yeats, William Butler. "The Celtic Element in Literature." *Ideas of Good and Evil*. 270–295. London, 1903.

About the Contributors

J.K. Bollard has various articles on Medieval Welsh narrative and Middle English romance and has published translations of the early Welsh Arthurian poetry in *The Romance of Arthur* (Garland, 1984), of *Peredur* in *The Romance of Arthur II* (Garland, 1986), and of the Myrddin prophecies in *The Romance of Merlin* (Garland, 1990). He has taught Medieval Welsh Language and Literature at the Universities of Massachusetts and Connecticut and at Yale and is currently an adjunct member of the English Department at the University of Amherst. He is also a lexicographer among whose work is included *A Pronouncing Dictionary of Proper Names* (Omnigraphics, 1993).

Rachel Bromwich is an Emeritus Reader in Celtic Language and Literature of the University of Cambridge, and an Honorary Professor of Welsh at St. David's University College, Lampeter. Her main publication is *Trioedd Ynys Prydein: The Welsh Triads* (1961), of which she is at present preparing a third edition. She has also published *Dafydd ap Gwilym* in the Writers of Wales series (1974), *Aspects of the Poetry of Dafydd ap Gwilym* (1986), and *Dafydd ap Gwilym: A Selection of Poems* (1982, 1993), as well as a number of essays. She was co-editor of *The Arthur of the Welsh* (1991) and of *Culhwch and Olwen: An Edition and Study of the Oldest Arthurian Tale* (1992).

T.M. Charles-Edwards is a Fellow and Tutor in Modern History at Corpus Christi College, Oxford. He is the author of *Early Irish and Welsh Kinship, The Welsh Laws,* and articles on Celtic and Anglo-Saxon history, and on Celtic language, law, and literature.

Patrick K. Ford received his Ph.D. in Celtic Languages and Literatures at Harvard University, where he is now the Margaret Brooks Robinson Professor of Celtic and chair of the department. His books include *The Poetry of Llywarch Hen* (University of California Press, 1974), *The Mabinogi and Other Medieval Welsh Tales* (University of California Press, 1977), *Ystoria Taliesin* (University of Wales Press, 1992), and *The Irish Literary Tradition* (with J.E.C. Williams, University of Wales Press, 1992). His essays on medieval Welsh and Irish literature have appeared in such journals as *Studia Celtica, Études celtiques, Zeitschrift für celtische Philologie,* and *Viator.* He is past president of the North American Branch of the International Arthurian Society and of the Celtic Studies Association of North America, and is a member of the editorial board of *Arthuriana.*

Jeffrey Gantz is the arts editor of the *Boston Phoenix,* a weekly newspaper, where he writes about film, theater, art, books, music, and ballet. He is the translator of *The Mabinogion* (1976) and *Early Irish Myths and Sagas* (1982), both from Penguin Classics.

Elizabeth Hanson-Smith has taught Chaucer and Medieval Literature for the past 25 years at California State University, Sacramento. She has published on strategies for teaching Old English poetry, on women's poetry of the Findern MS., and on computer analysis of medieval dialects. Until her retirement in July 1995, she also taught linguistics and pedagogy, and served as coordinator of the graduate program in TESOL, which she founded in 1983. As Professor Emeritus, she continues research in computer-assisted language teaching and serves as consultant to CSUS Regional & Continuing Education and the international TESOL professional organization.

Professor Emeritus **R.M. Jones** was head of the Department of Welsh in the University of Wales, Aberystwyth. Works of scholarship include *I'r Arch* (1959), *Cyflwyno'r Gymraeg* (1964),

About the Contributors

System in Child Language (1970), *Tafod y Llenor* (1974), *Llenydiaeth Gymraeg 1936-* (1975), *Llên Cymru a Chrefydd* (1977), *Seiliau Beirniadaeth,* 4 vols. (1984-1988), *Llenyddiaeth Gymraeg 1902-1936* (1987), *Blodeugerdd Barddas o'r Bedwaredd Ganrif ar Bymtheg* (1988), *Cyfriniaeth Gymraeg* (1994). A fellow of the British Academy, he has been chairman of Yr Academi Gymreig and is president of CYD and vice-president of the UCCF. Volume I of his *Selected Poems* (translated by Joseph P. Clancy) was published by Christopher Davies in 1987. His creative work includes ten volumes of verse, two novels, and six collections of short stories.

Sarah Larratt Keefer is Associate Professor of Medieval Literature at Trent University, Ontario. She has published two books on the relationship between Old English psalm-poetry and the interlinear glossed psalters of the tenth and eleventh centuries, and many articles on a variety of subjects pertaining to medieval history, liturgy, and literature. She is the designer of the Directory of Individual Liturgical Sources database and text-files that will supplement the international *Fontes Anglo-Saxonici* project, and is co-editor of a forthcoming volume on editing Old English verse.

Catherine A. McKenna is Professor of English and Comparative Literature at Queens College and at the Graduate School and University Center of the City University of New York. She is Coordinator of the Medieval Studies Certificate Program at the CUNY Graduate School, and President of the Celtic Studies Association of North America. She is the author of *The Medieval Welsh Religious Lyric: Poems of the Gogynfeirdd 1137–1282* (Ford and Bailie, 1991) and a contributing editor of the *Cyfres Beirdd y Tywysogion* published by the Centre for Advanced Welsh and Celtic Studies of the University of Wales.

Seán Ó Coileáin is Professor of Modern Irish at University College, Cork and a member of the Senate of the National University of Ireland. Deeply influenced by John Kelleher and Albert Lord while studying for his doctorate at Harvard, his research interests and publications range from the oral-literary and literary-historical relationships of early Irish materials to modern Irish literature and folklore, with particular emphasis on the legacy of the Great Blasket Island. For his biography of the leading Irish-language poet Seán Ó Ríordáin (1916–1977), entitled *Seán Ó Ríordáin: Beatha agus Saothar*, he received the literary award of the Irish-American Cultural Institute.

C.W. Sullivan III is Professor of English and Director of Graduate Studies in English at East Carolina University. He is the author of *Welsh Celtic Myth in Modern Fantasy* (Greenwood, 1989), editor of *Science Fiction for Young Readers* (Greenwood, 1993) and *As Tomorrow Becomes Today* (Prentice-Hall, 1974), and a co-editor of *Herbal and Magical Medicine: Traditional Healing Today* (Duke, 1992). He is the immediate past President of the International Association for the Fantastic in the Arts, editor of the *Children's Folklore Review*, and a member of the editorial board of *Para*doxa: Studies in World Literary Genres*. His articles on mythology, folklore, fantasy, and science fiction have appeared in a variety of anthologies and journals.

Roberta L. Valente studied medieval Celtic folklore in the U.S. and Wales, earning a Ph.D. from Cornell University in 1986. Her doctoral dissertation, "*Merched y Mabinogi:* Women and the Thematic Structure of the Four Branches," analyzed the role of women in the Four Branches in light of medieval Welsh law. After several years of teaching English and many years of advocacy on behalf of battered women, Ms. Valente traded in the joys of academic life for a law degree, earning her J.D. from the George Washington University in 1991. She has since worked in the Washington, DC, area as an advocate for battered women and now serves as the director of the American Bar Association's Commission on Domestic Violence, working for legislative reform and community action to end domestic violence.

Andrew Welsh is an Associate Professor of English and Comparative Literature at Rutgers University in New Brunswick, New Jersey, where he teaches courses in medieval literature, folklore, and poetry. He is the author of a book on the poetics of lyric poetry and folk poetry, *Roots of*

Lyric: Primitive Poetry and Modern Poetics (Princeton University Press, 1978), and of articles on Old English, Middle English, and Middle Welsh literature. His articles on the Four Branches have also appeared in *Cambridge Medieval Celtic Studies, Speculum,* and *Viator.*

Juliette Wood studied philosophy at the College of New Rochelle and folklore at the University of Pennsylvania, spent two years at the University of Wales, Aberystwyth, learning Welsh, and then received an M.Litt in Welsh at Oxford University. She is currently secretary of the Folklore Society and has edited two publications for them: *Aspects of British Calendar Customs* (with Theresa Buckland, 1993) and *Colour in Folklore* (with John Hutchings, 1991). She is a contributor to *The Feminist Companion to Mythology* (1992) and has just completed a new introduction and appendix to W. Jenkyn Thomas's *The Welsh Fairy Book* (University of Wales Press, 1995). She worked at the Welsh Folk Museum as University of Wales Fellow from 1986 to 1988 and is currently Honorary Lecturer at the Department of Welsh, University of Wales, Cardiff, and teaches folklore studies at the University of Reading.